SOCIOLOGICAL
METHODOLOGY
2002

SOCIOLOGICAL METHODOLOGY

2002

VOLUME 32

EDITOR: Ross M. Stolzenberg

ADVISORY EDITORS:

Kenneth A. Bollen

William Axinn

Phillip Bonacich

Steven Borgatti

Mitchell Duneier

Katherine Faust

Robert Groves

Jacques A.P. Hagenaars

Robert Hanneman

Edgar Kiser

Kenneth C. Land

Calvin Morrill

Martina Morris

Susan A. Murphy

Trond Petersen

Tom W. Smith

Elizabeth Stasny

Ross M. Stolzenberg

Bruce Western

Kazuo Yamaguchi

MANAGING EDITOR: Fabio Rojas

An official publication by Blackwell Publishing for

THE AMERICAN SOCIOLOGICAL ASSOCIATION

SALLY T. HILLSMAN, *Executive Officer*

Library of Congress Catalog Card Information
Sociological Methodology, 1969–85
San Francisco, Jossey-Bass. 15 v. illus. 24 cm. annual. (Jossey-Bass behavioral science
series)
Editor: 1969, 1970: E. F. Borgatta; 1971, 1972, 1973–74: H. L. Costner;
1975, 1976, 1977: D. R. Heise; 1978, 1979, 1980: K. F. Schuessler;
1981, 1982, 1983–84: S. Leinhardt; 1985: N. B. Tuma

Sociological Methodology, 1986–88
Washington, DC, American Sociological Association. 3 v. illus. 24 cm. annual.
Editor: 1986: N. B. Tuma; 1987, 1988: C. C. Clogg

Sociological Methodology, 1989–1992
Oxford, Basil Blackwell. 4 v. illus. 24 cm. annual.
Editor: 1989, 1990: C. C. Clogg; 1991, 1992: P. V. Marsden
"An official publication of the American Sociological Association."
1. Sociology—Methodology—Year books.   I. American Sociological
Association.   II. Borgatta, Edgar F., 1924– ed.

HM24.S55	301'.01'8	68-54940
	rev.	
Library of Congress	[r71h2]	

British Cataloguing in Publication Data
Sociological Methodology. Vol. 30
1. Sociology. Methodology
301'.01'8

ISBN 1-4051-0769-3
ISSN 0081-1750

REVIEWERS

Paul Allison
William Axinn
Kenneth Bailey
Richard Berk
Suzanne Bianchi
William Bielby
Ken Bollen
Phillip Bonacich
Stephen Borgatti
Norman Bradburn
Richard Breen
James Davis
Jan De Leeuw
John DeLamater
Norman Denzin
Robert Emerson
Jonathan Entin
Eugene Ericksen
David Firth
John Fox
Noah Friedken
Roger Gould
Larry Griffin
Shelby Haberman
Jacques Hagenaars

Charles Halaby
Robert Hanneman
David Heise
Dawn Iacobucci
F. Thomas Juster
Jee-Seon Kim
Hallie Kintner
Kenneth Land
Joel Levine
Daniel Lichter
Stanley Lieberson
James Lindgren
Roderick Little
John Logan
J. Scott Long
Jay Magidson
Elizabeth Ann Martin
Douglas Massey
Peter McCullagh
Stephen Morgan
Charles Mueller
William Parish
Phillipa Pattison
Pamela Paxton
Robert Petrin

Stanley Presser
Ken Rasinski
Sean Reardon
Mark Reiser
John Robinson
Steven Rytina
Marc Scott
John Skvoretz
Herbert Smith
Tom Smith
Michael Sobel
Frank Stafford
Arthur Stinchcombe
Jeffrey Timberlake
Jeroen Vermunt
Stanley Wasserman
David Weakliem
Kim Weeden
Alexander Weinreb
Michael White
James Wiley
Larry Wu
Yu Xie
Kazuo Yamaguchi
Yoosik Youm

CONTENTS

CONTRIBUTORS

Sean F. Reardon, Pennsylvania State University

Glenn Firebaugh, Pennsylvania State University

Paul D. Allison, University of Pennsylvania

Richard P. Waterman, University of Pennsylvania

Philippa Pattison, Department of Psychology, University of Melbourne

Garry Robins, Department of Psychology, University of Melbourne

Jeroen Bruggeman, University of Amsterdam

Ivar Vermeulen, University of Amsterdam

Ted Palys, School of Criminology, Simon Fraser University

John Lowman, School of Criminology, Simon Fraser University

Katherine Faust, University of South Carolina

John Skvoretz, University of South Carolina

László Pólos, Eotvos Lorand University, Budapest; Erasmus University, Rotterdam

Michael T. Hannan, Stanford University

Rick Grannis, University of California–Los Angeles

Lisa D. Pearce, University of Michigan

Geoffrey R. Stone, University of Chicago

James Lindgren, Northwestern University

Kazuo Yamaguchi, University of Chicago

SUBMISSION INFORMATION FOR AUTHORS

Sociological Methodology is an annual compendium of advances in the methodology of social research. These articles promise to advance the quality and efficiency of sociological research, or to make accessible to sociologists recent methodological advances in related disciplines. *Sociological Methodology* is an official publication of the American Sociological Association.

Sociological Methodology seeks contributions that address the full range of problems confronted by empirical work in the contemporary social sciences, including conceptualization and modeling, research design, data collection, measurement, and data analysis. Work on the methodological problems involved in any approach to empirical social science is appropriate for *Sociological Methodology*. Chapters present original methodological contributions, expository statements on and illustrations of recently developed techniques, and critical discussions of research practice.

The content of each annual volume of *Sociological Methodology* is driven by submissions initiated by authors; the volumes do not have specific themes. Editorial decisions about manuscripts submitted are based on the advice of expert referees. Criteria include originality, breadth of interest and applicability, and expository clarity. Discussions of implications for research practice are vital, and authors are urged to include empirical illustrations of the methods they discuss.

Authors should submit five copies of manuscripts to

Ross M. Stolzenberg
Sociological Methodology
The University of Chicago
Department of Sociology
307 Social Science Building
1126 East 59th Street
Chicago, Illinois 60637

Manuscripts should include an informative abstract of not more than one double-spaced page, and should not identify the author within the text. Submission of a manuscript for review by *Sociological Methodology* implies that it has not been published previously and that it is not under review elsewhere.

Inquiries concerning the appropriateness of material and/or other aspects of editorial policies and procedures are welcome; prospective authors should correspond with the editor by E-mail at r-stolzenberg@uchicago.edu.

ACKNOWLEDGMENTS

I thank the editorial board of *Sociological Methodology* and the many reviewers who gave generously of their time and effort to evaluate papers submitted for publication. I am very grateful to the previous editors, Michael Sobel and Mark Becker, for their unbending commitment to the scholarly quality of articles published in *Sociological Methodology*. Without the journal's well deserved reputation for quality, built by Sobel, Becker, and previous editors, it would be impossible for any subsequent editor to attract the first-rate submissions that the journal requires. I am also grateful to Sobel and Becker for their help in making the transition from their offices to mine. They showed me every courtesy and kindness, as did their managing editor, Carson Hicks. They gave me more help than I knew to ask for, and they responded instantly and fully to my every request for information or assistance. They set a high standard indeed for competence and good will. I thank them for their help. Members of the ASA publications committee provided much useful and constructive advice. I thank them for their candor and for their good nature. In the ASA office, Karen Edwards has cheerfully overlooked my administrative deficiencies and selflessly filled in the gaps left by them. I thank her for her generous, talented, and good-natured help. Stephanie Magean has copyedited the entire text of this volume with speed, skill, and care, but never a complaint. Margaret Walsh and Margaret Zusky at Blackwell have made this volume exist by cheerfully, competently, and creatively doing whatever it takes to produce a book from a set of manuscripts. I do not fully understand what they did, but I am very glad that they did it. Editing

Sociological Methodology has taken more time than I imagined, and I am enormously gratefuly to Craig Coelen, the president of NORC, for making available the resources that have permitted me to find that time among my other responsibilities. I give special thanks to Fabio Rojas, who has served as my able, hard-working, tolerant, and generally good-natured and vastly over-qualified managing editor. His term ends soon as he completes his doctoral dissertation. I hope to publish at least one of his papers in the pages of *Sociological Methodology* before my term as editor expires.

FOREWORD: PITY THE AUTHOR ...

Pity the writer of this introduction! While articles in *Sociological Methodology* are widely and frequently cited, even used in graduate teaching, I can locate no evidence that the editor's introduction is read by anyone but its author. My informal analysis finds no journal citations whatsoever to the editor's introduction to any volume of *Sociological Methodology*. With this finding in hand, I have reasonable certainty that if this essay takes the usual form, then it will be very private stuff, intended for many but unread by any; remembered by the author, but not by any other. Previous editors are all talented writers and researchers whose other work is widely cited, so the problem must be the topic rather than the authors. In particular, the usual topic of the editor's introduction is the editor's heartfelt argument that subsequent chapters of the volume are significant pieces of the highest quality. But readers know that editors have a lot of incentive to sincerely overstate these claims, even to themselves: Editors themselves are measured by the quality and significance of the articles that they publish, and they spend more time than they originally estimated on the inevitable emergencies and crises of getting a volume into print. And then there is the audience problem. The readership of *Sociological Methodology* is composed of academics and researchers. Academics always find lots to disagree about because, like lawyers, they are well-trained in the dark art of fault-finding and are rewarded for promoting their own judgments above all others. Researchers are in the business of testing opinions (presented as hypotheses), and their workday life is a series of lessons about how unlikely it is that a seemingly reasonable opinion will withstand an empirical test. Faced with readers who are so willing and able to disagree with assertions of the future value of articles written in the recent past, I think I had better let the chapters of this volume stand on their own very strong legs, and turn my attention to topics that I can claim with authority, at least until my term as editor concludes. So I now describe the current mission and domain of *Sociological Methodology*, in the hope that doing so will stimulate readers to contribute to future volumes.

The mission of *Sociological Methodology* is to publish articles that improve the methods available to contemporary sociologists for expanding sociological knowledge. This definition includes methods that are used in theory construction. This definition also includes methods that are used in theory testing, substantive analyses, and descriptive studies. And this definition also includes methods that are used to develop new methods. I believe that *any* method is an appropriate topic for *Sociological Methodology* if it improves (or could improve) the quality of sociological knowledge or the efficiency with which sociological knowledge is produced. This statement requires some clarification.

By "quality," I mean validity and reliability. Measurements and analyses always provide information about something, but that something is never completely the thing or process that the analyst has in mind. Roughly speaking, validity is the extent to which measurements and analytic methods provide information about the things and processes that we intend them to describe, rather than about some other thing or process. For example, a common source of invalidity in field studies is confounding of researchers' own cognitive maps and affective evaluations with their perceptions of their research subjects' cognitive maps and affective evaluations; when validity falls too low, these researchers inadvertently study themselves instead of their subjects. Reliability is the extent to which these measurements and analyses are free from random noise. When reliability falls too low, researchers have studied nothing more informative than a crapshoot. By "efficiency" I mean the amount of time and other resources that are required to produce a research result of a given degree of quality.

Finally, I mean very much to say that *Sociological Methodology* seeks methodological studies that contribute to any and every part of the sociological enterprise. Here are a few examples of topics that seem especially promising:

- *Statistical methods: Sociological Methodology* will continue to include statistical methods, of course. The growth of statistical methods in sociology has been propelled by trends that continue unabated. These are the increasingly available and rich datasets and archival records that have been produced by decades of survey research and much longer periods of organizational record-keeping; and increasingly powerful, convenient, and inexpensive electronic computers and computer programs with which to manipulate those big datasets.
- *Theory construction methods:* There are methods for theory construction too, and advances in symbolic manipulation, logical analysis, and simulation analysis show much promise for application to sociological theory construction.
- *Hybrid methodologies:* There is a long history of combining observational methods and unstructured interviews with survey research and statistical analysis techniques. Experimental and survey methods have a long and fruitful history. Considerable effort has been made to join archival analysis of administrative records with survey research techniques. The potential contributions of these hybrid methodologies are huge.
- *Observational studies, field studies, and unstructured interview studies:* Advances in image-processing techniques and automated speech recognition likely will soon hold much promise for improving the reliability, validity, and efficiency of field research. In the meantime, simpler tools, such as miniaturized cameras, television, voice recorders, and other sensing devices seem to hold much promise for improving these types of research, if only by improving the detail and accuracy of records, by permitting researchers to review and revise their observations, and by allowing multiple researchers, including assistants and subordinates, to gather and analyze in a consistent manner larger amounts of data than could be gathered and analyzed properly by one or two persons.
- *Archival studies:* Image processing offers huge opportunities to overcome the spectacular amounts of time consumed by analysis of paper archives. Once scanned by computers and digitized, images of documents often can be catalogued and organized electronically, and sometimes can be fully coded and subjected to textual analysis.

Finally, I want to consider what it takes to get a methodological paper published in *Sociological Methodology*. Submissions are peer-reviewed—a process that tends to reward precise measurement, to favor papers that employ accepted procedures, and to address well-recognized problems and make incremental but recognizable progress toward solving them. This editorial process does a fine (but not perfect) job of keeping bad research out of scientific journals, producing gradual but constant refinement of scientific knowledge and method, and controlling the idiosyncrasies or ill-informed impulses of editors. But peer review also seems to make it difficult for authors to publish work that considers big problems or that proposes creative, innovative, and unusual solutions to long-standing problems. I think that editors have some responsibility to overcome the conservative, incremental bias of the peer-review process by taking some risks to promote the publication of papers that propose bold solutions to big problems. The problem is to find a way to let such papers into the journals without giving them an unwarranted, premature, and misleading stamp of approval. One solution is to publish papers with accompanying evaluative commentary. I have used this strategy in this volume, and I hope to use it in future issues as well.

ANTICIPATING LAW: RESEARCH METHODS, ETHICS, AND THE LAW OF PRIVILEGE

Ted Palys*
John Lowman*

Our ethical obligation to protect the research confidentiality of individual participants is challenged when third parties use subpoenas in the context of criminal proceedings and civil litigation in an effort to order the production of confidential information. This paper discusses strategies researchers may employ in order to maximize their legal ability to maintain confidentiality in spite of those challenges. Use of existing statutory protections is the first choice, but these are available for only a subset of research related to health and criminal justice issues. In situations where statutory protections are not available, the Wigmore criteria may act as a guide for the design of research that maximizes researchers' ability to protect research participants by advancing a case-by-case claim for researcher-participant privilege. We discuss the legal basis for this conclusion and outline procedures that may be used to further strengthen confidentiality protections.

1. THE ETHICAL OBLIGATION TO PROTECT RESEARCH PARTICIPANTS

Survey research, field studies, and other contemporary social science research techniques involve construction of detailed, accurate records of

*Simon Fraser University

information about characteristics and behavior of specific, identified persons who serve as research participants. If divulged, some of these records can be used to harm research participants or others who are named in the records. Widely accepted ethical principles (e.g., such as those issued by the American Anthropological Association; American Political Science Association; American Society of Criminology; American Sociological Association) require researchers to conceal research information attributable to a particular individual from those who would use it for non-research purposes. In addition, the confidentiality of research records has been claimed as a pillar of the researcher's academic freedom, and that too has motivated academic researchers to restrict the access of others to research records (e.g., Wolfgang 1981).

Academic freedom and ethical principles of research scientists notwithstanding, third parties occasionally seek confidential research records concerning research participants. Historically, these threats have come from two major sources: (1) congressional committees, grand juries, prosecutors, and other law enforcement authorities who subpoenaed researchers in an effort to force them to divulge confidential research information to help prosecute research participants and/or others for offenses disclosed during the course of research; and (2) corporate litigants, including energy, tobacco, pharmaceutical, and computer giants who subpoenaed researchers either to discredit them or to enlist them in their litigious cause (Lowman and Palys forthcoming).

When social researchers have refused to divulge information about research participants to courts and governmental entities, subpoena powers backed by the threat of criminal penalties for noncompliance have been used to try to motivate researchers to reveal research records (Bond 1978; Caroll and Knerr 1975; Cecil and Wetherington 1996; Lowman and Palys forthcoming; Scarce 1994). Social science tradition in the face of such threats is to staunchly resist, both to protect research participants and to preserve academic freedom (Wolfgang 1981). In two celebrated cases—those of political scientist Samuel Popkin (Caroll and Knerr 1973) and sociologist Richard Scarce (Scarce 1994)—this involved being incarcerated on charges of contempt of court.

Researchers can preempt the possibility of legal challenge and the prospective consequences of refusal to obey a subpoena or other court order to divulge confidential research records by removing identifiers or destroying the records *before* governments or courts express interest in them.[1] Where this is not possible, researchers should design and conduct their research in ways that protect those records from disclosure to governments or courts by (1) establishing them as privileged (where that status is made possible by state or federal legislation); or (2) laying the foundation for that privilege to be recognized on a case-by-case basis in common law. This paper considers both strategies.

2. SHIELD LAWS

Because it bears many similarities to journalism, some types of social science research may enjoy confidentiality protection under the provisions of the First Amendment of the U.S. Constitution (McLaughlin 1999). Thirty-one states have enacted journalistic privilege laws, some of which could include researchers under their broad definition of "journalist." Delaware law explicitly includes scholars in its definition of "journalist" (McLaughlin 1999). But social science and journalism have obvious dissimilarities too, and this protection is absent or uncertain in many situations.

Some states have research shield laws. For example, New Hampshire protects data "obtained for the purposes of medical or scientific research by the commissioner [of Health and Human Services] or by any person, organization or agency authorized by the Commissioner to obtain such data" (*N.H. Rev. Stat. Ann.* §126-A:11). Minnesota (*Minn. Stat. Ann.* §144.053) and Michigan (*Mich. Comp. Laws* §333.2631 and -2632) have similar laws regarding health research (Fanning 1999).

Apparently in response to recognition that certain types of federally mandated research would not yield valid data unless research participants could be guaranteed confidentiality with respect to personal/identifying information, the U.S. Congress has enacted a series of research data confidentiality shield laws, beginning with legislation protecting the confidentiality of data supplied to the U.S. Bureau of the Census.

Later, to enable researchers to obtain information about drug abuse among soldiers returning from Vietnam, the Comprehensive Drug Abuse

---

[1]This is particularly appropriate when the destruction of records at the end of the study, or their anonymization at the earliest opportunity, is part of the researcher's pledge and consistent with the research participant's understanding at the time the record was created. We emphasize "before" because once that interest is expressed, the researcher likely would be considered in contempt of court for destroying evidence.

Prevention and Control Act of 1970 authorized the Secretary of Health Education and Welfare to issue to drug researchers "confidentiality certificates" that ensured immunity from compelled production of confidential research information (Madden and Lessin 1983).[2] Legislation in 1974 expanded confidentiality certificate coverage to mental health research in general, including studies of alcohol and other psychoactive drugs.[3] Currently, Section 301(d) of the Public Health Service Act (42 U.S.C. §241(d)) authorizes the Secretary of Health and Human Services to issue confidentiality certificates to researchers involved in any "health" research, whether funded by DHHS or not, where confidentiality is deemed essential for producing valid and reliable information. Authority to issue the certificates has been delegated to the individual agencies comprising DHHS. Receipt of a certificate protects the researcher from being compelled to produce confidential information in any court or other proceeding.[4]

In crime research, 42 U.S.C. §3789g provides that information collected using funds of the Office of Justice Programs (OJP) are immune from legal process and inadmissible as evidence "in any action, suit, or other judicial, legislative, or administrative proceedings." In addition, OJP-funded research is subject to 28 CFR Part 22 (§22.23), which requires all funding applicants to submit written certification that they not divulge confidential information pertaining to any identifiable private person. Once approved, confidentiality is guaranteed.

State shield laws can provide useful protection in certain circumstances, but the general utility of such laws is made uncertain by the combination of interstate differences in these laws (including their total absence in some states), and the common practice of researchers to use data that include research participants from several different states. The legal validity of federal research confidentiality certificate legislation has been challenged only once, and without success (*People of the State of New York* v. *Robert Newman* 1973; Nelson and Hedrick 1983). The decision referred to the confidentiality that the certificates provided as "absolute" (e.g., *People* v. *Newman* 1973 at par. 12, 15, 20, 43); the Supreme Court refused to hear an appeal.

[2] Comprehensive Drug Abuse Prevention and Control Act of 1970, Pub. L. No. 91-513, § 3(a).
[3] Comprehensive Alcohol Abuse and Alcoholism Prevention, Treatment, and Rehabilitation Amendments of 1974, Pub. L. No. 93-282, §122(b).
[4] For application instructions, see ⟨http://www.nimh.nih.gov/research/confidentapp.cfm⟩ and/or NIMH's "frequently asked questions" page at ⟨http://www.nimh.nih.gov/research/confidentfaq.cfm⟩.

3. ASSERTING RESEARCH-PARTICIPANT
PRIVILEGE IN COMMON LAW

In the absence of shield law protection, researchers must rely on tests of "reason and experience" in common law to protect confidential research information from government- and court-ordered disclosure. As Rule 501 of the *Federal Rules of Evidence* explains:

> Except as otherwise required by the Constitution of the United States or provided by Act of Congress or in rules prescribed by the Supreme Court pursuant to statutory authority, the privilege of a witness, person, government, state, or political subdivision thereof shall be governed by the principles of the common law as they may be interpreted by the courts of the United States in the light of reason and experience.

Similarly, in cases where no statutory privilege applies, state courts apply the same tests of reason and experience to adjudicate privilege claims
We now describe how the common law of privilege operates. The discussion focuses on the "Wigmore test"—four criteria that both federal and state courts use to adjudicate claims of privilege. We suggest that by designing their research to anticipate the evidentiary requirements of the Wigmore test, researchers can present the strongest possible evidence to sustain a claim of research-participant privilege. In the process, researchers not eligible for the guaranteed protection of confidentiality and privacy certificates can provide research participants with the fullest common law protection possible within the law as it stands today. State courts may differ in their application of the Wigmore test. Reliance on a particular state's peculiarities in this regard seems likely to have the same problems, discussed above, as reliance on a particular state's research and journalism shield laws. Our focus is thus on federal cases.

3.1. *The Wigmore Criteria*

When it was formulated at the start of the last century, the Wigmore test codified common law concerning claims of "a privilege against disclosure of communications between persons standing in a given relation"

(Wigmore 1905:3185). Privilege can exist on a class basis or it can be claimed on a case-by-case basis. A class-based privilege, such as attorney-client privilege, involves an assumption of privilege that places the onus of proof on any person who seeks to obtain confidential information to demonstrate why the privilege should be set aside. When the courts have not yet recognized a class privilege, privilege may still be claimed on a case-by-case basis, but here the onus of proof is on the person asserting the privilege. Research-participant privilege falls into the latter category; various courts have granted privilege to research participants when it has been claimed in particular cases (see Lowman and Palys forthcoming), but the U.S. Supreme Court has yet to hear a research-based case of privilege and make any pronouncement on the matter.

The Supreme Court of Canada has made it clear that anyone wanting to assert a case-by-case claim for privilege must do so using the Wigmore test (see *Inquest of Unknown Female* 1994; Jackson and MacCrimmon 1999; Lowman and Palys 2000; Palys and Lowman 2000; Sopinka, Lederman, and Bryant 1992). The test is also an accepted part of U.S. jurisprudence, having been used in 13 cases before the U.S. Supreme Court since 1900 and the U.S. Courts of Appeals since 1930,[5] and was used as a key basis for the federal rules of evidence regarding evidentiary privilege (see *In re Grand Jury Investigation* 1990 at par. 49). However, we know of no U.S. case in which the Wigmore criteria have been invoked to assert a claim for research-participant privilege. Indeed, in the literature describing these cases, the test is mentioned only in passing (e.g., Lempert and Saltzburg 1982; Nelson and Hedrick 1978; Traynor 1996). In contrast, in Canada, where only one researcher (Russel Ogden) has received a subpoena and been asked to divulge the identities of research participants, he successfully employed the Wigmore test to assert privilege. We will draw on his experience together with the experiences of several U.S. researchers in the process of describing the test's evidentiary requirements.

To qualify for case-by-case privilege, the Wigmore criteria require the following: "(1) The communications must originate in a *confidence* that they will not be disclosed; (2) This element of *confidentiality must be essential* to the full and satisfactory maintenance of the relation between

---

[5] *American Civil Liberties Union of Mississippi* v. *Finch* 1981; *Caesar* v. *Mountanos* 1976; *Falsone* v. *US* 1953; *Fraser* v. *US* 1944; *Garner* v. *Wolfinbarger* 1970; *In re Doe* 1983; *In re Grand Jury* 1997; *In re Grand Jury Investigation* 1990; *In re Grand Jury Proceedings Storer Communications* 1987; *In re Hampers* 1981; *Mullen* v. *US* 1958; *Radiant Burners* v. *American Gas* 1963; *Sandberg* v. *Virginia Bankshares* 1992.

the parties; (3) The *relation* must be one which in the opinion of the community ought to be sedulously *fostered*; and (4) The *injury* that would inure to the relation by the disclosure of the communications must be *greater than the benefit* thereby gained for the correct disposal of litigation" (Wigmore 1905:3185; italics in original). A successful claim of privilege by the Wigmore test necessitates evidence that speaks to all four requirements (e.g., Crabb 1996; Daisley 1994; Jackson and MacCrimmon 1999; O'Neil 1996; *R.* v *Gruenke* 1991; Traynor 1996; Wiggins and McKenna 1996).

To illustrate the depth of this responsibility, it is useful to recall the experiences of Mario Brajuha, a State University of New York graduate student writing a thesis on the sociology of the American restaurant while working as a waiter in the restaurant in which he was conducting his research. The restaurant burned, and the grand jury investigating the suspected arson subpoenaed Brajuha to testify and sought his field notes, for which he claimed privilege. At trial, the judge granted the privilege, noting that, "Affording social scientists protected freedom is essential if we are to understand how our own and other societies operate" (quoted in O'Neil 1996:41). However, while the U.S. Court of Appeals (Second Circuit) later accepted that a "scholar's privilege" *might* exist, they reversed the earlier court's decision on the grounds that the evidence presented was not sufficient to allow a decision on the claim in this case (Brajuha and Hallowell 1986; O'Neil 1996):

> Surely the application of a scholar's privilege, if it exists, requires a threshold showing consisting of a detailed description of the nature and seriousness of the scholarly study in question, of the methodology employed, of the need for assurances of confidentiality to various sources to conduct the study, and of the fact that the disclosure requested by the subpoena will seriously impinge upon that confidentiality. Brajuha has provided none of the above (*In re Grand Jury Subpoena Dated January 4* 1984:14).

We suggest that designing one's research in anticipation of meeting the requirements for privilege that are embodied in the Wigmore criteria will help the researcher address the court's concerns and thereby maximize the protection they can offer research participants through the common law. We now review the criteria and their implications for research design.

3.2. *Designing Research to Assert Research-Participant Privilege*

Establishing a Shared Understanding of Confidence. Wigmore (1905: 3233) wrote, "The moment confidence ceases, privilege ceases." In practical terms, this means that researchers should ensure there is a clear "expectation of confidentiality" that is shared by researcher and participant, and that the research record includes evidence that speaks to that understanding.

It is because of having poor evidence with respect to this criterion that subpoenaed researchers such as Mario Brajuha and Richard Scarce (see Brajuha and Hallowell 1986; Scarce 1994) faced an uphill legal battle right from the start.[6] In their cases, part of the problem was that they had not even clearly established that their interactions were part of a researcher-participant relationship; neither had completed a prospectus that had been subjected to ethics review. Consequently, there was no record of the pledge they had made to participants, or any affirmation that they were engaged in an activity that was university-approved and being executed in accordance with the canons of their discipline. Nor had either of the two kept records of their and participants' understanding regarding confidentiality in field notes. Brajuha, for example, could say only that he had guaranteed confidentiality to some but not all participants, and could not recall to whom he had guaranteed confidentiality, and to whom he had not (Brajuha and Hallowell 1986; O'Neil 1996).

In contrast, when the Vancouver Coroner subpoenaed Russel Ogden (see *Inquest of Unknown Female* 1994; Lowman and Palys 2000) and asked him to identify two of his research participants who may have witnessed a death, Ogden spoke directly to the first criterion. Evidence presented to the court showed that he had completed and revised several proposals in collaboration with his supervisory committee; that he had undergone research ethics review; and that he could produce copies of the pledge of confidentiality he had made to prospective participants. Taken together,

---

[6]Brajuha and Scarce both were unsuccessful in claiming privilege; indeed Scarce was incarcerated for 159 days. Our intention is not to chastise these two former students, who showed incredible strength and principle in situations where they clearly had received poor advice and were abandoned by their universities, but to learn from their experience.

this evidence made it abundantly obvious to the coroner reviewing his case that Ogden was indeed engaged in "research"; that officials at the university, both in criminology and on the University Research Ethics Review Committee, had read and approved his plan; that it reflected the highest ethical standards of his discipline; and that both he and his participants shared the understanding that their interactions were completely confidential. It is interesting that although there had never been a case in Canada where a legal authority had subpoenaed a researcher and asked him or her to reveal confidential information, Ogden and his supervisor correctly anticipated that if anyone were to challenge the confidentiality of their information it would be the Coroner. Part of Ogden's pledge was that he would refuse to divulge any identifying information even if threatened with contempt of court.

A matter of no small importance with respect to criterion one is that Ogden's pledge to participants was unequivocal; anything less could undermine the researcher's ability to meet the first Wigmore criterion because it runs the risk of being treated as a "waiver of privilege" by the courts. As this suggests, one implication of Wigmore is that the stronger the guarantee, the more clearly one "passes" this first part of the test. Conversely, protections for research participants can be substantially weakened by researchers' discussions with potential participants of the potential threat of court-ordered disclosure of confidential information—unless it is to reaffirm that they will continue to maintain confidentiality in the face of such legal force—and of any limits they would impose on confidentiality. For example, in *Atlantic Sugar* v. *United States* (1980), corporate respondents to an International Trade Commission questionnaire were told that the information they provided would not be disclosed "except as required by law." A U.S. Customs Court later used this exception to justify its order of disclosure of research information from researchers.

Establishing that the Confidence is Essential. Because common law assertions of researcher-participant privilege are decided on a case-by-case basis, general claims about the importance of confidentiality to research are helpful but not sufficient. Researchers should also be prepared to demonstrate that confidentiality was crucial to their ability to do the research *in the case in question* (Daisley 1994; Jackson and MacCrimmon 1999; Palys and Lowman 2000; Traynor 1996). Traynor (1996) suggests that evidence of the necessity of confidentiality should be created at the outset by addressing the issue in research proposals, in part to show that the pledge of confidentiality was part of a considered plan and neither capricious nor rote. For example, Ogden's research proposal explicitly discussed why he believed that it would be impossible to gather reliable and valid data and to meet the ethical standards of his discipline unless he was prepared to offer "absolute" confidentiality to those participants who wanted it.

Claims that confidentiality was "essential" can be weakened by researcher behavior that courts view as inconsistent with such claims. For example, Scarce's claims that confidentiality was essential to gather valid data concerning law violations by animal rights activists apparently were weakened by his non-research relationship with a particular participant, and by the presence of his wife at a key meeting where the court believed a confession may have been made, when the wife had not been shown in evidence to be conducting the research (*In re Grand Jury Proceedings: James Richard Scarce* 1993; O'Neil 1996; Scarce 1994, 1999).

Conversely, claims that confidentiality was essential can be strengthened by asking participants directly—and recording their answers—as to whether they would participate in the research if confidentiality were not guaranteed. Ogden specifically asked his two groups of research participants how important the provision of confidentiality was to their participation. Most members of the first group—persons with AIDS who merely reported their attitudes regarding assisted suicide and euthanasia—indicated that anonymity was *not* vital to their participation. However, members of the second group—persons who answered questions about actual deaths they had attended and participated in—were unanimous in stating they would divulge information to Ogden *only* if he were committed to maintaining their anonymity. The two individuals who had attracted the coroner's attention were members of the second group, and the coroner found this evidence persuasive in showing that the information he sought would never have existed in the first place had it not been for the strength of Ogden's guarantee, and that he was now obliged ethically to live by that pledge (*Inquest of Unknown Female* 1994).

In some cases it is possible that evidence comparable to Ogden's can be developed *after* a subpoena is served. For example, after being served with a subpoena for confidential research information including reports of sexual practices, researchers at the Center for Disease Control (CDC) contacted research participants and asked if they would object to disclosure of that information to the Proctor and Gamble Corporation (*Farnsworth* v. *Proctor and Gamble* 1985). The participants objected, and this was reported to the court, which agreed that the participants should not be identified.

Establishing that the Community Values the Relationship.   Criterion three asks whether the relationship under scrutiny is so socially valued that "the community" believes it warrants vigorous protection. There are many communities that can be considered here, including, for example, the research community itself; the community of which participants in the research at hand are members; the social policy communities seeking independent research information for policy formulation and implementation processes; and the broader citizenry, who benefit from the knowledge created through research. Although much of this information would come from expert testimony when and if the researcher is subpoenaed, there is evidence that can be gathered and material that should be retained as one goes through the process of preparing for and executing the research.

For example, with respect to the research community, any research that has satisfied peer review, secured funding, and/or undergone ethics review is clearly valued by the research community. Added to these sources of evidence is the extant jurisprudence on research-participant privilege, where an abundance of evidence from the courts themselves attests to the value to society of academic research (e.g., see *Dow Chemical v. Allen* 1982; *In re Michael A. Cusumano and David B. Yoffie* 1998; *Richards of Rockford v. Pacific Gas and Electric Co.* 1976).

A Balancing of Interests.   Well-designed social science research on sensitive topics that anticipates the evidentiary requirements of the Wigmore test should satisfy the first three criteria comfortably. In the case of the fourth criterion, the court balances the social values upheld in the researcher-participant relationship and the negative impacts to that relationship that would result from a violation of confidentiality against the costs that would be incurred by withholding relevant evidence in the case at hand. At one level, there is little the researcher can prepare for here, since one never knows for sure when a subpoena will arise, and hence what the other half of the equation will be. At the same time, it is instructive to consider the implications of this criterion for the way we go about research.

In general, U.S. courts have not ordered disclosure unless there is a compelling need for the information, the testimony or documents are directly relevant to the case at hand, and no alternative source of information exists. Even then, the court still must determine that its interest in the information outweighs the damage to research that would be done by disclosure. The challenge to the court is always to fashion a resolution that respects both sets of interests. In this regard, there are two distinguishable sets of interests that have fared very differently in court: the interests of researchers and of research participants.

We mention this distinction because we believe a misnomer characterizes much of the writing about privilege in the United States, where one often sees reference to "a researcher's privilege," "academic privilege," or "a scholar's privilege" (e.g., Levine and Kennedy 1999; O'Neil 1996). Stated briefly, we do not believe that one exists, nor that one necessarily should exist, over and above the protection that the research enterprise should have from interests that would engage in harassment and intimidation via litigation and thereby chill academic freedom or "punish" particular researchers or agencies for their independence. University research is a largely publicly funded enterprise whose canons extol the virtues of openness, accountability, and freedom of inquiry. As long as freedom of inquiry and the ability to do research are not affected, academics are obliged to disseminate the fruits of their labor and respond to critique. Decision-making in U.S. courts is consistent with that view (Lowman and Palys forthcoming).

With respect to research participant rights, however, we see a very different story, and suggest that the pattern of U.S. jurisprudence has made research-participant privilege a *de facto* reality. At times courts seem to go out of their way to protect participants (e.g., *In re Grand Jury Subpoena Dated January 4* 1984), apparently understanding that when volunteer participants can no longer trust their interests will be protected, the research enterprise is done.

Whether researcher-participant privilege, or any privilege, should be subject to the balancing considerations reflected in criterion four is itself a matter of some debate. In *Jaffee* v. *Redmond* (1996), the U.S. Supreme Court showed it was cognizant of the dilemma when it discussed the U.S. Court of Appeals argument that psychotherapist-patient privilege should be qualified:

> We part company with the Court of Appeals on a separate point. We reject the balancing component of the privilege implemented by that court and a small number of States. Making the promise of confidentiality con-

tingent upon a trial judge's later evaluation of the relative importance of the patient's interest in privacy and the evidentiary need for disclosure would eviscerate the effectiveness of the privilege. As we explained in *Upjohn*, if the purpose of the privilege is to be served, the participants in the confidential conversation "must be able to predict with some degree of certainty whether particular discussions will be protected. An uncertain privilege, or one which purports to be certain but results in widely varying applications by the courts, is little better than no privilege at all."

Researchers face exactly this dilemma. One of the basic principles of natural justice is that law should be known in advance. The problem with case-by-case analysis is that what we know in advance is that the law will be made after the fact while researchers must make their decisions ahead of time. However, after a five-year search of the literature describing the subpoenaing of researchers, we have yet to find a case where, in the absence of a research-participant waiver of privilege, violating a research confidence would have been the ethical thing to do. Whatever circumstances arise, using the Wigmore criteria as a guide to research design allows the researcher to anticipate the evidentiary concerns of the courts in a way that maximizes protection of research participants by creating the best case for recognition of a researcher-participant privilege.

4. CONCLUSION

The American Sociological Association ethics code asserts that researchers have an ethical obligation to be *aware* of relevant law, to make an *ethical* decision about the degree of confidentiality they are prepared to promise and then to abide by that pledge (Levine and Kennedy 1999). Understanding the law of privilege does not confine our ethical sensibilities, but is a prerequisite to using law in the service of ethics. This understanding will minimize the likelihood of law and ethics coming into conflict, and may even positively affect the future development of law.

To the extent that some statutory protections already exist, researchers should use them whenever they can. But the protections afforded by federal and state laws are limited. When statutory protections are not available, researchers must turn to the common law to assert privilege. An examination of U.S. jurisprudence suggests that the courts generally have respected research-participant privilege. When confidentiality is essential to the research, many U.S. courts have recognized that releasing the names of respondents would have a profoundly chilling effect on research participation, thereby jeopardizing research and the social benefits that flow from it (Lowman and Palys forthcoming). U.S. jurisprudence on research-participant privilege clearly recognizes that, without people willing to participate, there is no research enterprise (e.g., see Picou 1996).

We have argued that knowledge of the common law of privilege allows researchers to proactively design research in a way that maximizes legal protections for research participants. The primary advantage of a claim of privilege according to common law is that all researchers can assert it using criteria that can be anticipated. In this regard, we have suggested that the Wigmore test provides a useful framework for researchers to anticipate the evidentiary requirements of the courts.

The more that researchers use the Wigmore criteria as a guide to anticipate the evidentiary requirements of the courts, the more likely the courts will be to respond with positive decisions that may culminate in the formal recognition of research-participant privilege. Indeed, the next researcher to be subpoenaed might consider arguing that such a privilege has already been established in U.S. jurisprudence in all but name.

REFERENCES

Bond, K. 1978. "Confidentiality and the Protection of Human Subjects in Social Science Research: A Report on Recent Developments." *American Sociologist* 13: 144–52.

Brajuha, M., and L. Hallowell. 1986. "Legal Intrusion and the Politics of Field Work: The Impact of the Brajuha Case." *Urban Life* 14:454–78.

Caroll, J., and C. Knerr. 1973. "Confidentiality of Social Science Research Sources and Data: The Popkin Case." *Political Science Quarterly* 6:268–80.

———. 1975. "A Report of the APSA Confidentiality in Social Science Research Data Project." *Political Science Quarterly* 8:258–61.

Cecil, J., and G. T. Wetherington, eds. 1996. *Court-Ordered Disclosure of Academic Research: A Clash of Values of Science and Law*. Special Edition of *Law and Contemporary Problems* 59(3).

Crabb, B. B. 1996. "Judicially Compelled Disclosure of Researchers' Data: A Judge's View." *Law and Contemporary Problems* 59(3):9–34.

Daisley, B. 1994. "Clear Evidence Needed to Invoke Wigmore Rules." *Lawyer's Weekly*. December 9: 28.

Fanning, J. 1999. "Privacy and Research: Public Policy Issues." Office of the Assistant Secretary for Planning and Evaluation, U.S. Department of Health and Human Services. Unpublished paper.

Jackson, M., and M. MacCrimmon. 1999. "Research Confidentiality and Academic Privilege: A Legal Opinion." Submission prepared for the Simon Fraser University Ethics Policy Review Task Force. Available at ⟨http://www.sfu.ca/~palys/JackMacOpinion.pdf⟩.

Lempert, R. O., and S. A. Saltzburg. 1982. *A Modern Approach to Evidence: Text, Problems, Transcripts and Cases*, 2nd ed. St. Paul, MN: West Publishing.

Levine, F., and J. M. Kennedy. 1999. "Promoting a Scholar's Privilege: Accelerating the Pace." *Law and Social Inquiry* 24:967–76.

Lowman, J., and T. S. Palys. 2000. "Ethics and Institutional Conflict of Interest: The Research Confidentiality Controversy at Simon Fraser University." *Sociological Practice: A Journal of Clinical and Applied Sociology* 2(4):245–55.

———. Forthcoming. "The Ethics and Law of Confidentiality in Criminological Research." *International Journal of Criminal Justice*.

Madden, T. J., and H. S. Lessin. 1983. "Statutory Approaches to Ensuring the Privacy and Confidentiality of Social Science Research Information: The Law Enforcement Assistance Administration Experience." Pp. 263–72 in *Solutions to Ethical and Legal Problems in Social Research*, edited by R. F. Boruch and J. S. Cecil. New York: Academic Press.

McLaughlin, R. H. 1999. "From the Field to the Courthouse: Should Social Science Research be Privileged?" *Law and Social Inquiry* 24:927–66.

Nelson, R. L., and T. E. Hedrick. 1983. "The Statutory Protection of Confidential Research Data: Synthesis and Evaluation." Pp. 213–38 in *Solutions to Ethical and Legal Problems in Social Research*, edited by R. F. Boruch and J. S. Cecil. New York: Academic Press.

O'Neil, R. M. 1996. "A Researcher's Privilege: Does Any Hope Remain?" *Law and Contemporary Problems* 59(3):35–50.

Palys, T. S., and J. Lowman. 2000. "Ethical and Legal Strategies for Protecting Confidential Research Information." *Canadian Journal of Law and Society* 15(1): 39–80.

Picou, J. S. 1996. "Compelled Disclosure of Scholarly Research: Some Comments on "High Stakes" Litigation." *Law and Contemporary Problems* 59(3):149–57.

Scarce, R. 1994. "(No) Trial (But) Tribulations: When Courts and Ethnography Conflict." *Journal of Contemporary Ethnography* 23:123–49.

———. 1999. "Good Faith, Bad Ethics: When Scholars Go the Distance and Scholarly Associations Do Not." *Law and Social Inquiry* 24:977–86.

Sopinka, J., S. N. Lederman, and A. W. Bryant. 1992. *The Law of Evidence in Canada*. Toronto, Canada: Butterworths.

Traynor, M. 1996. "Countering the Excessive Subpoena for Scholarly Research." *Law and Contemporary Problems* 59(3):119–48.

Wiggins, E. C., and J. A. McKenna. 1996. "Researchers' Reactions to Compelled Disclosure of Scientific Information." *Law and Contemporary Problems* 59(3):67–94.

Wigmore, J. H. 1905. *A Treatise on the System of Evidence in Trials at Common Law, Including the Statutes and Judicial Decisions of All Jurisdictions of the United States, England, and Canada*. Boston, MA: Little, Brown.
Wolfgang, M. 1981. "Criminology: Confidentiality in Criminological Research and Other Ethical Issues." *Journal of Criminal Law and Criminology* 72:345–61.

Cases Cited

American Civil Liberties Union of Mississippi v. *Finch* (1981). 638 F.2d 1336 (5th Cir.).
Atlantic Sugar, Ltd v. *United States* (1980). 85 Cust. Ct. 128.
Caesar v. *Mountanos* (1976). 542 F.2d 1064 (9th Cir.).
Dow Chemical v. *Allen* (1982). 672 F.2d 1262 (7th Cir.).
Falsone v. *United States* (1953). 205 F.2d 734 (5th Cir.).
Farnsworth v. *Proctor and Gamble Company* (1985). 758 F.2d 1545, 1546-47 (11th Cir.).
Fraser v. *United States* (1944). 145 F.2d 139 (6th Cir.).
Garner v. *Wolfinbarger* (1970). 430 F.2d 1093 (5th Cir.).
Inquest of Unknown Female (1994). Oral Reasons for Judgment, the Honourable L.W. Campbell, Vancouver Coroner. Case file 91-240-0838.
In re Doe (1983). 711 F.2d 1187 (2nd Cir.).
In re Grand Jury (1997). 103 F.3d 1140 (3d Cir.).
In re Grand Jury Investigation (1990). 918 F.2d 374 (3rd Cir.).
In re Grand Jury Proceedings: James Richard Scarce (1993). 5 F.3d 397 (9th Cir.).
In re Grand Jury Proceedings Storer Communications (1987). 810 F.2d 580 (6th Cir.).
In re Grand Jury Subpoena Dated January 4 (1984). 750 F.2d 223. (2nd Cir.).
In re Hampers (1981). 651 F.2d 19 (1st Cir.).
In re Michael A. Cusumano and David B. Yoffie (1998). CA1-QL 567 (1st Cir.).
Jaffee v. *Redmond* (1996). 518 U.S. 1, 95-266.
M.(A.) v. *Ryan* (1997). 1 S.C.R. 157.
Mullen v. *United States* (1958). CADC-QL 156 No. 14663 (DC Cir.).
People of the State of New York v *Robert Newman* (1973). 32 N.Y.2d 379, 298 N.E.2d 651, 345 N.Y.S.2d 502 *cert. denied*, 414 U.S. 1163.
R. v. *Gruenke* (1991). 3 S.C.R. 263.
Radiant Burners v. *American Gas* (1963). 320 F.2d 314 (7th Cir.).

Richards of Rockford, Inc. v. *Pacific Gas and Electric Company* (1976).
71 F.R.D. 388 (N.D. Cal.).
Sandberg v. *Virginia Bankshares* (1992) 979 F.2d 332 (4th Cir.).
Upjohn Company v. *United States* (1981). 449 U.S. 383.

DISCUSSION: ABOVE THE LAW— RESEARCH METHODS, ETHICS, AND THE LAW OF PRIVILEGE

*Geoffrey R. Stone**

In *Anticipating Law*, Palys and Lowman set forth the rationale for a "researcher-participant privilege" and advise scholars how best to preserve the confidentiality of their research in the face of a legal system that has not looked kindly on such a privilege. Although I am inclined to agree with Palys and Lowman that a researcher-participant privilege would, on balance, be beneficial, the case for the privilege is hardly self-evident. Moreover, the advice Palys and Lowman offer researchers in the absence of such a privilege is, in my judgment, unwise. I will briefly address both of these points.

1. THE RESEARCHER-PARTICIPANT PRIVILEGE

Most of the rules of evidence, like most of the "rules" of research, are designed to get at the truth. For the most part, the rules of evidence exclude "unreliable" information from the consideration of the trier of fact. Privileges, however, are an exception. Privileges generally exclude reliable information in order to further a competing social policy. The effect of evidentiary privileges may thus be to increase the likelihood of erroneous fact-finding in criminal or civil proceedings. Because this is a high price to pay, the social policy furthered by a privilege must be quite weighty to justify the cost to the truth-finding function of the legal process.

The most well-entrenched evidentiary privilege, which is applicable in every American jurisdiction, protects confidential communications between a lawyer and a client for the purpose of legal advice. The rationale of the attorney-client privilege is that clients will not be candid with their attorneys if everything clients disclose to their attorneys can be used against them in court, and attorneys cannot give sound legal advice to their clients if clients are less than candid in their disclosures to their attorneys. Because this privilege facilitates full and candid discussion between

*University of Chicago.

19

the attorney and the client, the privilege arguably enhances the overall reliability of the legal process, even though it renders inadmissible some evidence that might be both relevant and reliable.

Other privileges, such as the marital privilege (which governs confidential communications between spouses), the physician-patient privilege, the psychotherapist-patient privilege, and the priest-penitent privilege are recognized in some jurisdictions, but not in others. Some of these privileges originated at common law; others are the result of legislation. Some jurisdictions have legislatively enacted a journalist-source privilege, although the Supreme Court has held that the First Amendment does not establish such a privilege as a constitutional right.[1]

Palys and Lowman argue that scholarly researchers should enjoy an evidentiary privilege for confidential information they learn from research participants in the course of their scholarly research. The argument is that such a privilege is necessary to protect both academic freedom and the confidentiality of research participants. More fundamentally, they maintain that such a privilege is necessary to ensure that research participants will feel free to disclose confidential information to researchers without fear that the information will later be made public.

Certainly, from the perspective of scholars, this is an appealing proposal. It may be less appealing, however, from the perspective of society as a whole. As with other privileges, whenever such a privilege is invoked it may increase the risk of erroneous fact-finding in criminal and civil cases. As a consequence, some individual whose life, liberty or property is on the line may face an increased risk of an inaccurate decision by the legal trier of fact. This is not to be taken lightly.

But we have other privileges, so why not a researcher-participant privilege as well? There may be several reasons why the researcher-participant privilege hasn't taken hold. First, unlike the attorney-client privilege, the disclosures involved in scholarly research rarely concern matters likely to come before the courts. Thus, it is only in unusual circumstances that the absence of the privilege will have a chilling effect on research. A much higher percentage of attorney-client communications concern matters that are, or could be, relevant to litigation. The absence of an evidentiary privilege would thus have a much more serious and more pervasively dampening effect on the candor of attorney-client communications than on the candor of researcher-participant communications.

[1]See *Branzburg v. Hayes*, 408 U.S. 665 (1972).

Second, most of the well-entrenched privileges implicate privacy interests that are deeply rooted in the very nature of the protected relationship. In a significant sense, these privileges are designed not only to encourage confidential communications but also to respect the inherent privacy of the marital, physician-patient, psychotherapist-patient, and clergyman-penitent relationship. The researcher-participant relationship typically lacks that essential characteristic.

Third, the general trend has been an increasing skepticism about privileges. The absence of empirical evidence that privileges actually serve their intended purpose (facilitating open communication), especially outside the attorney-client context, weighed against the loss of occasionally significant evidence in specific cases, has fueled a general hesitancy to add still more privileges to the list. Indeed, the trend has been to narrow rather than to broaden the scope of existing privileges; see Strong (1992).

Having said all this, I remain sympathetic to the idea of the researcher-participant privilege. In at least some circumstances, the absence of such a privilege could inhibit research participants from cooperating fully and candidly with a scholarly project; in at least some circumstances, the refusal of such individuals to participate, or to participate fully and candidly, could undermine the reliability of the study and perhaps even preclude the research entirely; in at least some circumstances, the loss of the research could be a significant loss for society; and in at least some circumstances, the "evidence" wouldn't have existed in the first place if the participant had not been ensured confidentiality, so recognition of the privilege (at least in those circumstances) would sacrifice little, if anything, of value to the legal process.

The closest analog, of course, is the journalist-source privilege, which has received only mixed support. My own view is that the Supreme Court was wrong to reject a constitutional basis for the journalist-source privilege, and that the First Amendment could readily be understood to embrace some form of researcher-participant privilege as well. But, at least for the moment, that is water over the dam. Short of a significant shift in the direction of the Supreme Court, proponents of the researcher-participant privilege, like supporters of the journalist-source privilege, will have to undertake the difficult and gritty work of persuading Congress and the state legislatures, one by one, that such a privilege is sound public policy. In the past, universities have demonstrated their capacity to work the legislative halls on matters of great importance to higher education.

That they haven't rallied the troops in this instance may speak volumes about the perceived need for such a privilege—at least relative to competing concerns in higher education.

It is important to note that the absence of a formal researcher-participant privilege does not mean that information conveyed to the researcher is freely available to every tomdickandharry litigant who wants it. To the contrary, courts exercise considerable discretion under Rule 45 of the Federal Rules of Civil Procedure and under the Wigmore test, as suggested by Palys and Lowman, to protect confidential information. Courts ordinarily will deny compelled disclosure of such material, and use protective orders and redaction to preserve confidentiality, unless the party seeking disclosure can demonstrate "a substantial need for the . . . material that cannot be otherwise met without undue hardship."[2] These are important protections that often will shield disclosure of confidential participant-researcher communications, even without a full-scale evidentiary privilege.

Even with these protections, however, there will inevitably be situations in which the absence of a formal privilege will impair scholarly research. Consider, for example, a social science study designed to explore the economic origins of crime, in which the researcher seeks information from individuals in the community about drug use, unlawful gun possession, and other criminal activity. If it is known that police can compel the researcher to disclose such information about specific individuals, the study will certainly be hindered. One partial solution to this dilemma, short of a full-scale privilege, would be for the courts to give real bite to the concept of "substantial need" upon a showing that disclosure will significantly undermine research. That is, courts could hold that it is inappropriate to compel disclosure of such information unless the stakes for the legal system are unusually high[3] and *clearly* outweigh the research need for confidentiality. This much could (in theory) be accomplished even without a formal privilege.

The key advantage of a full-scale privilege, analogous to the attorney-client privilege, is that it would admit of no case-by-case "bal-

[2] Federal Rules of Civil Procedure 45(c)(3)(B). See *Dow Chemical Co.* v. *Allen,* 672 F.2d 1262, 1275 (7th Cir. 1982) (to obtain confidential information in this context the interests of the moving party "must be strong and the extent of the intrusion carefully limited"). See also Crabb (1996:9, 25–30); Carrington and Jones (1996:51, 62–63); Wiggins and McKenna (1996:67, 79); Traynor (1996:119, 120, 128, 131).

[3] Suppose, for example, the police need the name of an individual who has participated in a research project in order to find a kidnapped child.

ancing" of the competing interests. It would provide absolute protection against compelled disclosure of any information protected by the privilege, regardless of anyone else's need for the information. This difference may be less significant than appears, however, for the trend has been to narrow even the established evidentiary privileges in this ad hoc direction.[4]

2. RESEARCHERS ABOVE THE LAW

In order to maximize the possibility that researchers will be able to assert confidentiality in this uncertain legal environment, Palys and Lowman advise scholarly researchers (1) to promise absolute confidentiality to research participants and (2) to be willing to go to prison for contempt of court rather than to breach that guarantee. There are several flaws in this advice.

First, a researcher following this advice would be considerably less than fully honest with research participants. In the absence of a legally recognized (and absolute) researcher-participant privilege, such a promise would create the distinctly misleading impression that the researcher has the *legal* authority to ensure confidentiality. In fact, however, the researcher will be able to honor such a promise only by violating the law. This unwittingly implicates the participant in an unlawful agreement. Whether or not this exposes the participant to possible criminal liability, it is unethical to deceive a research participant in this manner.

Second, a researcher who follows this advice places his employer (typically a university) in an exceedingly difficult position, presumably without its permission. If the researcher expressly sought the university-employer's authorization to mislead research participants in this manner, a responsible university would likely deny permission. But if the researcher takes it upon himself to follow the authors' advice, his conduct may expose the university to (1) considerable public embarrassment for employing a researcher who misleads research participants and then violates the law, (2) possible civil liability to the research participant if the researcher (either at the university's direction or otherwise) ultimately discloses the information to the court—in breach of the "absolute" guarantee of confiden-

---

[4] See Crabb (1996:9, 24); Strong (1992:107). Indeed, even those courts that have considered a researcher-participant privilege have tended to define them in terms of a balancing of competing interests. See In re *Grand Jury Subpoena Dated January 4, 1984*, 750 F.2d 223 (2d Cir. 1984). See also Traynor (1996:119, 129).

tiality,[5] or (3) possible criminal or other government sanction if the researcher-employee refuses to obey a court order to disclose the information.

Moreover, the researcher who makes such a promise places himself in a serious dilemma. He risks losing his job for knowingly making an ethically questionable promise that may place his university-employer in legal jeopardy; if he ultimately discloses the information because of a court order, he breaches his unqualified promise of confidentiality and thus renders himself vulnerable to possible civil liability to the participant for breach of contract; and if he refuses to obey a court order to disclose the information, he may be fined and/or imprisoned.

All of which brings me to the most basic question. Is it ethical for researchers to promise absolute confidentiality if the only way they can fully honor such promises is by refusing to comply with a lawful judicial order? The answer, in my judgment, is "no."

The essence of the authors' claim is that considerations of "academic freedom" and professional "ethics" support their conclusion as the necessary extension of a higher law. This is unpersuasive. Scholars and universities in this nation operate in a privileged environment. But even scholars and universities are not above the law. It is not for scholars and universities to judge for themselves which laws they will obey and which they will flout. Such an attitude, if embraced in practice, would disserve higher education and threaten the distinctive position scholars and universities enjoy. Such an approach would be arrogant, self-righteous, and misguided.

I do not mean to suggest that violation of the law is never ethical, either as a form of civil disobedience or otherwise. But it should be a last resort and reserved for matters of high principle. Before reaching that point, researchers and universities must decide whether recognition of a researcher-participant privilege is truly a matter of fundamental concern to the research community. If so (and this conclusion is far from obvious), they must then make a serious and sustained effort *within* our political and legal system to educate and persuade voters, courts, and legislators to enact such a privilege as essential to the ability of researchers and universities to fulfill their responsibilities to society.

[5] See *Cohen* v. *Cowles Media Co.*, 501 U.S. 663 (1991) (upholding civil liability for a newspaper whose reporter breached promise of absolute confidentiality to a source). See also Traynor (1996:119, 121–22) ("if a court refuses to uphold such an assurance, researchers and their sponsors may be liable for the ensuing breach of confidentiality").

If they undertake such an effort, they may succeed. Increasing numbers of states have enacted the journalist-source privilege in recent years. But in the absence of such an effort, law violation by individual researchers is an inappropriate and self-aggrandizing response to the challenge. And if the community of universities and researchers is not willing to make this matter a high priority for sustained political and legal action, then courts and legislators should not recognize the privilege and researchers should conform their behavior to the requirements of the law.

What about the individual researcher who believes she *needs* to guarantee absolute confidentiality to her participants in order to undertake her research? Is she justified in making such a promise? For the reasons noted above, such conduct would be unethical with respect to both the participants and the employer-university. But even putting those issues aside, let's suppose we reach the moment of truth. The judge orders the researcher to disclose information because it is of substantial importance to an on-going legal proceeding. If the researcher has expressly promised participants absolute confidentiality, she may feel a strong moral obligation to honor her promise, and even to go to jail if necessary. This may be thrilling. The researcher will likely fancy herself a martyr and may even make it into the *Times*. After all, she is standing on principle in honoring her sacred promise to the participant. But this is all circular. The researcher had no business—professionally, legally, or ethically—making the promise in the first place. By making the initial promise, the researcher falsely constructs the role of martyr. If she hadn't offered the unwarranted guarantee of absolute confidentiality, the dilemma—and the drama—would not exist.

Palys and Lowman see this situation differently both because they think recognition of a researcher-participant privilege would be good public policy (I agree) and because they embrace a troubling view of the citizen's responsibility to comply with the law. They seem to think that it is appropriate and ethical for an individual to calculate whether the benefit of pursuing his self-interest exceeds the cost imposed upon him for violating the law. If so, it's apparently acceptable to violate the law. It is not so simple. An individual does not act ethically or responsibly if he kills his business partner because he's willing to spend 20 years in jail. And a researcher does not act ethically or responsibly if he subverts the legal process by unlawfully refusing to disclose relevant information to a court because he's willing to serve six months in jail.

How would we draw the line if we were to embrace such an approach to the law? If Palys and Lowman can disobey this law because they think it unduly interferes with their ability to undertake their research, what about a law against wiretaps? Is it ethical for a researcher unlawfully to wiretap phone calls in order to enhance his research? Is it ethical for a scholar to break into a subject's home in order to find information that might advance her study? What is the *ethical* principle that grants the scholar the right to violate some of these laws but not others? Or are we free to violate them all? Except as a last resort, the way to change "bad" laws is to change them.

Finally, suppose we get to the last resort. Suppose over the next ten years universities and researchers make a concerted effort to educate and persuade voters, courts, and legislators to adopt the researcher-participant privilege—without success. Is it then appropriate for scholars to take matters into their own hands and unconditionally promise confidentiality to participants, knowing that they will have to violate the law to fulfill the promise? No. Civil disobedience (if that's what this is) is not appropriate whenever one "loses" in the political and legal process. Such action may be ethical when the moral stakes are high and when the "system" is oppressive, unjust and illegitimate, but there is no ethical basis for such action merely because citizens, courts and legislators don't do what scholars think is in their best interests. To compare the moral plight of the researcher who cannot promise absolute confidentiality to that of African-Americans who refused to leave segregated lunch counters or to that of individuals subpoenaed by congressional committees to disclose Communist affiliations is to profoundly inflate the moral dimension of the researcher's dilemma. Yes, it would be good if scholars could ensure research participants absolute confidentiality. And, yes, it would be good if the government were to fund all worthwhile research. But neither is a right of high moral dimensions.

Ironically, all of this is largely unnecessary. The proper course for a researcher who cannot count on the protection of an absolute researcher-participant privilege is not to promise unconditional confidentiality, but to promise unconditional confidentiality *within the limits allowed by the law*. Although some research-participants may not be satisfied by this, they will be few and far between. In any event, this is the most one can responsibly promise, and it is thus the most one *should* promise.

Palys and Lowman argue that if researchers cast their promise in this form it may discourage courts from protecting confidentiality. The great weight of opinion is that this concern is without foundation.[6] Courts are highly unlikely to disadvantage a researcher because he promises confidentially "within the limits allowed by law." Making a promise that one cannot honor without violating the law is not likely to prove an effective way to win over the courts. The proper course is to make the case on the merits—both case-by-case and legislature-by-legislature—that sound public policy justifies the protection of confidentiality when it is necessary to the research enterprise.

REFERENCES

Carrington, P., and T. Jones. 1996. "Reluctant Experts." *Law and Contemporary Problems* 59:51–63.
Cecil, J., and G. T. Wetherington. 1996. "Foreward." *Law and Contemporary Problems* 59:1–5.
Crabb, B. 1996. "Judicially Compelled Disclosure of Researchers' Data: A Judge's View." *Law and Contemporary Problems* 59:9–30.
Strong, J. W. 1992. *McCormick on Evidence* (4th ed.). St. Paul, MN: West.
Traynor, M. 1996. "Countering the Excessive Subpoena for Scholarly Research." *Law and Contemporary Problems* 59:119–32.
Wiggins, E., and J. McKenna. 1996. "Researchers' Reactions to Compelled Disclosure of Scientific Information." *Law and Contemporary Problems* 59:67–82.

Cases Cited

Atlantic Sugar Ltd. v. *United States*, 85 Customs Court 128 (1980).
Branzburg v. *Hayes*, 408 U. S. 665 (1972).
Cohen v. *Cowles Media Co.*, 501 U.S. 663 (1991).
Dow Chemical Co. v. *Allen*, 672 F.2d 1262 (7th Cir. 1982).
Farnsworth v. *Proctor and Gamble Co.*, 758 F.2d 1545 (11th Cir. 1985).
In re *Grand Jury Subpoena Dated January 4, 1984*, 750 F.2d 223 (2d Cir. 1984).
Lampshire v. *Proctor and Gamble Co.*, 94 F.R.D. 58 (N.D. Ga. 1982).

[6]See, e.g., Cecil and Wetherington (1996:1, 5); O'Neil (1996:35, 36, 40, 46); Wiggins and McKenna (1996:67, 82); Traynor (1996:119, 132). See also *Farnsworth* v. *Proctor & Gamble Co.*, 758 F.2d 1545, 1547 (11th Cir. 1985) ("Even without an express guarantee of confidentiality there is still an expectation, not unjustified, that when highly personal and potentially embarrassing information is given for the sake of medical research, it will remain private."); *Lampshire* v. *Proctor & Gamble Co.*, 94 F.R.D. 58 (N.D. Ga 1982). The one decision the authors cite in support of this concern in no way suggests that the court would have granted any greater confidentiality to the documents in question if the questionnaire had not said "except as provided by law." *Atlantic Sugar Ltd.* v. *United States*, 85 Customs Court 128 (1980.)

DISCUSSION: ANTICIPATING PROBLEMS— DOING SOCIAL SCIENCE RESEARCH IN THE SHADOW OF THE LAW

James Lindgren *

As a social science researcher, should you promise full confidentiality to the people that you are studying? If the government or a private plaintiff wants your research notes or records, will you be put to the choice of either breaking your confidences or going to jail? In their provocative article, *Anticipating Law*, Ted Palys and John Lowman suggest that those researchers who design their projects so as to maximize the need for confidences and who actually make stronger promises of confidentiality may be able to give both their participants and themselves more legal protection.

This strategic use of the law is both the paper's strength and its primary danger. While many (if not most) researchers blithely promise their participants absolute confidentiality, the more sophisticated among them have been promising much less. During my own Ph.D. training at the University of Chicago, Professor Norman Bradburn, who was also the Research Director of the National Opinion Research Center, instructed his graduate students not to promise any more than you can deliver. He recommended promising to keep information confidential only to the extent that the law allows.

In some fields, such as sociology, the code of ethics requires that researchers go one step further, determining the extent of legal protection and ("as appropriate") explaining their findings to the participants. The current provision of the American Sociological Association's code provides these guidelines: "Sociologists inform themselves fully about all laws and rules which may limit or alter guarantees of confidentiality. They determine their ability to guarantee absolute confidentiality and, as appropriate, inform research participants, students, employees, clients, or others of any limitations to this guarantee at the outset" (ASA 1997, Principle E). The ASA also provides an important exception: Researchers may break

*Northwestern University of Law
This paper was supported by the Searle Fund of Northwestern University.

confidences to prevent future death or damage to the health of the subject or others (ASA 1997, 11.02(b); Levine and Kennedy, 1999, p. 973).

The earlier ASA Code went further: "Confidential information provided by research participants must be treated as such by sociologists, even when this information enjoys no legal protection or privilege and legal force is applied" (ASA 1989, IB7; Scarce 1999). This had the potential of putting researchers above the law, mandating that they violate court orders (Levine and Kennedy, 1999).

Palys and Lowman offer an interesting partial solution to this dilemma: Design the research and elicit participation in such a way that the participants have a reasonable expectation of privacy, in part because that is what they were promised by the researchers. That way courts are more likely to recognize a privilege. Then both the participants and the researchers win—the researchers are not sent to jail and the participants' confidences are preserved.

Palys and Lowman (this volume, p. 9) explain their approach in the context of the case of Russel Ogden, a Canadian researcher who refused to divulge possible information about a murder:

> A matter of no small importance . . . is that Ogden's pledge to participants was unequivocal; anything less . . . runs the risk of being treated as a "waiver of privilege" by the courts. As this suggests, one implication of Wigmore is that the stronger the guarantee, the more clearly one "passes" this first part of the test. Conversely, protections for research participants can be substantially weakened by researchers' discussions with potential participants of the potential threat of court-ordered disclosure of confidential information—unless it is to reaffirm that they will continue to maintain confidentiality in the face of such legal force—and of any limits they would impose on confidentiality.

This is a version of the approach mandated by the 1989 ASA Code, but it is invoked, not just for moral reasons but for strategic ones. Promising more than the law might allow could create more protection for researchers and participants.

This is not the only contribution of the paper. They emphasize the greater legal protection researchers can give to confidences when their practices are more regular, their records better, their compliance with human subjects review procedures more scrupulous, and so on.

The problem with Palys and Lowman's approach is that its legal status is more doubtful than their paper suggests. In their conclusion (p. 13), they assert:

> To the extent that some statutory protections already exist, researchers should use them whenever they can. But the protections afforded by federal and state laws are limited. When statutory protections are not available, researchers must turn to the common law to assert privilege. An examination of U.S. jurisprudence suggests that the courts generally have respected *research-participant privilege*.

Other scholars who share Palys and Lowman's desire for a limited researcher privilege have reviewed the cases and concluded that no such privilege is generally recognized in the United States (Levine and Kennedy 1999; McLaughlin 1999). For example, Levine and Kennedy assert: "Despite some helpful court opinions over the past three decades, no general recognition of a social science research privilege in criminal or civil legal proceedings has emerged" (p. 968).

In legal scholarship, it is quite common to combine normative and descriptive arguments in the same paper (as Palys and Lowman do). It is important, however, to understand that Palys and Lowman are not only arguing what researchers should do when designing their research projects in the shadow of the law; they are also arguing what the law should be. It is not clear just how serious the risk is of going to jail if you take their suggestions and promise more confidentiality than many other researchers would in the same situation. You will probably, as they argue, increase your chances of legally conferring the confidentiality you promised the participants, which would both protect their secrets and protect you from jail for refusing to turn them over. But you will probably also increase the chances that you will go to jail—at least until the court decides that you will not relent. Rik Scarce spent 159 days in jail protecting his research from government intrusion (Scarce 1999), though Palys and Lowman plausibly argue that he might have fared much better if he had followed their prescriptions—especially making his promises of confidentiality explicit and documenting them.

A further reason to be cautious about the state of the current law in the United States is that common law privileges are primarily a matter of state law (as for example, journalist privileges usually are). It is quite likely that, even if the law develops as Palys and Lowman hope it does, some states would respect a researcher privilege while others would not.

In Daniel Ellsberg's famous 1959 Rand essay on nuclear blackmail (Ellsberg [1959] 1975), he considered a massive response to a nuclear attack as irrational. Working from that premise, he argued that it was necessary to persuade the other side in a situation of nuclear deterrence that you were just crazy enough to respond massively to an attack even when such a response would just invite more devastation of your own country. He discussed ways to accomplish this deterrence besides just persuading the other side that you were unstable. For example, you could delegate the response decision or you could tie your hands in what we today call pre-commitment strategies.

Palys and Lowman are suggesting something similar for researchers. If you can persuade the courts that you will go to jail for five months, as did Rik Scarce (Scarce 1999), rather than divulge the participants' secrets, the courts are more likely to back down and respect your position. But Palys and Lowman demonstrate that your actions are more likely to succeed if they are supported, not just by the courage of your defiant convictions, but by strategies that both tie your hands and make the need for confidentiality manifest—through explicit commitments to participants, good record-keeping, and strong principles.

REFERENCES

American Sociological Association (ASA). 1989. Code of Ethics. Washington, D.C.: American Sociological Association.
———. 1997. Code of Ethics. Washington, D.C.: American Sociological Association. (http://www.asanet.org/ecoderev.htm).
Ellsberg, Daniel. [1959] 1975. "The Theory and Practice of Blackmail." Pp. 343–58 in Bargaining: Formal Theories of Negotiation, edited by Oran R. Young. Champaign: University of Illinois Press.
Levine, F., and J. M. Kennedy. 1999. "Promoting a Scholar's Privilege: Accelerating the Pace." Law and Social Inquiry 24:967–76.
McLaughlin, R. H. 1999. "From the Field to the Courthouse: Should Social Science Research be Privileged?" Law and Social Inquiry 24:927–66.
Scarce, R. 1999. "Good Faith, Bad Ethics: When Scholars Go the Distance and Scholarly Associations Do Not." Law and Social Inquiry 24:977–86.

MEASURES OF MULTIGROUP SEGREGATION

Sean F. Reardon*
Glenn Firebaugh*

In this paper we derive and evaluate measures of multigroup segregation. After describing four ways to conceptualize the measurement of multigroup segregation—as the disproportionality in group (e.g., race) proportions across organizational units (e.g., schools or census tracts), as the strength of association between nominal variables indexing group and organizational unit membership, as the ratio of between-unit diversity to total diversity, and as the weighted average of two-group segregation indices—we derive six multigroup segregation indices: a dissimilarity index (D), a Gini index (G), an information theory index (H), a squared coefficient of variation index (C), a relative diversity index (R), and a normalized exposure index (P). We evaluate these six indices against a set of seven desirable properties of segregation indices. We conclude that the information theory index H is the most conceptually and mathematically satisfactory index, since it alone obeys the principle of transfers in the multigroup case. Moreover, H is the only multigroup index that can be decomposed into a sum of between- and within-group components.

This paper was supported by a Spencer Foundation Small Grant to Reardon and NSF grants (NSF SBR-9515153 and SBR-9870870) to Firebaugh. All errors remain the responsibility of the authors. Address all correspondence to Sean F. Reardon, 310F Rackley Building, Pennsylvania State University, University Park, PA 16802 (sean@pop.psu.edu).
*Pennsylvania State University

1. INTRODUCTION

The measurement of segregation has a venerable history in U.S. sociology, dating back to the late 1940s and early 1950s, when a variety
of segregation indices were proposed and discussed in a series of articles in the *American Sociological Review* (Bell 1954; Cowgill and
Cowgill 1951; Duncan and Duncan 1955; Jahn 1950; Jahn, Schmid, and
Schrag 1947; Williams 1948). With few exceptions (Theil 1972; Theil
and Finezza 1971), however, the major methodological developments
in segregation measurement have been limited to measuring segregation between two population groups—between blacks and whites, for
example, or men and women (James and Taeuber 1985; Massey and Denton 1988).

As U.S. society becomes more racially diverse, two-group measures of segregation will become increasingly inadequate for describing
complex patterns of racial segregation and integration. In this paper we
take up the challenge of extending dichotomous indices of segregation to
the multigroup case. First, however, we present a brief summary of prior
work on segregation measurement.

1.1. *A Brief History of Segregation Measurement*

The first systematic analysis and critique of segregation indices was Duncan and Duncan's seminal 1955 article in the *American Sociological
Review*. The problem, as the Duncans saw it, was that segregation measures were often constructed from "naive" notions of segregation rather
than being derived from clearly articulated conceptualizations of segregation and its processes:

> [Segregation] is a concept rich in theoretical suggestive-
> ness and of unquestionable heuristic value. Clearly we
> would not wish to sacrifice the capital of theorization and
> observation already invested in the concept. Yet this is
> what is involved in the solution offered by naive opera-
> tionalism, in more or less arbitrarily matching some con-
> venient numerical procedure with the verbal concept of
> segregation . . . (1955, p. 217).

Despite the Duncans' call for careful theoretical grounding of segregation measurement, no comprehensive approach to segregation measurement was put forth until the 1980s.[1]

The 1980s saw two important developments in the theory of segregation measurement. First, James and Taeuber (1985)—drawing on Schwartz and Winship's (1980) work on inequality measurement—developed a set of criteria against which segregation measures could be evaluated and used these criteria to demonstrate that indices that are highly correlated in empirical studies may nonetheless behave very differently under certain circumstances, such as when the population shares of groups change. Second, Massey and Denton (1988) used factor analysis to classify segregation indices into five distinct dimensions, which they named *evenness, exposure, concentration, centralization,* and *clustering.* Measures of evenness (e.g., Gini and Dissimilarity) and exposure (P^*) have been most commonly used to measure segregation. These measures describe the distribution of groups among organizational units (e.g., schools, census tracts) without regard for their spatial proximity. The spatial dimensions of segregation are measured by indices of concentration, centralization, and clustering.

The importance of the work of James and Taeuber and of Massey and Denton lies in the clarity they bring to the operationalization of the concept of "segregation." However, neither article discusses measures of multigroup segregation. While several authors have suggested multigroup measures, these indices have been rarely used or discussed. Consequently, the development of multigroup segregation measures lacks the conceptual sophistication of dichotomous measures.

---

[1]Prior to the mid-1980s, sociologists relied on a variety of indices, most commonly the dissimilarity index (popularized by Taeuber and Taeuber 1965), the P^* exposure indices (Bell 1954; Farley 1984; Farley 1977; Lieberson and Carter 1982a; Lieberson and Carter 1982b), and the variance ratio index (Bell 1954; Coleman, Hoffer, and Kilgore 1982; Duncan and Duncan 1955; Zoloth 1976) to measure residential and educational segregation. A lively debate in the 1970s and 1980s centered on the merits and flaws of these and other segregation indices (Cohen, Falk, and Cortese 1976; Coleman, Hoffer and Kilgore 1982; Cortese, Falk, and Cohen 1976; Falk, Cortese, and Cohen 1978; James and Taeuber 1985; Kestenbaum 1980; Lieberson and Carter 1982b; Morgan 1983; Taeuber and Taeuber 1976; Winship 1977; Winship 1978).

1.2. *Our Objectives*

This article derives and evaluates a set of six multigroup segregation indices. To this point, multigroup segregation indices have been constructed in an ad hoc fashion, without a general set of principles to guide their development.[2] Moreover, there has been no systematic effort to evaluate the properties of these multigroup indices. This article provides such an evaluation.

2. MEASURES OF MULTIGROUP SEGREGATION

2.1. *Notation*

Throughout this paper, we use the following notation: t denotes size and π denotes proportion; subscripts i and j index organizational unit (e.g., school, census tract); and subscripts m and n index group (e.g., racial group). Hence:

t_j = number of cases (individuals) in organizational unit j

T = total number of cases (note that $\Sigma_j (t_j / T) = 1$)

π_m = proportion in group m (e.g., proportion black)

π_{jm} = proportion in group m, of those in unit j

      (e.g., proportion black in school j)

Because segregation measures are functions of the group proportions (the π_m's and the π_{jm}'s), two measures of the variation in group membership figure prominently in the measurement of segregation—

---

[2]The first measure to be used as a multigroup segregation index, H—the information theory index, also called the entropy index—was defined by Theil (1972; Theil and Finezza 1971). Derived from a branch of mathematics known as information theory, H has an undeserved reputation for being hard to interpret, and has been rarely used in empirical research (for examples, see Kulis 1997; Miller and Quigley 1990; Reardon and Yun 2001; Reardon, Yun, and Eitle 2000; White 1986). A number of other multigroup indices have been proposed but even less often used. Morgan (1975) and Sakoda (1981) have provided generalizations of the dissimilarity index. Reardon (1998) defined a multigroup generalization of the Gini index. James (1986) defined an exposure-based multigroup generalization of V, the variance ratio index. Carlson (1992) used Goodman and Kruskal's τ_b (Goodman and Kruskal 1954) to measure race/sex occupational segregation; τ_b reduces to V in the two-group case, and so can be seen as a multigroup generalization of V.

Simpson's Interaction Index, denoted I (Lieberson 1969; White 1986) and
Theil's Entropy Index, denoted E (Theil 1972):

$$I = \sum_{m=1}^{M} \pi_m(1 - \pi_m) \tag{1}$$

$$E = \sum_{m=1}^{M} \pi_m \ln\left(\frac{1}{\pi_m}\right), \tag{2}$$

where ln is the natural logarithm (here and throughout the article).[3] Both I
and E can be seen as measures of the "diversity" of a population since
both are equal to zero if and only if all individuals are members of a single
group ("no diversity") and both are maximized if and only if individuals
are evenly distributed among the M groups ($\pi_m = 1/M$ for all m).

2.2. Criteria for Evaluating Measures of Multigroup Segregation

First we state the four James and Taeuber (1985) criteria—organizational
equivalence, size invariance, the principle of transfers, and composition
invariance—which specify how segregation indices should respond to
changes in the distribution of groups among organizational units. Because
two-group indices respond the same way to transfers (one-way transfers
from unit i to unit j) and exchanges (two-way transfers between units i
and j), James and Taeuber (1985) conflate the two under the rubric "transfers." However, multigroup segregation indices can respond differently to
exchanges than to transfers, so we add a fifth criterion, the principle of
exchanges.[4]

1. *Organizational equivalence*: If an organizational unit is divided into
    k units, each with the same group proportions as the original unit,
    segregation remains unchanged. Likewise, if k organizational units

---

[3] Note that we define $0 \cdot \ln(1/0) = \lim_{\pi \to 0} (\pi \cdot \ln(1/\pi)) = 0$. Note also that E can
be defined using logarithms to any base; we use the natural logarithm for simplicity
throughout this article.
[4] In addition to the criteria described here, a multigroup segregation index
should (1) be bounded between 0 (no segregation) and 1 (complete segregation); (2)
be a continuous function of the within-unit group proportions and the unit sizes; and
(3) allow the calculation of segregation among M groups, where $M \geq 2$. The multigroup indices we derive below meet all three criteria.

      with identical group proportions are combined into a single unit, seg-
regation is unchanged.

2.   *Size invariance*: If the number of persons of each group m in each
organizational unit j is multiplied by a constant factor p, segregation
is unchanged.

3.   *Transfers*: If an individual of group m is moved from organizational
unit i to unit j, where the proportion of persons of group m is greater
in unit i than in j ($\pi_{im} > \pi_{jm}$), then segregation is reduced.

4.   *Exchanges*: If an individual of group m in organizational unit i is
exchanged with an individual of group n from organizational unit j,
where the proportion of persons of group m is greater in unit i than in
j ($\pi_{im} > \pi_{jm}$) and the proportion of persons of group n is greater in
unit j than in i ($\pi_{jn} > \pi_{in}$), segregation is reduced.

5.   *Composition invariance*: In James and Taeuber's formulation, the
composition invariance criterion states that if the number of persons
of group m in each unit increases by a constant factor p and the number and distribution of persons of all other groups is unchanged, segregation is unchanged. This definition corresponds to the "margin-
free" criterion discussed in the sex segregation literature (e.g., Charles
and Grusky 1995; Grusky and Charles 1998; Watts 1992; Watts 1994).
Not all scholars of segregation agree, however, that composition
invariance is a desirable property for segregation measures (e.g., see
Coleman, Hoffer, and Kilgore 1982).

In addition to the James and Taeuber criteria, we define two decomposability properties that are desirable for segregation indices—organizational
and group decomposability.

6.   *Additive organizational decomposability*: If J organizational units
are clustered in K clusters, then a segregation measure should be
decomposable into a sum of independent within- and between-
cluster components.

7.   *Additive Group Decomposability*: If M groups are clustered in N supergroups, then a segregation measure should be decomposable into a
sum of independent within- and between-supergroup components.

Although not necessary for defining a meaningful segregation measure,
organizational and group decomposability are useful properties for many
analyses, since organizational units (schools, census tracts) and/or groups
(ethnic groups) are often clustered.

2.3. *Four Approaches to Deriving Multigroup Segregation Measures*

Multigroup segregation indices can be derived from different starting points, reflecting alternative ways to think about segregation. First, segregation can be thought of as a function of the disproportionality in group proportions across organizational units. This conceptualization links the measurement of segregation to the measurement of inequality, since inequality can also be conceptualized as a function of the disproportionality in the distribution of some good (Firebaugh 1998; Firebaugh 1999). Second, segregation can be thought of as association between groups and organizational units, so segregation indices can be related to association measures such as χ^2 and G^2. Third, segregation can be conceptualized as variation in the diversity of units (e.g., variation in the racial diversity of schools). This suggests a variance decomposition approach to the measurement of segregation, in which we first define a measure of the total diversity of a population and then define segregation as the share of this total diversity accounted for by the between-unit (e.g., school-to-school) differences in group proportions. A fourth approach is to construct a multigroup segregation measure as a weighted average of dichotomous segregation indices.

2.3.1. *Segregation as Disproportionality in Group Proportions*
We start with segregation as disproportionality. The disproportionality approach begins with the observation that segregation relates to the ratio of π_{jm} to π_m:

Disproportionality Axiom for Segregation. Segregation is zero when and only when $\pi_{jm}/\pi_m = 1$ for all j and m; otherwise, segregation is greater than zero.

The ratio $r_{jm} = \pi_{jm}/\pi_m$ reflects the extent to which group m is disproportionately represented in unit j ($r_{jm} < 1.0$ indicates group m is underrepresented; $r_{jm} > 1.0$ indicates group m is overrepresented). We can define segregation as the average disproportionality across all units and groups— that is, the average of the deviations of the r_{jm} from 1.0, where "deviation" is measured according to some function f such that $f(1) = 0$. In particular, we can define the weighted average disproportionality, W, as the average value of $f(r_{jm})$ across all units and groups, weighted by unit size and group proportions:

$$W = \sum_{m=1}^{M} \pi_m \sum_{j=1}^{J} \frac{t_j}{T} f(r_{jm}). \tag{3}$$

While there are many possible disproportionality functions f, an appropriate function f will have the property that W obtains its minimum value of zero if and only if $r_{jm} = 1.0$ for all j and m (if $\pi_{jm} = \pi_m$ for all j and m). The maximum value of W will depend on the specific function f. Therefore, to define an index of segregation that is bounded between 0 and 1, we divide W by its maximum possible value (the value in the case of complete segregation) to set the upper bound to 1.0:

$$Segregation = \frac{W}{\max(W)} = \frac{W}{W^*}, \tag{4}$$

where W^* is the value of W obtained in the case of complete segregation. Equations (3) and (4) define a general class of segregation indices, each member of which is derived from a different disproportionality function f.

Firebaugh (1998, 1999) has shown that many inequality indices can be thought of as measures of the average deviation of X_j from μ (the mean of the X_j), where deviation is defined by some disproportionality function f. Different inequality indices give different results because they employ different disproportionality functions—the function used to measure distance from 1.0. Columns 1 and 2 of Table 1 list the disproportionality functions for four standard inequality indices. We can derive four segregation indices from these four disproportionality functions (Table 1).[5]

[5] Our approach here to deriving segregation indices from the disproportionality functions used in inequality indices relies on calculating the disproportionality of within-unit group proportions (π_{jm}) relative to overall group proportions (π_m). Earlier discussions define segregation indices in terms of proportions, rather than ratios, or define segregation in terms of the disproportionality of within-unit black/white or male/female ratios, relative to overall ratios (e.g., see Deutsch, Flückiger, and Silber 1994; James and Taeuber 1985). James and Taeuber (1985) note that some black/white racial segregation indices (e.g., the dissimilarity, Gini, and Atkinson indices) can be derived from inequality measures simply by calculating the inequality, across all whites, in the black/white ratios of their schools or tracts. However, this approach has several limitations. First, formulations based on black/white ratios will sometimes encounter the problem of division by zero (James and Taeuber 1985, footnote 7). The r_{jm}-ratio approach avoids this problem since the pertinent ratio is π_{jm}/π_m, and by definition $\pi_m > 0$ for groups in the data. Second, James and Taeuber do not generalize their approach to the case of multiple groups, since there is no clear multigroup analog to the black/white ratio they employ. Finally, while the James and Taeuber approach gives meaningful two-group results for D, G, and the Atkinson index, our disproportionality approach yields not only multigroup versions of D and G, but also yields H and a multigroup version of V.

TABLE 1

Derivation of Disproportionality-Based Multigroup Segregation Indices from Disproportionality Functions

Disproportionality Function $f(r_{jm})$	Corresponding Inequality Index	Maximum[a] of $\sum_{m=1}^{M}\pi_m\sum_{j=1}^{J}\frac{t_j}{T}f(r_{jm})$	Multigroup Segregation Index	Relationship to Association Measure
$\lvert r-1\rvert/2$	Mean relative deviation	I[b]	$D=\dfrac{1}{2I}\sum_{m=1}^{M}\pi_m\sum_{j=1}^{J}\dfrac{t_j}{T}\lvert r_{jm}-1\rvert$	n/a
$\lvert r_i-r_j\rvert/2$	Gini coefficient	I[b]	$G=\dfrac{1}{2I}\sum_{m=1}^{M}\pi_m\sum_{i=1}^{J}\sum_{j=1}^{J}\dfrac{t_i t_j}{T^2}\lvert r_{im}-r_{jm}\rvert$	n/a
$r\ln r$	Theil	E[c]	$H=\dfrac{1}{E}\sum_{m=1}^{M}\pi_m\sum_{j=1}^{J}\dfrac{t_j}{T}r_{jm}\ln r_{jm}$	$H=\dfrac{G^2}{2TE}$
$(r-1)^2$	Squared coefficient of variation	$(M-1)$	$C=\dfrac{1}{M-1}\sum_{m=1}^{M}\pi_m\sum_{j=1}^{J}\dfrac{t_j}{T}(r_{jm}-1)^2$	$C=\dfrac{\chi^2}{T(M-1)}$

[a]See Appendix A for proofs.
[b]I denotes the Simpson Interaction Index (Equation [1]).
[c]E denotes Theil's Entropy index (Equation [2]).

41

Table 1 shows the derivation of four multigroup segregation indices from four disproportionality functions. The mean relative deviation disproportionality function leads to a multigroup measure we call the generalized dissimilarity index (D), since it reduces to the familiar binary dissimilarity index when $M = 2$. This generalized D is equivalent to the generalizations of the dissimilarity index given by others (Morgan 1975; Reardon 1998; Sakoda 1981) and can be interpreted as the percentage of all individuals who would have to transfer among units to equalize the group proportions across units, divided by the percentage who would have to transfer if the system started in a state of complete segregation.

Likewise, the Gini disproportionality function produces a multigroup segregation measure we call the generalized Gini index (G), also defined by Reardon (1998), that reduces to the familiar Gini index of segregation in the two-group case, and can be interpreted as the weighted sum, over M groups, of the weighted average absolute difference in group proportions between all possible pairs of units, divided by the maximum possible value of this sum, obtained if the system were in a state of complete segregation.

The Theil disproportionality function yields the Theil information theory index (H), though Theil derived H using a different approach (Theil 1972; Theil and Finezza 1971). As we shall see below, H can be interpreted as a normalized likelihood-ratio measure of association between two nominal variables indexing group and unit memberships, respectively. It can also be interpreted as one minus the ratio of the average within-unit population diversity to the diversity of the total population.

Finally, the squared coefficient of variation function gives a multigroup segregation measure that we denote by C. This index has not been previously defined in the multigroup case, although it does reduce to the familiar V in the two-group case. It can be interpreted as a measure of the variance of the r_{jm}'s or, as we will see below, as a normalized chi-squared measure of association between groups and units.

2.3.2. *Segregation Indices as Measures of Association*
An alternative approach to deriving segregation indices comes from noting that segregation can be thought of as a measure of association for two-way contingency tables (White 1986, p. 208). Conceptualize the cross-classification of a nominal variable indexing M groups (e.g., racial groups) with a nominal variable indexing J organizational units (e.g., schools). Then define a class of association measures A as

$$A = \sum_{m=1}^{M} \sum_{j=1}^{J} E(t_{jm}) \cdot f\left(\frac{t_{jm}}{E(t_{jm})}\right), \tag{5}$$

where t_{jm} denotes the number of cases in the jm^{th} cell, and $E(t_{jm})$ is the expected count in the jm^{th} cell under the assumption of no association (the expected number of members of group m in unit j in the case of no association or, equivalently, zero segregation). Equation (5) defines a general class of association measures A, where A is the average deviation of the observed cell counts from the expected cell counts, weighted by the expected cell counts, where the deviation is defined by some distance function f. Hence the greater the weighted-average distance of the t_{jm} from the $E(t_{jm})$, the greater is the value of A.

Note that equation (5) subsumes χ^2 and G^2, from which most measures of association are derived. If $f(r)$ measures the squared distance from r to 1.0—that is, if $f(r) = (r-1)^2$—we get $A = \chi^2$, the chi-squared statistic. If $f(r) = r \ln r$, as in the Theil index, we get $A = G^2/2$, or one-half the likelihood ratio chi-squared statistic. Note also that $E(t_{jm}) = \pi_m t_j$ and that $t_{j\,m}/E(t_{jm}) = r_{jm}$. Hence

$$A = \sum_{m=1}^{M} \sum_{j=1}^{J} \pi_m t_j f(r_{jm}) = TW. \tag{6}$$

If we divide an association measure A by its maximum possible value (obtained in the case of complete segregation), we get a class of segregation measures bounded between 0 (in the case of no segregation) and 1 (in the case of complete segregation). Since $max(A) = max(TW) = Tmax(W) = TW^*$, we get:

$$\frac{A}{max(A)} = \frac{TW}{TW^*} = \frac{W}{W^*}. \tag{7}$$

The association approach to deriving segregation indices, then, yields exactly the same class of segregation indices as does the disproportionality approach. This relationship between the W- and A-class measures makes explicit two potentially useful facts. First, it demonstrates that conventional measures of association (χ^2 and G^2) are functions of the weighted-average distance of the r_{jm} from 1.0, where $r_{jm} = t_{j\,m}/E(t_{j\,m})$. Measures of association, like measures of inequality and segregation, can be based on a general class of disproportionality functions. Second, in the case where

j indexes organizational unit and *m* indexes group, measures of association (once normalized) are also measures of segregation (see also White
1986; Zoloth 1976).[6] Since considerably more is known about the statistical properties of association measures than of segregation measures, this
connection may be useful in applying inferential statistics to segregation
measures.

2.3.3. *Segregation Measures as Diversity Ratios*
Our third approach to constructing multigroup segregation measures relies
on the calculation and decomposition of diversity. Our approach here is
similar in some ways to variance decomposition methods, except that we
substitute the idea of "diversity" for variance. In this approach, we define
a measure of the "diversity" of a population, and then define segregation
as the share of this diversity accounted for by differences in group proportions across units.

We begin by defining more precisely the notion of "diversity." In a
population where each individual is a member of exactly one of M mutually exclusive and unordered groups, the diversity d should be defined as
a function of the π_m's, the population shares of each of the groups ($d =
d(\pi_1, \pi_2, \ldots, \pi_m)$). Moreover, in the case where all individuals are mem-
bers of the same group ($\pi_n = 1$ for some n and $\pi_m = 0$ for all $m \neq n$),
diversity has its minimum value of zero; conversely, diversity is maximized if and only if each group is equally represented in the population
($d_{max} = d(1/M, 1/M, \ldots, 1/M)$). Two such diversity indices are the Simpson Interaction Index (I) and the Entropy (E) (equations [1] and [2] above).

Now suppose we have a population of M groups, with T individuals distributed among J organizational units. Let d be the diversity of the
total population, and d_j be the diversity within unit j. From the mean value
theorem of calculus, it can be shown that if d is a continuous, differentiable, concave-down function of the π_m's,[7] then

$$0 \leq \sum_{j=1}^{J} \frac{t_j}{T} d_j \leq d, \tag{8}$$

---

[6]In particular, we can derive the following equalities: $G^2 = 2TEH$ and $\chi^2 = T(M-1)C$.
[7]That is, for all m, the second partial derivative of d with respect to π_m must
be negative on $0 < \pi_m < 1$.

with the left-hand equality holding if and only if $d_j = 0$ for all j and the right-hand equality holding if and only if $\pi_{jm} = \pi_m$ for all j and m. The left-hand side of this inequality states that the weighted average of the within-unit diversities will always be greater than or equal to zero, with equality holding only if each unity has no diversity (e.g., each unit is monoracial, in the case of racial diversity). The right-hand inequality states that the weighted average within-unit diversity will always be less than or equal to the total diversity of the population, with equality holding here only if each unit has the same group proportions as the population as a whole. Both I and E are continuous, differentiable, concave-down functions on $0 < \pi_m < 1$, so both satisfy this inequality.

We can use this inequality to construct a general class of segregation indices. Let $S(d)$—the segregation measure based on the diversity index d—be defined as

$$S(d) = 1 - \frac{\bar{d}_j}{d} = \sum_{j=1}^{J} \frac{t_j}{Td} (d - d_j), \qquad (9)$$

where $\bar{d}_j$ is the weighted average within-unit diversity. From equations (8) and (9), it is clear that $S(d) = 0$ if and only if each unit has the same group proportions as the total population, and $S(d) = 1$ if and only if each unit has no diversity. $S(d)$ can be interpreted as the average difference between total and within-unit diversity, divided by the total diversity. Since this residual diversity can be attributed only to between-unit differences in group proportions, $S(d)$ can also be seen as a measure of the proportion of total diversity attributable to between-unit differences.[8]

Substituting the diversity index I into equation (9), we get

$$S(I) = \sum_{j=1}^{J} \frac{t_j}{TI} (I - I_j). \qquad (10)$$

We will refer to $S(I)$ as the *relative diversity index*, and denote it as R. R is equivalent to Goodman and Kruskal's τ_b (Carlson 1992; Goodman and Kruskal 1954), and it can be interpreted as one minus the ratio of the probability that two individuals from the same unit are members of differ-

---

[8] To see the relationship between the S-class measures and variance decomposition methods, note that if we substituted σ^2, the variance of a continuous variable x, for d in equation (9), then $S(d)$ would simply be R^2, the between-unit proportion of the variance in x.

ent groups to the probability that any two individuals are members of different groups.

Substituting the entropy index E into equation (9) yields

$$S(E) = \sum_{j=1}^{J} \frac{t_j}{TE} (E - E_j). \tag{11}$$

This is simply Theil's information theory index H (Theil 1972; Theil and Finezza 1971), although written in a different form than shown in Table 1. Although Theil originally derived H using information theory, and we have derived it above from a disproportionality approach, equation (11) shows that H—like R—can also be seen as a measure of the ratio of within-unit diversity to total diversity (see also Zoloth 1976).

2.3.4. *Multigroup Segregation Measures Constructed from Dichotomous Indices*

Each of the three approaches described so far derives multigroup indices of segregation directly from a general mathematical operationalization of the idea of "segregation." A fourth method of constructing a multigroup segregation index derives multigroup indices as weighted averages of dichotomous indices. Suppose we have a population with M groups and S_m is a dichotomous index measuring the segregation of group m from all other groups. We can then define a multigroup segregation index S as a weighted average (where the weights—the W_m's—are positive and sum to 1) of the S_m's:

$$S = \sum_{m=1}^{M} W_m S_m. \tag{12}$$

In equation (12), $S = 0$ only in the case of no segregation and $S = 1$ only in the case of complete segregation. A multigroup index constructed this way necessarily reduces to its dichotomous counterpart when $M = 2$.

We can use equation (12) to derive James's (1986) "generalized segregation index"—a multigroup segregation index that cannot be derived from any of the three approaches described above. James derives this index from the P^*, or exposure, indices (Bell 1954; Farley 1984) by taking a simple weighted average of the normalized exposures of each group to all other groups.[9] Since the normalized exposure index is identical to the variance ratio index V, James's index is simply

$$P = \sum_{m=1}^{M} \pi_m V_m, \tag{13}$$

where V_m is the dichotomous version of V computed between group m and all other groups combined.

P is not, of course, the only multigroup index derivable from equation (12). In principle, we could use equation (12) to generate any number of multigroup indices from existing dichotomous indices, simply by constructing a set of weights (the W_m's) that sum to 1. For example, we could define $W_m = \pi_m$ (to weight groups proportionally to their relative sizes) or $W_m = (1 - \pi_m)/(M - 1)$ (to weight groups proportionally to the relative size of their complement) or $W_m = 1/M$ (to weight all groups equally, regardless of size) or $W_m = \pi_m(1 - \pi_m)/I$ (to weight groups most heavily when $\pi_m = 0.5$ and least heavily when π_m is close to 0 or 1). In fact, in addition to P, four of the five indices derived earlier (all but H) can be written in the form of equation (12).

$$D = \sum_{m=1}^{M} \frac{\pi_m(1 - \pi_m)}{I} D_m; \tag{14}$$

$$G = \sum_{m=1}^{M} \frac{\pi_m(1 - \pi_m)}{I} G_m; \tag{15}$$

$$R = \sum_{m=1}^{M} \frac{\pi_m(1 - \pi_m)}{I} V_m; \tag{16}$$

$$C = \sum_{m=1}^{M} \frac{(1 - \pi_m)}{M - 1} V_m. \tag{17}$$

It is instructive to compare the formulas for C, P, and R. Comparing equations (13), (16), and (17), we see that C, P, and R are each weighted aver-

---

[9] Although James calls this the "generalized segregation index" and denotes it as GSI, we will call it the normalized exposure index and denote it as P to suggest its relationship to the P^* indices.

ages of the V_m's; they differ only in the weight terms.[10] All three indices reduce to V, the variance ratio index, in the two-group case.

Although this approach to deriving multigroup segregation indices as weighted averages of M dichotomous indices appears useful, since it allows us to derive a limitless number of potential indices, including many of those derivable from other approaches, it has serious flaws. The S_m's in equation (12) are not independent of one another—a redistribution of persons that affects S_m necessarily affects at least one S_n, where $n \neq m$. Thus the idea that equation (12) allows us to "weight" the segregation of group m in some way that depends on its relative size is misleading, since the weights do not apply to independent quantities. Put another way, while equation (12) may seem to allow the decomposition of total segregation into M components—each indicating the contribution to total segregation made by the segregation of group m from all other groups—it is meaningless to talk of a single group's contribution to segregation. Segregation is defined by the *relationships* among the groups' distributions across organizational units—not by the distribution across units of each group in isolation.

A second flaw of this approach is that defining multigroup segregation as a weighted average of dichotomous indices may divorce an index from its substantive interpretation. For example, the multigroup dissimilarity index defined earlier based on the disproportionality approach retains the original substantive interpretation of the dichotomous dissimilarity index: it is the proportion of individuals who would have to transfer among units in order to eliminate segregation. A generalized dissimilarity index defined from equation (12) would meet the minimal requirements of a segregation index and would reduce to the dichotomous D when $M = 2$,

[10] Note that C, P, and R can also be written as

$$C = \sum_{m=1}^{M} \sum_{j=1}^{J} \frac{t_j}{T} \frac{(\pi_m - \pi_{jm})^2}{(M-1)\pi_m},$$

$$P = \sum_{m=1}^{M} \sum_{j=1}^{J} \frac{t_j}{T} \frac{(\pi_m - \pi_{jm})^2}{1 - \pi_m},$$

$$R = \sum_{m=1}^{M} \sum_{j=1}^{J} \frac{t_j}{TI} (\pi_m - \pi_{jm})^2.$$

These equations indicate that C, P, and R are each measures of the squared difference between the π_{jm}'s and π_m's; they differ only in their denominators.

but it would not retain the substantive meaning of D in the multigroup case (except in the special case where we set $W_m = \pi_m(1 - \pi_m)/I$, as in equation [14]). Likewise, a generalized Gini index derived from equation (12) would lose the substantive interpretation of the generalized Gini index derived from the disproportionality approach.

Because of these flaws, we suggest that multigroup segregation indices not be derived exclusively from equation (12). It may, however, prove computationally useful to write a multigroup index as a weighted sum of dichotomous indices, but this computational convenience should not substitute for substantive meaning.

Table 2 summarizes the six indices we have defined. In addition, we include in Table 2 a formula for each of the indices. In some cases, of course, other expressions of the formulas are possible (e.g., H is often written as in equation [11]).[11]

3. EVALUATION OF THE MULTIGROUP MEASURES

We now turn to evaluating the indices against the seven criteria articulated earlier. Simple algebra shows that all six indices satisfy the organizational equivalence and size invariance criteria. The other criteria, however, require more careful analysis.

Transfers. Of the six indices, only the information theory index H obeys the principle of transfers. For each of the others, it is possible (albeit counterintuitive) to *increase* measured segregation by transferring an individual of group m from organizational unit i to unit j, where the proportion of persons of group m is greater in unit i than in j ($\pi_{im} > \pi_{jm}$) (proofs are shown in Appendix B).

Exchanges. Following James and Taeuber (1985), we evaluate the six indices' compliance with the exchange principle by taking the derivative with respect to an exchange of persons x, where x involves a transfer of persons of group m from unit i to j and a complementary transfer of an equal number of persons of group n from unit j to i. If this derivative is always negative when both $\pi_{im} > \pi_{jm}$ and $\pi_{jn} > \pi_{in}$, the index satisfies

---

[11] The six multigroup segregation indices defined here can be calculated by a program (-seg-) that runs under the STATA statistical software program and can be downloaded without charge from http://ideas.uqam.ca/ideas/data/bocbocode.html.

TABLE 2
Summary of Six Multigroup Segregation Measures

Multigroup Index	Type	Two-Group Form	Formula	Original Citations for Multigroup Form
Dissimilarity (D)	Disproportionality	D	$D = \sum_{m=1}^{M} \sum_{j=1}^{J} \frac{t_j}{2TI} \left| \pi_{jm} - \pi_m \right|$	Morgan 1975; Sakoda 1981
Gini (G)	Disproportionality	G	$G = \sum_{m=1}^{M} \sum_{i=1}^{J} \sum_{j=1}^{J} \frac{t_i t_j}{2T^2 I} \left| \pi_{im} - \pi_{jm} \right|$	Reardon 1998
Information Theory (H)	Disproportionality, association, and diversity ratio	H	$H = \sum_{m=1}^{M} \sum_{j=1}^{J} \frac{t_j}{TE} \pi_{jm} \ln \frac{\pi_{jm}}{\pi_m}$	Theil 1972; Theil and Finezza 1971
Squared Coefficient of Variation (C)	Disproportionality association	V	$C = \sum_{m=1}^{M} \sum_{j=1}^{J} \frac{t_j}{T} \frac{(\pi_{jm} - \pi_m)^2}{(M-1)\pi_m}$	New
Relative Diversity (R)	Diversity ratio	V	$R = \sum_{m=1}^{M} \sum_{j=1}^{J} \frac{t_j}{TI} (\pi_{jm} - \pi_m)^2$	Carlson 1992; Goodman and Kruskal 1954; Reardon 1998
Normalized Exposure (P)	Weighted average	V	$P = \sum_{m=1}^{M} \sum_{j=1}^{J} \frac{t_j}{T} \frac{(\pi_{jm} - \pi_m)^2}{(1 - \pi_m)}$	James 1986

the principle of exchanges (see Appendix B for the calculation of the derivatives).

The dissimilarity index fails to satisfy the principle of exchanges when $M > 2$ since the index remains constant in the case of exchanges that move individuals between units where the groups are either over- or underrepresented in both units (see James and Taeuber 1985, for $M = 2$ and Appendix B, below, for $M > 2$).

The derivative of the generalized Gini index with respect to x is

$$\frac{dG}{dx} = \frac{-2}{IT^2} \left[t_i + t_j + \sum_{r=i_m+1}^{j_m-1} t_r + \sum_{s=i_n+1}^{j_n-1} t_s \right], \tag{18}$$

where i_m, j_m, i_n, and j_n are the ranks of schools i and j ranked by decreasing proportions of groups m and n, respectively. Because dG/dx is negative when $i_m < j_m$ and $i_n < j_n$, G satisfies the principle of exchanges (for discussion of the sensitivity of G to exchanges, see James and Taeuber 1985).

Differentiating H with respect to x gives

$$\frac{dH}{dx} = \frac{1}{TE} \left(\ln \frac{\pi_{jm}}{\pi_{im}} + \ln \frac{\pi_{in}}{\pi_{jn}} \right). \tag{19}$$

Clearly $dH/dx < 0$ when $\pi_{im} > \pi_{jm}$ and $\pi_{jn} > \pi_{in}$, so the information theory index complies with the principle of exchanges. The effect of an exchange x on H has two components, one for each of the two groups involved in the exchange. The magnitude of each component is proportional to the difference in logged proportions between the two units. James and Taeuber discuss the sensitivity of H to exchanges in the two-group case (1985, p. 14).

The other three indices—C, P, and R—also obey the principle of exchanges. Differentiating each in turn with respect to x gives

$$\frac{dC}{dx} = \frac{-2}{T(M-1)} \left(\frac{\pi_{im} - \pi_{jm}}{\pi_m} + \frac{\pi_{jn} - \pi_{in}}{\pi_n} \right); \tag{20}$$

$$\frac{dP}{dx} = \frac{-2}{T} \left(\frac{\pi_{im} - \pi_{jm}}{1 - \pi_m} + \frac{\pi_{jn} - \pi_{in}}{1 - \pi_n} \right); \tag{21}$$

$$\frac{dR}{dx} = \frac{-2}{TI} \left[(\pi_{im} - \pi_{jm}) + (\pi_{jn} - \pi_{in}) \right]. \tag{22}$$

Again, the effect of an exchange x has two components, one for each of the two groups involved in the exchange. The magnitude of each of these components is proportional to the difference in proportions between the two units. For C, the magnitude of each component is also *inversely* proportional to a group's share of the overall population, while for P the effect is *proportional* to a group's share of the overall population. Thus C is most sensitive to transfers of individuals of small groups while P is most sensitive to transfers of individuals of large groups. Because R does not share this dependence on relative group size, it is preferable to C and P in cases where change in index values should not be sensitive to the relative sizes of the groups involved in the exchanges.

Composition Invariance.   James and Taeuber show that the dichotomous H and V fail to satisfy their version of the composition invariance criterion. Consequently, the multigroup H and the three multigroup generalizations of V (C, P, and R) fail to satisfy the criterion. Although the dichotomous D and G do satisfy the James and Taeuber composition invariance condition, simple algebra shows that the multigroup D and G do not. Thus none of the six measures defined here satisfy the composition invariance criterion as defined by James and Taeuber.[12]

Additive Organizational Decomposability.   Recall that organizational decomposability refers to the situation where the J organizational units are grouped into K clusters (where $K < J$), such as the grouping of schools within districts, or census tracts within counties or metropolitan areas. A full organizational decomposition should allow us to partition total segregation into $K + 1$ independent additive components—a between-cluster component and K within-cluster components. The portion of total segregation due to segregation within cluster k should be the amount by which total segregation would be reduced if segregation within cluster k were eliminated by rearranging individuals among its units while leaving all

[12] It may seem then that we could easily construct a composition-invariant multigroup index from equation (12) simply by letting S_m be a composition-invariant dichotomous index (such as the dichotomous D or G) and $W_m = 1/M$. However, suppose S_m is a composition-invariant dichotomous index and that the number of members of group 1 is multiplied by a constant p in every unit. Although S_1 (the segregation between group 1 and all other groups combined) will be unchanged, S_2, $S_3, \ldots S_M$ will, in general, change (and thus S will change). So a multigroup index defined as the average of M dichotomous composition-invariant indices will not itself be composition-invariant.

other units unchanged. Evaluating whether an index S can be decomposed, then, requires evaluating whether we can write

$$S = S_K + \sum_{k=1}^{K} g(S_k),$$ (23)

where S_K is the between-cluster segregation among the K clusters, S_k is the segregation within cluster k, and g is a strictly increasing function on the interval $[0,1]$ with $g(0) = 0$.

Of the six multigroup indices described here, only two can be decomposed this way. It is straightforward to show that any S-class measure (equation [9]) can be written as

$$S = S_K + \sum_{k=1}^{K} \frac{t_k d_k}{Td} S_k,$$ (24)

where d_k and d are the diversity within cluster k and in the total population, respectively. From this, we get expressions for the decomposition of H and R:

$$H = H_K + \sum_{k=1}^{K} \frac{t_k E_k}{TE} H_k;$$ (25)

$$R = R_K + \sum_{k=1}^{K} \frac{t_k I_k}{TI} R_k.$$ (26)

These clearly satisfy the organizational decomposition property, since each of the k within-cluster components is an increasing function of the within-cluster segregation. For both H and R, within-cluster segregation is proportional to the relative size of the cluster (t_k/T), the relative diversity of the cluster (E_k/E or I_k/I), and the level of within-cluster segregation between units (H_k or R_k). Larger, more diverse, and more segregated clusters contribute more to overall segregation than do smaller, more homogeneous, and less segregated clusters.[13]

The dissimilarity index, because it does not satisfy the principle of exchanges, cannot be appropriately decomposed into within- and between-cluster components—it is possible to reduce within-cluster segregation and leave the total segregation unchanged. Although Rivkin

---

[13] Reardon, Yun, and Eitle (2000) provide an alternative proof of this decomposition for H.

(1994) has claimed otherwise, the Gini index also cannot be satisfactorily decomposed, since it is possible to reduce within-cluster segregation while increasing the total Gini index, a highly unsatisfactory result. While C and P are decomposable in the dichotomous case—in that case they are equivalent to R, which *is* decomposable—C and P are *not* decomposable for $M > 2$.[14]

Additive Group Decomposability.   Recall that group decomposability refers to the situation where M groups are themselves grouped into N mutually exclusive supergroups, where $N < M$. For example, ethnic groups may be grouped into larger groups (Mexicans, Puerto Ricans, Cubans, etc., grouped together into a Hispanic supergroup).

The group decomposability criterion can be formulated analogously to the organizational decomposability criterion. An index S meets the grouping decomposability criterion if we can write

$$S = S_N + \sum_{n=1}^{N} g(S_n), \tag{27}$$

where S_N is the segregation calculated among the N supergroups, S_n is the segregation among the groups making up supergroup n, and g is a strictly increasing function on the interval $[0,1]$ with $g(0) = 0$.[15]

---

[14] Note that C can be written as

$$C = C_K + \sum_{k=1}^{K} \frac{t_k}{T} \left[\sum_{m=1}^{M} \sum_{j \in k} \frac{t_j \pi_{km}}{t_k \pi_m} \frac{(\pi_{jm}^2 - \pi_{km}^2)}{(M-1)\pi_{km}} \right].$$

The bracketed term is not equal to C_k because of the additional π_{km}/π_m term. Similarly, P can be written as

$$P = P_K + \sum_{k=1}^{K} \frac{t_k}{T} \left[\sum_{m=1}^{M} \sum_{j \in k} \frac{t_j(1 - \pi_{km})}{t_k(1 - \pi_m)} \frac{(\pi_{jm}^2 - \pi_{km}^2)}{(1 - \pi_{km})} \right].$$

Again, the term in the bracket is not equal to P_k because of the additional $(1 - \pi_{km})/(1 - \pi_m)$ term. The multigroup C and P have no organizational decomposition of the form given in equation (23).

[15] It is important to distinguish this type of decomposition from the decomposition of segregation into a weighted sum of dichotomous indices, since the latter "decomposition" contains no independent between- and within-group components.

Of the six indices, apparently only H can be decomposed in this manner.[16] Reardon, Yun, and Eitle (2000) show that H can be written as

$$H = H_N + \sum_{n=1}^{N} \frac{t_n E_n}{TE} H_n, \qquad (28)$$

where H_N is the segregation calculated among the supergroups, T and E are the size and entropy of the population as a whole, and t_n, E_n, and H_n are the size, entropy, and segregation within supergroup n, respectively. The contribution of within-supergroup segregation to the total segregation is proportional to the relative size of the supergroup (t_n/T), the relative diversity of the supergroup (E_n/E), and the level of within-supergroup segregation between groups (H_n). Larger, more diverse, and more segregated supergroups contribute more to overall segregation than do smaller, more homogeneous, and less segregated supergroups.

Table 3 summarizes the compliance of the six indices with the seven criteria. The first four criteria are generally agreed on as essential to any meaningful segregation index. In that light, H is the superior index, since it alone satisfies all four criteria for both the two-group and multigroup cases. While all the indices save D satisfy the principle of exchanges, only H satisfies the stronger principle of transfers in the multigroup case. None of the indices satisfies the composition invariance principle in the multigroup case—which is not necessarily a flaw, as we have noted. Finally, while R and H satisfy the organizational decomposition property in the multigroup case (and C and P also satisfy it in the dichotomous case), only H satisfies both the organizational and the grouping decomposition properties.

4. DISCUSSION AND CONCLUSION

Taking our cue from scattered work suggesting that some binary indices can be generalized to the multigroup case, we develop methods for deriving and evaluating measures of multigroup segregation. We begin by describing alternative ways to *conceptualize* segregation: as disproportionality in group proportions, which links segregation measures to inequal-

---

[16]We have no formal proof that a group decomposition of the other indices is impossible, but we are unable to find any such decompositions after considerable algebraic manipulation.

TABLE 3
Properties of Multigroup Segregation Indices

	Dissimilarity (D)	Gini (G)	Information Theory (H)	Squared Coefficient of Variation (C)	Relative Diversity (R)	Normalized Exposure (P)
Organizational equivalence	✓	✓	✓	✓	✓	✓
Size invariance	✓	✓	✓	✓	✓	✓
Transfers						
2-Group	X[a]	✓	✓	✓	✓	✓
M-Group	X	X	✓	X	X	X
Exchanges						
2-Group	X[a]	✓	✓	✓	✓	✓
M-Group	X[a]	✓	✓	✓	✓	✓
Compositional invariance						
2-Group	✓	✓	X	X	X	X
M-Group	X	X	X	X	X	X
Additive organizational decomposability						
2-Group	X	X	✓	✓	✓	✓
M-Group	X	X	✓	X	✓	X
Additive group decomposability	X	X	✓	X	X	X

[a]The dissimilarity index satisfies only a weak form of the principles of transfers and exchanges: transfers and exchanges that move individuals from units of higher to lower proportions may result in no change in D, but they will never result in an increase in D.

ity measures; as association between group and organizational unit, which links segregation measures to χ^2 and G^2; as between-unit diversity relative to total diversity, which links segregation measures to variance decomposition methods; and as a weighted average of two-group segregation, which links multigroup segregation measures to dichotomous measures.

From these approaches we derive a dissimilarity index D, a Gini index G, an information theory index H, a squared coefficient of variation index C, a relative diversity index R, and a normalized exposure index P. D, G, and H are extensions of binary measures bearing the same names, whereas C, P, and R reduce to a single binary measure that is variously known as the variance ratio index (V), eta^2, the normalized exposure index, and Bell's revised index of isolation. Each of these measures captures the dimension of segregation that Massey and Denton (1988) call "evenness"— the extent to which mutually exclusive groups are evenly distributed among organizational units.[17]

Other multigroup measures are possible. In fact, equation (12) suggests that a limitless number of new multigroup indices can be derived from any dichotomous index S_m, though measures derived from the weighted average index approach embodied in equation (12) do not necessarily have any meaningful interpretation. We suggest that proposed indices be evaluated against a conceptually derived set of mathematical criteria, as we have done here. While there may be reasonable disagreement about the desirability of specific criteria or about the completeness of our particular list, it is nonetheless important that segregation indices be defined so that their mathematical behavior matches key conceptual and analytic needs, whatever those may be.

What do our seven criteria show regarding the six indices here? The most important finding is that Theil's information theory index H is the only one of the six that obeys the principle of transfers in the multigroup case. Failure to obey the principle is problematic for a segregation measure, since it means that the measure cannot be trusted to register a decline in segregation when an individual of group m moves from unit i to unit j, where the proportion of persons of group m is higher in unit i than in unit j. All five indices other than H may *increase* when a member of group m moves from a higher-π_m to a lower-π_m unit. H is also the only

---

[17] The point that segregation measures pertain to mutually exclusive groups is worth noting in light of the recent change in U.S. Census Bureau procedures for classifying race. To measure segregation based on 2000 census data, researchers will need to convert census tabulations into mutually exclusive groupings.

index that permits grouping decomposition, and it is one of only two indices that permits organizational decomposition in the multigroup case. Our overarching recommendation, then, is that researchers use the information theory index H for measuring multigroup segregation, at least when evenness is the conceptual dimension of segregation of interest.

Finally, while H appears superior to the other indices evaluated here, several important methodological issues in the study of multigroup segregation remain. First, we do not know at this point whether the violation of the principle of transfers seriously undermines the non-H indices, or instead is of little practical consequence in most research applications. However, the answer may become clearer in practice, as a new generation of research literature emerges on multigroup segregation. Second, the measures we describe here do not account for spatial dimensions of segregation. Future work should generalize spatial measures of segregation (concentration, clustering, and centralization) to the multigroup case. Third, the link between several of the multigroup measures and familiar measures of statistical association suggests possibilities for applying inferential statistics to segregation measurement, making possible the estimation of segregation levels from sample data rather than population data as well as hypothesis testing regarding differences in segregation levels between populations and over time.

APPENDIX A: MAXIMUM VALUES FOR THE MULTIGROUP SEGREGATION INDICES

The denominators of the disproportionality-based segregation indices have this common form:

$$W^* = \max\left[\sum_{m=1}^{M} \pi_m \sum_{j=1}^{J} \frac{t_j}{T} f(r_{jm}) \right]. \qquad (A\text{-}1)$$

The maximum value of W (for the four functions f that we use) is obtained under complete segregation—when each unit contains members of only a single group (no individual shares a unit with any member of any other group).[18] That is, when

---

[18] The proofs that, for each of the four disproportionality functions f that we use, W obtains its maximum value only under the condition of complete segregation require relatively straightforward, albeit tedious, applications of calculus. We omit the proofs here in the interest of space. Note that, by our definition, complete segregation is possible only when there are at least as many units as groups. Thus the derivations here assume $J \geq M$.

$$r_{jm} = \frac{\pi_{jm}}{\pi_m} = \begin{cases} \dfrac{1}{\pi_m} & \text{for } \pi_m \text{ proportion of the population} \\ 0 & \text{for } (1 - \pi_m) \text{ proportion of the population} \end{cases}. \quad \text{(A-2)}$$

This yields

$$W^* = \sum_{m=1}^{M} \pi_m \left[\pi_m f\left(\frac{1}{\pi_m}\right) + (1 - \pi_m) f(0) \right]. \quad \text{(A-3)}$$

We derive the maximum values for each index by substituting the four disproportionality functions into equation (A-3).

Dissimilarity Index (D). If $f(r) = |r - 1|/2$, equation (A-3) yields:

$$W^* = \sum_{m=1}^{M} \pi_m \left[\pi_m \frac{\left|\dfrac{1}{\pi_m} - 1\right|}{2} + (1 - \pi_m) \frac{|0 - 1|}{2} \right] = I. \quad \text{(A-4)}$$

So the denominator of D is Simpson's Interaction Index I.

Theil's Information Theory Index (H). If $f(r) = r \ln r$, equation (A-3) yields the following (recall we define $0 \cdot \ln 0 = 0$):

$$W^* = \sum_{m=1}^{M} \pi_m \left[\pi_m \left(\frac{1}{\pi_m}\right) \ln\left(\frac{1}{\pi_m}\right) + (1 - \pi_m) \cdot 0 \ln 0 \right] = E. \quad \text{(A-5)}$$

So the denominator of H is Theil's Entropy Index E.

Squared Coefficient of Variation Index (C). If $f(r) = (r - 1)^2$, equation (A-3) yields

$$W^* = \sum_{m=1}^{M} \pi_m \left[\pi_m \left(\frac{1}{\pi_m} - 1\right)^2 + (1 - \pi_m)(0 - 1)^2 \right] = M - 1. \quad \text{(A-6)}$$

So the denominator of C is M-1.

Gini Index (G). If $f(r) = |r_{im} - r_{jm}|/2$, the derivation is slightly more complicated. The value of $|r_i - r_j|/2$ depends on the group proportions within both units i and j, so

$$
\frac{|r_{im} - r_{jm}|}{2} = \begin{cases} |0 - 0|/2 = 0 & \text{for } (1 - \pi_m)^2 \text{ proportion of the} \\ & \text{population (when } \pi_{im} = \pi_{jm} = 0) \\ |1/\pi_m - 0|/2 = 1/2\pi_m & \text{for } \pi_m (1 - \pi_m) \text{ proportion of the} \\ & \text{population (when } \pi_{im} = 1; \pi_{jm} = 0) \\ |0 - 1/\pi_m|/2 = 1/2\pi_m & \text{for } \pi_m (1 - \pi_m) \text{ proportion of the} \\ & \text{population (when } \pi_{im} = 0; \pi_{jm} = 1) \\ |1/\pi_m - 1/\pi_m|/2 = 0 & \text{for } \pi_m^2 \text{ proportion of the popul-} \\ & \text{tion (when } \pi_{im} = \pi_{jm} = 1) \end{cases}
$$

$$(\text{A-7})$$

Substituting this into a modified version of equation (A-3) and simplifying, we get

$$
W^* = \sum_{m=1}^{M} \pi_m \left[(1 - \pi_m)^2 \cdot 0 + \pi_m(1 - \pi_m) \cdot \frac{1}{2\pi_m} \right.
$$

$$
\left. + \pi_m(1 - \pi_m) \cdot \frac{1}{2\pi_m} + \pi_m^2 \cdot 0 \right] = I. \qquad (\text{A-8})
$$

So the denominator of G is Simpson's Interaction Index I.

APPENDIX B: PROOFS OF TRANSFER AND EXCHANGE PROPERTIES

We can evaluate each index's compliance with the principles of transfers and exchanges by taking the derivative of the index with respect to a transfer or exchange x. The four indices derived from the disproportionality approach share the general form below, given in equation (4). (We change the subscripts here since we will use m, n, i, and j to refer to the specific groups and units involved in the transfer or exchange.)

$$
S = \frac{1}{W^*} \sum_{r=1}^{M} \sum_{k=1}^{J} \pi_r \frac{t_k}{T} f(r_{kr}). \qquad (\text{B-1})
$$

Note that any transfer or exchange does not affect the π_r's or T. We can write the derivative of S with respect to a transfer or exchange x as

$$
\frac{dS}{dx} = \frac{1}{W^*} \sum_{r=1}^{M} \sum_{k=1}^{J} \left[\pi_r \frac{t_k}{T} \frac{df}{dr_{kr}} \frac{dr_{kr}}{d\pi_{kr}} \frac{d\pi_{kr}}{dx} + \pi_r \frac{1}{T} \frac{dt_k}{dx} f(r_{kr}) \right]. \qquad (\text{B-2})
$$

Note also that $dr_{kr}/d\pi_{kr} = 1/\pi_r$. In the case where x indicates a transfer of persons of group m from unit i to j, we get the following expressions:

$$\frac{dt_k}{dx} = \begin{cases} -1 & \text{when } k = i \\ 1 & \text{when } k = j \\ 0 & \text{when } k \neq i, j \end{cases} \qquad \text{(B-3)}$$

$$\frac{d\pi_{kr}}{dx} = \begin{cases} \dfrac{t_{kr}}{t_k^2} & \text{when } k = i \text{ and } r \neq m \\[2mm] -\dfrac{t_{kr}}{t_k^2} & \text{when } k = j \text{ and } r \neq m \\[2mm] \dfrac{t_{kr} - t_k}{t_k^2} & \text{when } k = i \text{ and } r = m \\[2mm] \dfrac{t_k - t_{kr}}{t_k^2} & \text{when } k = j \text{ and } r = m \\[2mm] 0 & \text{when } k \neq i, j \end{cases} \qquad \text{(B-4)}$$

We calculate dS/dx for any of the four segregation indices derived from the disproportionality approach by substituting equations (B-3), (B-4), and the appropriate disproportionality function $f(r)$ into equation (B-2). Using $f(r) = r \ln r$ yields

$$\frac{dH}{dx} = \frac{1}{TE} \ln \frac{\pi_{jm}}{\pi_{im}}. \qquad \text{(B-5)}$$

When $\pi_{jm} < \pi_{im}$, $dH/dx < 0$, so H satisfies the principle of transfers.

   For each of the other five indices, the derivative with respect to a transfer x results in a more complicated function. In each case, the derivative may be positive when $\pi_{jm} < \pi_{im}$, so none of the other functions satisfy the principle of transfers. Rather than compute the derivative of each of these functions, however, we instead provide proofs by counterexample. Two examples suffice to demonstrate that each of the indices other than H does not satisfy the principle of transfers.

   Example 1 (Table B1) shows the distribution of members of three groups among three organizational units, and the subsequent distribution following a transfer of a member of group A from unit 2 to unit 1. Since unit 2 begins with a greater proportion of members from group A, this transfer should result in a decrease in the segregation if the principle of transfers is satisfied. However, four of the six indices (D, G, R, and P)

TABLE B1
Failure of Multigroup D, G, R, and P to Obey the Principle of Transfers

	Time 1			
	Unit 1	Unit 2	Unit 3	Total
Group A	6	8	10	24
Group B	181	193	378	752
Group C	12	0	12	24
Total	199	201	400	800

	Time 2			
	Unit 1	Unit 2	Unit 3	Total
Group A	7	7	10	24
Group B	181	193	378	752
Group C	12	0	12	24
Total	200	200	400	800

Index	D	G	H	C	R	P
Time 1	0.1537	0.2085	0.0419	0.0084	0.0073	0.0063
Time 2	0.1636	0.2182	0.0412	0.0082	0.0083	0.0084
Change	+0.0099	+0.0097	−0.0007	−0.0002	+0.0010	+0.0019

show an increase in segregation following the transfer. Clearly then, these indices do not obey the transfer criterion. Example 2, likewise, illustrates that C may increase as a result of a transfer from a unit of higher proportion to one of lower proportion (Table B2).

In the case where x indicates an exchange rather than a transfer, the indices behave differently. Equation (B-2) still applies, but when x is an exchange where an individual of group m in organizational unit i is exchanged with an individual of group n from organizational unit j, we get the following values for dt_k/dx and $d\pi_{kr}/dx$:

$$\frac{dt_k}{dx} = 0, \tag{B-6}$$

$$\frac{d\pi_{kr}}{dx} = \begin{cases} -1/t_k & \text{when } k = i \text{ and } r = m \\ +1/t_k & \text{when } k = j \text{ and } r = m \\ +1/t_k & \text{when } k = i \text{ and } r = n \\ -1/t_k & \text{when } k = j \text{ and } r = n \\ 0 & \text{when } k \neq i, j \text{ or } r \neq m, n \end{cases} \tag{B-7}$$

TABLE B2
Failure of Multigroup C to Obey the Principle of Transfers

	Time 1			
	Unit 1	Unit 2	Unit 3	Total
Group A	99	101	100	300
Group B	0	100	0	100
Group C	100	0	100	200
Total	199	201	200	600

	Time 2			
	Unit 1	Unit 2	Unit 3	Total
Group A	100	100	100	300
Group B	0	100	0	100
Group C	100	0	100	200
Total	200	200	200	600

Index	D	G	H	C	R	P
Time 1	0.3655	0.3664	0.31468	0.2494	0.18183	0.1501
Time 2	0.3636	0.3636	0.31467	0.2500	0.18182	0.1500
Change	−0.0019	−0.0028	−0.00001	+0.0006	−0.00001	−0.0001

Substituting equations (B-6) and (B-7) into (B-2), we get

$$\frac{dS}{dx} = \frac{1}{TW^*}\left(\frac{df}{dr_{jm}} - \frac{df}{dr_{im}} + \frac{df}{dr_{in}} - \frac{df}{dr_{jn}}\right). \tag{B-8}$$

Again, we calculate dS/dx in the case of an exchange for any of the indices derived from the disproportionality approach used in equation (B-1) by substituting the appropriate disproportionality function $f(r)$ into equation (B-8). Using $f(r) = |r - 1|/2$ yields

$$\frac{dD}{dx} = \frac{z_m + z_n}{TI} \tag{B-9}$$

where

$$z_m = \begin{cases} -1 & \text{if } \pi_{im} > \pi_m > \pi_{jm} \\ 1 & \text{if } \pi_{im} < \pi_m < \pi_{jm} \\ 0 & \text{otherwise} \end{cases}$$

$$
z_n = \begin{cases}
-1 & \text{if } \pi_{jn} > \pi_n > \pi_{in} \\
1 & \text{if } \pi_{jn} < \pi_n < \pi_{in} \\
0 & \text{otherwise}
\end{cases}
$$

Since $dD/dx = 0$ if, for example $\pi_{im} > \pi_{jm} > \pi_m$ and $\pi_{in} < \pi_{jn} < \pi_n$, D does not strictly satisfy the principle of exchanges.

Substituting $f(r) = r \ln r$ into equation (B-8) yields the derivative of H with respect to an exchange x (equation [19]), while substituting $f(r) = (r-1)^2$ into equation (B-8) yields the derivative of C with respect to an exchange x (equation [20]):

$$
\frac{dH}{dx} = \frac{1}{TE}\left(\ln\frac{\pi_{jm}}{\pi_{im}} + \ln\frac{\pi_{in}}{\pi_{jn}}\right);
$$

$$
\frac{dC}{dx} = \frac{-2}{T(M-1)}\left(\frac{\pi_{im} - \pi_{jm}}{\pi_m} + \frac{\pi_{jn} - \pi_{in}}{\pi_n}\right).
$$

When $\pi_{jm} < \pi_{im}$ and $\pi_{in} < \pi_{jn}$, $dH/dx < 0$ and $dC/dx < 0$, so both H and C satisfy the principle of exchanges.

The derivative of G with respect to an exchange x is obtained by recalling that we can write G as a weighted sum of dichotomous G_m's (equation [15]). Taking the derivative of G in equation (15), and noting that $dG_r/dx = 0$ for all $r \neq m, n$, we get

$$
\frac{dG}{dx} = \frac{\pi_m(1 - \pi_m)}{I}\frac{dG_m}{dx} + \frac{\pi_n(1 - \pi_n)}{I}\frac{dG_n}{dx}. \tag{B-10}
$$

James and Taeuber (1985) show that the derivative of the dichotomous Gini index with respect to an exchange x is given by

$$
\frac{dG_r}{dx} = \frac{-1}{\pi_r(1 - \pi_r)T^2}\left[t_i + t_j + 2\sum_{k=i_r+1}^{j_r-1} t_k\right], \tag{B-11}
$$

where i_r and j_r are the ranks of schools i and j ranked by decreasing proportions of group r. Substituting this expression into equation (B-10) yields equation (18):

$$
\frac{dG}{dx} = \frac{-2}{IT^2}\left[t_i + t_j + \sum_{r=i_m+1}^{j_m-1} t_r + \sum_{s=i_n+1}^{j_n-1} t_s\right]
$$

Because dG/dx is negative when $i_m < j_m$ and $i_n < j_n$, G satisfies the principle of exchanges.

Since R is not derived from the disproportionality approach, we cannot obtain its derivative from equation (B-9). Instead, we take its derivative directly from the expression for R in footnote 10:

$$\frac{dR}{dx} = \frac{1}{TI} \sum_{r=1}^{M} \sum_{k=1}^{J} \left[2t_k(\pi_{kr} - \pi_r) \frac{d\pi_{kr}}{dx} \right]. \qquad \text{(B-12)}$$

Substituting equation (B-7) into this expression gives us equation (22):

$$\frac{dR}{dx} = \frac{-2}{TI} \left[(\pi_{im} - \pi_{jm}) + (\pi_{jn} - \pi_{in}) \right].$$

When $\pi_{jm} < \pi_{im}$ and $\pi_{in} < \pi_{jn}$, $dR/dx < 0$, so R satisfies the principle of exchanges.

Using a similar approach for P—differentiating P with respect to an exchange x and substituting equation (B-7) into the result—yields equation (21):

$$\frac{dP}{dx} = \frac{-2}{T} \left[\frac{(\pi_{im} - \pi_{jm})}{(1 - \pi_m)} + \frac{(\pi_{jn} - \pi_{in})}{(1 - \pi_n)} \right].$$

When $\pi_{jm} < \pi_{im}$ and $\pi_{in} < \pi_{jn}$, $dR/dx < 0$, so P satisfies the principle of exchanges.

REFERENCES

Bell, W. 1954. "A Probability Model for the Measurement of Ecological Segregation." *Social Forces* 43:357–64.

Carlson, Susan M. 1992. "Trends in Race/Sex Occupational Inequality: Conceptual and Measurement Issues." *Social Problems* 39:269–90.

Charles, Maria, and David B. Grusky. 1995. "Models for Describing the Underlying Structure of Sex Segregation." *American Journal of Sociology* 100:931–71.

Cohen, Jack K., R. Frank Falk, and Charles F. Cortese. 1976. "Reply to Taeuber and Taeuber." *American Sociological Review* 41:889–93.

Coleman, James, Thomas Hoffer, and Sally Kilgore. 1982. "Achievement and Segregation in Secondary Schools: A Further Look at Public and Private School Differences." *Sociology of Education* 55:162–82.

Cortese, Charles F., R. Frank Falk, and Jack K. Cohen. 1976. "Further Considerations on the Methodological Analysis of Segregation Indices." *American Sociological Review* 41:630–37.

Cowgill, Donald O., and Mary S. Cowgill. 1951. "An Index of Segregation Based on Block Statistics." *American Sociological Review* 16:825–31.

Deutsch, Joseph, Yves Flückiger, and Jacques Silber. 1994. "Measuring Occupational Segregation: Summary Statistics and the Impact of Classification Errors and Aggregation." *Journal of Econometrics* 61:133–46.

Duncan, Otis Dudley, and Beverly Duncan. 1955. "A Methodological Analysis of Segregation Indexes." *American Sociological Review* 20:210–17.

Falk, R. Frank, Charles F. Cortese, and Jack Cohen. 1978. "Utilizing Standardized Indices of Residential Segregation: Comment on Winship." *Social Forces* 57:713–16.

Farley, John E. 1984. "'P* Segregation Indices: What Can They Tell Us About Housing Segregation in 1980?" *Urban Studies* 21:331–36.

Farley, Reynolds. 1977. "Residential Segregation in Urbanized Areas of the United States in 1970: An Analysis of Social Class and Racial Differences." *Demography* 14:497–518.

Firebaugh, Glenn. 1998. "Measuring Inequality: A Convenient Unifying Framework." Presented at the annual meeting of the Population Association of America, Chicago, IL.

———. 1999. "Empirics of World Income Inequality." *American Journal of Sociology* 104:1597–630.

Goodman, Leo, and William H. Kruskal. 1954. "Measures of Association for Cross-Classifications." *Journal of the American Statistical Association* 49:732–64.

Grusky, David B., and Maria Charles. 1998. "The Past, Present, and Future of Sex Segregation Methodology." *Demography* 35:497–504.

Jahn, Julius A. 1950. "The Measurement of Ecological Segregation: Derivation of an Index Based on the Criterion of Reproducibility." *American Sociological Review* 15:100–104.

Jahn, Julius A., Calvin F. Schmid, and Clarence Schrag. 1947. "The Measurement of Ecological Segregation." *American Sociological Review* 12:293–303.

James, David R., and Karl E. Taeuber. 1985. "Measures of Segregation." *Sociological Methodology* 14:1–32.

James, Franklin J. 1986. "A New Generalized "Exposure-Based" Segregation Index." *Sociological Methods and Research* 14:301–16.

Kestenbaum, Bert. 1980. "Notes on the Index of Dissimilarity: A Research Note." *Social Forces* 59:275–80.

Kulis, Stephen. 1997. "Gender Segregation Among College and University Employees." *Sociology of Education* 70:151–73.

Lieberson, Stanley. 1969. "Measuring Population Diversity." *American Sociological Review* 34:850–62.

Lieberson, Stanley, and Donna K. Carter. 1982a. "A Model for Inferring the Voluntary and Involuntary Causes of Residential Segregation." *Demography* 19:511–26.

———. 1982b. "Temporal Changes and Urban Differences in Residential Segregation: A Reconsideration." *American Journal of Sociology* 88:296–310.

Massey, Douglas S., and Nancy A. Denton. 1988. "The Dimensions of Racial Segregation." *Social Forces* 67:281–315.

Miller, Vincent P., and John M. Quigley. 1990. "Segregation by Racial and Demographic Group: Evidence from the San Francisco Bay Area." *Urban Studies* 27:3–21.

Morgan, Barrie S. 1975. "The Segregation of Socioeconomic Groups in Urban Areas: A Comparative Analysis." *Urban Studies* 12:47–60.

———. 1983. "A Temporal Perspective on the Properties of the Index of Dissimilarity." *Environment and Planning A* 15:379–89.

Reardon, Sean F. 1998. "Measures of Racial Diversity and Segregation in Multigroup and Hierarchically Structured Populations." Presented at the annual meeting of the Eastern Sociological Society, Philadelphia, PA.

Reardon, Sean F., and John T. Yun. 2001. "Suburban Racial Change and Suburban School Segregation, 1987–1995." *Sociology of Education* 74:79–101.

Reardon, Sean F., John T. Yun, and Tamela McNulty Eitle. 2000. "The Changing Structure of School Segregation: Measurement and Evidence of Multi-racial Metropolitan Area School Segregation, 1989–1995." *Demography* 37:351–64.

Rivkin, Steven G. 1994. "Residential Segregation and School Integration." *Sociology of Education* 67:279–92.

Sakoda, J. 1981. "A Generalized Index of Dissimilarity." *Demography* 18:245–50.

Schwartz, Joseph, and Christopher Winship. 1980. "The Welfare Approach to Measuring Inequality." *Sociological Methodology* 9:1–36.

Taeuber, Karl E., and Alma F. Taeuber. 1965. *Negroes in Cities: Residential Segregation and Neighborhood Change.* Chicago, IL: Aldine Publishing.

———. 1976. "A Practitioner's Perspective on the Index of Dissimilarity." *American Sociological Review* 41:884–89.

Theil, Henri 1972. *Statistical Decomposition Analysis.* Amsterdam: North-Holland.

Theil, Henri, and Anthony J. Finezza. 1971. "A Note on the Measurement of Racial Integration of Schools by Means of Informational Concepts." *Journal of Mathematical Sociology* 1:187–94.

Watts, Martin. 1992. "How Should Occupational Sex Segregation be Measured?" *Work, Employment and Society* 6:475–87.

———. 1994. "A Critique of Marginal Matching." *Work, Employment and Society* 8:421–31.

White, Michael J. 1986. "Segregation and Diversity Measures in Population Distribution." *Population Index* 52:198–221.

Williams, Josephine J. 1948. "Another Commentary on So-called Segregation Indices." *American Sociological Review* 13:298–303.

Winship, Christopher. 1977. "A Reevaluation of Indexes of Residential Segregation." *Social Forces* 55:1058–66.

———. 1978. "The Desirability of Using the Index of Dissimilarity or Any Adjustment of it for Measuring Segregation: Reply to Falk, Cortese, and Cohen." *Social Forces* 57:717–20.

Zoloth, Barbara S. 1976. "Alternative Measures of School Segregation." *Land Economics* 52:278–98.

DISCUSSION: SEGREGATION INDICES AND THEIR FUNCTIONAL INPUTS

Rick Grannis *

MULTIGROUP INDICES

Reardon and Firebaugh's (2002) advocacy of multigroup segregation indices is an important contribution to the index debate, a debate of central importance to understanding segregation. Indices guide and circumscribe all comparisons both over time and between cities, all correlations with other variables, and all classifications (Jahn, Schmid, and Schrag 1947). More importantly, they operationalize segregation theory itself and thus circumscribe all substantive understandings. Reardon and Firebaugh's (2002) review of multigroup indices highlights the fact that two-group indices have guided our thinking about segregation.

Indices reduce huge data arrays into simpler, more readily understandable numbers. Regardless of the formula one uses to reduce such arrays, the formula itself is merely a function of those arrays and only those arrays. Before choosing formulas, segregation researchers need to consider how their choice of inputs guides their theoretical development. Only when they have correctly determined which variables are appropriately included in the discussion of segregation can they proceed to develop indices and build definitions and theories.

Reardon and Firebaugh's (2002) formula-based criterion for segregation indices excluded other potentially important multigroup indices. They identified six measures that they evaluated against desirable properties of segregation indices adapted from Schwartz and Winship's (1980) and James and Taeuber's (1985) original four criteria: the principle of transfers, compositional invariance, size invariance, and organizational equivalence. These criteria, however, concern only the racial populations of each neighborhood and thus have no meaning for indices that include other variables. In fact, all of Reardon and Firebaugh's (2002) multigroup

*Cornell University and RAND
Direct all correspondence to Rick Grannis, Department of Sociology, Cornell University, Ithaca, New York 14853 (rdg25@cornell.edu).

measures can be derived from exactly the same set of data, a matrix whose rows consist of neighborhoods, whose columns consist of groups, and whose cell entries consist of the number of persons of the group represented by the column in the neighborhood represented by the row.

1. MULTIDIMENSIONAL INDICES

The distinction of considering multigroup segregation instead of dichotomous segregation is profound; it involves including new variables in the functions (one for each additional racial group) or adding new columns to the data matrix being reduced. However, the decision to include or to exclude other variables such as neighborhood contiguity, tract area, or proximity to the central city is as fundamental to the understanding of segregation data as is the choice of whether or not to restrict the scenario to a majority race and a single minority race or to allow for a multiple-race scenario. This is the issue of multidimensional inputs to segregation indices, and it reflects the multidimensional nature of spatial segregation. This is a topic that Reardon and Firebaugh (2002) do not address, and it is at least as important as their distinction between two-group and multigroup segregation.

Below, I consider some properties of multigroup segregation indices with multidimensional inputs. I show that indices can best be understood in terms of the variables they are functions of and that accounting for the location of neighborhoods with respect to each other is as important as analyzing multiple racial groups. I conclude by proposing a multigroup spatial proximity index.

2. INDICES AS FUNCTIONS

In addition to the racial population of each neighborhood, what other variables might we consider? In addition to Reardon and Firebaugh's (2002) six multigroup indices, Massey and Denton's (1988) classic survey of segregation indices identified 20 more distinct formulas used to measure aspects of segregation. We can reduce these 26 indices to a set of simple functions and illustrate them in terms of the variables they use as inputs to show how our choice of indices defines segregation and profoundly influences our understanding of this phenomenon.[1] Table 1 lists the indices

[1] An appendix, available from the author on request, discusses how analyzing functional inputs relates to factor analyses.

TABLE 1
Original Citation of Segregation Indices

Segregation Index	Citation
Absolute centralization	Massey and Denton (1988)
Absolute clustering	Massey and Denton (1988) adapted from Geary (1954) and Dacey (1968)
Absolute concentration	Massey and Denton (1988)
Atkinson	Atkinson (1970)
Correlation ratio	Bell (1954); White (1986)
Delta	Duncan, Cuzzort, and Duncan (1961) adapted from Hoover (1941)
Dissimilarity	Duncan and Duncan (1955)
Distance-decay isolation	Morgan (1983)
Entropy	Theil and Finezza (1971); Theil (1972)
Gini	Duncan and Duncan (1955)
Isolation	Bell (1954); Lieberson (1981)
Multigroup dissimilarity	Morgan (1975); Sakoda (1981)
Multigroup Gini	Reardon and Firebaugh (2002)
Multigroup information	Theil and Finezza (1971); Theil (1972)
Multigroup normalized exposure	James (1986)
Multigroup relative diversity	Goodman and Kruskal (1954); Carlson (1992)
Multigroup squared coefficient of variation	Reardon and Firebaugh (2002)
Proportion in central city	Massey and Denton (1988)
Relative centralization	Duncan and Duncan (1955)
Relative clustering	Massey and Denton (1988)
Relative concentration	Massey and Denton (1988)
Spatial proximity	White (1986)

and cites their original appearance in the literature.[2] Table 2 displays their computational formulas; Table 3 lists the indices as functions of the variables they use as inputs.[3]

Each index is a function of between two and 11 variables. Through inspection alone, some patterns are obvious and algebra makes

[2] For simplicity's sake, I use only the generalized version of the Atkinson index. The three versions of it used by Massey and Denton (1988) are easily derivable by substitution. I also use only the interaction index, and its distance-decay counterpart. The isolation index and its distance-decay counterpart are corollaries equaling unity minus the interaction indices.

[3] An appendix, available from the author on request, discusses how these variables were identified and summarizes the algebraic transformations.

TABLE 2

Computational Formulas for Segregation Indices

Segregation Index	Formula
Absolute centralization	$(\Sigma X_{i-1} A_i) - (\Sigma X_i A_{i-1})$
Absolute clustering	$\{[\Sigma(x_i/X)\Sigma(c_{ij}x_j)] - [X/n^2\Sigma\Sigma c_{ij}]\}/$ $\{[\Sigma(x_i/X)\Sigma c_{ij}t_j] - [X/n^2\Sigma\Sigma c_{ij}]\}$
Absolute concentration	$1 - \{[\Sigma(x_i a_i/X) - \Sigma_{i=1}^{n1}(t_i a_i/T_1)]/$ $[\Sigma_{i=n2}^{n}(t_i a_i/T_2) - \Sigma_{i=1}^{n1}(t_i a_i/T_1)]\}$
Atkinson	$1 - [P/(1-P)]|\Sigma[(1-p_i)^{(1-k)}p_i^k t_i/PT]|^{(1/(1-k))}$
Correlation ratio	$(_x P_x^* - P)/(1-P)$, where $_x P_x^* = \Sigma[x_i/X][x_i/t_i]$
Delta	$\frac{1}{2}\Sigma|[x_i/X - a_i/A]|$
Dissimilarity	$\Sigma[t_i|p_i - P|/2TP(1-P)]$
Distance-decay isolation	$\Sigma x_i/X\Sigma K_{ij} y_j/t_j$, where $K_{ij} = c_{ij}t_j/\Sigma c_{ij}t_j$
Entropy	$\Sigma[t_i(E - E_i)/ET]$, where $E = (P)\log[1/P] + (1-P)\log[1/(1-P)]$ $E_i = (p_i)\log[1/p_i] + (1-p_i)\log[1/(1-p_i)]$
Gini	$\Sigma\Sigma[t_i t_j|p_i - p_j|/2T^2P(1-P)]$
Isolation	$\Sigma[x_i/X][x_i/t_i]$
Multigroup dissimilarity	$(1/2TI)\Sigma\Sigma t_j|\pi_{jm} - \pi_m|$
Multigroup Gini	$(1/2T^2I)\Sigma\Sigma\Sigma t_i t_j|\pi_{im} - \pi_{jm}|$
Multigroup information	$(1/TE)\Sigma\Sigma t_j \pi_{jm}\ln[\pi_{jm}/\pi_m]$
Multigroup normalized exposure	$(1/T)\Sigma\Sigma t_j(\pi_{jm} - \pi_m)^2/(1 - \pi_m)$
Multigroup relative diversity	$(1/TI)\Sigma\Sigma t_j(\pi_{jm} - \pi_m)^2$
Multigroup squared coefficient of variation	$(1/T(M-1))\Sigma\Sigma t_j(\pi_{jm} - \pi_m)^2/\pi_m$
Proportion in central city	X_{cc}/X
Relative centralization	$(\Sigma X_{i-1} Y_I) - (\Sigma X_i Y_{i-1})$
Relative clustering	$P_{xx}/P_{yy} - 1$, where $P_{xx} = \Sigma\Sigma x_i x_j c_{ij}/X^2$ $P_{yy} = \Sigma\Sigma y_i y_j c_{ij}/Y^2$
Relative concentration	$\{[\Sigma(x_i a_i/X)]/[\Sigma(y_i a_i/Y)] - 1\}/$ $\{[\Sigma_{i=1}^{n1}(t_i a_i/T_1)]/[\Sigma_{i=n2}^{n}(t_i a_i/T_2)] - 1\}$
Spatial proximity	$(XP_{xx} + YP_{yy})/TP_{tt}$, where $P_{tt} = \Sigma\Sigma t_i t_j c_{ij}/T^2$ $P_{xx} = \Sigma\Sigma x_i x_j c_{ij}/X^2$ $P_{yy} = \Sigma\Sigma y_i y_j c_{ij}/Y^2$
Notation	
a_i	Each neighborhood i's land area
A	Urban region's land area
c_{ij}	Dichotomous variable that equals 1 when neighborhoods i and j are contiguous and 0 otherwise*

continued

TABLE 2
Continued

Segregation Index	Formula
Notation (continued)	
E	$\sum_{m=1}^{M} \pi_m (1 - \pi_m)$
I	$\sum_{m=1}^{M} \pi_m \ln[1/\pi_m]$
M	Number of groups being considered
n	Number of neighborhoods i in the urban area
p_i	Neighborhood i's minority proportion
P	Urban region's minority proportion
t_i	Neighborhood i's total population
T	Urban region's total population
x_i	Neighborhood i's minority population
X	Urban region's minority population
X_{cc}	Number of minorities living within the boundaries of the central city
y_i	Neighborhood i's majority group population
Y	Urban region's majority population
π_{Jm}	Proportion in group m
π_m	Proportion in group m, of those in unit j

When Neighborhoods Are Ordered by Land Area, from Smallest to Largest

n_1	Rank of the neighborhood where the cumulative population of neighborhoods equals X, the study area's minority population, summing from the smallest neighborhood up
n_2	Rank of the neighborhood where the cumulative population of neighborhoods equals Y, the study area's majority group population, summing from the largest neighborhood down
T_1	Cumulative population of neighborhoods 1 to n_1
T_2	Cumulative population of neighborhoods n_2 to n

When Neighborhoods Are Ordered by Increasing Distance from Central Business District

A_i	Cumulative proportion of land area through neighborhood i
X_i	Cumulative proportion of minorities through neighborhood i
Y_i	Cumulative proportion of majority group members through neighborhood i

---

*Massey and Denton (1988) used $\exp(-d_{ij})$, or the negative exponential of the distance between the centroids of i and j, to estimate contiguity.

TABLE 3
Input Variables for Segregation Indices

Segregation Index	Input Variables			
	Constants	Vectors	Matrices	Orderings
Absolute centralization		**a, x**		O_2
Absolute clustering	n, X	**t, x**	**C**	
Absolute concentration	$n_1, n_2, T_1 T_2, X$	**a, t, x**		O_1
Atkinson	P, T	**p, t**		
Correlation ratio	P, X	**t, x**		
Delta	A, X	**a, x**		
Dissimilarity	P, T	**p, t**		
Distance-decay isolation	X	**t, x, y**	**C**	
Entropy	P, T	**p, t**		
Gini	P, T	**p, t**		
Isolation	X	**t, x**		
Multigroup dissimilarity	T, I	**t, π**		
Multigroup Gini	T, I	**t, π**		
Multigroup information	T, E	**t, π**		
Multigroup normalized exposure	T	**T, π**		
Multigroup relative diversity	T, I	**T, π**		
Multigroup squared coefficient of variation	M, T	**t, π**		
Proportion in central city	X, X_{cc}			
Relative centralization		**x, y**		O_2
Relative clustering	X, Y	**x, y**	**C**	
Relative concentration	$n_1, n_2, T_1 T_2, X, Y$	**a, t, x, y**		O_1
Spatial proximity	T, X, Y	**t, x, y**	**C**	

Notation
a $= [a_i]$
cc $= [cc_i]$
t $= [t_i]$
π $= [\pi_{im}] = [\pi_m]$
x $= [x_i]$
y $= [y_i]$
C $= [c_{ij}]$
n_1 (see Table 1)
n_2 (see Table 1)
O_1 Ordering of the neighborhoods by land area, from smallest to largest
O_2 Ordering of the neighborhoods by increasing distance from the central business district

numerous other patterns apparent. Table 4 lists the indices as functions of this reduced set of input variables. Table 5 categorizes indices by their common input variables and describes their inputs more fully.

TABLE 4
Reduced Set of Input Variables for Segregation Indices

	Input Variables		
Segregation Index	Vectors	Matrices	Orderings
Absolute centralization	**a, x**		O_2
Absolute clustering	**x, y**	C	
Absolute concentration	**a, x**, y		
Atkinson	**x, y**		
Correlation ratio	**x, y**		
Delta	**a, x**		
Dissimilarity	**x, y**		
Distance-decay isolation	**x, y**	C	
Entropy	**x, y**		
Gini	**x, y**		
Isolation	**x, y**		
Multigroup dissimilarity	$t_1, t_2, \ldots$		
Multigroup Gini	$t_1, t_2, \ldots$		
Multigroup information	$t_1, t_2, \ldots$		
Multigroup normalized exposure	$t_1, t_2, \ldots$		
Multigroup relative diversity	$t_1, t_2, \ldots$		
Multigroup squared coefficient of variation	$t_1, t_2, \ldots$		
Proportion in central city	**cc, x**		
Relative centralization	**x, y**		O_2
Relative clustering	**x, y**	C	
Relative concentration	**a, x**, y		
Spatial proximity	**x, y**	C	

This new list represents those variables, and only those variables, that a segregation researcher would have to find values for in order to calculate these indices.[4]

Some indices (dissimilarity, Gini, entropy, Atkinson, isolation, and the correlation ratio) are functions of the minority population and the majority population of each neighborhood, and only those variables. These indices are more widely used than any other segregation measures and many of

[4] For example, one counts the number of minorities in a neighborhood or the number of majority group members in a neighborhood, but one does not count a proportion. One calculates a proportion from counted values. Similarly, the sums of neighborhood populations are just that, sums. One had to identify neighborhoods and count their populations.

TABLE 5
Segregation Indices Grouped by Shared Variables

Input Variables	Indices
Minority and majority populations of individual neighborhooods (x, y)	Atkinson
	Correlation ratio
	Dissimilarity
	Entropy
	Gini
	Isolation
Racial populations of individual neighborhoods $(t_1, t_2, \ldots)$	Multigroup dissimilarity
	Multigroup Gini
	Multigroup information
	Multigroup squared coefficient of variation
	Multigroup relative diversity
	Multigroup normalized exposure
Minority and majority populations of individual neighborhoods and neighborhood contiguity (C, x, y)	Absolute clustering
	Distance-decay isolation
	Relative clustering
	Spatial proximity
Minority and majority populations and land area of individual neighborhoods (a, x, y)	Absolute concentration
	Relative concentration
Minority population and land area of individual neighborhoods (a, x)	Delta
Minority population and land area of individual neighborhoods and neighborhood ordinal distance from central business district (a, O_2, x)	Absolute centralization
Minority and majority populations of individual neighborhoods and neighborhood ordinal distance from central business district (x, O_2, y)	Relative centralization
Minority population of neighborhood and whether neighborhood is in central city (cc, x)	Proportion in the central city

the debates about indices refer only to these. By considering only members of this group, most segregation researchers have implicitly argued that only two arrays of numbers—the majority population of the neighborhoods and the population of a single minority group of each neighborhood—are important for understanding segregation and that no other information is necessary. Reardon and Firebaugh's (2002) multigroup indices are extensions of these indices to the multigroup case.

3. SPATIAL PROXIMITY

Some indices (absolute and relative clustering, distance-decay isolation, and spatial proximity) are primarily concerned not with the distribution of the minority and majority populations across neighborhoods but with the distribution of minority and majority neighborhoods with respect to each other. White (1983) termed this the "checkerboard problem." If one allows the squares on a checkerboard to represent neighborhoods, once the composition of each square is given, any spatial rearrangement of them will result in the same calculation for most segregation indices. Thus, "A city in which all the nonwhite parcels were concentrated into one single ghetto would have the same calculated segregation as a city with dispersed pockets of minority residents" (White 1983, pp. 1010–11).

These "clustering" indices can all be rewritten in terms of a single function:

$$f(x_i, y_j) = \Sigma_{i=1} \Sigma_{j=1} c_{ij} x_i y_j \tag{1}$$

This function focuses on the potential for interactions and is explicitly defined in terms of the product of the number of individuals of the specified groups in the set of neighborhoods defined by the contiguity matrix $\mathbf{C}$. All of these indices can be thought of as interaction measures, except that instead of assuming the potential for interaction exists only among residents of a single neighborhood (e.g., a census tract), they assume the potential for interaction exists between residents of neighborhood i and all other neighborhoods defined as contiguous to i by the contiguity matrix $\mathbf{C}$. $\mathbf{C}$ could also be defined as a weight such as inverse distance so that neighborhoods that were closer were weighted more heavily while neighborhoods that were farther away were weighted less heavily.

The formulas for the clustering indices then translate as follows:

Distance-decay isolation $= f(x_i/X, y_j)/f(t_j, 1)$ (2)

Absolute clustering $= \{f(x_i, x_j) - f(X^2, n^{-2})\}/$

$$\{f(x_i, t_j) \quad f(X^2, n^{-2})\} \tag{3}$$

Relative clustering $= Y^2 f(x_i, x_j)/X^2 f(y_i, y_j) - 1$ (4)

Spatial proximity $= \{f(x_i, x_j)/X + f(y_i, y_j)/Y\}/\{f(t_i, t_j)/T\}$ (5)

The distance-decay isolation index can be interpreted as the probability that the next person a group X member meets is from group Y. The absolute clustering index measures how much group x members are clustered so that they interact with each other more than one would expect as a proportion of how much opportunity group x members have to interact with anyone more than one would expect. The relative clustering index compares the average proximity of members of group X to the average proximity of members of group Y. The spatial proximity index is the average of intragroup proximities weighted by each group's fraction in the population. In short, the distance between groups, or the geographic level at which they are segregated, as well as the fact that they are separated, has been a concern of previous research. It would be useful to combine Reardon and Firebaugh's (2002) focus on multiple groups with this concern for the dimension of distance.

4. AN EXAMPLE

Although segregation researchers are certainly aware of the presence and importance of ghettos and the spatial patterning of neighborhoods, there is a tendency to revert to more simplistic measures when analyzing more complex relationships. I illustrate one such complexity by reexamining some data from an article by Farley et al. (1994) that began by examining "residential segregation scores" (using the dissimilarity index) for metropolitan Detroit in 1990, controlling separately for household income and for educational attainment. Since Farley et al. used only the dissimilarity index, their analysis utilized only two arrays of numbers to compute their index scores for each subset. Using their data, I computed the dissimilarity index (to replicate their results), the isolation index, and the spatial proximity index for each of their income and educational subsets. The isolation index is perhaps the second most commonly cited index and, like the dissimilarity index, uses only information about the number of white and black households in the tract. Computing the spatial proximity index required using one additional array of numbers: those tracts in the Detroit metropolitan area that were contiguous and those that were not. Figures 1 and 2 display the results.

In both figures, the line represented by long dashes and triangles represents the dissimilarity index scores, the line with short dashes and circles represents the isolation index, and the solid line with squares represents the spatial proximity index. As Farley et al. (1994) noted, the

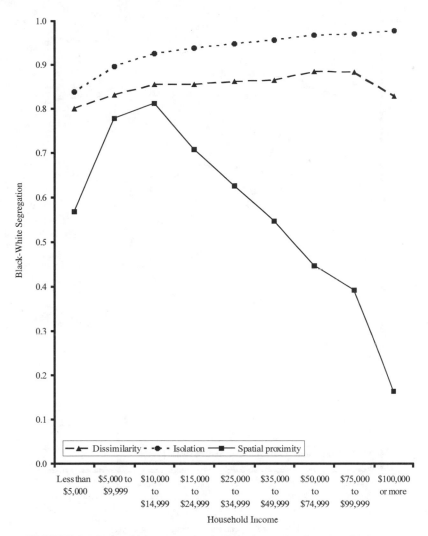

FIGURE 1. Black-white segregation in Detroit metropolitan area by income.

dissimilarity index is essentially unaffected by changes in income; the isolation index behaves similarly. Using one or both of these indices, which only use information about the numbers of white and black households in each tract, one might reasonably conclude that segregation is unaffected by changes in income or educational attainment, as did Farley et al. (1994). Segregation as measured by the spatial proximity index,

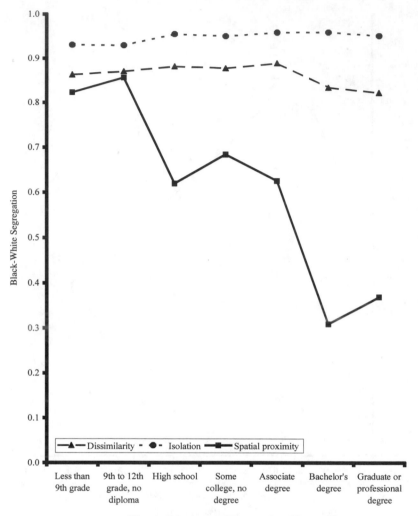

FIGURE 2. Black-white segregation in Detroit metropolitan area by educational attainment.

however, drops dramatically with increases in income or educational attainment.

Thus two findings emerge from these figures. First, in Detroit, blacks with high incomes and high education are just as likely to be segregated at the tract level as blacks with low incomes and little education (as shown by the dissimilarity or isolation indices). Second, the tracts that blacks with high incomes and high education live in are much more likely to be adjacent to white tracts than are the tracts occupied by blacks with low incomes and little education. While income and education do not allow blacks in Detroit easy access into white tracts, they do allow them access into tracts in larger white areas. Segregated neighborhoods of 1300 households (the average tract size in this region) may be sufficiently large to segregate most face-to-face interactions but may not be sufficiently large to segregate supermarkets, school districts, or churches. Upper-class blacks live in smaller "mostly black" communities than do their less well-to-do counterparts. Using indices that only account for the distribution of whites and blacks at the tract level misses this second important and powerful finding.

5. MULTIGROUP SPATIAL PROXIMITY

While Reardon and Firebaugh (2002) use "organizational units" instead of neighborhoods to maximize generality (for example, with school districts, etc.), this simplification ignores important differences between neighborhoods and schools, not the least of which is that school districts are often much bigger than the neighborhood equivalents by which we typically measure residential segregation (e.g., a high school feeder zone may include several census tracts and numerous census block groups). Much of the theorizing done about residential segregation would not have any meaning at the micro-level at which Reardon and Firebaugh's (2002) indices (as well as many traditional segregation indices) would measure it, concerning only very small communities of a few hundred or a thousand households, oblivious to larger patterns. This has not been a critical issue in the past since segregation has primarily been measured in a two-group scenario, black and white. Given the ghettoization of blacks throughout America, segregation at the neighborhood level typically implied larger-scale segregation (Massey and Denton 1993). As we begin to consider more complex, multigroup cases, however, the disparity between micro-level segregation and larger patterns may become more acute.

As we begin to consider more widespread use of multigroup measures, it is appropriate that we simultaneously consider using spatial proximity measures more. The spatial proximity index has an obvious adaptation to the multigroup case:

Multigroup spatial proximity $= \Sigma_m \{ f(x_{im}, x_{jm})/X_m \}/\{ f(t_i, t_j)/T \}$ (6)

$$= \Sigma_m (1/X_m)(\Sigma_i \Sigma_j x_{im} x_{jm} c_{ij})/$$

$$(\Sigma \Sigma t_i t_j c_{ij}/T) \qquad (7)$$

This new index is the average of intragroup proximities weighted by each group's fraction of the population. The numerator is the sum of several terms, one for each racial group. Each term is the total number of potential interactions among members of each racial group averaged over the number of members of that racial group. The denominator equals the total number of potential interactions between all individuals averaged over the total number of people in the study area. Since this index is a sum of an independent term for each racial group, this index could be used effectively to measure spatial proximity among a single racial group, two racial groups, or several. It could also be expanded to measure spatial proximity among different subcategories (e.g., income, educational level) within a single racial group or among multiple racial groups.

Researchers need to consider indices that account for nearby neighborhoods unless they are certain the boundaries of census tracts, block groups, or other neighborhood proxies completely confine the experience of segregation. Using clustering indices, such as the multigroup spatial proximity index proposed above, also allows one to deal with the Modifiable Areal Unit Problem (MAUP), which results from the imposition of artificial boundaries on a geographically correlated phenomenon (Openshaw and Taylor 1979). Analytical results may be highly sensitive to the size and boundaries of the zones used. Dramatically different results may be obtained from the same set of data when the information is grouped in different levels of spatial resolution (scale effect) or by merely altering the boundaries or configurations of the zones at a given scale of analysis (zone effect). Using the smallest possible neighborhood equivalent in combination with a clustering index would allow one to account for segregation patterns at or above the level of analysis. While the availability of data limits our analyses, we should not allow our analytic tools to be more limiting than our data.

6. CONCLUSION

In choosing the indices by which they measure segregation, sociologists define segregation itself and induce particular substantive understandings. When we use indices, we are trying to reduce huge data arrays into simpler, more readily understandable numbers. While no index will be useful for every study of segregation, the importance of measuring both neighborhood-level and larger-level segregation patterns clearly shows that indices that include distance or contiguity as an input should be used more often in future segregation research. Furthermore, the definition of contiguity (or distance), as used in these measures, needs to remain adaptable, to account not only for geographic distance or adjacency but also for the actual probabilities of contact.[5]

When researchers choose to ignore information about the racial composition of nearby neighborhoods, they are making assertive theoretical claims that segregation only occurs at (or below) the level of the neighborhood they are using (e.g., a census tract) and that life in a minority community of a few hundred or a thousand households in the midst of a majority population is not conceptually different from life in a minority community of a hundred thousand households since they fail to incorporate data that would allow them to distinguish these two situations. Just as multigroup segregation indices are important for understanding complex demographic patterns, so indices that include data on neighborhood contiguity are important for understanding segregation patterns occurring at levels larger than a census tract.

REFERENCES

Atkinson, A. B. 1970. "On the Measurement of Inequality." *American Sociological Review* 43:865–80.

Bell, Wendell. 1954. "A Probability Model for the Measurement of Ecological Segregation." *Social Forces* 32:357–64.

Carlson, Susan M. 1992. "Trends in Race/Sex Occupational Inequality: Conceptual and Measurement Issues." *Social Problems* 39:269–90.

Dacey, Michael F. 1968. "A Review on Measures of Contiguity for Two and K-Color Maps." Pps. 479–95 in *Spatial Analysis: A Reader in Statistical Geography*, edited by Brian J. L. Berry and Duane F. Marble. Englewood Cliffs, NJ: Prentice-Hall.

Duncan, Otis D., and Beverly Duncan. 1955. "A Methodological Analysis of Segregation Indices." *American Sociological Review* 20:210–17.

[5] For example, Grannis (1998) has argued that, in addition to mere geographic contiguity, it is important to note whether residential streets connect neighborhoods to each other. Therefore, one could let the contiguity or distance variables in these indices refer to residential street connectivity or distance, or any other appropriate measure of the actual potential for interaction.

Duncan, Otis D., Ray P. Cuzzort, and Beverly Duncan. 1961. *Statistical Geography: Problems in Analyzing Area Data.* Glencoe, IL: Free Press.

Farley, Reynolds, Charlotte Steeh, Maria Krysan, Tara Jackson, and Keith Reeves. 1994. "Stereotypes and Segregation: Neighborhoods in the Detroit Area." *American Journal of Sociology* 100:750–80.

Geary, R. C. 1954. "The Contiguity Ratio and Statistical Mapping." *Incorporated Statistician* 5:115–41.

Goodman, Leo, and William H. Kruskal. 1954. "Measures of Association for Cross-Classifications." *Journal of the American Statistical Association* 49: 731–64.

Grannis, Rick. 1998. "The Importance of Trivial Streets: Residential Streets and Residential Segregation." *American Journal of Sociology* 103:1530–64.

Hoover, Edgar M. 1941. "Interstate Redistribution of Population, 1850–1940." *Journal of Economic History* 1:199–205.

Jahn, Julius A., Calvin F. Schmid, and Clarence Schrag. 1947. "The Measurement of Ecological Segregation." *American Sociological Review* 103:293–303.

James, David R., and Karl E. Taeuber. 1985. "Measures of Segregation." *Sociological Methodology* 14:1–32.

James, Franklin J. 1986. "A New Generalized "Exposure-Based" Segregation Index." *Sociological Methods and Research* 14:301–16.

Lieberson, Stanley. 1981. "An Asymmetrical Approach to Segregation." Pp. 61–82 in *Ethnic Segregation in Cities*, edited by Ceri Peach, Vaughn Robinson, and Susan Smith. London: Croom Helm.

Massey, Douglas S., and Nancy A. Denton. 1988. "The Dimensions of Residential Segregation." *Social Forces* 67:281–305.

Massey, Douglas S., and Nancy A. Denton. 1993. *American Apartheid: Segregation and the Making of the Underclass.* Cambridge, MA: Harvard University.

Morgan, Barrie S. 1975. "The Segregation of Socioeconomic Groups in Urban Areas: A Comparative Analysis." *Urban Studies* 12:47–60.

———. 1983. "An Alternate Approach to the Development of a Distance-Based Measures of Racial Segregation." *American Journal of Sociology* 88:1237–49.

Openshaw, S., and P. Taylor. 1979. "A Million or so Correlation Coefficients: Three Experiments on the Modifiable Area Unit Problem." Pp. 127–44 in *Statistical Applications in the Spatial Sciences*, edited by Neil Wrigley. London: Pion.

Reardon, Sean F., and Glenn Firebaugh. Forthcoming. "Measures of Multigroup Segregation." *Sociological Methodology.*

Sakoda, J. 1981. "A Generalized Index of Dissimilarity." *Demography* 18:245–50.

Schwartz, J., and C. Winship. 1980. "The Welfare Approach to Measuring Inequality." *Sociological Methodology* 9:1–36.

Theil, Henri. 1972. *Statistical Decomposition Analysis.* Amsterdam: North-Holland.

Theil, Henri, and Anthony J. Finezza. 1971. "A Note on the Measurement of Racial Integration of Schools by Means of Informational Concepts." *Journal of Mathematical Sociology* 1:187–94.

White, Michael J. 1983. "The Measurement of Spatial Segregation." *American Journal of Sociology* 98:1008–19.

———. 1986. "Segregation and Diversity Measures in Population Distribution." *Population Index* 52(2):198–221.

RESPONSE: SEGREGATION AND SOCIAL DISTANCE—A GENERALIZED APPROACH TO SEGREGATION MEASUREMENT

Sean F. Reardon*
Glenn Firebaugh*

The study of segregation is a fundamentally sociological enterprise, defined by a concern with the social distance between members of different groups. The groups of interest may be categorized by race and ethnicity, by sex, by religion, by income or wealth, or by any number of other social characteristics. Social distance may be based on spatial locations, social institutions—such as schools, organizations, or occupations—social networks, or some other aspect of the social terrain. In any case, however, the motivation behind the study of segregation is generally driven by the understanding that individuals' location in social space is linked to their access to resources of some kind—economic rewards, social networks, cultural capital, political power, physical safety, quality schools and instruction, social status, and so on.

Regardless of the specific segregation phenomenon under examination, however, the sociological study of segregation always depends on two key elements: (1) methods of producing meaningful and analytically useful descriptions of the social distance between groups; and (2) sociological theory that illuminates the relationship between individuals' location in social space to their access to social resources. Our concern in our paper in this volume and in this reply to Grannis's commentary is with the first of these elements, the need for theoretically appropriate and meaningful measures of segregation. This requires the reduction of often massive amounts of information about the location of individuals within the social terrain and about the social distance among them. As in much of sociology, careful measurement of social phenomena is the prerequisite to careful analysis.

The field of segregation research has long been hampered by its general reliance on a set of simple, two-group, aspatial measures of seg-

*Pennsylvania State University

regation. Our paper in this volume removes the *two-group limitation* by extending a traditional set of measures of segregation to the case where the population of interest contains more than two mutually exclusive groups (Reardon and Firebaugh 2002, this volume). Grannis (2002, this volume) points out that although we address the two-group limitation, we have ignored the *aspatial* aspect of traditional segregation indices, since the measures we examine do not take into account the spatial location of the organizational units (e.g., census tracts) in which individuals are located. This is true, and Grannis is right in calling for more attention to spatial measures of segregation, particularly in the field of residential segregation. Here we take up Grannis's suggestion that we attend to "the dimension of distance," although we consider the more general notion of "social distance" rather than simply considering spatial distance.

Our response here addresses four main points: (1) We argue that a segregation measure should incorporate a theoretically appropriate social distance metric; (2) we suggest several approaches to developing social distance-based multigroup segregation measures; (3) we discuss the need for criteria against which to evaluate such measures, and present a tentative list of such criteria; and (4) we suggest an agenda for the field of segregation measurement.

1. SOCIAL DISTANCE AND SOCIAL PROXIMITY

The dichotomy between spatial and aspatial indices is a somewhat false one, since both types of measures incorporate implicit notions of social distance. Traditional, "aspatial" measures imply that the social distance between any two organizational units is equal, while "spatial" measures take the social distance between two units to vary according to some function of the spatial location of units. We formalize these notions below.

From the social location information, we must define a social distance metric. More specifically, we must define, for each pair of individuals i and j, the social distance d_{ij} between individuals i and j. (Note that we change notation slightly from our earlier paper; here i, j, and k index individuals, while I, J, and K index organizational units.) Standardizing the social distance metric to range from 0 to 1, we will have $d_{ij} = 0$ if i and j are in the same social location and $d_{ij} = 1$ if i and j are at the maximum possible social distance from one another. From this it follows as well that the social distance metric should give $d_{jj} = 0$ for all j and $0 \leq d_{ij} \leq 1$ for all $i \neq j$. In cases where it is more convenient to use social proximity rather than social distance, we can define the social proximity of individuals i and j as $c_{ij} = 1 - d_{ij}$.

In practice, however, we rarely have the individual-level data that allow us to compute the social distance or proximity of two *individuals*. Instead, we usually have data tabulated by some organizational units (schools, census tracts), among which we may have some measure of social distance/proximity (such as spatial distance, spatial contiguity). Consider the case where the population is divided among discrete organizational units (such as schools or tracts) and individual j is in unit J while individual k is in unit K. Now if we define $d_{ik} = d_{jk} = d_{JK}$ for all j in J, k in K, and $J \neq K$, then d_{JK} is the social distance between units J and K (with $d_{JJ} = 0$ for all J and $0 \leq d_{JK} \leq 1$ for all $J \neq K$). Moreover, for simplicity's sake, we can (though we need not) define $d_{ij} = 0$ for all i and j in the same unit J—when we do this we are in effect saying the organizational units bound social relations in such a way that the effective social distance between individuals in the same organizational unit is negligible.

Note that the social distance metric need not be defined by *spatial* distance, though there are clearly cases where spatial factors may play a role in social distance. The concept of social distance (or proximity) is more general than that of spatial distance. Consider, for example, the following different ways of conceptualizing and operationalizing social distance.

Social Distance and Residential Segregation.   As Grannis and others have pointed out, in the study of residential segregation, distance matters. It matters because greater spatial proximity is assumed to mean greater social proximity, a greater probability of social interaction. However, scholars have suggested a variety of ways of operationalizing a social distance metric based on spatial distance or proximity.

One common way of doing this is to define the social distance matrix—as Grannis does in this volume—as based on contiguity of residential areas (tracts, block groups), so that $d_{ij} = d_{IJ} = 0$ for all i in I and j in J if $I = J$ or if I is adjacent to J, and $d_{ij} = 1$ otherwise (Morrill 1991). Wong (1993) suggests refining this so that d_{ij} depends on the length of the shared boundary between I and J or on the area and perimeter of the two areas, since these factors may influence the probability of interaction among members of adjacent areas. Grannis, however, suggests that social distance may be in part a function of the presence of connecting tertiary street networks; this would lead to defining d_{ij} as a function of street networks connecting I and J (Grannis 1998). Another approach is to define the social distance matrix as some function of the spatial distance between individuals. For example, if r_{ij} is the spatial (Euclidean) distance between i and j, we might define $d_{ij} = ar_{ij}$, where a is some standardizing constant, so that social distance increases linearly as a function of spatial distance (Jakubs 1981; Morgan 1983a). Other scholars have suggested $d_{ij} = 1 - e^{-r_{ij}}$, so that social proximity decays exponentially with spatial distance (Massey and Denton 1988; Morgan 1983b; White 1983).

One potential problem with contiguity-based distance metrics is that they will generally result in cases where $d_{ij} + d_{jk} < d_{ik}$ for some i, j, and k, which may lead to somewhat uninterpretable results (e.g., negative segregation). However, it is not our goal in this paper to discuss the merits or flaws of these different approaches to measuring social distance based on spatial distance. Rather, we wish to point out the need to use segregation measures that capture a theoretically appropriate dimension of social distance.

An additional point merits attention here. Because studies of residential segregation are generally based on data aggregated by tracts or blocks, measured levels of segregation may be confounded somewhat by the somewhat arbitrary definition of the size and boundaries of the areal units employed. This issue is known as *the modifiable areal unit problem* (MAUP) in the literature (Openshaw and Taylor 1979). Although Grannis claims that using segregation indices that incorporate a spatial distance metric "allows one to deal with" MAUP issues (page 82, this volume), this is not necessarily so. In our framework, MAUP arises not from the aspatial nature of traditional segregation indices but from the assumptions that $d_{ij} = 0$ for all i and j in J and that $d_{jk} = d_{JK}$ for all j and k in $J \neq K$. This assumption is valid only to the extent that it is reasonable to assume that all individuals in a given areal unit are located at the same place in the social/spatial geography. The smaller the areal units, and the more closely boundaries between units correspond to real social barriers, the more reasonable this assumption. Nonetheless, we should keep in mind that spatial measures are not immune from MAUP, though they may be less sensitive to MAUP-induced measurement error than aspatial measures.

Social Distance and School Segregation.   In describing school segregation, there is little justification for attending to the physical distance between two schools, since school boundaries circumscribe social relations and the provision of resources and instruction far more clearly than spatial distance among schools. Conversely, school segregation research has rarely attended to differences in levels of social distance among different pairs of students within schools—all students within a school are assumed to be in the same social location. While this may seem an over-simplification in a school with substantial grade and curricular differentiation (since a pair of students in kindergarten and twelfth grade, for example, presumably have far less social interaction than a pair of students in the same grade and classroom), it makes sense from the point of view of the allocation of school resources, policies, curricula, and so on, since many such aspects of schooling operate at the level of the school rather than the level of the classroom or grade.

Given the assumption that all students within a given school occupy the same location in the social geography of schooling, and that all schools are equally distant from one another, we get a social distance metric that has $d_{ij} = 0$ if i and j are in the same school, and $d_{ij} = 1$ otherwise. (Note that in the school segregation literature, there is no concern with MAUP, since the assumption that all students within a school are located in the same place in the social geography of schools is fairly reasonable.)

Social Distance and Social Network Segregation. Suppose we are interested in measuring the segregation of social or friendship networks. We might define social proximity based on the "degrees of separation" between individuals. For example, suppose we have a population of adolescents, each of whom identifies their five "best friends" in the population. From this information, we may draw a social network map (e.g., see Coleman 1961), with "best friends" indicated by (one- or two-way) links. From this network, we can define some measure of the social distance d_{ij} between i and j as a function of the number, length, and directionality of the network path(s) connecting i and j. For example, let n_{ij} be the length of (the number of links in) the shortest path connecting individual i to j and then define $d_{ij} = 1 - a^{-n_{ij}}$, where a is some constant greater than 1. More complex measures of social distance might incorporate information on the number of distinct paths connecting i and j, as well as information on whether friendship links are mutually nominated or not. Again, our goal here is not to evaluate the merits of different definitions of social distance within friendship networks, but only to point out (1) that "social distance" may apply to other dimensions of distance than spatial distance; and (2) the need for careful attention to how social distance is operationalized.

Social Distance and Occupational Segregation.   As a final example of
social distance, consider the study of occupational segregation. In the occupational segregation literature, occupations are generally thought of in the
same way as schools are in the school segregation literature—as distinct
organizational units, each equally socially distant from one another (e.g.,
see Charles and Grusky 1995; Watts 1992; Watts 1997). In our notation,
the social distance between occupations is $d_{JK} = 1$ for all occupations $J \neq$
K, and the social distance within an occupation J is $d_{ij} = 0$ for all i and j
in J. In some cases, this may be a somewhat unreasonable assumption. It
may make sense to define d_{JK} to account for the fact that professional
occupations are more similar to one another ("closer" in social distance)
than a professional occupation is to a service or labor occupational category. The exact definitions of social distance one might employ should
derive from theoretical understandings of the occupational structure and
social relations among members of different occupations.

    In each of these examples, the exact definition of "social distance"
should follow from theoretical consideration of the social processes of
interest. Grannis and others who have argued against the use of aspatial
measures of residential segregation do so because sociological theory suggests that the probability of social interaction decreases with spatial distance. In order to provide the basis for meaningful analysis of segregation
and its processes, segregation measures must incorporate an appropriate
metric of social distance.

2. INCORPORATING SOCIAL DISTANCE INTO
SEGREGATION MEASURES

Even given a theoretically appropriate social distance matrix, we still
require a mathematical formulation for computing segregation levels based
on this social distance matrix. Although a complete derivation and evaluation of segregation indices that incorporate notions of social distance or
proximity is beyond the scope of our comments here, we nonetheless wish
to suggest several approaches that might profitably lead to useful measures of segregation.

2.1. *Segregation Measures Using Proximity-Weighted Group*
Proportions

Think of segregation as a measure of the extent to which the composition
of each individual's social environment deviates from the composition of

the average social environment of the total population. We can formally define the composition of the social environment of individual k as follows. Suppose m is one of M distinct groups (e.g., race/ethnic groups) in the population. Let k and j index individuals, and define $c_{kj} = 1 - d_{kj}$ as the "social proximity" of individuals k and j. Let $x_{jm} = 1$ if individual j is in group m and $x_{jm} = 0$ otherwise. Then define

$$\tilde{\pi}_{km} = \frac{\sum_j x_{jm} c_{kj}}{\sum_j c_{kj}}. \tag{1}$$

Now $\tilde{\pi}_{km}$ is the proximity-weighted proportion of members of group m in the social environment of individual k. Likewise, the average proximity-weighted proportion of members of group m in the social environment of the population is $\tilde{\pi}_m$, which is simply the average of the $\tilde{\pi}_{km}$ over all individuals.

As we noted above, however, in practice we rarely have the individual-level data that allow us to compute the social proximity of two *individuals*. To compute $\tilde{\pi}_{km}$ in the case where we have data tabulated by some organizational units (schools, census tracts), among which we may have some measure of social proximity (distance, contiguity), consider individuals j and k in organizational units J and K, respectively. Now if c_{jk} is equal to some constant c_{JK} for all j and k in J and K, then c_{JK} is the social proximity of unit J to unit K (with $c_{JJ} = 1$ for all J and $0 \leq c_{JK} \leq 1$ for all $J \neq K$). From this, we get

$$\tilde{\pi}_{km} = \tilde{\pi}_{Km} = \frac{\sum_J t_J \pi_{Jm} c_{KJ}}{\sum_J t_J c_{KJ}}, \tag{2}$$

where t_J is the number of individuals in unit J and π_{Jm} is the proportion of J made up of group m (for example, proportion Latino in census tract J). Now $\tilde{\pi}_{km}$ is constant for all individuals k in K, and this constant can be computed from the sizes, compositions, and proximities of each of the units relative to K.

Now consider the special case where each organizational unit has no social proximity to any other unit—as in the case where the organizational units are schools. In this case $c_{JJ} = 1$ for all J and $c_{KJ} = 0$ for all $J \neq K$. From this, we get $\tilde{\pi}_{Km} = \pi_{Km}$, where π_{Km} is the proportion of unit K in group m. In other words, if we assume that all individuals in a given unit have maximum social proximity to each other and minimum (zero) proximity to individuals in other units, then the composition of the social environment of individual k is simply the composition of his or her organizational unit.

If we return to our definition of segregation above—a measure of the extent to which the composition of each individual's social environment deviates from the composition of the total population—we can use equation (2) to extend the set of multigroup segregation indices in Reardon and Firebaugh (2002, this volume) to a more general set of indices that can accommodate any number of forms of social proximity. To do this, we simply replace π_{jm} and π_m with $\tilde{\pi}_{jm}$ and $\tilde{\pi}_m$ in Table 2 in Reardon and Firebaugh (2002, this volume). A note of caution regarding this approach is warranted however; it is not immediately clear whether constructing social distance-based segregation measures in this way leads to mathematical difficulties. However, we leave the evaluation of these and all measures suggested here to future consideration. Our goal here is simply to suggest different possible approaches to incorporating social distance into measures of multigroup segregation.

2.2. Segregation Measures as Distance-Weighted Average Differences in Group Proportions

A second possible approach to constructing segregation indices that incorporate a social distance metric is to take the sum, over all groups and all pairs of organizational units, of a measure of the difference in group proportions between units, weighted by the size of the group, the size of the units, and the social distance between the units. This gives

$$W = \sum_{m=1}^{M} \pi_m \sum_{J} \sum_{K} \left[\frac{t_J t_K}{T^2} \cdot f(r_{Jm}, r_{Km}, d_{JK}) \right], \tag{3}$$

where $f(r_{Jm}, r_{Km}, d_{JK})$ is a function that measures the difference between r_{Jm} and r_{Km} as an increasing function of d_{JK} with $f(r_{Jm}, r_{Km}, d_{JK}) = 0$ if $r_{Jm} = r_{Km}$. Following our approach in deriving the disproportionality-based segregation indices described in our paper in this volume, we then divide W by its maximum possible value (obtained in the case of complete segregation) to get plausible distance-weighted measures of segregation. For example, if $f(r_{Jm}, r_{Km}, d_{JK}) = d_{JK}|r_{Jm} - r_{Km}|/2$, we get a distance-weighted Gini index. Similarly, if $f(r_{Jm}, r_{Km}, d_{JK}) = d_{JK}(r_{Jm} - r_{Km})^2$, we get a distance-weighted squared coefficient of variation index. In the case when $d_{JK} = 1$ for all $J \neq K$ (which is the case when we think of all organizational units as equally distant from one another, as is the case with aspatial segregation measures), these two distance-weighted measures reduce to the G and C we define in our paper in this volume. The spatially adjusted versions of the dissimilarity index suggested by Morrill (1991) and Wong (1993) can also be derived from this approach, if we define $f(r_{Jm}, r_{Km}, d_{JK}) = (|r_{Jm} - 1| + |r_{Km} - 1| - (1 - d_{JK})|r_{Jm} - r_{Km}|)$ and use $d_{JK} = 1 - W_{JK}$ (where W_{JK} is Wong's boundary weight term—a measure of social proximity in our terminology). In the aspatial case (where $W_{JK} = 0$ for all $J \neq K$), these indices reduce to D.

2.3. Segregation Measures as Average Social Proximity Ratios

A third general approach to developing segregation measures that incorporate a social distance metric is to compute a set of average within- and between-group social proximity measures and then to define segregation as some appropriate function (most likely a ratio) of these average social proximities. White (1983) was the first to take this approach, applying it to the measurement of spatial segregation.

In this approach, for each pair of groups m and n, we compute the average social proximity of a member of group m and group n. In particular, the average social proximity of two individuals of groups m and n is

$$C_{mn} = \sum_J \sum_K \frac{t_J \, t_K \, \pi_{Jm} \, \pi_{Kn}}{T^2 \pi_m \pi_n} (1 - d_{JK}). \tag{4}$$

Similarly, the average social proximity of any two individuals is

$$C_{tt} = \sum_J \sum_K \frac{t_J \, t_K}{T^2} (1 - d_{JK}). \tag{5}$$

Grannis, following White in his comment, suggests a segregation measure based on these measures. His multigroup spatial proximity index is simply

$$SP = \sum_{m=1}^{M} \pi_m \frac{C_{mm}}{C_{tt}}, \tag{6}$$

which is a multigroup extension of White's two-group proximity statistic P (White 1983). One potential disadvantage of this measure, however, is that it is not bounded between zero and one, as are other segregation measures. Instead, it is bounded between 0 and $1/C_{tt}$, where $0 < C_{tt} \leq 1$. A value of SP greater than 1.0 indicates that individuals have a greater social proximity, on average, to members of their own group than to other groups; a value of 1.0 indicates zero segregation; and a value less than 1.0 indicates that individuals have a greater social proximity, on average, to members of other groups than to their own (a result that can arise if the social distance metric is defined in a way that allows cases where $d_{ij} + d_{jk} < d_{ik}$ for some i, j, and k).

A related index can be constructed if we simply replace C_{mm} and C_{tt} by D_{mm} and D_{tt} in equation (6) and subtract the resulting ratio from 1. This index measures the ratio of the average social distances among members of the same groups to the average social distance among the population. One advantage of this index over Grannis's is that it is normally bounded between 0 and 1 (although negative values, indicating negative segregation, are possible if the social distance metric is not defined so that $d_{ij} + d_{jk} \geq d_{ik}$ for all i, j, and k). Finally, other approaches to deriving multigroup segregation indices that incorporate measures of social distance are possible (e.g., see Jakubs 1981; Morgan 1983a; Morgan 1983b), but we leave a fuller discussion of these for another time.

3. EVALUATING MEASURES OF SEGREGATION THAT INCORPORATE SOCIAL DISTANCE

Grannis implies that the appropriateness of a segregation index can be reasonably inferred based on its "functional inputs"—the information used to compute it. "Indices can best be understood in terms of the variables they are functions of," he argues (page 70, this volume), but never makes clear the justification for this statement. While true at a relatively crude level—an index that does not use information on the spatial location of census tracts cannot be said to be a spatial measure—this method of analyzing segregation indices seems to miss key issues in the measurement of segregation, notably the need for segregation measures that allow mathematically valid comparisons among different populations.

We agree with Grannis that a segregation measure must rely on an appropriate social distance metric, yet, given a definition of social distance, a variety of measures of segregation are possible. We have suggested several general approaches to deriving segregation indices that incorporate a social distance metric. Each of these approaches yields multiple potential indices that derive from different functional definitions of segregation and different operationalizations of the concept of "social distance." In addition, there are at least several other measures of spatial segregation in the literature that we have not discussed and that do not fall under these general types (e.g., see Jakubs 1981; Morgan 1983a; Morgan 1983b). In all, we are presented with a wide array of apparently meaningful segregation measures that incorporate a social distance metric, each of which is potentially a useful measure of spatial segregation. All of the indices we have described above include information on social distance; and all allow for multiple groups. How are we to decide which to use?

To see if an index permits mathematically valid comparisons among different populations, we must determine whether the index responds appropriately to changes in the distribution of individuals across social space. That insight is the basis for the criteria we established for evaluating the aspatial multigroup indexes in our earlier paper. As we show there, not every mathematical operationalization of the concept of segregation possesses the mathematical properties to allow meaningful comparisons among different populations and useful segregation decomposition analyses.

Thus, while Grannis's suggestion of a multigroup spatial proximity index is a useful contribution to the field of residential segregation research, his index, as well as all of those we have suggested above, should be carefully evaluated according to some theoretically appropriate set of mathematical criteria to ensure that they allow meaningful comparisons among populations. This task is well beyond the scope of our discussion here, however. We would like to suggest that researchers take up in the future the task of both specifying an appropriate set of criteria—as James and Taeuber (1985) and we have done for aspatial measures—and evaluating the many social distance-based measures of segregation against these criteria.

As a start toward this goal, we present here a tentative list of appropriate criteria to use for evaluating social distance-based segregation measures. Although Grannis states that the four James and Taeuber (1985) criteria that we use in our paper "concern only the racial populations of each neighborhood and thus have no meaning for indices that include other variables" (like a social distance metric), we fail to see the rationale for this statement. Even in the case of spatial segregation indices, we would still like an index to remain invariant under a doubling of the population in every neighborhood, for example. While some criteria may require a more general statement in the case of social distance-based indices, the idea that indices ought to respond in conceptually appropriate ways to changes in the population distribution among organizational units remains valid. Finally, the criteria we present here are meant as a starting place for discussion; more thorough consideration than we can give them here is necessary before setting them in stone.

Nonspatial Analog.   If $c_{ij} = 1$ for all i and j in the same organizational unit, and $c_{ij} = 0$ for all i and j in distinct units, then a segregation measure should reduce to a meaningful aspatial measure. Traditional aspatial measures of segregation are a special case of social distance-based measures, defined as the case where the social proximity of any two distinct units is zero.

Definitions of Minimum and Maximum Segregation.   Though arguable, we suggest the following definitions of maximum and minimum segregation. A spatial segregation index should be bounded between 0 (obtained only in the case of no segregation) and 1 (obtained in the case of complete segregation). Segregation should be zero when the group proportions are the same at all points in the social terrain. This means that segregation is zero if either of the following conditions are met, and greater than zero otherwise: (a) if $\pi_{Jm} = \pi_{Km} = \pi_m$ for all J, K, m, regardless of the distances among the units; or (b) if $c_{ij} = 1$ for all i, j, regardless of the group proportions in the units. Segregation is maximized if there is no social proximity between any members of different groups. That is, for any pair of individuals i and j who are members of different groups, the social proximity c_{ij} equals zero.

   Note in particular that these definitions appear to be invalid for the social proximity measures we describe above, because these measures allow measured segregation to be negative, at least given certain definitions of social distance. What it means for segregation to be negative, and whether a meaningful measure should allow such a result, merit further consideration.

Social Distance Scale Invariance.   If the social distance between each pair of units is multiplied by a constant, then segregation is unchanged. This criterion is debatable, however, as it views segregation as a measure of the relative distribution of individuals across social space. In this perspective, a street with all whites at one end and all blacks at the other end would be as segregated as a metropolitan area with all whites on one side and all blacks on the other. There may be cases where such a result is inappropriate, however. More generally, a segregation index should respond appropriately to a change in the social distance scale, though the definition of "appropriate" must derive from some theoretical understanding of the social processes of interest.

Organizational Equivalence. If $\pi_{Jm} = \pi_{Km}$ for all m, $c_{JK} = 1$, and $c_{JI} = c_{KI}$ for all I, then segregation is unchanged if units J and K are combined into a single unit. Likewise, if a unit is divided into two units J and K such that $\pi_{Jm} = \pi_{Km}$ for all m, $c_{JK} = 1$, and $c_{JI} = c_{KI}$ for all I, then segregation is unchanged.

Size Invariance. If the number of members of each group m in each unit J is multiplied by a constant p, then segregation is unchanged.

Transfers, Exchanges, and Mobility A key criterion for a segregation measure is a definition of how segregation should change in response to the movement of individuals (or units) in social space. Transfers and exchanges, as we define them in our paper in this volume, are a specific type of movement of individuals within the social space. In the case of more generalized social distance-based measures of segregation, however, it is not exactly clear what should be the appropriate formulation of these criteria. We suggest the following formulations as a starting point, though more careful thought needs to be given to this issue.

Transfers. If a member x of group m is transferred from unit J to K, such that the average distance of x from all other members of group m is increased while the average distance of x from members of other groups is unchanged or reduced, then segregation is reduced.

Exchanges. If a member x of group m from unit J is exchanged with a member y of group n from unit K, such that the average distance of x from all other members of group m is increased and the average distance of y from all other members of group n is increased while the average distance of x and y from members of groups other than their own is unchanged or reduced, then segregation is reduced.

Mobility.   An appropriate mobility criterion should describe what happens if the social distance between two organizational units is changed while their social distances from all other units are unchanged. It seems that the effect of moving units J and K should depend not only on the change in d_{JK}, but also on the group proportions in J and K. In particular, if each group m is either overrepresented in both J and K or underrepresented in both J and K, then segregation should be increased if d_{JK} is reduced. Conversely, if each group m is overrepresented in one of J and K and underrepresented in the other, then segregation should be decreased if d_{JK} is reduced.

Additive Grouping Decomposability.   If M groups are clustered in N supergroups, then a segregation measure should be decomposable into a sum of independent within- and between-supergroup components.

Additive Spatial Decomposition.   A segregation measure should be decomposable into a sum of independent within- and between-cluster components.

4. AN AGENDA FOR FUTURE DEVELOPMENTS IN SEGREGATION MEASUREMENT

The field of segregation research has long been hampered by an inappropriate reliance on a limited set of two-group measures that lack explicit attention to theoretically appropriate social distance metrics. And while Grannis is not the first to suggest the need for more attention to spatial dimensions of segregation, he is right to reiterate the point, since much work remains to be done in developing appropriate spatial measures, particularly multigroup spatial measures. Here we would like to suggest an agenda for future developments in segregation measurement.

First, segregation measures must be developed that appropriately incorporate a social distance metric. This requires careful attention to the theoretical processes that define the appropriate social distance metric. Grannis's taxonomy of segregation measures illustrates the aspatial nature of many indices, but a focus on functional inputs alone is insufficient for developing theoretically valid segregation measures. In addition, the functional form of both the social distance metric and the segregation measures must be conceptually appropriate to the phenomenon under examination.

Second, a set of criteria describing the appropriate mathematical behavior of the social distance-based measures is needed. We have suggested some tentative criteria above, but these need more careful consideration and formulation in some cases. A full discussion of the criteria is beyond the scope of our comments here. These criteria can then be used to evaluate the many social distance-based segregation measures available in the literature.

Careful development and evaluation of social distance-based segregation measures will go a long way toward improving the field of segregation research. There are, however, several other areas where further work is needed. In particular, all existing segregation measures require that the groups of interest be mutually exclusive and unordered. Third, then, work is also needed in the development of segregation indices for groups that are not mutually exclusive. Given the new procedures for racial and ethnic classification (in the United States), which allow respondents to identify themselves as members of multiple groups, segregation measurement must be extended to allow the measurement of segregation among members of overlapping groups. No work that we are aware of has addressed this issue, though it is clearly one of growing importance in the United States.

Fourth, the field needs segregation indices—both aspatial and social distance-based—that measure segregation among ordered groups, such as groups defined by income categories or educational attainment, for example. Grannis suggests that multigroup measures, such as his multigroup spatial proximity index, can be used to measure segregation among groups defined by income or educational level, but this ignores the ordered nature of these groups. Grannis is not alone in missing this point, however; studies of socioeconomic segregation have often ignored the ordering of income categories in measuring segregation (e.g., Fong and Shibuya 2000; Telles 1995). Jargowsky (1997) develops a measure of income segregation that respects the ordered nature of income categories, but his measure is aspatial. However, measures of spatial autocorrelation—such as Moran's I and Geary's c (Cliff and Ord 1973; Cliff and Ord 1981; Odland 1988)—and Chakravorty's NDI (1996) provide useful approaches to measuring spatial segregation among ordered income groups.

A final set of issues that we would like to see addressed concern the need to think about the implications of data collection and aggregation approaches for segregation measurement. As we have argued above, the aggregation of data generally necessitates that we treat all individuals within an organizational unit (especially a census tract or block group) as located at the same point in the social geography. This assumption gives rise to MAUP issues and leads to an unknown amount of error in segregation computations.

Gathering social location data at an individual level would alleviate these problems, and allow more precise measurement of segregation. Particularly in residential and social network research, more fine-grained, individual-level data would be useful. A major obstacle to using individual-level data, however, is that segregation measurement relies on having data on the full population under examination, since little or nothing is known about the sampling properties of segregation measures. It would be very useful to examine these properties, to determine whether it might be feasible to get measures of individual-level segregation from a population sample.

REFERENCES

Chakravorty, Sanjoy. 1996. "A Measurement of Spatial Disparity: The Case of Income Inequality." *Urban Studies* 33:1671–86.

Charles, Maria, and David B. Grusky. 1995. "Models for Describing the Underlying Structure of Sex Segregation." *American Journal of Sociology* 100:931–71.

Cliff, A. D., and J. K. Ord. 1973. *Spatial Autocorrelation*. London: Pion.

———. 1981. *Spatial Processes: Models and Applications*. London: Pion.

Coleman, James S. 1961. *The Adolescent Society : The Social Life of the Teenager and Its Impact on Education*. New York: Free Press of Glencoe.

Fong, Eric, and Shibuya, Kumiko. 2000. "The Spatial Separation of the Poor in Canadian Cities." *Demography* 37:449–59.

Grannis, Rick. 1998. "The Importance of Trivial Streets: Residential Streets and Residential Segregation." *American Journal of Sociology* 103:1530–64.

Grannis, Rick. 2002. "Segregation Indices and Their Functional Inputs." *Sociological Methodology* 32:69–84.

Jakubs, John F. 1981. "A Distance-Based Segregation Index." *Journal of Socioeconomic Planning Sciences* 15:129–36.

James, David R., and Karl E. Taeuber. 1985. "Measures of Segregation." *Sociological Methodology* 14:1–32.

Jargowsky, Paul A. 1997. *Poverty and Place: Ghettos, Barrios, and the American City*. New York: Russel Sage Foundation.

Massey, Douglas S., and Nancy A. Denton. 1988. "The Dimensions of Racial Segregation." *Social Forces* 67:281–315.

Morgan, Barrie. 1983a. "An Alternate Approach to the Development of a Distance-Based Measure of Racial Segregation." *American Journal of Sociology* 88:1237–49.

———. 1983b. "A Distance-Decay Interaction Index to Measure Residential Segregation." *Area* 15:211–16.

Morrill, Richard L. 1991. "On the Measure of Spatial Segregation." *Geography Research Forum* 11:25–36.

Openshaw, S., and P. Taylor. 1979. "A Million or So Correlation Coefficients: Three Experiments on the Modifiable Areal Unit Problem." Pp. 127–44 in *Statistical Applications in the Spatial Sciences*, edited by Neil Wrigley. London: Pion.

Odland, J. 1988. *Spatial Autocorrelation*. Newbury Park, CA: Sage.

Reardon, Sean F., and Glenn Firebaugh. 2002. "Measures of Multigroup Segregation." *Sociological Methodology* 32:33–67.

Telles, Edward E. 1995. "Structural Sources of Socioeconomic Segregation in Brazilian Metropolitan Areas." *American Journal of Sociology* 100:1199–223.

Watts, Martin. 1992. "How Should Occupational Sex Segregation Be Measured?" *Work, Employment and Society* 6:475–87.

———. 1997. "Multidimensional Indexes of Occupational Segregation: A Critical Assessment." *Evaluation Review* 21:461–82.

White, Michael J. 1983. "The Measurement of Spatial Segregation." *American Journal of Sociology* 88:1008–18.

Wong, David S. 1993. "Spatial Indices of Segregation." *Urban Studies* 30:559–72.

INTEGRATING SURVEY AND ETHNOGRAPHIC METHODS FOR SYSTEMATIC ANOMALOUS CASE ANALYSIS

Lisa D. Pearce*

This paper describes how the salience of research findings can be enhanced by combining survey and ethnographic methods to draw insights from anomalous cases. Using examples from a research project examining the influence of religion on childbearing preferences in Nepal, the author illustrates how survey data can facilitate the selection of ethnographic informants and how semistructured interviews with these deviant cases leads to improved theory, measures, and methods. A systematic sample of 28 informants, whose family size preferences were much larger than a multivariate regression model predicted, were selected from the survey respondent pool for observation and in-depth interviews. The intent was to explore relationships between religion and fertility preferences that may not have been captured in the initial multivariate survey data analyses. Following intensive fieldwork,

Support for this research was provided by a Mellon International Demographic Research and Training Grant, a National Science Foundation Research Traineeship, and a National Institute of Child Health and Human Development (Grant No. 5 T32 HD0714-02) Interdisciplinary Training Grant in Demography to the Population Research Institute, Penn State University. Many thanks to the staff of the Population and Ecology Research Laboratory in Rampur, Chitwan, Nepal, for their help with the fieldwork described in this paper. I would also like to thank William Axinn, Jennifer Barber, Hart Nelsen, Nancy Landale, Glenn Fircbaugh, Shannon Stokes, Maria Krysan, Elizabeth Rudd, N. E. Barr, and Marida Hollos for their feedback on earlier drafts of this paper. I take sole responsibility for any errors. Direct correspondence to Lisa D. Pearce, Institute for Social Research, 426 Thompson Street, Ann Arbor, MI 48106–1248, email: lisapear@umich.edu.
*University of Michigan

the author revised theories about religion's influence, coded new measures from the existing survey data, and added these to survey models to improve statistical fit. This paper discusses the author's research methods, data analyses, and resulting insights for subsequent research, including suggestions for other applications of systematic analyses of anomalous cases using survey and ethnographic methods in tandem.

1. INTRODUCTION

Researchers sometimes elect to study a single research question using multiple methods. Using more than one approach reveals multiple pieces of evidence that serve as "building blocks" in the research endeavor (Lieberson 1992). Also, methods that vary in form and focus act as checks on one another, adding supplementary features and compensatory strengths to the mix (Axinn, Fricke, and Thornton 1991; Burgess 1982; Denzin 1970; Massey 1987; Sieber 1973). This complementarity may be achieved by allowing a set of different research methods to interactively evolve, using one to inform the other, strengthening the overall research process, yielding richer data, and increasing the depth of insight for interpreting the findings. This paper demonstrates how using survey methods to systematically select anomalous cases for ethnographic study can lead to improved theories, suggest alternative measures, and reveal sources of error in the methods being used.

Studying anomalous cases often leads to important refinement of social theories and measurement strategies (Kendall and Wolf 1949; Lazarsfeld and Rosenberg 1949–1950). This approach of studying anomalous cases has been coined *deviant case analysis*. A well-cited example of this approach is the analysis of a union organization characterized by a high level of democratic procedures in Lipset, Trow, and Coleman's (1956) *Union Democracy*. The authors highlight how the "internal politics" of the union cause it to deviate from the predictions of Michels's iron law in an attempt to refine theories of organizational power structures. Other examples include Burgess and Cottrell's (1939) study of couples for which marital adjustment was incorrectly predicted. They found that personality factors played a big role in marital adjustment and needed to be included in the theories and models leading to prediction. Merton (1946) found that not all radio listeners with close relatives in the armed services were vulnerable to the Kate Smith war-bond selling marathon accounts of sacrifices that soldiers were making in the war. He discovered that those who were unaffected by the accounts of soldier sacrifice were unaffected because their close relatives were stationed in safe areas such as the United States or other inactive theaters. This led Merton to readjust his classification scheme and compare respondents with close relatives serving in the armed forces in places of danger to all other respondents. Through intensive interviews with a subgroup of a large sample, Kahl (1953) discovered that parental pressure to attend college had as much influence on some young men as the more common predictors—socioeconomic status and IQ. These are examples of how deviant cases inform researchers about how predictive schemes can be expanded and how inadequate measurement strategies can limit predictive power.

The logic behind deviant case analysis continues to motivate a wide variety of ethnographic studies aimed at developing and/or refining theories. In studies of criminal motives and emotions, Katz (1988, 1999) advocates an analytically inductive approach that invites the confrontation of negative cases so that theory can be continuously revised. Agar (1996) speaks of continually "checking" recurrent themes and using falsifications to revise theories. Burawoy et al. (1991) suggest an approach called the *extended case method* in which a researcher finds a case that contradicts an existing theory and then uses findings from an in-depth study of the case to reconstruct the theory instead of rejecting it. These approaches are all useful applications of the logic that studying anomalous cases can lead to valuable knowledge regarding the shortcomings of theories and models.

The majority of studies employing the logic of deviant case analysis to improve theories are of an intensive nature, focusing on one or two individuals, groups, organizations, and/or countries. In this paper, I suggest that further applications of deviant case analysis can be developed by combining survey analysis and sampling techniques with ethnographic methods to identify and study cases that seem anomalous to predicted patterns. The suggestions for ways to identify and sample anomalous cases from representative survey data provide a unique way for ethnographers to pinpoint subgroups of a population that are difficult to locate. The rich information provided by ethnographic analysis of these anomalous cases reveals a depth of understanding rarely achieved by standard survey research methods. This is not to say that other approaches to studying deviant cases or to combining survey and ethnographic methods are flawed. Instead, this paper is meant to inspire new methodological possibilities that can widen the range of options for studying social dynamics.

The procedures discussed here are illustrated with a study of fertility preferences in Nepal; however, the approach itself can be tailored to fit other substantive research interests. In addition, while the study described in this paper ultimately uses insights from semistructured interviews to modify survey measures and models, other situations may call for different ethnographic methods to be used or for the ethnographic analysis itself to be the core focus. In other words, I hope that readers will see a set of possibilities that could be applied to their primary research interests and methods while reading this piece.

The approach presented here is motivated by ideas that surfaced a few decades ago to encourage continued creativity in the interaction of survey and ethnographic methods. Kendall and Wolf (1949) suggest that, "Through careful analysis of the cases which do not exhibit the expected behavior, the researcher recognizes the oversimplification of his theoretical structure and becomes aware of the need for incorporating further variables into his predictive scheme" (pp. 153–54). Commenting on this, Sieber (1973) writes, "But often the researcher does not have in hand the additional information necessary for measuring the further variables. Since it is extremely rare for a survey researcher to reenter the field for intensive interviewing after the completion of a survey, the needed information is almost never collected." The approach described in this paper explicitly searches out the "additional information necessary" by using information available from regression diagnostic techniques employed during initial survey analyses to locate anomalous cases and then sending the researcher back into the field to do follow-up interviews with these cases. The results support the call for continued creativity in the design of multimethod research projects in the advancement of a holistic social science.

The outline of this paper is as follows. I first briefly describe the background for the specific research project in which I used systematic anomalous case analysis; I will continue to refer to this example throughout the paper. Second, I discuss the mechanics of and benefits to systematically sampling anomalous cases from survey data analyses for further investigation. Third, I describe the fieldwork I conducted. Fourth, I illustrate three types of useful insights that can be drawn from in-depth study of anomalous cases. I show how findings from this ethnographic part of the study can help revise theory, suggest new measurement strategies for subsequent survey analyses, and reveal sources of measurement error. Finally, I conclude with suggestions for how this type of approach can be applied in a wide variety of settings.

2. SETTING UP THE STUDY: RELIGION AND CHILDBEARING PREFERENCES IN NEPAL

The research used in this paper to demonstrate this particular application of combining methods examines the influence of religion and other factors on childbearing preferences in Nepal. The basic sequence of methods went as follows. First, multivariate models of factors affecting family size preferences were designed and tested using survey data. Second, regression diagnostic tests of these models were used to identify a list of statistical outliers as potential ethnographic informants. From this list, 28 ethnographic informants were selected. Next, in-depth interviews and observations were carried out with these informants. Insights gained from these interviews were then used to recode survey data and to suggest additional predictors in the multivariate survey analyses.

The survey data used in the survey analyses described here are from the 1996 Chitwan Valley Family Study (CVFS). These data come from a survey administered to a probability sample of 5,271 men and women between the ages of 15 and 59 living in the Chitwan Valley of south-central Nepal. The survey collected data on current attitudes and preferences as well as past experiences and behaviors regarding a variety of demographic and social processes.

For the study here, I focus on two groups among the CVFS survey respondents: a *pre-family formation group* of unmarried men and women, aged 16–25 years ($n = 959$), and a *completed fertility group* of married men and women, aged 45–59 years, who had at least one child ($n = 864$). For each group, I specified a preliminary model to predict family size preferences.

The dependent variable for both preliminary statistical models was a scale created from a set of questions designed by Lolagene Coombs (1974) to ascertain ideal family size. The first item in the Coombs Scale measure was as follows: "People often do not have exactly the same number of children they want to have. If you could have exactly the number of children you want, how many children would you want to have?" Using this ideal number as a basis, subsequent questions attempted to further delineate preferences. The second item was: "If you could not have exactly [the number the respondent gave] children, would you want to have [one number lower] or [one number higher]?" The answer to the second question was then used in a third question: "If you could not have [the second choice number] of children, would you want to have [one number lower] or [one number higher]?" Figure 1 displays the options a respondent has when answering the Coombs Scale questions. Depending on the path a respondent followed in answering these questions, she or he was coded as somewhere between a 1, representing the lowest underlying ideal family size preference, and a 25, representing the highest underlying family size preference. Treating the Coombs Scale as an interval level measure, I developed ordinary least squares (OLS) regression models to predict Coombs Scale scores for each of these two groups.

For the pre-family formation group, the model takes into account religio-ethnic identity, the importance of religion, gender, age, number of siblings, parents' ability to read, education, media exposure, travel to the capital city or another country, expectance of an inheritance, and the hours from the home to the nearest urban area. The estimates from this model are displayed in the first column of estimates in Table 1.

The preliminary model used to predict family size preferences among the completed fertility group of CVFS respondents is displayed in the second column of estimates in Table 1. The predictors used in this model are similar to those used in the model for younger, unmarried respondents, except that age at marriage and number of children ever born to the respondent are included as control variables.

In developing these preliminary models, I tested a variety of models to arrive at one that best explained the relationship between religion and childbearing preferences for each group. This process began with simple models and then moved on to model the influence of religion as a combination of one's religio-ethnic identity and the importance of religion in one's life. In the end, two dummy variables were created for each of the five religio-ethnic groups in these models, one representing those in each group who felt religion was very important, and a second for those who placed little or no importance on religion. The reference category in this model is High Caste Hindus who find religion very important. The other variables in the models are controls selected on the basis of theories of fertility preferences and results of previous research. The adjusted R^2 is .09 for the pre-family formation group model and .12 for the completed fertility group model. Because the focus of this paper is not on these substantive results, they are not discussed in detail here. The focus is instead given to how this multimethod approach for studying childbearing preferences was conducted.

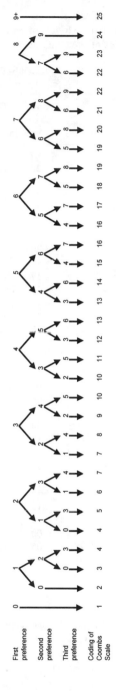

FIGURE 1. Response alternatives and coding scheme for Coombs Scale family size preference measure.

TABLE 1

Preliminary OLS Estimates from Models of Family Size Preferences
Among Two Subsamples of the Chitwan Valley Family Study

Religio-Ethnic Group by Importance of Religion[a]	Coombs Family Size Preference Scale			
	Pre-Family Formation Group (Unmarried, Ages 15–29)		Completed Fertility Group (Married, Ages 45–59)	
High Caste Hindu				
Finds religion unimportant (0,1)	−.20	(1.22)[b]	−.26	(.65)
Low Caste Hindu				
Finds religion important (0,1)	−.74*	(2.18)	−.34	(.93)
Finds religion unimportant (0,1)	−.75**	(2.42)	−.76	(1.29)
Hill Tibeto-Burmese				
Finds religion important (0,1)	−.56*	(2.18)	−.22	(.70)
Finds religion unimportant (0,1)	−.20	(.88)	.39	(.72)
Newar				
Finds religion important (0,1)	.17	(.45)	.49	(1.09)
Finds religion unimportant (0,1)	−.14	(.50)	−.35	(.41)
Terai Tibeto-Burmese				
Finds religion important (0,1)	.22	(.86)	1.18***	(3.22)
Finds religion unimportant (0,1)	.19	(.75)	2.61***	(4.97)
Controls				
Gender (female = 1)	−.59***	(4.68)	.03	(.11)
Respondent's age	−.05*	(1.98)	.05*	(2.07)
Number of mother's children	.06*	(1.93)	.05	(1.46)
Mother and/or father could read				
(1 = yes, 0 = no)	−.04	(.38)	−.45*	(1.90)
Education (highest grade completed)	−.11***	(4.80)	.01	(.27)
Age at marriage	.03	(1.21)		
Number of respondent's children ever born	.16***	(3.49)		
Newspaper and radio exposure scale	−.19*	(2.28)	−.33*	(1.92)
Travel to Kathmandu or other country				
(1 = yes, 0 = no)	−.19	(1.48)	−.22	(1.01)
Expecting inheritance from parents				
(1 = yes, 0 = no)	.00	(.01)	−.43*	(1.86)
Travel time to Narayanghat	−.05	(.78)	.22*	(1.86)
Intercept	8.05		3.61	
Adj R-squared	.09		.12	
N	959		864	

[a]Reference group is High Caste Hindus who find religion important.
[b]T-ratios in parentheses.
*p < .05
**p < .01
***p < .001 for one-tailed t-tests

3. SYSTEMATICALLY SAMPLING ANOMALOUS CASES

Researchers wanting to be able to reliably generalize findings from any type of study to a larger population must achieve a representative sample of that population (Kish 1965). For many ethnographic studies, a representative sample is not the goal and other types of sampling procedures are useful (Babbie 1992; Strauss and Corbin 1990). However, when the ability to safely generalize about the anomalous cases in a study is desirable, one approach is to systematically select a sample of these deviant cases using regression diagnostic tests from survey data analyses to provide a sampling frame. Information available from the data and diagnostic tests of its analysis can help identify subgroups of the population who are of great interest and who are otherwise very difficult to locate.

The aim of this project was to gain a deeper understanding of the relationship between religion and childbearing preferences by identifying cases that were incorrectly predicted and studying these cases in depth to look for limitations in theory, measures, and methods. Although data analysts may view statistical outliers as dubious in value and may even exclude them from their analyses, I show here that outlier respondents may offer information that can help researchers improve preliminary models and increase their scope of applicability. Therefore, for this study, I randomly selected, interviewed, and observed a set of informants drawn from CVFS survey respondent outliers with the intent of uncovering new factors linked to religion and family size preferences in this region.

For all CVFS respondents in both the pre-family formation and completed fertility groups, I computed residual values, or the difference between the Coombs Scale Score predicted by the preliminary model and their actual answers to the survey questions. The residual value distributions for both models were graphed using SAS. Figure 2 displays the distribution of residual values for the pre-family formation group.

I was particularly interested in learning more about respondents in both groups who desired more children than the preliminary statistical model predicted. Therefore, respondents from the right tail of the residual distribution were selected for further study. For both groups, respondents whose residual values were approximately two or more standard deviations to the right of the mean residual, zero, were identified as outliers. Among the pre-family formation group, the outliers consisted of 31 respondents with residual values of +3 and higher, or those who scored at least 3 points higher on the Coombs Scale than the statistical model predicted.

112

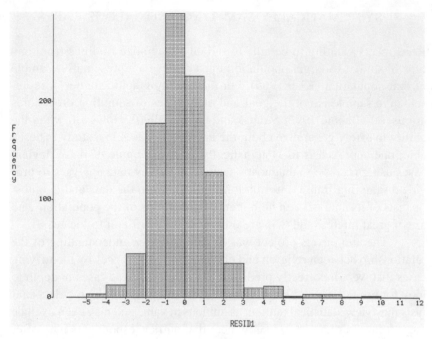

FIGURE 2. SAS Graph displaying the distribution of residual values for Coombs Scale
measure of family size preference among pre-family formation group (ages
15–29).

Among the completed fertility group, the outliers consisted of 31 respondents with residual values of +6 and higher.

To check for spatial patterns among the outliers, each outlier's
neighborhood was plotted on a map of the study area (Figure 3). Clusters
of outliers in a particular area may suggest residential variations in the
social processes under study. No strong spatial patterns were found for
either set of outliers in this case, but for other topics of study, this may be
a useful technique to identify key locations for ethnographic inquiry.

To generate random samples from each of the preliminary regression models, I first categorized each group of outliers by gender; seven
men and seven women were then randomly selected from each of the two
groups. These 28 informants served as the sample of ethnographic informants used to learn more about religion and childbearing preferences from
the perspective of model outliers.

In addition to providing a sampling frame, another way that survey
data can be a useful tool for beginning fieldwork is by providing a source

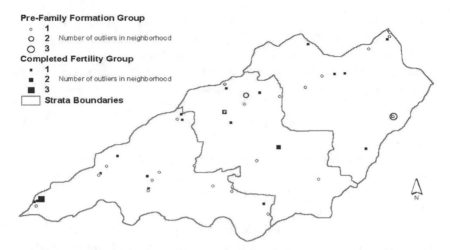

FIGURE 3. Residential location in the CVFS study area of statistical outliers from two preliminary regression models of family size preference.

of valuable information about informants. This can help in preparing for interviews by suggesting important topics to discuss, making it easier to physically locate informants, and providing a preestablished rapport with the informants. For example, before meeting informants, I examined and made notes to myself about their completed questionnaires and life history calendars from the 1996 CVFS survey. Although spending time with informants and members of their social world is vital to understanding the dynamics of their lives, and certainly influences the direction and shape of the interview, the availability of biographical information before an interview allows for important preparation. A life history calendar, for instance, reveals past events such as moves, parental separations, or periods of school dropout that can be explored in greater detail during an interview.

The maps and records kept by the survey project staff made locating respondents relatively easy. Also, the selected informants were familiar with the staff interviewers who accompanied me to the field and served as interviewing assistants. Because a good rapport had been established with the informants during previous CVFS data collection projects, the informants were more open and at ease during my fieldwork. Of course, these kinds of benefits are only as good as the survey research project with which a more qualitative study is linked. If the CVFS records had been incomplete or wrong, or if the interviewing staff had established poor rapport with respondents, the survey study would have made my field-work harder, not easier, and perhaps would have tainted my findings. For this type of integrated design, it is important to carefully choose a survey research project with which to collaborate.

4. THE FIELDWORK

Once the anomalous cases are sampled, the ethnographic fieldwork begins. This is when cases that have not been predicted correctly can speak back to the process and suggest improvements in theory, measures, and meth-ods (Horst 1955). A variety of intensive methods—such as participant observation, unstructured interviews, content analysis, archival studies, and others—can be employed at this stage to gain a full and rich under-standing of the factors involved with these anomalous cases.

For the project discussed in this paper, I spent five months living in the field, observing, and carrying out semistructured interviews. Analysis of these interviews is the main focus here. Averaging about 90 minutes, the interviews took place in Nepali and a native Nepali-speaking assistant came to each interview in case translation problems arose. Each interview began with the three structured survey questions on ideal family size that make up the Coombs Scale, the dependent variable from the analyses of CVFS survey data. A substantive issue was how informants' answers to these questions in this interview would vary from their answers during the original survey, nearly two years earlier. After this structured inquiry, I probed in an unstructured manner about the informant's personal family size preference and issues related to family size in general. I also engaged informants in a discussion of religious beliefs and practices, asking them about their own as well as those of their family and friends, and making note of the specific words they used to compare people. By the end, 27 of the 28 selected informants were interviewed.

During each interview, I took detailed notes.[1] Interview or field notes have two important uses. First, the researcher can examine the notes many times during and following the interview phase, exploring content for themes and meanings common among the anomalous cases (Agar 1996;

---

[1] In initial interviews I tried using a tape recorder, but the informants seemed distracted by its presence. This led me to rely on interview notes. However, I would recommend, whenever possible, using a quality recorder to tape interviews and mak-ing full transcripts for data analysis.

Spradley 1979; Strauss and Corbin 1990). In a comparative approach, non-deviant cases could be selected for in-depth analysis as well, and the themes and meanings could be compared to those found when studying the deviant cases. Second, the researcher can code and count themes that emerge in the unguided reading of notes to quantify various meanings or phenomena (Emerson, Fretz, and Shaw 1995; Miles and Huberman 1984). For example, I used my notes to count the number of times a particular phrase was used or idea mentioned to gauge the strength of an attitude, belief, or behavior. Both kinds of analysis helped identify underlying issues and the common language of informants, and thus informed subsequent hypotheses. Because I was interested in applying these findings in subsequent survey measurement and analysis, I used the ethnographic findings to improve statistical analyses and their interpretations. It is the analysis of these in-depth interviews, or other ethnographic methods used to study deviant cases, that reveals the knowledge needed to refine theories, measures, and/or methods for whatever the next research step may be.

5. USING ETHNOGRAPHIC INSIGHTS TO REVISE THEORIES, MEASURES, AND METHODS

The in-depth study of anomalous cases can provide meaningful insights on three levels. First, researchers may be able to uncover additional factors that had not previously been considered (Kendall and Wolf 1949; Sieber 1973). Second, intensive deviant case analysis can reveal ideas for refining the measurement of key variables if further survey data analyses will be conducted (Kendall and Wolf 1949). Third, the ethnographic study of anomalous cases can reveal methodological phenomena responsible for the cases' deviance and suggest ways to correct for these problems in the future (Horst 1955).

Gathering and analyzing field notes sharpened the project examined here in several ways. First, I learned more about the dynamics of religious influence in Nepal, and from this deepened understanding, I was able to code new, more informed measures of religion from the survey data for further analyses. Second, I realized the pervasive effect of family planning media messages on individuals in Nepal, which also led to new measurement strategies in my statistical analyses. Finally, I was reminded of important methodological issues and how they can influence the fit of survey data to a statistical model. I developed a better understanding of sources of error and what they mean for the study of anomalous cases.

5.1. *Revising Theories*: *New Dimensions of Religion*

For the preliminary survey data analyses of religion and childbearing preferences, relying on theories about religion's impact, I had hypothesized
about how various dimensions of religion would influence childbearing
preferences. First, I expected that each different religio-ethnic group was
characterized by a distinct formulation of religious meanings. Next, I
hypothesized that respondents in all religio-ethnic groups would vary in
the extent to which religion was a salient part of their identity. I also rea-
soned that, above and beyond an individual's religious identity, the level
of religious belief and activity within the community in which the respondent lives would have an influence on childbearing preferences. Initial
findings did not support the hypothesis about community-level effects.
Also individual-level beliefs and practices did not have the effect I had
hypothesized among the younger respondents. Therefore, one priority of
my fieldwork was to ask questions and explore issues around the form,
function, and meaning of religion in the study area.

 Throughout my interviews and observations, I often noted the influence of the religious beliefs and practices of senior members of households. Especially during my interviews with the pre-family formation
group, I realized that young people define their religious identity mostly
as a reflection of their mother, father, or a grandparent. If a young person
visits a temple or performs a religious rite in the home, it is often with
other family members. When I asked informants where they learned their
religious beliefs, or why they worship a particular god or goddess, they
most often cited the traditional beliefs and practices of their parents and
other family members. When I asked if they saw themselves as more religious or less religious than their parents, all the pre-family formation informants responded that one or both of their parents were more religious.
The majority of religious activity was either led or practiced alone by the
matriarchs of the family, although in many cases fathers and grandfathers
were quite religious as well.

 Shanti,[2] an 18-year-old High Caste Hindu, described how religious
worship of Hindu gods and goddesses within her home was a form of
religious education.

---

[2] All personal names have been changed to protect the identity of my
informants.

> My parents teach *dharma* (religion) to me. Each morning I do *puja* (worship) with my mother to *Ganesh* (a Hindu god). Then, in the evening, I worship five *devis* (gods) with my father. When I pray with my mother or father, *ghan* (knowledge of religion) comes to me.

From conversations like this one, I learned that religion in Nepal is very family-centered, and that young family members were expected to gradually learn from time to time rather than always being preoccupied with religious activities or thoughts. Particularly for young adults in this setting, religious identity seemed to be based largely on the religious practices and beliefs demonstrated in their families. This led me to reevaluate my theoretical framework and incorporate more ideas about the levels of religious influence above individuals' own religiosity, especially about the impact of family members' religiosity.

Discovering the importance of religion at the family level, I used the survey data to create measures reflecting the household religious environment. Because the CVFS contains interviews with all members of a household between the ages of 15 and 59, it was possible to use the survey responses of all family members on their religious practices and beliefs to create average household-level measures. For example, I created household measures for the average frequency of visiting religious temples and the average importance given to death rituals.[3] I used these measures to predict childbearing preferences.

Model 1 in Table 2 displays the results from a revised model, predicting family size preferences among the younger age group, which includes a measure of the average frequency with which household members visit religious temples and the measure of average importance of death rituals among household members. Both measures have a positive and statistically significant effect on family size preferences. That is, the more often family members visit temples and the more strongly they believe in the importance of death rituals, the more children an individual desires. These measures contribute to the higher adjusted R^2 for this model (.11) than for the preliminary model in Table 1 (.09), suggesting that these measures help explain the influence of religion on childbearing preferences.

---

[3] I also created measures of mothers' religiosity and the religiosity of the oldest female in the household. The measures of average household religiosity had stronger effects, so I chose to use those in my analyses. In addition, this allowed me to keep respondents who had no elder female relatives living in the household in the analyses.

TABLE 2

Revised OLS Estimates from Models Predicting Family Size Preferences Among Two Subsamples of the Chitwan Valley Family Study

	Coombs Family Size Preference Scale			
	Pre-Family Formation Group (Unmarried, Ages 15–29)		Completed Fertility Group (Married, Ages 45–59)	
Religio-Ethnic Group by Importance of Religion[a]	Model 1	Model 2	Model 3	Model 4
High Caste Hindu				
Finds religion unimportant (0,1)	−.05 (.31)[b]	−.01 (.07)	−.20 (.50)	−.19 (.48)
Low Caste Hindu				
Finds religion important (0,1)	−.65* (1.91)	−.69* (2.04)	−.30 (.76)	−.26 (.65)
Finds religion unimportant (0,1)	−.52* (1.67)	−.57* (1.83)	−.72 (1.20)	−.26 (.65)
Hill Tibeto-Burmese				
Finds religion important (0,1)	−.49* (1.91)	−.50* (1.94)	−.12 (.39)	−.09 (.28)
Finds religion unimportant (0,1)	.01 (.03)	.03 (.13)	.48 (.87)	.46 (.83)
Newar				
Finds religion important (0,1)	.27 (.67)	.29 (.77)	.50 (1.10)	.49 (1.09)
Finds religion unimportant (0,1)	.02 (.07)	.05 (.17)	−.40 (.46)	−.42 (.49)
Terai Tibeto-Burmese				
Finds religion important (0,1)	.49* (1.84)	.55* (2.08)	1.29*** (3.32)	1.21*** (3.07)
Finds religion unimportant (0,1)	.56* (2.07)	.03 (.13)	2.74*** (4.93)	2.25*** (3.82)

Household Religiosity

	Model 1		Model 2		Model 3		Model 4	
Household members' average temple visits per month	.68***	(3.76)	.70***	(3.87)	.30	(1.00)	.40	(1.32)
Household members' average importance of death rites	.43*	(1.70)	.45*	(1.79)	-.13	(.30)	-.17	(.40)

Controls

	Model 1		Model 2		Model 3		Model 4	
Gender (female = 1)	-.60***	(4.74)	-.62***	(4.89)	.01	(.05)	.03	(.10)
Respondent's age	-.05*	(1.95)	-.06*	(2.14)	.05	(2.00)	.05*	(1.81)
Number of mother's children ever born	.05*	(1.85)	.05*	(1.89)	.05	(1.34)	.05	(1.30)
Mother and/or father could read (1 = yes, 0 = no)	-.04	(.33)	-.05	(.39)	-.48*	(2.03)	-.46*	(1.91)
Education (highest grade completed)	-.12***	(4.75)	-.11***	(4.80)	.01	(.18)	.00	(.03)
Age at marriage					.03	(1.24)	.03	(1.21)
Number of respondent's children ever born					.16***	(3.58)	.17***	(3.63)
Newspaper and radio exposure scale	-.23**	(2.76)			-.33*	(1.89)		
Newspaper, radio, and TV exposure scale			-.33***	(3.40)			-.34*	(1.77)
Travel to Kathmandu or other country (1 = yes, 0 = no)	-.19	(1.48)	-.17	(1.36)	-.23	(1.06)	-.22	(1.01)
Received/expects inheritance (1 = yes, 0 = no)	-.02	(.10)	-.03	(.16)	-.45	(1.93)	-.45*	(1.91)
Travel time to Narayanghat	-.02	(.28)	-.02	(.27)	.24*	(1.99)	.20*	(1.67)
Intercept	6.90		7.16		3.45		3.68	
Adj R-squared	.11		.12		.12		.10	
N	958		953		859		827	

[a]Reference group is High Caste Hindus who find religion important.

[b]T-ratios in parentheses.

*p<.05, **p<.01, ***p<.001 for one-tailed t-tests

An *F*-test comparing these two models confirms that the revised model is a statistically significant improvement over the initial model at the $p < .001$ level.

Model 3 in Table 2 displays the revised model of family size preference for the married, older respondents. Including the household-level measures of temple visits and the importance of death rituals did not change the adjusted R^2 (.12), and thus does not improve the predictive value of this model over the preliminary model. This is not particularly surprising given that interviews with the pre-family formation group brought the influence of elder relatives' religiosity to my attention.

5.2. *Revising Existing Measures*: *Media Influence*

Every informant in both groups who responded to the Coombs Scale questions during the interview with me (22 of the 27 interviewed) gave an answer lower than the response they had given two years earlier. In many cases the answer they gave was very close to what the statistical model predicted for them. Figure 4 plots three scores for 12 of the 14 members

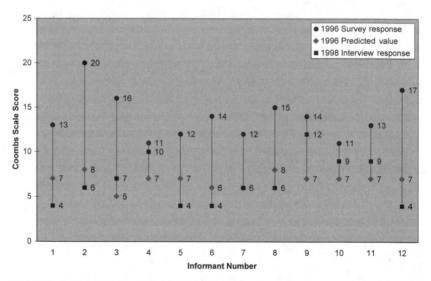

FIGURE 4. Comparison of Coombs Scale scores for 1996 survey responses, 1996 predicted values, and 1998 interview responses of unmarried informants (ages 16–25).

TABLE 3

Mean Coombs Scale Responses for Two Subsamples of Outliers:
1996 Survey Response, 1996 Predicted Value, and 1998 Interview Response

	Coombs Scale Score (1–25)		
	1996 Survey Response Mean	1996 Predicted Value Mean	1998 Interview Response Mean
Pre-family formation group	13.64	6.86	6.75
Completed fertility group	22.86	10.64	9.00

of the pre-family formation group:[4] the original score derived from their responses to the Coombs Scale questions on the 1996 survey, the predicted score derived from my preliminary model, and the score derived from their responses to the Coombs Scale questions in the 1998 interview. The 1998 Coombs Scale scores for all these informants are significantly lower than those calculated from the 1996 survey data, and match much more closely the score predicted by the preliminary model. Table 3, which presents group means for the three scores, provides an overall picture of this pattern.

Figure 5 plots the three Coombs Scale scores (1996 survey score, predicted score, and 1998 interview score) for 10 of the 14 members of the completed fertility group.[5] The same pattern is evident for these respondents: Their scores fall significantly two years after the survey, coming very close to the score that the statistical model predicted for them. The means for the three Coombs Scales scores, presented in the bottom row of Table 3, illustrate this. Drawing on my analysis of interview texts, I determined that one possible cause of this uniform decrease in preferences might be the influence of recent family planning media campaigns.

During the unstructured portion of all of the interviews, I initiated discussions with informants about ideal family size and the changes in their responses over time. I noticed similarities in how informants described their reasons for wanting a small number of children during the inter-

[4] There was one informant I could not locate and one who repeatedly refused to give answers to the Coombs Scale questions.

[5] Four informants were uncomfortable answering the Coombs Scale questions; their interviews provided insight on the cognitive challenges these questions can pose.

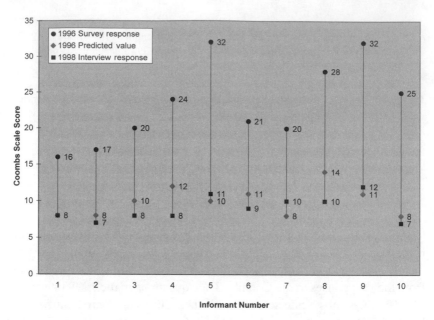

FIGURE 5. Comparison of Coombs Scale scores from 1996 survey responses, 1996
predicted value, and 1998 interview responses for married respondents
with children (ages 45–59).

views. For instance, 5 of the 13 unmarried young adults used exactly the
same phrase, *dui jana thikai chha* (two children are good), and several
other informants used similar phrases. One informant remarked, "Having
two children will bring me happiness." Several unmarried informants who
had taken English language courses used the words "quality versus quantity" in the midst of sentences in Nepali. One informant spoke of a teacher
at her school who had explained the benefits of investing in fewer children; another stated that she wanted only two children who would both be
thulo manche (important people). Overall, 20 informants discussed the
financial advantages of raising fewer children, such as cutting down on
the cost of food, clothes, and schooling, and distributing land among fewer
adult children.

In probing the source and significance of these phrases and common language, I learned that informants were aware of family planning
slogans featured in newspapers and magazines, on billboards, and on radio
or television. These messages overtly encourage families to limit their

family size to two children. The one that was most often quoted word for word during my interviews was the one mentioned above: *Dui jana thikai chha*. Three other messages that were common in the media and expressed in different variants during my interviews were *Dui bhanda badi santan dhann dhau dhau parchha* (It is difficult to raise more than two children), *Buddhiman babu ama le dui bhanda badi santan janmaudainan* (Wise parents do not give birth to more than two children), and *Dui bhai thikka; dherai bhai dikka* (Two children are just right; many children mean trouble). On the radio, a thrice-weekly drama promotes small families as happier than large families because more can be invested in each child and it is easier to feed them, send them to school, and keep them healthy.

It is logical to posit that if exposure to these kinds of messages influenced the language with which informants discussed their attitudes about family size, it may also have influenced their responses to the Coombs Scale questions. And if media exposure to these messages affected responses, then perhaps the outliers had less exposure in 1996 than they did in 1998. Therefore, the ethnographic findings suggested going back to examine more survey data for answers.

The CVFS data provide evidence that outlier respondents had less media exposure than other survey respondents in 1996. Table 4 reports the means and statistical tests of difference for various media-related mea-

TABLE 4

Average Media Exposure of the Outliers and Nonoutliers from
Preliminary Models of Family Size Preferences

	Outliers (N = 62)	Nonoutliers (N = 1792)	Difference of Means T-Test Results
Frequency of reading the newspaper (0–3)	.82	1.04	+
Frequency of listening to the radio (0–3)	2.06	2.21	+
Ever listened to family planning programs (0,1)	.63	.72	+
Frequency of watching television (0–3)	1.34	1.64	*
Household owns a radio (0,1)	.42	.48	

$+P < .10$, $*P < .05$

sures for the original group of all outliers from which I sampled informants and for all other CVFS respondents. The outlier respondents had significantly less exposure than all other CVFS respondents on four of the five measures. Outliers read the newspaper less often, listened to the radio less often, watched television less often, and were less likely to listen to family planning programs on the radio. Their households were also less likely to own a radio, but this difference is not statistically different. Therefore it is possible that the media campaigns promoting small families, and two-child families in particular, had less influence on these outlier respondents than on other participants in the 1996 survey. Another possibility is that the frequency of family planning messages in the media increased from 1996 to 1998 and so even if these respondents' frequency of media exposure was unchanged, they became exposed to more messages about fertility limitation.

No survey data are available to examine changes in media content or exposure among outlier respondents during the two years between the CVFS survey and the interviews. However, given the wide use of phrases and rationales for small families in my interviews that echoed those in the family planning media, it is likely that media exposure had some reductive influence on their Coombs Scale scores in 1998.

Although my preliminary models included measures of newspaper reading and radio listening, I was convinced by what I learned from the interviews and my observations of television programming to expand the measure of media exposure to include data on the frequency of television watching. I had not initially included television in my media measure because I did not know how common it was to watch television in this area, and I did not realize that there were such overt messages on television regarding ideal family size. This is an example of how ethnographic observation and interviewing corrected the false assumptions that I had made about the situation. This is one of the most valuable benefits ethnographic fieldwork brings to the research process; being able to put the researcher more directly in the shoes of those being studied helps avoid fatal biases (Becker 1996; Blumer 1969).

Models 2 and 4 in Table 2 incorporate the revised measure of media exposure. As shown in Model 2, when television watching is added to media exposure for the pre-family formation group, the coefficient increases from $-.23$ to $-.33$, and the adjusted R^2 increases from .11 to .12, suggesting that this revised measure improves the predictive value of the model for the unmarried group. For the completed fertility group, however, adding television viewing to the measure increases the coefficient only slightly, from $-.33$ to $-.34$, and decreases the adjusted R^2 from .12 to .10. Overall, this age group may watch less television than the younger group, which would lessen the impact of adding it to the media exposure measure.

At this point, some would argue it was not necessary to have used multiple research methods to arrive at the findings about the importance of family members' religion and the wide reach of media campaigns. It is possible that these ideas could have emerged from an independent ethnographic study in a Nepalese village or from running survey data analyses on every possible variable in the data set, but the possibility remains they would not. In fact, an experiment by Sieber (1973) indicates that both surveys and ethnographic fieldwork tend to miss findings that the other type of method can more easily bring to light. For example, high-quality survey research provides the power to do a variety of comparisons across large groups but is limited in its ability to find new ideas or suggest misunderstandings of concepts. Ethnographic methods are better at revealing new information and the rich context of issues under study (Brannen 1992).

5.3. *Understanding the Methods: Sources of Error*

When considering other reasons for obtaining different responses to the same questions at two points in time, another factor to be weighed is survey error and its various sources. Survey data are subject to errors in validity, errors in reliability, and interviewer effects. These different types of error hold important implications for studying extreme cases from survey data.

Validity.   A survey item is considered valid if it measures what it is intended to measure (Carmines and Zeller 1979). Problems of differential validity arise when some respondents have a different way of understanding a survey question than others. For example, some respondents may misunderstand the question or may not be used to the cognitive process involved in formulating an answer (Caldwell 1985; Caldwell, Hill, and Hull 1985; Sudman and Bradburn 1974).

Evidence from the interviews conducted here suggests that a few of the outlier respondents from the survey did not fully understand the Coombs Scale questions or how to formulate responses. For a few of the older completed fertility group informants, the confusion over the questions seemed to be based in their skepticism that fertility could (or should) be planned. This may emanate both from the fatalistic nature of the dominant Hindu culture in Nepal (Bista 1994) and from the relative novelty of modern birth control methods in this setting. An older man named Shyam typified the response of five other older informants to the questions about family size preference. He chuckled and replied: "People cannot have the exact number of children they want. It is not up to us. We have the number of children that we have." When these informants were asked to consider whether they would want one more or one less child if they could not have the number they had in reality, they seemed uninterested in rethinking their past and how they would do it differently if they could. Even those who formulated a response to the Coombs Scale questions often added a condition. This happened in five out of 14 cases. For example, an older High Caste Hindu woman said that she would choose two sons and one daughter as her ideal, but that "people do not usually get what they wish for."

When members of the completed fertility group had a difficult time answering questions about the ideal number of children to have, I asked them questions about their own children and what it was like raising them. During these discussions, a few informants said that they would have done things differently if they could have, or if they had known what they know now. In fact, some of them said they advise their children to have smaller families and use family planning methods. Therefore, some of these informants were probably outliers in the original survey because they had not understood how to answer a question about the ideal number of children when asked by a survey interviewer. However, once they discussed many of the issues surrounding childbearing in an unstructured way they were more comfortable discussing the possibility of a family size different from the one that they had.

In the larger research process, one benefit that can emanate from this mixed-method approach is the researcher's ability to use the intensive interviews as an opportunity for detecting problems of differential validity. During fieldwork, a researcher can adapt the interview process to make the measuring tool more valid for all respondents and incorporate this in subsequent surveys or interviews.

Reliability.   The reliability of a survey item is the degree to which repeated measures will yield similar responses. Problems with reliability come from random errors. Sometimes a random shock will result in an unexpected response to a particular survey item (Carmines and Zeller 1979). For example, a respondent may be tired, not pay attention to a question and give a nonsensical answer, or a coder might make an error. For some of the outliers selected in the project described here, the high residual value may have been due to a random shock causing an accurate measurement of an atypical state in the subject, an inaccurate measurement of a typical state in the subject, or a combination of both. Revisiting these types of outlying respondents, either with a repeated survey or ethnographic interviews, helps us to understand how to reduce these types of random error.

For the research project discussed in this paper, one explanation for the change in family size preferences given between the two interviews may be the phenomenon of regression to the mean. This occurs when a random shock causes an extreme value response once, but repeated observations result in more expected or consistent results. For example, among my informants, there may have been someone who heard the question wrong and thought they were being asked to state the number of children they actually had, which may have been more than they now feel is ideal. In biomedical clinical trials, researchers have found that subjects selected on the basis of having unusually high or low values of a particular measurement will tend to have values closer to the population mean in subsequent measurements (Beath and Dobson 1991). To test this effect among the outliers, similar interviews would need to be conducted with a subset of CVFS left-tail outliers whose family size preferences were much lower than predicted in 1996. If an increase in media exposure was playing a role, I would expect to see still lower Coombs Scale scores. If regression to the mean was at work, I would expect these left-tail outliers to have higher scores that were closer to the population mean. A test of this effect is beyond the scope of this paper, but I find it plausible that both factors are at work, meaning there may be some regression to the mean *and* increased media exposure may be lowering fertility preferences in this context.

The possibility that regression to the mean is partly responsible here suggests that a more complex sample design is desirable for systematically sampling anomalous cases. The limit to the particular sampling approach used in my case was that no informants were selected from the opposite tail of the residual distribution or from the small residual cases. This limited the ability for comparisons between the informants I interviewed and others who wanted fewer children than the model predicted, or others who wanted exactly the number of children the model predicted.

For future studies of this kind, unequal probability sampling may be a better approach. One could pick respondents for ethnographic reexamination by randomly sampling the original survey data cases, giving each case a sample selection probability proportional to the error (or squared error) of its residual in the statistical model. This type of approach would generate ample extreme cases, from both ends of the continuum, while simultaneously including cases with less extreme residual values that would make it possible to distinguish regression to the mean effects from other types of change.

Interviewer Effects.   Research methods that require face-to-face interaction inherently involve interviewer effects (Bradburn 1983; Lyberg and Kasprzyk 1991). Interviewer effects can lead to response bias. Therefore, another hypothesis for why all 22 informants who responded gave lower answers during the 1998 interviews than they did two years prior is that my presence in the interview had an effect. The 1996 CVFS survey interviews were conducted in person by a trained staff of local Nepali interviewers. In the case of my unstructured interviews, the informants probably had few, if any, prior interactions with a woman from the United States, which may have made them feel less open with their responses. Also, any similar interactions would probably have been with Westerners working for nongovernmental organizations promoting family planning and/or development projects, which may have motivated them to describe a low family size preference to me. In addition, whether or not they had any such previous interactions, the informants may have known about low fertility rates in countries such as the United States, and they were probably aware that I was studying population issues. Although I tried to establish a nonjudgmental presence, the outlier informants may have felt that the desired response was to express preference for a smaller number of children (Bradburn 1983; DeMaio 1984).

When methodological errors produce outlier respondents in survey data, subsequent ethnographic interactions with these respondents may provide little substantive insight for theoretical or analytical revisions of the sort discussed earlier. However, these types of cases do bring to light important ideas for improving sampling, survey instruments, and data collection efforts in the future. Therefore, a value still exists in sampling these types of deviant cases, and it is important to try to understand the processes leading to the definition of each particular case as anomalous.

6. CONCLUSION

As described in this paper, there are several benefits to integrating survey and ethnographic methods to learn from anomalous cases in a population. First, a large-scale survey can provide a useful sampling frame from which to systematically select deviant cases as ethnographic informants. Regression diagnostics are a unique way to identify a sampling frame from which one can systematically select a sample of ethnographic informants who can provide much theoretical and methodological insight. Second, access to informant characteristics measured in the survey data enables researchers to learn valuable information prior to observations or interviews. This information can help researchers prepare for interviews by suggesting conversation topics or probes and by providing background and context descriptions. Also, survey data collections can help by establishing prior rapport with informants and by providing records explaining where to locate them. Finally, the insights that emerge from ethnographic study lead to improved theories, measures, and methods which can then inform subsequent survey data collection and/or analysis. In the example used here, developing new measures of religion and media exposure significantly improved a regression model's ability to explain variance in family size preferences among the young, unmarried adults in the sample.

The lessons learned from this specific study can benefit those interested in using a similar approach for their own work. First, careful attention must be given to the sampling procedures. Unequal probability sampling is strongly suggested to obtain informants from both extremes as well as from the pool of cases for which the model works well. This allows for the comparisons that are necessary to understand the sources of each anomalous case's deviance. Second, during the ethnographic field study of the selected informants, attempts must be made to distinguish which cases are anomalous because theories were misspecified and which cases are results of errors in validity, reliability, or interviewer influence. There is much to be learned from the multiple types of outliers.

In this study, anomalous cases were selected based on their residual values. In other words, these are cases in which the observed value of the dependent variable was very different from the value predicted by the model. These are the types of cases referred to in most standard deviant case analyses. However, based on a modern regression diagnostics modeling framework, cases can also warrant investigation when their independent variable values give them undue influence over the model.[6] Future systematic analyses of anomalous cases should sample cases with both large residuals and values for independent variables that have disproportionate influence. This is because a large residual is not as much of a concern if the values of the independent variables do not exert undue influence on the model, and disproportional influence of independent variable values is not worrisome when the case's residual is low. Selecting anomalous cases requires careful consideration of the statistical issues surrounding extreme cases.

Hopefully, this paper encourages others to think of ways to tackle other research topics and questions with similar methods. There are many studies in the United States and abroad that could incorporate these methods in an attempt to push theoretical and analytical processes further than what can be achieved with one method.[7] The opportunities are great for using the well-designed methods of regression diagnostic techniques to suggest cases that could teach us more about a wide variety of phenomena in the social world.

REFERENCES

Agar, Michael H. 1996. *The Professional Stranger*. San Diego, CA: Academic Press.
Axinn, William G., Thomas E. Fricke, and Arland Thornton. 1991. "The Microdemographic Community-Study Approach: Improving Survey Data by Integrating the Ethnographic Method." *Sociological Methods and Research* 20(2):187–217.
Babbie, Earl. 1992. *The Practice of Social Research*. Belmont, CA: Wadsworth.
Beath, Kenneth J., and Annette J. Dobson. 1991. "Regression to the Mean for Nonnormal Populations." *Biometrika* 78(2):431–35.
Becker, Howard S. 1996. "The Epistemology of Qualitative Research." Pp. 53–72 in *Ethnography and Human Development. Context and Meaning in Social Inquiry*, edited by Richard Jessor, Anne Colby, and Richard A. Shweder. Chicago: University of Chicago Press.

[6] When using the statistical package SAS for data analysis, the DFBETA test statistics will identify cases that are having undue influence on the model due to a particular independent variable value.

[7] For example, an anonymous reviewer of this paper has suggested that one might run models using an existing representative data set to predict the probability of marriage for black women. This would involve performing regression diagnostics and selecting a range of informants using unequal probability methods to generate enough anomalous cases for ethnographic analysis. Then, an ethnographic study of these cases could lead to a better understanding of the meaning of marriage and relationships for these women. A study like this could point to factors that cause current predictive models to fall short.

Bista, Dor B. 1994. *Fatalism and Development* . Calcutta, India: Orient Longman.

Blumer, Herbert. 1969. *Symbolic Interactionism*. Englewood Cliffs, NJ: Prentice Hall.

Bradburn, Norman M. 1983. "Response Effects." Pp. 289–328 in *Handbook of Survey Research*, edited by Peter H. Rossi, James D. Wright, and Andy B. Anderson. New York: Academic Press.

Brannen, Julia, editor. 1992. *Mixing Methods: Qualitative and Quantitative Research*. Aldershot, England: Avebury.

Burawoy, Michael, et al. 1991. *Ethnography Unbound Power and Resistance in the Modern Metropolis*. Berkeley: University of California Press.

Burgess, E. W., and Leonard S. Cottrell Jr. 1939. *Predicting Success or Failure in Marriage*. New York: Prentice Hall.

Burgess, R. G. 1982. "Multiple Strategies in Field Research." In *Field Research: A Sourcebook and Field Manual*, edited by R. G. Burgess. London: George Allen and Unwin.

Caldwell, John C. 1985. "Strengths and Limitations of the Survey Approach for Measuring and Understanding Fertility Change." Pp. 45–62 in *Reproductive Change in Developing Countries*, edited by John Cleland, John Hobcraft, and Betzy Dinesen. Oxford, England: Oxford University Press.

Caldwell, John C., Allan G. Hill, and Valerie J. Hull, eds. 1985. *Micro-Approaches to Demographic Research*. London: Kegan Paul International.

Carmines, Edward G., and Richard A. Zeller. 1979. "Reliability and Validity Assessment." In *Quantitative Applications in the Social Sciences*, edited by John L. Sullivan. Newbury Park, CA: Sage.

Coombs, Lolagene C. 1974. "The Measurement of Family Size Preferences and Subsequent Fertility." *Demography* 11(4):587–611.

DeMaio, T. J. 1984. "Social Desirability and Survey Measurement: A Review." Pp. 257–82 in *Surveying Subjective Phenomena*, edited by C. F. Turner and E. Martin. New York: Russell Sage.

Denzin, N. 1970. *The Research Act in Sociology*. London: Butterworth.

Emerson, Robert M., Rachel I. Fretz, and Linda L. Shaw. 1995. *Writing Ethnographic Fieldnotes*. Chicago, IL: University of Chicago Press.

Horst, Paul. 1955. "The Prediction of Personal Adjustment and Individual Cases." In *The Language of Social Research*, edited by Paul F. Lazarsfeld and Morris Rosenberg. Glencoe, IL: Free Press.

Kahl, Joseph A. 1953. "Educational and Occupational Aspirations of 'Common Man' Boys." *Harvard Educational Review* 23(Summer):186–203.

Katz, Jack. 1988. *Seductions of Crime: Moral and Sensual Attractions in Doing Evil*. New York: Basic Books.

———. 1999. *How Emotions Work*. Chicago, IL: University of Chicago Press.

Kendall, Patricia L., and Katherine M. Wolf. 1949. "The Analysis of Deviant Cases in Communications Research." In *Communications Research, 1948–1949*, edited by Paul F. Lazarsfeld and Frank W. Stanton. New York: Harper.

Kish, Leslie. 1965. *Survey Sampling*. New York: Wiley.

Lazarsfeld, Paul F., and Morris Rosenberg. 1949–1950. "The Contribution of the Regional Poll to Political Understanding." *Public Opinion Quarterly* 13(4): 569–86.

Lieberson, Stanley. 1992. "Einstein, Renoir, and Greeley: Some Thoughts About Evidence in Sociology." *American Sociological Review* 57 (February):1–15.

Lipset, Seymour Martin, Martin A. Trow, and James S. Coleman. 1956. *Union Democracy*. Glencoe, IL: Free Press.

Lyberg, Lars, and Daniel Kasprzyk. 1991. "Data Collection Methods and Measurement Error: An Overview." Pp. 237–58 in *Measurement Errors in Surveys*, edited by Paul Biemer, Robert M. Groves, Lars E. Lyberg, Nancy A. Mathiowetz, and Seymour Sudman. New York: Wiley.

Massey, Douglas S. 1987. "The Ethnosurvey in Theory and Practice." *International Migration Review* 21 (4):1498–522.

Miles, M., and A. Huberman. 1984. *Qualitative Data Analysis*. Beverly Hills, CA: Sage.

Merton, Robert K., Marjorie Fiske, and Alberta Curtis. 1946. *Mass Persuasion*. New York: Harper.

Sieber, Sam D. 1973. "The Integration of Fieldwork and Survey Methods." *American Journal of Sociology* 78 (6):1335–59.

Spradley, James P. 1979. *The Ethnographic Interview*. Fort Worth, TX: Harcourt Brace.

Strauss, Anselm, and Juliet Corbin. 1990. *Basics of Qualitative Research Grounded Theory Procedures and Techniques*. Newbury Park, CA: Sage.

Sudman, Seymour, and Norman M. Bradburn. 1974. *Response Effects in Surveys*. Chicago, IL: Aldine.

4

REASONING WITH PARTIAL KNOWLEDGE

*László Pólos**
Michael T. Hannan†

We investigate how sociological argumentation differs from classical first-order logic. We focus on theories about age dependence of organizational mortality. The overall pattern of argument does not comply with the classical monotonicity principle: Adding premises overturns conclusions in an argument. The cause of nonmonotonicity is the need to derive conclusions from partial knowledge. We identify metaprinciples that appear to guide the observed sociological argumentation patterns, and we formalize a semantics to represent them. This semantics yields a new kind of logical consequence relation. We demonstrate that this new logic can reproduce the results of informal sociological theorizing and lead to new insights. It allows us to unify existing theory fragments, and it paves the way toward a complete classical theory.

Observed inferential patterns which seem "wrong" according to one notion of inference might just as well signal that the speaker is engaged in correct execution of another style of reasoning.
—Johan van Benthem (1996)

We appreciate the support of the Centre for Formal Studies in the Social Sciences at Eötvös Loránd University, ERIM Institute of Erasmus University, the Business School Trust of the Stanford Graduate School of Business, and the Netherlands Institute for Advanced Study. Glenn Carroll, Igor Douven, Uskali Mäki, Susan Olzak, and Gábor Péli made extremely useful comments on earlier versions.
*Eötvös Loránd University, Budapest; Erasmus University, Rotterdam
†Stanford University

133

1. INTRODUCTION

When instances of sociological theorizing are examined from the perspective of formal logic, a confusing picture emerges. The argumentation seems to be erroneous; the sets of explanatory principles used in different parts of a theoretical program often seem inconsistent. A key difficulty originates from incompleteness. Typical theories are in flux. Carefully constrained explanatory principles are not (yet) available. Formally minded people can easily conclude that the sociological theories are unsystematic and unreliable.

Surely the logic of argumentation in sociology does not always follow the principles of classical logic. Nonetheless, we contend that argumentation might fail some classical test and yet still follow systematic logical principles. In the spirit of van Benthem (1996), we want to identify some of these principles, show how they operate in the normal routines of sociological theorizing, and provide a methodology for building theories and testing theoretical claims that fits the actual patterns of argumentation. This effort entails use of a new nonmonotonic logic developed specifically to fit sociological argumentation. We show that this logic sometimes allows systematic and consistent arguments to be formed even when different fragments of a theory seem to warrant opposing conclusions. In addition, we try to demonstrate that theory building with this logic can strengthen theories in progress and yield novel insights.

We hasten to note that, although our objectives are methodological in a broad sense, we do not deal with issues of empirical verification of theoretical claims. Instead, we focus on *patterns of argumentation*, how definitions, assumptions, and insightful causal stories are stitched together to reach conclusions when empirical knowledge is partial. Nonetheless, we think that the proposed strategy of theory building can ease the task of making connections between abstract theory and empirical findings. We try to demonstrate this conjecture in a sustained substantive application of our method.

Studying these issues in full generality entails a vast—perhaps intractable—task. Therefore, we narrow the focus and examine theories in organization sociology concerning age dependence in mortality processes. Empirical research provided three different tendencies to be explained. Historically, these divergent patterns were explained by separate theory fragments, each selected to explain a subset of empirical findings. Theory fragments were developed under the label of liability-of-newness theories to explain the fact that many populations of organizations exhibited a negative relationship between organizational age and the hazard of mortality. In other populations, organizations were most vulnerable not at founding but somewhat later. Liability-of-adolescence theory was developed to account for this pattern, especially the initial rise of mortality. Finally, research on some other populations found that older organizations have the highest hazard. Theory fragments, called theories of obsolescence, senescence, and network saturation, were designed to explain these findings.

No one claims that these theory fragments hold simultaneously. Even if each fragment is consistent and supported by some substantial empirical research, the picture is disquieting. The key underlying processes have not been established empirically. Rather, the relevant empirical work operates at the surface level by establishing parametric relationships between age and the mortality hazard and arguing that certain deeper processes give rise to these relationships. In other words, empirical knowledge on this subject is very incomplete. The present state of knowledge does not supply an answer to the fundamental question: What should be expected of a not-yet-studied population of organizations? Getting to the point where we can answer this question requires some kind of unification of the fragments. However, first-order logic does not give enough room to keep all of these theory fragments on board; at most one of them can be true. Hannan (1998) formalized these theory fragments in first-order logic but was only partly successful in unifying them. The resulting formulation integrated two—but not all three—of the fragments. In other words, the formalization yielded two internally consistent fragments that seemingly cannot be reconciled in a classical logic. Making sense of this situation and making headway in refining the theories demands a different approach. Perhaps this entails use of a logic that imposes less stringent constraints. We argue that a nonmonotonic approach provides a valuable alternative methodology.

Use of nonmonotonic logic in theory building constitutes a substantial departure from long-standing practice in sociology. When sociologists examine the logic of argumentation in their field, they invariably employ (often informally) a classical logic—either propositional logic or, if quantification is needed, first-order logic.[1] Such classical logics offer only one way to eliminate inconsistencies: Restrict the scope of (some)

---

[1] We have occasionally encountered the (surprising) reaction that sociologists do not rely on logic, even informally. We disagree. Standard forms of theoretical criticism in sociology, as in science generally, argue that some conclusion does not follow from the stated premises or that a set of theoretical claims is inconsistent (thereby warranting all possible conclusions).

explanatory principles. According to this methodology, the price to be paid for consistency is the limitation of explanatory power. Although we accept that, under certain circumstances, such a price is well worth paying, restricting the scope of premises appears to be justified only if the restrictions can be well motivated substantively. Otherwise the cure is ad hoc, and it does not contribute to understanding. Indeed, a highly developed theoretical and empirical understanding is needed to state precise restrictions on the scope of arguments—scope limits too are universally quantified statements. One might well question whether sociology and other social sciences can supply such precise information.

We show that nonmonotonic reasoning offers an appealing alternative methodology. The explanatory principles might remain intact if there is no substantive reason to restrict their scope. Two different lines of explanation pointing in opposite directions might not yield any conclusions, but they might also not yield any contradictions in specified circumstances. In addition, the absence of conclusions might be cured by knowledge showing that (under the specific circumstances) one line of argumentation is more specific than the other. Because the explanatory principles remain intact, so too does the explanatory power of the theory. In fact, we show that the situation is even better in the case of one sociological theory in which explanatory power increases when its theory fragments are integrated using a nonmonotonic logic.

In logic, monotonicity means that the set of conclusions that follows from a set of premises grows monotonically as premises are added. In other words, monotonicity means that adding premises cannot overturn conclusions that follow from the original (smaller) set of premises. In contrast, nonmonotonic logics allow the addition of new premises (reflecting new knowledge) to overturn existing conclusions. In such logics, introduction of premises that would result in contradictions according to first-order logic do not necessarily create inconsistency. Switches between explanatory principles follow the generic guidelines: When different principles give conflicting results, inferences should be based on the most specific principles that apply; and when conflicting principles do not differ in specificity, no inference should be drawn.

During the last 15 years, logicians working on applications in computer science designed and studied many nonmonotonic logics. Due to this frantic activity, a vast array of alternatives is now available.[2]

[2] Standard technical references on the subject include McCarty (1980), Makinson (1994), and Veltman (1996); Brewka, Dix, and Konolige (1997) provide an accessible overview of the field of nonmonotonic logic.

However, given their typical computer-science motivation, most of these logics are suitable tools for studying reasoning in databases but much less desirable tools for studying patterns of argumentation in theory building. There are two key differences. First, it obviously matters for representing theoretical arguments whether the "rules" are definitions, universally quantified propositions, metaprinciples, or insightful causal stories. These distinctions ought to be marked in the syntax used to represent a theory. However, these distinctions were not important in modeling computer-science applications, and therefore they do not appear in the syntaxes developed in this approach. Second, the database approach treats old information as less valid than new information: One normally updates an entry in a database to override old information that has been found to be incorrect. But we will argue that argumentation patterns are different, that updates add new information but do not vitiate existing information. Hence we decided that many available logics are less than ideal for representing patterns of argumentation and theory building.

As far as we know, only Frank Veltman (1996) rigorously maintained the desired distinctions (among the different kinds of elements that comprise an argument) in designing his nonmonotonic language for update semantics. In formulating our approach, we followed Veltman as closely as possible. Nonetheless, we found a number of features of his update semantics that needed to be altered to fit our problem.[3] So, despite some qualms about introducing yet another type of nonmonotonic logic, we decided that a new logic was needed for representing patterns of theory building. Below we sketch the broad outlines of the logic we developed. But first we describe the substantive context for our application.

---

[3] First, Veltman developed the semantics for a propositional language. Theory building requires quantification—that is, at least first-order logic. Second, for Veltman, the key generic quantifier "normally implies" must always be the outmost operator in forming sentences. We found this limitation to be too restricting, especially in forming definitions. Third, Veltman considers inconsistency and incoherence to be similarly damaging. In his context—i.e., in the study of (relatively) short natural language discourse—this is indeed justified. For our subject (theory building over several decades), consistency is the most one can hope for. Fourth, Veltman regards discourses with the property that generalizations (our "causal stories") can be overridden by more specific considerations to be incoherent. On the other hand, this can (and in fact does) happen to explanatory principles in the course of theory building over several decades. So a logic designed to describe reasoning in theory building should not exclude this possibility.

2. THEORIES OF AGE DEPENDENCE

2.1. *The Liability of Newness*

We pick up the history of the relevant arguments with the famous paper of Stinchcombe (1965), which makes four distinct arguments for a liability of newness. First, new organizations normally lack the technical and social requirements for smooth functioning. In old organizations, the members might have learned the relevant specialized knowledge and might have developed loyalty to the organization. Even when members get replaced, incumbents can convey the necessary knowledge to newer entrants. In contrast, new organizations have to get by with the generalized skills produced outside the organization, which normally fit the organizational context less than perfectly, or they have to invest in training. Second, new organizations must invent roles and role relationships and structure rewards and sanctions. The need for much learning by doing lowers performance in young organizations. Third, in new organizations, most social relations are relations among strangers. Thus new organizations pose more uncertainty than old ones. Compensating for such uncertainties takes away vital resources from the young organizations. Fourth, young organizations normally lack strong ties to external constituencies, which makes it harder to mobilize resources and ward off attacks.

Stinchcombe makes clear that this story applies best to the beginning of the industrial age or to the beginnings of the histories of particular industries. He mentions explicitly that the growing availability of general skills, socially induced capacities to learn, and ease of recruitment might eliminate this effect. So the liability of newness might be only an historical observation that need not (in principle) be supported by facts of the contemporary world. Nonetheless, researchers exposed the liability-of-newness theorem to testing in many populations of organizations. Much early research found supporting evidence (Carroll and Hannan 2000) and made relevant the arguments that, from one premise-set or another, pointed toward negative age dependence.

The empirical validity of this story (at least with size not taken into account—see below) presents a theoretical dilemma. What makes this claim an empirically justified theorem? We see at least two possibilities. First, some research that covers entire histories of longstanding organizational populations brings into the picture data on organizations that were founded in the premodern period that (in accordance with Stinchcombe's argument) were exposed to the liability of newness. Furthermore, the great proliferation of organizations in the early history of most populations means that small and vulnerable organizations get high representation in data on complete populations. According to this interpretation, the liability of newness is indeed a premodern phenomenon; but fossil records of the early history of organizational populations preserved it for us. Alternatively, the findings might not be limited to the premodern phase. In this case, the theorem requires a different explanation, one that applies to modern/contemporary organizations.

One argument put forward by Hannan and Freeman (1984) establishes the continuing relevance of the liability of newness. It can be recapitulated as follows:

1. Selection favors reliable and accountable organizations.
2. Reliability and accountability require highly reproducible structures.
3. Structural reproducibility rises with age.
4. Whenever a particular type is favored over another, then the mortality hazard of organizations of the favored type is lower than that of organizations of the less favored type.

Despite some prior claims to the contrary, these assumptions do imply the liability of newness (Péli, Pólos, and Hannan 2000).

2.2. The Liability of Adolescence

After the liability of newness had been demonstrated empirically and successfully integrated into theory, the empirical picture became clouded. Some researchers found evidence that the hazard starts low, then rises to a peak, and finally declines again as organizations age (Carroll and Hannan 2000), a pattern sometimes called a *liability of adolescence*. The standard story for this pattern holds that new organizations are endowed; they begin with a given amount of capital (financial and social) and a position in a more or less given network of ties. Surviving the initial period does not depend on smooth functioning, because endowments provide (partial) immunity. As endowments get spent down, performance matters more and the hazard increases. The mortality hazard in a population peaks when most organizations have exhausted their endowments. From then on, the normal process takes over: The hazard declines as organizations accumulate reliability, accountability, and organization-specific human capital.

2.3. *Aging, Obsolescence, Senescence, and Network Saturation*

Empirical work on organizational mortality began to show a more serious divergence during the past decade, depending upon how researchers handled organizational size. Freeman, Carroll, and Hannan (1983) noted that negative age dependence might reflect the operation of unobserved heterogeneity rather than aging and that organizational size, which was not measured in early studies, could serve as the heterogeneous force. When researchers found data that allowed them to control for initial sizes and subsequent growth/decline, more than half of the studies produced evidence of positive age dependence (Carroll and Hannan 2000). These empirical findings motivated examination of processes that generate *positive* age dependence.

Barron, West, and Hannan (1994) offered several explanatory schema. One emphasizes alignment. If organizations tend to be aligned with their environments at founding and structural inertia makes it unlikely that they can keep pace with changing environments, then the quality of alignment worsens with passage of time. Poor alignment with environments elevates the hazard for old organizations; there is a liability of obsolescence.

A second story focuses on daily (more or less routine) procedures. As organizations age, frictions accumulate and procedures become slower and perhaps also less accurate. Without maintenance, routines tend to deteriorate; and the accumulated inertia makes routine maintenance both more difficult and more expensive to complete. Old organizations lose on speed and efficiency, and they eventually vanish. This pattern has been called a liability of senescence.

A third explanation builds on the saturation of possible network ties (Barron 1992). If extending the web of ties is vital (say, for the recruitment of new customers and key staff), then saturation of the space of possible ties lowers vitality. As organizations age, the possibilities for adding ties generally declines. Therefore, older organizations have higher mortality hazards.

3. NONMONOTONICITY IN THEORY BUILDING

We distilled some guidelines for both syntax and semantics from these examples. Theory building (at least in this case) conforms to the principle of *informational monotonicity*: Explanatory principles are not withdrawn, even when their first-order consequences get falsified. Instead, they are maintained; and their effects are controlled by more specific arguments. Thus explanatory principles clearly differ from classical first-order (universal) generalizations, because they show an informational stability.

What are explanatory principles? When we look at their grammatical surface, we see that explanatory principles are typically bare plural sentences and that their normal interpretation is as generic sentences (Krifka et al. 1995). Explanatory principles are responsible for the empirical content of a theory.[4] For these two reasons, we called these explanatory principles *empirical generalizations* in some previous publications. Even though such a classification is fully justified, it is not quite specific enough. Explanatory principles are informationally stable in the sense that already established explanatory principles are maintained in further developments of a theory. Neither their empirical nature nor their genericity accounts for such persistence. The reason why explanatory principles are persistent in the process of theory building is that these principles are the key ingredients of theory, the specific causal explanations. In short, they are *causal stories*. To drop a causal story might be exactly the right thing to do in the process of theorizing. But, once a causal story is dropped, the theory is replaced by a different theory. In theory *building*, causal stories are persistent.

The details of our approach differ from previous developments in nonmonotonic logic in how we define specificity orderings of arguments. In particular, we build formal models of arguments involving causal stories (in terms of sequences of intensions of open formulas, as we explain in the next section).

What should be expected of a suitable nonmonotonic logic? To develop some intuition, we begin with a famous example of simple inference pattern with a failure of monotonicity.[5]

Premise 1: Birds fly.
Premise 2: Tweety is a bird.
Proposition: Tweety flies.

Suppose we add three new premises:

---

[4]Metaprinciples are not theory specific, and definitions express only analytical conventions.
[5]This stylized example and the Nixon Diamond (discussed below) are ubiquitous in the technical literature.

Premise 3: All penguins are birds.
Premise 4: Penguins do not fly.
Premise 5: Tweety is a penguin.

What happens to the conclusion that seemed justified based on the first two premises alone? Not only does it now seem unjustified, but we are tempted to derive the *opposite* conclusion: "Tweety does not fly."

What is going on here? Compare the two possible arguments about flying. One builds on a premise about birds; the other builds on a premise about penguins. Tweety is both a bird and a penguin; so both premises apply. But, the premise about penguins seems to be more relevant for Tweety than the premise about birds. The premise about penguins seems to be more specific than the premise about birds. This difference in the specificity of the premises accounts for the difference in the relevance of the arguments. We want to use the most relevant arguments available. So, we go for the conclusion: "Tweety does not fly."

What is the source of this (implicit) specificity ordering? We argue that it is the third premise, "All penguins are birds." One might object that the presence/absence of this premise should not matter much, because our common background knowledge holds that penguins are birds. Yet, another of the logicians' favorite examples—the Nixon Diamond—shows that common background knowledge does not always clarify inferences:

Premise 1: Quakers are doves.
Premise 2: Republicans are hawks.
Premise 3: Dick is a Republican.
Premise 4: Dick is a Quaker.
Proposition: ???

Our background knowledge tells us that no one can be both a hawk and a dove. Indeed, the argumentation implicitly assumes that "x is a hawk" is the negation of "x is a dove." But background knowledge does not inform us about the specificity of the premises. Lacking a dependable specificity order, we cannot conclude either that "Dick is a dove" or that "Dick is a hawk."

Seeing all this, one might go back to the previous example and decide that the original conclusion was perhaps unjustified.[6] "Birds fly"

---

[6] Without doubt, this would be the reaction of some classically minded logicians.

is a rule—a rule with exceptions; and we did not know whether Tweety was an exception. Although we should have waited until we learned something about this, we just jumped to the conclusion.

Well, sometimes conclusions must be drawn before all relevant facts are known—there is an urgency of action (Descartes 1897–1913). This kind of urgency almost always arises in theory building. A theorist cannot wait until all relevant things about the subject are known but instead must take what is known and draw conclusions on the basis of available evidence. In fact, this very feature of theorizing accounts for the nonmonotonicity of much argumentation in sociology and other fields.

Before turning to a description of our formal languages, it is worth pointing out that stories about "Tweety" and "Dick," though time-honored exemplars of nonmonotonic reasoning in logic, raise red flags for sociologists. Any quantitatively oriented scholar surely would object that the statement "birds fly" lacks the specificity needed for a prop in a scientific argument. This is surely true. The logicians were examining naturally occurring conversations. Scientists operate with semiformal languages. Given our interest in theory building, we naturally focus on the latter. Indeed, the sociological theory fragments that we model have such a semiformalized nature (involving statements about probability distributions).

4. A CAPSULE SUMMARY OF THE FORMAL APPROACH

We introduce two languages. The first serves to represent causal stories. Its central contribution to the approach is a new kind of quantifier, which we denote by $\mathfrak{N}$. Formulas quantified by $\mathfrak{N}$ state what is expected to "normally" be the case according to a causal story (in the absence of more specific information to the contrary). (Appendix A defines all of the relevant logical symbols.) We formalize such causal accounts in terms of what logicians call the intensions of the formulas that compose them. Intensions provide a formal means of characterizing the abstract meaning of the formulas, and thus also of the sentences stating the causal stories.

Theories can be seen to consist of two parts: the first-order or classical part (which contains those statements that are claimed to hold without exception) and the causal stories (which are rules with possible exceptions). We claim that both components ought to be preserved as a theory develops. Because new knowledge might introduce new casual accounts or limit the scope of existing ones, it is helpful to think in terms of the stages of a theory, defined in terms of the premises available at a given time in the development of a theory. This distinction is important because the nonmonotonic inferences are specific to a theory stage.

The second language serves to represent the consequences of a stage of a theory, "provisional theorems" that depend upon causal stories (perhaps in combination with first-order rules). We think of such provisional theorems as having a haphazard existence in that they might be wiped out by the development of new knowledge. That is, what can be derived at one stage might not be derivable in a later stage. So the status of a provisional theorem differs from that of a causal story. The syntax of the second language codes this difference. It introduces a "presumably" quantifier, denoted by $\mathcal{P}$. Sentences quantified by $\mathcal{P}$ are potential provisional theorems. If they do follow from the premises of a theory stage, then they are proved to be provisional theorems (at that stage).

We need some formal machinery for testing what really follows from the premises in a stage of a theory. We build a representation of arguments in the form of rule chains. These chains are composed of links that state strict rules or causal stories. The chains are constructed so that they start with the subject of the argument and terminate with the purported conclusion of the argument (the consequence to be derived). In nonmonotonic inference, different rule chains—each representing an argument embodied in the state of the theory—might lead to opposing conclusions. The testing procedure determines whether any inference can be drawn at all and, if so, which one. This procedure involves standards for assessing whether a pair of relevant rule chains is comparable in specificity and so determining specificity differences for comparable chains. It thus provides a method of constructing proofs of the claims of a theory.

The next section supplies the details (but still in a somewhat informal manner). Readers who are not interested in these details can get a good sense of how the methodology works from the substantive application.

5. FORMAL LANGUAGES FOR SOCIOLOGICAL THEORIZING

A logic is a formal definition of a consequence relation. In theorizing, the consequence relations hold among sentences of a language. So it is natural to start the formal characterization of a logic with a definition of a language. We are focusing on nonmonotonicity, the uncertainty that conclusions really follow from the theory as such, although they appear to be conclusions of a given stage of the theory. This possibility is frightening, and we would like to avoid it if we could. If these dangerous beasts are here to stay, they should be marked clearly. We do so by defining separate languages for the well-behaved part of the theory and the part that misbehaves in the sense of showing signs of nonmonotonicity.

Two kinds of sentences generate failures of monotonicity: causal stories and provisional theorems (propositions derived from causal stories). The difference between them becomes clear from their roles in theorizing. Serious causal stories capture some relevant (and valid) insight about the underlying causal mechanisms; they yield the "a ha!" feeling that good theories can provide. Neither their validity nor their relevance gets automatically undermined by any accidental counterexample—not even by some systematic exceptions. In fact, the meaning of these causal accounts cannot be properly reproduced by their truth conditions, expressed in term of the number or proportion of positive instantiations. They do not talk about what *is* the case. Rather, their main semantic contribution lies in shaping our expectations.

We need extra tools to express defaults. Because they provide insight, we want to treat causal stories as informationally stable in the sense that extensions of a theory keep them intact. As a theory develops, all that can happen to a causal story is that new insights might restrict its domain of applicability, if knowledge about exceptions develops. Even new knowledge should not lead us to discard them. Instead, new rules get added to the body of knowledge; and new, more specific rules can—and occasionally do—override older, more general rules.

Provisional theorems, on the other hand, have a haphazard existence. New knowledge might wipe them out without a trace, as we will see in modeling organizational mortality. The provisional theorems belong to particular stages of a developing theory—they represent the predictions that can be sensibly formed at that stage.

These considerations set a methodological agenda. "Official" causal stories of a theory should be those that the theorist (or theory group) regards as sufficiently dependable and insightful to serve as permanent assumptions of the theory. If there are doubts about future acceptability, then a claim does not deserve this status.

In the context of an evolving theory, part of the theory can normally be expressed in the language of first-order logic ($\mathcal{L}_F$, for short), which follows monotonicity. For instance, definitions and strict rules (universally quantified sentences) are generally expressed in this way. Premises stated in $\mathcal{L}_F$ provide the firm foundation for a theory. Any sentence that can be derived by classical rules from them counts as a dependable proposition of a theory. In formal terms, the deductive closure of these assumptions is part of a theory.

Study of the linguistic forms of the sentences expressing causal stories shows that it is unlikely that they can be expressed in $\mathcal{L}_F$. Generic sentences are general but not universal. Their truth conditions cannot be expressed in terms of particular cases. To return to a classic example, even if most birds do not fly, the claim "birds fly" would still be an acceptable causal story, *provided* that this is a justifiable expectation of a creature with only one known property: It is a bird. Causal stories cannot be expressed adequately in first-order logic, where generality means universal quantification.

5.1. *Syntax*

In previous work (Pólos and Hannan (2000, 2001)) we defined two languages, assigned meaning to their (well-formed) sentences, and spelled out the consequence notions that fit these semantics. Here we give an informal sketch.[7]

It is important for understanding our approach to distinguish between open and closed formulas. To fix ideas, consider a small example, involving the one-place predicate $O(\cdot)$, where $\cdot$ is the placeholder in the argument slot. $O(o)$ is formula, which reads "o is an organization." Such a formula holds that an object possesses a property. As stated, the truth of this formula cannot be established because the object in question has not been identified. In technical terms, the variable o is free (not bound), and $O(o)$ is an open formula. In $\mathcal{L}_F$, we can get a closed formula from an open one in several ways. For instance, we can replace the variable with the proper name of an object (or individual constant)—for example, $O(\text{Eötvös University})$. In this case, the truth of the statement can be checked by examining the named object, Eötvös University, to ascertain whether it is in fact an organization. Alternatively, we can quantify over the variable o (thereby binding it) by forming sentences such as $\exists o[O(o)]$—i.e., "some object (in the universe of discourse) possesses the property of being an organization" or $\forall o[O(o)]$—i.e., "every object (in the universe of discourse) has the property of being an organization." In each of these three revised formulas, all

---

[7]This section assumes familiarity with $\mathcal{L}_F$ at the level of such standard texts as Barwise and Etchemendy (1992). Mastery of these technical details is not needed for understanding the general method and its applications.

variables are bound and the formulas are said to be closed. Henceforth, we will refer to closed formulas as sentences.

Sociological applications usually emphasize connections between predicates. For example, take the predicates $Y(\cdot)$ and $RA(\cdot)$, which state the properties of "being young" and "having reliability/accountability." Many sociological propositions assert a relation of material implication: if A then B, usually expressed formally as $A \rightarrow B$ (or, alternatively, $\neg[A \wedge \neg B]$). Consider the open formula $Y(o) \wedge O(o) \rightarrow \neg RA(o)$. A closed version can be gained by, for example, universal quantification: $\forall o[Y(o) \wedge O(o) \rightarrow \neg RA(o)]$. This sentence states that it is the case for every object (in the universe of discourse) that if the object is both young and an organization then it does not possess the property of reliability/accountability. In defining syntax and semantics, we refer to formulas with shorthand expressions such as ϕ and ψ. For example, the last mentioned sentence can be expressed as $\forall o[\phi \rightarrow \psi]$, where ϕ stands for $Y(o) \wedge O(o)$ and ψ stands for $\neg RA(o)$.

The Language of Working Theory $(\mathcal{L}_W)$. We constructed the language of working theories $(\mathcal{L}_W$, for short) to provide expression for generic sentences. These are sentences formed by applying a generic "normally" quantifier, denoted by $\mathfrak{N}$, to link two open formulas that share free variables.

We defined $\mathcal{L}_W$ as the smallest extension of $\mathcal{L}_F$ such that, for any pair of open formulas $\langle \phi, \psi \rangle$, the language contains a new type of formula

$$\mathfrak{N}\bar{x}[\phi(\bar{x},\ldots) \rightarrow \psi(\bar{x},\ldots)],$$

where $\bar{x}$ denotes a subset of the free variables shared by ϕ and ψ and the ellipses indicate that there might be more free variables that are not being quantified. This expression reads "ϕs normally are ψs" or "ϕ normally implies ψ."

The Language of Theory Testing $(\mathcal{L}_T)$. We also defined a language for expressing nonmonotonic presumptions. We can explain our reasons for developing this third language with a simple example. Suppose that we have two causal stories:

$$\phi \text{ normally implies } \psi: \mathfrak{N}\bar{x}[\phi(\bar{x}) \longrightarrow \psi(\bar{x})];$$

$$\psi \text{ normally implies } \chi: \mathfrak{N}\bar{x}[\psi(\bar{x}) \longrightarrow \chi(\bar{x})].$$

We obviously want to have something parallel to first-order logic's "cut rule," which allows ψ to be cut out, giving an implication from ϕ to

χ. But what should be the status of the provisional theorem linking ϕ to χ? One answer might be that this too should be regarded as a causal story:

$$\phi \text{ normally implies } \psi\colon \mathfrak{N}\bar{x}[\phi(\bar{x}) \longrightarrow \chi(\bar{x})].$$

However, recall that we want to reserve the status of a causal story for the deep insights of a theory. If the rule linking ϕ to χ is not already in the set of causal stories, then it is presumably not known but is to be discovered (as an inference). So we need another semantics to express presumptions.

We defined a "presumably" quantifier, denoted by $\mathfrak{P}$, for this purpose. In the context of the example introduced above, we express the result of applying the cut rule to the pair of causal stories as

$$\phi \text{ presumably implies } \chi\colon \mathfrak{P}\bar{x}[\phi(\bar{x}) \longrightarrow \chi(\bar{x})],$$

In formal terms, we defined the language of theory testing $\mathcal{L}_T$ as the smallest extension of $\mathcal{L}_F$ that satisfies two conditions.

1. If ϕ is a first-order formula with n free variables and $a_1,\ldots,a_n$ are individual constants (proper names), then $\mathfrak{P}[\phi(\langle a_1,\ldots,a_n\rangle)]$ is a sentence that reads "the sequence $\langle a_1,\ldots,a_n\rangle$ presumably satisfies the (open) formula ϕ." A looser, but intuitive, reading is "the sequence $\langle a_1,\ldots,a_n\rangle$ presumably has the complex property ϕ."
2. If ϕ and ψ are first-order formulas with the shared free variables $\bar{x}$, then $\mathfrak{P}\bar{x}[\phi(\bar{x},\ldots) \to \psi(\bar{x},\ldots)]$ is a formula of $\mathcal{L}_T$ and the elements of $\bar{x}$ are bound by the quantifier $\mathfrak{P}$. This sentence reads "ϕ presumably implies ψ."

Our use of the expressions normally implies, presumably, and presumably implies reflects the influence of Veltman (1996). Although our research questions led us to a different formal semantics, the credit for developing some basic, dependable intuitions about a domain, which is normally recognized as very slippery, should go to Veltman.

5.2. Possible-Worlds Semantics

We now turn to the task of assigning meanings to the sentences of these new languages. We do so using what is called *possible-world semantics*.[8]

---

[8] Valuable background material on the semantics can be found in Dowty, Wall, and Peters (1980) and Gamut (1991).

Assigning meaning to sentences in $\mathcal{L}_F$ requires specifying: what objects the individual constants refer to, what the variables stand for, and what properties/relations the predicates denote. Individual constants refer to—and variables stand for—elements of the universe of discourse $(\mathcal{U})$. One-place predicates refer to properties that can be represented as subsets of the universe of discourse. Two-place predicates refer to relations represented by subsets of pairs of objects/elements of $\mathcal{U}$, three-place predicates to relations represented by subsets of triplets of objects/elements, and so forth.

We can define the semantics for the new languages in a systematic manner in terms of *interpretation functions*, which map individual constants to elements of the universe of discourse (and n-place predicates to sets of n-long sequences of elements of the universe of discourse). For example, $O(\cdot)$ is a one-place predicate. The interpretation function assigns to it the set of objects that—according to an interpretation—qualify as organizations. This set is called the *extension* of the predicate. Extensions obviously depend upon interpretations.

Not all interpretations are equally useful; some might have very little to do with the real world. Factual knowledge is required to tell which sets the predicates denote. It is not logic that tells which creatures are organizations or which creatures have acquired which other creatures. One has to go into the world and find out. If no factual information is available, then all denotations are equally possible. In other words, we have the whole set of different interpretations—possible worlds, in the usual formal language (see Gamut 1991)—but we know nothing about which of these possible worlds is the *actual* world. When more relevant facts and strict rules become known, the set of (still) possible worlds is made smaller.

The next step is to tell what sets the predicates denote in the various possible worlds. A generalized interpretation of the language assigns references to individual constants and denotation to all predicates in *every* possible world. We use interpretation functions to characterize the semantics of possible worlds.

The concept of *intension* plays a very important role in possible-world semantics and in the proposed logic. In formal terms, the intension of a predicate is the function that tells the extension of the predicate (the set of those objects for which the predicate is true) in every possible world. Intensions of expressions give abstract representations of their meanings. As Gamut (1991, p. 14) put it, "The intension of an expression is something like its conceptual content, while its extension comprises all that

exemplifies that conceptual content." Two predicates are considered to
have the same meaning if and only if they have the same intension.

We defined causal stories as generic sentences. As we noted above,
a generic sentence is either true or false, but its truth/falsity generally
cannot usefully be expressed in terms of the proportion of positive and
negative instances in a world (the so-called inductivist view). We regard
a generic sentence to be true if the regularity it expresses operates in
the world. Carlson (1995:225) calls this view the rules-and-regulations
approach:

> According to this approach, generic sentences depend for
> their truth and falsity upon whether or not there is a cor-
> responding structure in the world, structures being not
> the episodic instances but rather the causal forces behind
> those instances.

We take advantage of linguistic knowledge in building a formal
representation of such regularities. The linguistic research has concluded that the underlying structure of generic sentences contains two
open formulas (Carlson 1977; Diesing 1995; Kratzer 1995). Like generic
sentences, causal stories have some kind of conditional nature, relating
antecedents to consequents. Given that we construe the relation between
the antecedents and consequents in causal stories as open formulas, we
extended the definition of intension to apply to open formulas, specified with a list of (some of) its free variables. The intension of the open
formula $\phi(\bar{x})$, denoted by $\mathcal{I}(\phi(\bar{x}))$, is the function that gives, for every
possible world,[9] the (sequences of) objects for which this formula is
true in that world.

We can now specify a core idea underlying our modeling strategy.
We propose that the ordered pair whose first element is the intension of
the antecedent and whose second element is the intension of the consequent provides a useful semantic representation of the regularity expressed
by a causal story. (The ordering tells the direction of the relation.)

Semantics for $\mathcal{L}_W$.   With these preliminaries in hand, we can define a
stage of a theory as a pair of sets: $\langle \mathbf{W}, \mathbf{C} \rangle$. Here $\mathbf{W}$ denotes the set of (still)
possible worlds, the worlds that can be the real world as far as the first-

---

[9] If there are more free variables in $\phi(\bar{x})$ than are listed in $\bar{x}$, then they too
should be valuated.

order part of the theory is concerned; and **C** denotes the set of the semantic representations of the causal stories (and nothing else). The idea that a stage of a theory has both of these components corresponds to the view that both strict rules and causal stories matter. Strict rules exclude some of the otherwise possible worlds; and causal stories express regularities that are just as real as objects, properties, or relations.

Sentences in $\mathcal{L}_W$ are to be evaluated in theory stages. The sentences of the first-order part of the theory (the classical premises) can be true, false, or undefined in any stage. Intuitively speaking, a first-order sentence is true in a stage if it is true in all of the still-possible worlds, false if it is false in all still-possible worlds, and undefined otherwise. As noted above, a causal story ought to be modeled semantically by the presence of the corresponding regularity, because its truth or falsity cannot be characterized in terms of a universally quantified proposition about the world. Instead of dealing with truth, we treat sentences expressing causal stories as true if they represent explicit causal claims of the theory and as false otherwise. Their logical impact will be characterized by their role in inference—i.e., in terms of the conclusions they (along with the first-order premises) support: $\mathfrak{R}x[\phi(\bar{x}) \rightarrow \psi(\bar{x})]$ is true in a stage of a theory if the ordered pair of the intensions of ϕ and ψ are in **W** in that stage, and it is false otherwise.

It is important to realize that universal rules and causal stories are treated as stable elements of the theory. If they are true in a given theory stage, then they remain true in any extension. In contrast, their consequences can change from stage to stage—a consequence (provisional theorem) in one stage might be overruled in another.

Semantics for $\mathcal{L}_T$.   Lacking a rich semantics for causal stories, we leave the job of characterizing the basic intuitions about inference to the semantics of the sentences of $\mathcal{L}_T$. We call an argument based on a causal story a *rule chain*. Loosely speaking, a nonmonotonic test succeeds if a tentative[10]—but convincing—argument can be constructed from the causal stories (and strict rules) and if the rule chain expressing it is more specific than those representing all (tentative) counterarguments.

Because strict comparisons of chains are needed to test arguments, we must define carefully the proper construction of the chain: which rule can follow which other rule in the chain. As a preparatory step, we defined

---

[10] By tentative, we mean depending upon causal stories instead of simply first-order premises.

a specificity relation for intensions. Think of the following possible causal claim: Old and small organizations are vulnerable. The formal counterpart is

$$\mathfrak{N}o[O(o) \wedge Old(o) \wedge Small(o) \to Vul(o)].$$

In this case, the antecedent is the formula $O(o) \wedge Old(o) \wedge Small(o)$. The intension of this formula is the function that tells for every possible world which objects are the old and small organizations in that world. Suppose some class of organizations is believed to be an exception to this rule, say handcraft producers (in some industry).

All craft producers are old, small organizations:
$\forall o[Craft(o) \to O(o) \wedge Old(o) \wedge Small(o)];$
Craft producers are normally not vulnerable: $\mathfrak{N}o[Craft(o) \to \neg Vul(o)].$

   If these premises tell all that we know, then we cannot conclude that the extension of the predicate "Craft (o)" is smaller than that of the complex predicate "old and small organization" in the actual world. It might be smaller, or it might be equal. Yet we might be convinced that the "craft-producer" rule is more specific than the "old-and-small-organization" rule. If so, the relation between the two rules is this: In all still-possible worlds, the extension of the "craft-producer" predicate is a subset of the extension of the "old-and-small-organization" predicate; and the extension of the "craft" predicate is a proper subset in some worlds (where one sees, say, small, old liberal-arts colleges). This relation can be represented with the following *specificity relation*. The formula ϕ is at least as specific as the formula ψ, formally $\mathcal{I}(\phi) \sqsubseteq_{\mathbf{W}} \mathcal{I}(\psi)$, if and only if ϕ's intension is a subset of ψ's intension in every still-possible world.
   We want to represent arguments as chains of rules (strict rules and causal stories). We do so by defining $\phi\text{–}\psi$ rule chains. The first component of a chain, γ_1, identifies the subject of the argument. In the case of a $\phi\text{–}\psi$ chain, the first element is the intension of the antecedent ϕ; that is, $\gamma_1 = \mathcal{I}(\phi)$. We build the chain by representing the first-order rules and causal stories to produce a chain of the form $\Gamma = \langle \gamma_1, \gamma_2, \ldots, \gamma_k \rangle$, where for each γ_i, γ_{i+1} $(i \geq 1)$, the two components appear in the argument as related by either a first-order rule or a causal story. In addition, the last element in the chain, γ_k, is either $\mathcal{I}(\psi)$—which means that the rule chain is positive—or $\mathcal{I}(\neg\psi)$—which means that the rule chain is negative. In other words, positive chains correspond to (tentative) arguments, negative chains to (tentative) counterarguments.

The machinery of first-order logic allows all sorts of lengthening of arguments (for instance, by adding tautologies). Adding such irrelevant material to an argument would destroy the possibility of comparing the specificities of arguments sensibly using the length of the chains of argument. In the full-blown statement of the languages, we defined minimal rule chains for which the irrelevant first-order part is cut out. Once rule chains are stated in minimal form, specificities can be compared sensibly. Consider the two rule chains: $\Gamma = \langle \gamma_1, \gamma_2, \ldots, \gamma_k \rangle$ and $\Gamma' = \langle \gamma'_1, \gamma'_2, \ldots, \gamma'_l \rangle$. Comparison of the first elements in different chains tells only whether the arguments concern the same subject. Unless all of the chains have identical first elements ($\gamma_1 = \gamma'_1$ in the case under discussion), it does not make sense to compare them. If the first elements are the same, then start with the second elements in the chains. If $\gamma_2 \sqsubseteq_W \gamma'_2$ and $\neg(\gamma'_2 \sqsubseteq_W \gamma_2)$, then Γ is more specific. If these relations are reversed, then Γ' is more specific. If the two sets are incomparable, then specificity cannot be assessed and no conclusions can be drawn. If the sets are comparable and the specificities are the same (e.g., $\gamma_2 = \gamma'_2$), then compare the specificities of the third elements, and so on.

We used these ingredients to define the semantics for the language of working theories. Consider the semantics for the presumably-implies connective. Note that two-element chains can always be constructed for logically true statements, making $\mathfrak{P}$ tests succeed for them.[11] Such a first-order argument (a two-element chain) will always overrule tentative arguments (minimal chains having at least three elements).

The key to the semantics for this language is the following truth condition for sentences involving $\mathfrak{P}$. The presumably-implies relation $\mathfrak{P}\bar{x}[\phi(\bar{x}) \to \psi(\bar{x})]$ is true in a stage of a theory if (1) there exist minimal positive two-element ϕ–ψ chains (which means that the relationship is a strict, first-order, rule), or (2) there exist minimal positive ϕ–ψ chains, and, if there also exist minimal negative ϕ–ψ chains, then all minimal positive chains must be more specific than all minimal negative chains. It is false otherwise.

Figure 1 illustrates a pair of ϕ–ψ rule chains that produce a Nixon Diamond. The first element in each chain tells the subject of the argument: "Dick." The second elements are the intensions of "Quakers" and "Republicans," and the third elements are the intensions of "doves" and

---

[11] A sentence is logically true if there is no interpretation that would make it false in any possible world.

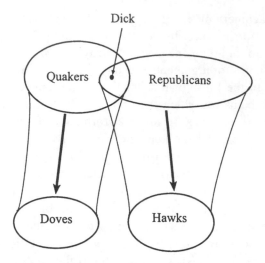

FIGURE 1. Illustration of the rule chains for an argument containing a Nixon Diamond.

"hawks." The "funnels" connecting the intensions represent the regularities that connect the complex properties—they illustrate that a causal story
is modeled as an ordered pair of intensions. The heavy arrows represent
the flow of the arguments, linking antecedents to consequents. Here the
two rule chains differ in their implications: The one on the left side of the
figure leads to the conclusion "Dick is a dove" and the one on the right of
the figure leads to the opposite conclusion (assuming that "hawk" is the
negation of "dove"). The two chains have the same length and their specificity cannot be compared (neither "Quakers" nor "Republicans" is a
proper subset of the other). Therefore, no conclusion is warranted.

Figure 2 illustrates the Penguin Principle for ϕ–ψ rule chains. The
situation is just as it is in Figure 1, except that the intension of "Penguin"
is a proper subset of the intension of "Birds." In other words, the argument represented in the chain on the right side of the figure is more specific than the opposing argument on the left. Therefore we conclude:
"Tweety does not fly."

Inference within Working Theories. The form of inference in most sociological work starts with premises that can be expressed in $\mathcal{L}_F$ and $\mathcal{L}_W$
and builds conclusions that can be expressed in $\mathcal{L}_T$. That is, the argumentation takes definitions and premises (stated as strict rules and causal
stories) and seeks to establish consequences (theorems). A semantic con-

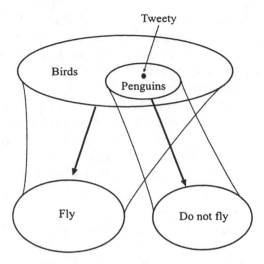

FIGURE 2. Illustration of rule chains for an argument subject to the Penguin Principle.

sequence relation is needed to make sense of such argumentation. In the formal statement of the approach, we defined a *rule-minimal* stage of a theory. Loosely speaking, this is a version of the theory for which **C** is stripped down to the bare minimum needed to make true all of the sentences of the theory expressing causal stories. In our applications, it suffices to regard the rule-minimal stage of the theory as the collection of the premises of the theory (and nothing else). We can then state the consequence relation as follows. The sentence ϕ is a consequence of a stage of theory if and only if all of the rule-minimal stages of the theory make ϕ true.

6. FORMALIZING THE LIABILITY OF NEWNESS

This formal logic for theory building might be interesting for its own sake. But does it contribute to our understanding of sociological processes? Here we try to show that it does, by extending Hannan's (1998) formalization of alternative formulations of age dependence. The key extensions involve unifications of the fragments that could not be unified with a classical approach.

   Use of default reasoning relies heavily on considerations of the specificity. We use an intuitive notion of specificity in the following formalization. The antecedents of the premises describe (partially) positions of a (half-open) segment on the age scale: $[t_1, t_2)$. Suppose that the antecedent of one causal story says, for instance, that t_1 falls in a given set, and the antecedent of another causal story says that t_1 lies within a *proper subset* of the same given set. Then arguments that use the latter causal story are more specific than those that use the former. Formalizing what is required to show that this intuition is correct would not add much to the understanding of the issues under discussion. Therefore, we simply assume that these intuitions provide sufficient guidelines to decide specificity issues.

Issues of age dependence in mortality processes concern properties of probability distributions of lengths of lifetimes. Modern work on organizational mortality analyzes the *hazard* (Carroll and Hannan 2000). Let t be a random variable that tells the length of an organizational lifetime. Then the lifetime distribution is given by $F_T(t) = \Pr\{T \le t\}$, the lifetime density by $f_T(t)$, and the survivor function by $G_T(t) = 1 - F_T(t)$.

Definition 1: The hazard of mortality for organization o in population p [12] is defined as

$$\mu_{o,p}(t) = \frac{f_T(t)}{G_T(t)} = \lim_{\delta \downarrow 0} \frac{\Pr\{Y_{o,p}(t + \delta) = 1 \mid Y_{o,p}(t) = 0\}}{\delta}, \quad t > 0,$$

where $Y_{o,p}(t)$ is a random variable equal to 0 if organization o (in population p) is still functioning as an independent entity at age t and equals 1 otherwise.

Given this definition, it should be clear the arguments being formalized are built on statements about the properties of *probability distributions*. So, although our formalization of the theoretical reasoning does not take a probabilistic form, the substantive application shows that our approach easily fits a probabilistic view of the social phenomena being modeled. Thus it does not make sense, in our view, to regard nonmonotonic reasoning (about arguments) and probabilistic reasoning (about realizations of stochastic processes) as rivals.

6.1. *Fragment 1: Reliability/Accountability*

At least six clearly distinguishable arguments claim the liability of newness. Because logical analyses using each yield similar results, we treat

---

[12] Comparisons of mortality hazards among organizations generally make substantive sense only within organizational populations, because both the overall levels of the hazards and the exact forms of age dependence vary considerably among populations (Carroll and Hannan 2000).

TABLE 1
Notation: Key parameters, functions, and predicates in the formalization
of theories of age dependence.

Functions	
$\alpha_{o,p}(t)$	Organization o's age at time t
$\epsilon_{o,p}(t)$	Organization o's endowment at age t
$\iota_{o,p}(t)$	Organization o's strength of immunity at age t
$\mu_{o,p}(t)$	Organization o's hazard of mortality at t
$\rho_{o,p}(t)$	Organization o's reliability/accountability at age t
$\omega_{o,p}(t)$	Organization o's (socially perceived) obsolescence t

Parameters	
ξ	Age at which an endowment normally ends in population p
σ	Age at which environmental drift normally destroys alignment

Predicates	
$AL_{o,p}(t)$	o is aligned with its environment at age t
$DS_{o,p}(t_0, t)$	o's environments at ages t_0 and t are dissimilar
$EE_{o,p}(t)$	o's endowment ends at age t
$o \in p$	o is a member of organizational population p
$O(o)$	o is an organization
$OB_{o,p}(t)$	o becomes obsolete at age t
$P(p)$	p is a population of organizations

only one: the argument about reliability/accountability. (Table 1 summarizes our notation.)

Let $O(o)$ and $P(p)$ be predicates stating that specified objects are organizations and populations, respectively; and $M(o,p)$ be a predicate stating that "o is a member of population p." To simplify expressions, we use the following notational convention: $o \in p \longleftrightarrow \{O(o) \wedge P(p) \wedge M(o,p)\}$. We also introduce a function, $\rho_{o,p}(t)$, that records the level of reliability/accountability of o at age t.

In what follows, we usually quantify (nonmonotonically) over populations, organizational members of populations, and age intervals. Thus we treat the causal stories as holding for all populations of organizations and for all of the organizations that comprise them.

Premise F_1.1: Reliability/accountability normally increases with age.

$$\mathfrak{N} o, p, t_1, t_2 [\{(o \in p) \wedge (\alpha_{o,p}(t_1) < \alpha_{o,p}(t_2))\} \longrightarrow \{\rho_{o,p}(t_1) < \rho_{o,p}(t_2)\}].$$

(This formula reads as follows: It is normally the case for all organizations, in all organizational populations, and at all pairs of ages that the reliability/accountability at an older age exceeds that at a younger age.) According to the standard argument, reliability/accountability lowers the hazard of mortality.

Premise F_1.2: Higher reliability/accountability normally lowers the mortality hazard.

$$\mathfrak{N} o, p, t_1, t_2 [\{(o \in p) \land (\rho_{o,p}(t_1) < \rho_{o,p}(t_2))\} \longrightarrow \{\mu_{o,p}(t_1) > \mu_{o,p}(t_2)\}].$$

These two premises imply the strong-form version of the liability of newness:

Theorem F_1.1: Mortality hazards presumably decline with age at all ages.

$$\mathfrak{P} o, p, t_1, t_2 [\{(o \in p) \land (\alpha_{o,p}(t_1) < \alpha_{o,p}(t_2))\} \longrightarrow \{\mu_{o,p}(t_1) > \mu_{o,p}(t_2)\}].$$

Proof: The step is to examine all of the rule chains in the argument that start with the intension of the open formula $(o \in p) \land \alpha_{o,p}(t_1) < \alpha_{o,p}(t_2)$ and end with the intension of $\mu_{o,p}(t_1) > \mu_{o,p}(t_2)$. At this stage, the argument is so simple that there is only such chain. The second step is to identify the shortest chain. But there is only one chain. The final step is to check whether the shortest chain is positive, which means that the claimed connection holds. This chain is indeed positive.   ∎

We treat this first stage as the default theory. Its premises will be included in every subsequent stage. Notice that, because (provisional) Theorem F_1.1 applies to any age interval, its scope of applicability is extremely *nonspecific*. It will turn out that it usually gets overridden by more specific premises in the more developed theories over at least part of the age range.

6.2. *Fragment 2: Endowment*

The next development introduced the notion of endowments. An organization is founded with a given level of endowment if it possesses immunity after founding, at least for a time. Endowment lasts as long as this initial immunity does. Furthermore there is a monotonic relation between the level of endowments and the strength of immunity. The higher the level of endowment the stronger the immunity. Let $\epsilon_{o,p}(t)$ state the level of endowment of organization o in population p age t, let $\iota_{o,p}(t)$ give the level of immunity, and let the predicate $EE_{o,p}(\xi)$ state that "the age ξ is the ending of the period of endowment for organization o." (Note that $\xi = 0$ means there is normally no initial endowment; $\xi = \infty$ means that the endowment normally never ends.)

Definition F$_2$.1: The age at the ending of initial endowment is expressed as

$$EE_{o,p}(\xi) \longleftrightarrow \forall o, t, \xi [\{\epsilon_{o,p}(t) > 0\} \leftrightarrow \{O(o) \wedge (\alpha_{o,p}(t) < \xi)\}].$$

The standard argument holds that organizations normally spend down their initial endowments.

Premise F$_2$.1: Endowments normally decline over endowment periods.

$$\mathfrak{N}o, p, t_1, t_2 [\{(o \Subset p) \wedge (\alpha_{o,p}(t_1) < \alpha_{o,p}(t_2)) \wedge (\alpha_{o,p}(t_1) < \xi) \wedge EE_{o,p}(\xi)\}$$
$$\longrightarrow \{\epsilon_{o,p}(t_1) > \epsilon_{o,p}(t_2)\}].$$

Moreover, endowments provide immunity and that immunity implies a reduction in mortality chances. We express these claims as strict (first-order) rules, because they have more the standing of "fact" than tendency. These premises hold both for comparisons of an organization at different ages (say before and after the ending of endowment) and for pairs of organizations (say, with different levels of immunity). Therefore, we quantify over pairs of organizations as well as pairs of ages.

Premise F$_2$.2: During a period of endowment, the higher the level of endowment, the stronger the immunity.

$$\forall o_1, o_2, p, t_1, t_2 [\{(o_1 \Subset p) \wedge (o_2 \Subset p) \wedge (t_1 < t_2 < \xi) \wedge EE_{o,p}(\xi) \wedge$$
$$(\epsilon_{o_1,p}(t_1) > \epsilon_{o_2,p}(t_2))\} \longrightarrow \{\iota_{o_1,p}(t_1) > \iota_{o_2,p}(t_2)\}].$$

Premise F$_2$.3: The stronger the immunity, the lower the mortality hazard.

$$\forall o_1, o_2, p, t_1, t_2 [\{(o_1 \Subset p) \wedge (o_2 \Subset p) \wedge (\iota_{o_1,p}(t_1) > \iota_{o_2,p}(t_2))\}$$
$$\longrightarrow \{\mu_{o_1,p}(t_1) < \mu_{o_2,p}(t_2)\}].$$

These definitions and premises imply a pair of provisional theorems.[13]

Theorem $F_2.1$: Mortality hazards presumably increase with age within endowment periods.

$$\wp\, o, p, t_1, t_2[\{(o \Subset p) \wedge (\alpha_{o,p}(t_1) < \alpha_{o,p}(t_2) < \xi) \wedge EE_{o,p}(\xi)\}$$

$$\longrightarrow \{\mu_{o,p}(t_1) < \mu_{o,p}(t_2)\}].$$

Theorem $F_2.2$: Mortality hazards are presumably lower within endowment periods than afterward.

$$\wp\, o, p, t_1, t_2[\{(o \Subset p) \wedge (\alpha_{o,p}(t_1) < \xi \leq \alpha_{o,p}(t_2)) \wedge EE_{o,p}(\xi)\}$$

$$\longrightarrow \{\mu_{o,p}(t_1) < \mu_{o,p}(t_2)\}].$$

6.3. *The First Unification Attempt* (U_1)

At this stage, the two arguments run in opposite directions. According to the default liability-of-newness theory, the hazard declines over all ages; and, according to the endowment fragment, the hazard rises over the initial part of the age axis for endowed organizations and is lower during endowment than afterward. How can these stories be reconciled?

The usual way is to restrict the scope of applicability of *both* theories. Hannan (1998) posited that the default theory applies *only* to periods of nonendowment and (obviously) that the endowment theory applies *only* to periods of endowment. This makes the theory consistent, but it does not really unify. The scope-restriction approach seems less satisfying than alternatives that allow the default theory to apply at all ages.

A second classic alternative would formulate parametric models of the functions relating endowments and immunity to age and reliability to age that yield precise functional forms of the relationship between age and the mortality hazard under various parameter settings. That is, if available data would allow, one might be able to estimate how organizations of a given population gain reliability and accountability as they age and similarly how their levels of endowment decline with age. Of course, the reality in the case under discussion is that no one has yet succeeded in establishing these relationships. It is important to realize that the empirical work has not managed to measure endowments, immunity, or

---

[13] 1The proofs are straightforward; they follow exactly the lines of the proof of Theorem $F_1.1.1$.

reliability/accountability and that, as a result, we have no empirical knowledge about even the functional forms of the underlying processes. What we know comes from studies that establish functional forms in the relationship of age and the mortality hazard and from reasoning about the underlying processes that likely generate these relationships. In other words, our empirical knowledge is partial at best.

Suppose, contrary to fact, that the task of modeling the subprocesses had been accomplished. Even then, completing the modeling task is far from simple. There are two credible causal stories to tell about how endowment level and reliability/accountability influence mortality hazards, all other things being equal, of course. One other element would be needed for exposing the combined theory to any reality check: a composition function that tells how to aggregate the contributions of the two component theories.[14] Such a full-blown theory could then be used to predict patterns of age dependence of mortality in not-yet-studied populations of organizations, once it is known how levels of reliability/accountability and endowment vary in those populations. Getting all the relevant knowledge components at the present state of the research is close to impossible. So it is worth trying to milk the existing parts of the theory, the causal stories. Perhaps they play the crucial role in theorizing and therefore can serve as a reliable basis for predicting patterns of age dependence patterns of mortality hazards in not-yet-studied populations. Of course, any such prediction will rely on certain population characteristics, but these characteristics are less numerous and definitely less detailed than the functions the full-blown theory would require.

We have two theory fragments, two lines of argumentation. The subject of each theory fragment is the same: mortality hazards at the beginnings and ends of age intervals. The theory fragments offer opposing propositions. If the arguments are equally specific or their specificity is not comparable, then we have a Nixon-Diamond situation: No theorems are derivable. But, we see a straightforward specificity difference. Endowment considerations apply only before the end of the endowment period while the default theory applies universally. In other words we have a penguin scenario.

So we go for a nonmonotonic approach. A key step in developing such a modeling procedure involves systematic translation of the verbal

---

[14] To find such an aggregation function is not at all a trivial task. For example, the natural choice of addition as a way to combine opposing forces does not work: To get a zero sum of two functions at least one of which is positive, one needs a negative component, but negative mortality hazards do not make sense.

argument into a formal language that enables nonmonotonic testing. It is easy to realize that the claim "Endowment considerations apply only before the end of the endowment period" is not specific enough. Time intervals are extended objects, defined by starting and ending times. Figure 3 gives a two-dimensional representation. The horizontal dimension in each gives the start of the interval to be considered, and the vertical dimension gives the end of the interval. So a given interval is a point in this space. Because the ending must follow the beginning, only the region above the 45-degree line is meaningful.

We need to consider three cases. An age interval might lie completely within an endowment period—that is both its start and end times lie before the end of the endowed period (ξ), the region labeled type I in Figure 3. They might lie after ξ completely (type II in Figure 3). Or, they might begin before ξ and end after ξ (type III in Figure 3). The sentence "Endowment considerations apply only before the end of the endowment period" says that endowment considerations apply to type-I intervals but not to type-II. What about type-III intervals? Both possible translations (that the considerations apply and that they do not apply to type-III intervals) are consistent with the nonmonotonic approach; and in both cases we are going to see a penguin scenario. Still, one of them might be more in line with the concept of the mortality hazard than the other.

Let us consider first the option that holds that endowment considerations do not apply to type-III intervals. Then the only line of argument that applies is the default theory: the liability of newness. According

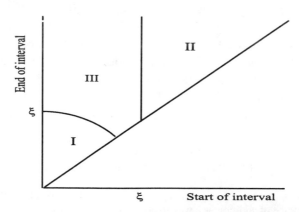

FIGURE 3. Classification of age intervals for translating the endowment theory (ξ denotes the age of ending of endowment).

to this theory, the mortality hazard at the beginning of the interval is greater then the mortality hazard at the end of the interval. Due to the immunity considerations, the hazard of mortality at the very beginning of an (endowed) organization's life is zero, according to the first translation of the key claim. Now take an interval that begins immediately after the founding of the organization and ends some time after the end of the endowment period. At the end of such a period, the hazard must be *negative*. Although this is a logical possibility, it violates the definition of a hazard.[15] Therefore, this approach does not meet the most basic requirement for a modeling procedure for mortality processes. The second translation holds that endowment considerations do apply to type-III intervals. This translation does not generate the undesirable result of implying negative hazards. Moreover, we will show that it yields interesting results.

The decision to choose the second translation might engender an objection. Is the endowment rule really as specific as we claim? Note that this rule has implications beyond the ending of endowment in the sense that it predicts that hazards after endowment fall above those during endowment (in the case of type II intervals). The answer is straightforward: The endowment rule is indeed more specific than the default. The default theory applies to any pair of ages. The endowment theory applies only to those age intervals that start *within* the endowment period (regardless of when they end). In particular, the endowment theory has no prediction for an interval that begins after the endowment period. So our claims about specificity are safe.

The first attempt at unification uses all four premises in the two theory fragments (according to the strategy we outlined).

Premises: $F_1.1$, $F_1.2$, $F_2.1\text{--}3$, and Definition $F_2.1$. At this second stage of the theory, we have the following:

Theorem $U_1.1$: Mortality hazards presumably increase with age over intervals that begin within endowment periods.

$$\mathcal{P}o, p, t_1, t_2 [\{(o \Subset p) \land (\alpha_{o,p}(t_1) < \alpha_{o,p}(t_2)) \land (\alpha_{o,p}(t_1) < \xi) \land EE_{o,p}(\xi)\}$$

$$\longrightarrow \{\mu_{o,p}(t_1) < \mu_{o,p}(t_2)\}].$$

[15] As indicated in Definition 1, the hazard is defined as the ratio of two non-negative functions, the density of the ending durations and the survivor function. Therefore, a negative value of a hazard entails a contradiction.

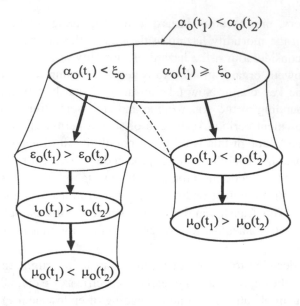

FIGURE 4. Rule chains in the first unification: combining the first and second fragments.

Proof: Figure 4 depicts the relevant rule chains. One begins with the intension defined for any pair of ages (drawn as the large ellipse at the top of the figure). This rule chain leads to the conclusion of negative age dependence. The rule chain drawn on the left emanates from the smaller (more specific) intension that applies only to those age intervals that begin before the ending of endowment. This rule chain leads to a conclusion of positive age dependence. According to the nonmonotonic inference rule, the more specific argument holds.[16]   ■

Theorem U_1.2: Mortality hazards presumably decrease with age after endowments are exhausted.

$$\mathfrak{P}\, o, p, t_1, t_2 [\{(o \Subset p) \wedge (\xi \leq \alpha_{o,p}(t_1) < \alpha_{o,p}(t_2)) \wedge EE_{o,p}(\xi)\}$$

$$\longrightarrow \{\mu_{o,p}(t_1) > \mu_{o,p}(t_2)\}].$$

[16] It might seem from this example that the less specific rule chain should dominate because it is shorter. However, this is not the case. Length of chains matters for testing only when the chains being compared have the same specificity.

Proof: Examine the most specific rule chains that connect $\mathcal{I}((\xi < \alpha_{o,p}(t_1) < \alpha_{o,p}(t_2)) \wedge EE_{o,p}(\xi))$ with $\mathcal{I}(\mu_{o,p}(t_1) > \mu_{o,p}(t_2))$. The antecedent falls only in the right-hand portion of the ellipse at the top of Figure 4. So the only rule chain that applies is the less specific one (on the right side of the figure) that leads to the conclusion of negative age dependence.   ■

A corollary also follows from Theorems $U_1.1$ and $U_1.2$: an overall tendency toward *positive* age dependence, as sketched in Figure 5. We regard this result as somewhat surprising in the sense that organizational theorists, in focusing on the different fragments, did not notice this implication. We shared this limited vision when we set out to construct a model, and we were pleasantly surprised to learn that the premises as formulated in nonmonotonic logic delivered more than we had expected.

In retrospect, we can see that the "surprise" arises because the standard endowment story has been told in terms of unobserved heterogeneity: Organizations differ in endowments and therefore in the lengths of periods of immunity. If one assumes an appropriate mixing distribution on the lengths of immunity periods, then the initial rise in the *average*

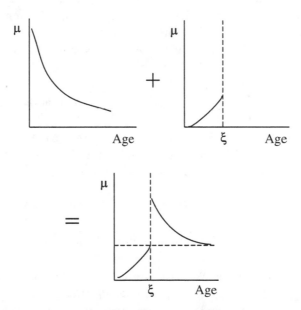

FIGURE 5. The pattern of age dependence of mortality according the first unification (ξ denotes the age of ending of endowment).

hazard in a population can be specified as due only to the monotonic decline with age of the fraction of organizations that still possess immunity. In this setup, the organizational-level hazard during immunity can be lower than at any subsequent age (as we assume) but the average hazard in the population can also decline from the peak. Our model differs in two important ways. First, we do not mix organization-level and population-level arguments. Second, we introduce age-dependence in the level of endowment. So our endowment effect is not just age-invariant unobserved heterogeneity. The effort to unify fragments in a consistent manner (at the same level of analysis) makes clear the importance of these subtle differences in assumptions.

Theorem U_1.3: An organization's mortality hazard presumably jumps to its maximum when its endowment ends.

Proof: In Theorem U_1.1, $\alpha_{o,p}(t_2)$ can be arbitrarily close to ξ, and then $\mu_{o,p}(t_2)$ presumably approximates the least upper bound of the hazard before age ξ. Similarly, $\alpha_{o,p}(t_2)$ in Theorem U_1.2 can be arbitrarily far above ξ; then, $\mu_{o,p}(t_2)$ will presumably approximate the greatest lower bound of the hazard beyond ξ. According to Theorem U_1.1, the greatest lower bound of the hazard beyond ξ presumably either equals or exceeds the least upper bound of the hazard before ξ. From Theorem U_1.2, we know that the hazard above, but (infinitely) close, to ξ presumably approximates the least upper bound of the values beyond ξ. Furthermore, we know that the set of the values of the hazard beyond ξ has several elements, and therefore the greatest lower bound of this set is strictly less than the least upper bound. If we put all these considerations together, we can then conclude that the hazard presumably jumps at ξ and the height of the jump is presumably at least as big as the difference between the greatest lower bound and the least upper bound of the hazard values beyond ξ. They also show that the hazard reaches its maximum at ξ.   ∎

7. SUPERIMPOSING A LIABILITY OF OBSOLESCENCE

Now we turn to the other main branch of the theory, which concerns positive age dependence. We concentrate on the version that relies on assumptions about obsolescence. We assume that the quality of the alignment between organizations and their environments affects mortality chances. We also assume that organizations are relatively inert, that, in the long run, their structures cannot follow environmental changes. So, after a period of given length, they will normally no longer be aligned with the environment. Following Hannan (1998), we parameterize this process in terms of environmental drift: Organizations are normally best aligned with the environments in which they first appear; but environments drift over time. Due to inertia, drift causes alignment to decline steadily over time (age, from the perspective of an organization). The drift is such that, within a period of length σ, the quality of alignment for organization o (in population p) does not change so much from the founding conditions that it affects the hazard. However, beyond σ, the environment has normally drifted far enough as to drive the quality of alignment below a threshold that affects the hazard. Further drift, beyond σ, continually degrades alignment.

7.1. Fragment 3: Obsolescence

The key modeling issue here is how to formalize the relevant part of the imprinting hypothesis. We focus on external alignment, the fit between an organization's structural features and capabilities and the demands of its external environment. We introduce the predicate $AL_{o,p}(t)$ to express that "organization o (in population p) is aligned with its environment at time t" and the predicate $OB_{o,p}(\sigma)$ to express that "σ is the age at which organization o becomes obsolete."

Environmental change drives the obsolescence process. Suppose that the environment can occupy different states at different times, in the sense that it imposes different adaptive demands at different times. Two states of an environment impose dissimilar adaptive demands if an organization cannot be aligned with both. The predicate $DS_{o,p}(t_0, t)$ states that the environments facing a given organization at times t_0 and t are dissimilar.

Definition F$_3$.1: Environmental dissimilarity is defined as:

$$\forall t_0, t[DS_{o,p}(t_0, t) \longleftrightarrow \forall x[\mathsf{O}(o) \wedge \neg(AL_{o,p}(t_0) \leftrightarrow AL_{o,p}(t))]].$$

The strong-form version of the imprinting hypothesis holds that alignment is maximal at (or shortly after) founding. This is because organization-builders can use state-of-the art designs and adapt to prevailing cultural understandings.

Premise F$_3$.1: Organizations are normally aligned with their environments at founding.

$$\mathfrak{N}o, p, \tau[\{\mathsf{O}(o) \wedge (\alpha_{o,p}(\tau) = 0)\} \longrightarrow AL_{o,p}(\tau)].$$

A drifting environment might remain in the neighborhood of a given position for some time, but it will eventually move beyond the neighborhood. Suppose the neighborhood boundary encloses the set of similar environmental states. As long as the environment stays within the neighborhood, the various states of the environment are similar. But, once it leaves the neighborhood, it does not return. If there is an age, σ, at which the environment drifts beyond a given initial neighborhood, then age and dissimilarity are linked. We specialize the theory to deal with drifting environments by introducing the following premise.

Premise $F_3.2$: Organizational environments normally drift.

$$\mathfrak{N} o, p, t_0, t_1 [\{O(o) \wedge (\alpha_{o,p}(t_0) = 0) \wedge (\alpha_{o,p}(t) > \sigma)\} \longrightarrow DS_{o,p}(t_0, t)].$$

The onset of obsolescence presumably varies among organizations (and populations). At one extreme, the environment is so volatile that even a new organization cannot achieve alignment, that is, $\sigma = 0$. At the other extreme, the environment changes so slowly that the threshold of poor alignment will normally not be reached in an organization's lifetime—that is, $\sigma = \infty$.

Definition $F_3.2$: Age of obsolescence (ending of alignment).

$$OB_{o,p}(\sigma) \longleftrightarrow \forall o, t_0, t, \sigma [\neg AL_{o,p}(t) \leftrightarrow$$

$$\{(O(o) \wedge (\alpha_{o,p}(t_0) = 0) \wedge (\alpha_{o,p}(t) > \sigma)\}].$$

Once organizations lose alignment with their environments, they start to become devalued by relevant evaluators as "obsolete." The longer an organization has been obsolete, the stronger is this devaluation process. Let $\omega_{o,p}(t)$ be a function that tells the degree to which organization o's relevant constituency regards it as obsolete at age t.

Premise $F_3.3$: After the onset of obsolescence, organizations are normally judged to be increasingly obsolete with further aging.

$$\mathfrak{N} o, p, t_1, t_2 [\{(o \Subset p) \wedge (\alpha_{o,p}(t_1) < \alpha_{o,p}(t_2)) \wedge (\alpha_{o,p}(t_2) > \sigma) \wedge OB_{o,p}(\sigma)\}$$

$$\longrightarrow \{\omega_{o,p}(t_1) < \omega_{o,p}(t_2)\}].$$

Premise F$_3$.4: The more obsolete an organization is judged to be, the higher is its mortality hazard.

$$\forall o_1, o_2, p, t_1, t_2 [\{(o_1 \Subset p) \land (o_2 \Subset p) \land (\omega_{o_1,p}(t_1) < \omega_{o_2,p}(t_2))\}$$

$$\longrightarrow \{\mu_{o_1,p}(t_1) < \mu_{o_2,p}(t_2)\}].$$

These definitions and premises imply a pair of theorems; again we omit the straightforward proofs.

Theorem F$_3$.1: Mortality hazards are presumably higher after the onset of obsolescence than before.

$$\wp o, p, t_1, t_2 [\{(o \Subset p) \land (\alpha_{o,p}(t_1) < \sigma \leq \alpha_{o,p}(t_2)) \land OB_{o,p}(\sigma)\}$$

$$\longrightarrow \{\mu_{o,p}(t_1) < \mu_{o,p}(t_2)\}].$$

Theorem F$_3$.2: Mortality hazards presumably increase with age after the onset of obsolescence.

$$\wp o, p, t_1, t_2 [\{(o \Subset p) \land (\upsilon < \alpha_{o,p}(t_1) < \alpha_{o,p}(t_2)) \land OB_{o,p}(\sigma)\}$$

$$\longrightarrow \{\mu_{o,p}(t_1) < \mu_{o,p}(t_2)\}].$$

7.2. The Second Unification Attempt (U$_2$)

The second unification uses all of the definitions and premises in the three theory fragments.

Premises: Premises F$_1$.1, F$_1$.2, F$_2$.1—3, and F$_3$.1–4, and Definitions F$_1$.1, F$_2$.1, and F$_2$.2. We again confront the issue of what to do with intervals for which a specific rule applies to part but not all (and, by definition, the default applies to the whole interval). Again, to avoid having the specific rule made irrelevant, we posit that whenever the more specific obsolescence rule applies to the *end point* of an age interval, the hazard increases over the interval.

In this third stage of the theory, the first theorem from the first unification is still valid. Although it is retained, the substantive reasoning has gotten more complex, because we have introduced obsolescence processes. We can illustrate its proof in this unified context with a graphical representation of the argument. Note that all of the theorems concern age intervals, which (as noted above) are two-dimensional objects. Figure 6

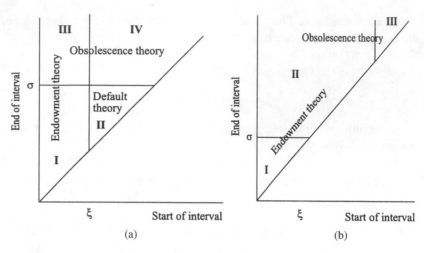

FIGURE 6. Domains of application of the various theory fragments in the second
unification when $\xi < \sigma$ (panel a) and when $\xi > \sigma$ (panel b); ξ denotes
the age of ending of endowment, and σ denotes the age of onset of obsolescence.

gives a two-dimensional representation of the domains of the various arguments. Consider this to be a "slice" from the set of possible worlds.[17] The
panel on the left represents the case where endowment ends before obsolescence begins; the panel on the right represents the opposite case.

Theorem $U_2.1$: Mortality hazards presumably increase with age
over intervals that begin within endowment periods.

Proof: Intervals that fall in zone I in each panel of Figure 6 fit the
pure endowment story: The entire interval falls within an endowment
period. The only specific rule that applies is "hazards increase within
endowment periods." Therefore, the theorem holds in Zone I. Zone III in
Figure 6(a) and Zone II in (b) contain the intervals that start during endow-

---

[17] The "official" proofs examine pairs of intensions. However, this substantive
application allows these simpler proofs because functions of the real line (the inequal-
ities involving ages) are identical in every possible world. And, given a particular
(named) organization in a particular population, the other functions in these theorems
are also constants over possible worlds. Thus we can conduct nonmonotonic tests in
terms of extensions rather than intensions.

ment and terminate after the onset of obsolescence. Two specific rules apply: the endowment and obsolescence rules. However, the two rules give the same conclusion: positive age dependence. So the theorem holds in this zone as well. Since these are the only zones relevant to the theorem, it is proved. ∎

Theorem $U_2.2$: Mortality hazards presumably decrease over intervals that begin at or after the end of the endowment and terminate before the onset of obsolescence.

$$\wp o, p, t_1, t_2 [\{(o \Subset p) \wedge (\alpha_{o,p}(t_1) < \alpha_{o,p}(t_2)) \wedge (\alpha_{o,p}(t_1) \geq \xi) \wedge$$

$$(\alpha_{o,p}(t_2) < \sigma) \wedge EE_{o,p}(\xi) \wedge OB_{o,p}(\sigma)\}$$

$$\longrightarrow \{\mu_{o,p}(t_1) < \mu_{o,p}(t_2)\}].$$

Proof: This theorem applies only if $\xi < \sigma$. Only Figure 6(a) is relevant; the intervals that fit the antecedent in this theorem fall in zone II. Here only the default theory applies. ∎

Theorem $U_2.3$: Mortality hazards presumably increase over intervals that end at or after the onset of obsolescence.

$$\wp o, p, t_1, t_2 [\{(o \Subset p) \wedge (\alpha_{o,p}(t_1) < \alpha_{o,p}(t_2)) \wedge$$

$$(\alpha_{o,p}(t_2) \geq \sigma) \wedge OB_{o,p}(\sigma)\}$$

$$\longrightarrow \{\mu_{o,p}(t_1) < \mu_{o,p}(t_2)\}].$$

Proof: This proof is similar to the proof of Theorem $U_2.1$. In zone IV in Figure 6(a) and zone III in (b), the only specific rule that applies is the obsolescence rule. This rule gives positive age dependence. In zone III in (a) and zone II in (b), both the endowment and obsolescence rules apply. Both lead to the conclusion of positive age dependence. Thus the theorem goes through. ∎

Again we can derive implications about jumps and maxima in the process—but only when obsolescence follows the end of endowment.

Theorem $U_2.4$: When the onset of obsolescence does not occur after the end of endowment ($\sigma \leq \xi$), an organization's mortality hazard

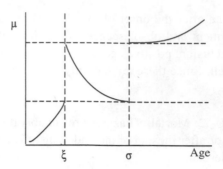

FIGURE 7. Age dependence of mortality according to the second unification for cases in which obsolescence strikes after the ending of endowment (ξ denotes the age of ending of endowment, and σ denotes the age of onset of obsolescence).

presumably jumps at the end of endowment and at the onset of obsolescence. (The proof follows the lines of the proof of Theorem $U_1.2$.)

Our model of the local behavior of the process yields an unexpected pattern: global positive age dependence. Two cases need to be considered. In the simpler case, when obsolescence strikes before endowments end at the same time ($\xi \leq \sigma$), then mortality hazards *increase* at all ages. It is clear in the Figure 6(a) that the default theory (the only one that entails negative age dependence) is overruled everywhere.

The second, more complex case, involves a delay between the ending of endowment and the onset of obsolescence ($\xi < \sigma$). Inspection of Figure 6(b) shows that there is an age range in which the default is not overridden (zone II). So there is a period in which the hazard falls with increasing aging. But, due to Theorem $U_2.4$, the hazard over this range must always exceed the maximum hazard during endowment. The overall pattern for this case has the general form shown in Figure 7.

8. FORMULATING A POPULATION-LEVEL THEORY

Although we insisted that comparisons of hazards make substantive sense only within organizational populations, to this point we have modeled the mortality process only at the organizational level. We next show that the new logic allows organization-level arguments to be aggregated meaningfully to the population level when certain uniformity premises hold as causal stories.[18]

Suppose that we treat the normal ages of ending of endowment and of onset of obsolescence as population characteristics and we define the relevant population parameters.[19] As in the organization-level theory, we do this in two steps. First, we define properties at the population level. These properties state the conditions that must be satisfied for a population to have normal ages of ending of endowment and onset of obsolescence.

Definition F$_4$.1: Common ages of ending of initial endowment and of onset of obsolescence.

1. $\forall p[\mathfrak{N}o[(o \Subset p) \rightarrow \{\forall t[(\epsilon_{o,p}(t) > 0) \leftrightarrow (\alpha_{o,p}(t) < \xi_p)]\}] \longleftrightarrow EE_p(\xi_p)];$
2. $\forall p[\mathfrak{N}o[(o \Subset p) \rightarrow \{\forall t[(\omega_{o,p}(t) > 0) \leftrightarrow (\alpha_{o,p}(t) > \sigma_p)]\}] \longleftrightarrow OB_p(\sigma_p)].$

Notice that these sentences, unlike those in the other theory fragments, combine classical and nonmonotonic quantification. It might be useful to supply a read for the first formula: For every population, the (population-specific) parameter ξ_p is the normal age of ending of endowment, $EE_p(\xi_p)$, if it is normally the case that every organization in the population is endowed until age ξ_p.[20]

We complete the construction of this part of the argument by introducing causal stories holding that organizational populations normally possess the property of uniform endowment and the onset of obsolescence.

Premise F$_4$.1: Organizational populations normally have a common age of ending of endowment and a common age of onset of poor alignment.

$$\mathfrak{N}p[P(p) \longrightarrow \{\exists \xi_p[EE_p(\xi_p) \wedge \exists \sigma_p[OB_p(\sigma_p)]]\}].$$

---

[18] We are using the term *population* here loosely to specify the unit within which the uniformity holds. It might be an organizational population in the formal sense (Pólos, Hannan, and Carroll 2002), or it might be a birth cohort, or some other unit.

[19] Of course, empirical research might be able to specify the sizes of endowments at the organizational level. In such a case, the more specific information should overrule the population-level default.

[20] Here the causal stories are those that justify treating a collection of organizations as a meaningful population.

Adding this definition and premise to the second unification yields theorems parallel to those in U_2 but expressed in terms of population parameters. This link allows us to link the unified theory (U_2) to the observed empirical patterns of age dependence in the diverse populations studied. Under specific conditions, the general picture reproduces the patterns of age-dependence found in empirical research, as can be seen by consulting Figure 7.

1.   If the organizations in a population lack endowments and occupy environments that change so gradually that obsolescence never strikes, then the default is never overridden: Age dependence is presumably uniformly negative.
2.   If the exhaustion of endowments is not completed within an observation period or obsolescence strikes before endowments are exhausted, then age dependence is presumably uniformly positive.
3.   If the organizations in a population are endowed and do not face obsolescence, then the mortality hazard presumably peaks in adolescence.
4.   If the organizations in a population are endowed and do face obsolescence at a time later than the ending of endowment, then the mortality hazard presumably has the age profile illustrated in Figure 7.

9. REFLECTIONS

Now after seeing how nonmonotonic logic applies in the context of theory construction, it is time to ask whether the new notion of the consequence relation changes our understanding of theory. It does not. Tarski's view of theory—a deductively closed system of sentences, where deductive closure means closure under the first-order notion of logical consequence—still applies.

The analysis presented in this paper did not deal with a theory in the Tarskian sense. Instead, it dealt with a theory in flux. And, just as a former dean is not a dean any longer, a theory in flux is not yet a Tarskian theory. Instead, it provides raw material for such a theory. Future research might provide evidence that would gainsay its present conclusions.

How can such a classical theory be built from this raw material? Suppose that enough high-quality empirical work clarified the conditions of occurrence of all the observed patterns of age dependence. Then one would likely feel tempted to declare that all the relevant facts are in hand. We would then want to construct a complete classical theory.

Nonmonotonic formalization of a theory in flux can be used to construct a Tarskian theory that is not contradicted by any known tendencies. Take all of the causal stories, restrict them to those domains where they were not overridden, and universally quantify them (with antecedents that provide the required restrictions). With this revision, all the derived expectations ("presumably implies" statements) turn into universally quantified—though highly restricted—theorems.

For example, suppose that a theory in flux had been frozen into a restricted classical theory after accommodating (only) considerations about the liability of newness and endowments—that is, at the second stage of the theory. The former causal stories $F_1.1$, $F_1.2$, and $F_2.1$ will then need to be reformulated as (constrained) universal sentences. The applicability domain of each process must be restricted to the age intervals in which it is not overridden. The result is a trio of restricted, but universally quantified, theorems that apply to the different relevant segments of the age domain. In other words, the frozen theory yields the pattern shown in Figure 7 as holding without exceptions. (Appendix B gives the details.) Since this process freezes the theory in flux into a theory proper, these new versions of what had been merely presumptions can freely be used in further derivations. Their inferential behavior follows first-order logic.

Partly contradictory arguments about age dependence in organizational mortality could be combined by means of a nonmonotonic logic to provide interesting (in part, unexpected) patterns. But extensive further research is needed before freezing a theory becomes a tempting possibility for a research program.

To regain consistency, the argument based on reliability/accountability has been restricted to ages above the endowment-protected youth of organizations. It is not at all obvious that this restriction is well motivated substantively. Strong intuition suggests the contrary: Reliability and accountability grows more in youth than in old age. So this frozen theory seems both less general and less tuned to substantive considerations than the nonmonotonic version.

To find a consistent way of unifying the arguments and avoiding contradiction of basic intuitions would require dependable knowledge of four functional forms (for all populations of organizations). How (exactly) does aging relate to reliability/accountability? How (exactly) does reliability/accountability influence the hazard? How (exactly) does aging relate to the level of endowment? How (exactly) does the level of endowment influence the hazard? As we emphasized in motivating our approach, the empirical research cannot yet deliver these functional forms.

In defining the outcome to be modeled, the hazard of mortality, we emphasized that the new logical machinery is well suited for modeling probabilistic phenomena. Indeed, when probabilistic constructs like the hazard are embedded in a nonmonotonic argument with its "presumably implies" and "normally" connectives, then a theory has a doubled representation of uncertainty. The underlying stochastic nature of the phenomenon gives rise to uncertainty about the timing of mortality events (given a specified hazard). The nonmonotonic reasoning admits uncertainty about what exactly might be the case for the hazard (given what is "normally" the case). Moreover, in our approach, arguments built on causal stories are to be treated as tentative, surely less informative than those built on universal quantification.

10. CONCLUSION

We have proposed a new approach to unifying fragments of theory programs undergoing development. This approach requires the use of some logical tools not yet deployed in sociology, as well as some innovation in shaping the tools themselves.

We tried to illustrate the potential value of these developments by applying them to a well-studied—yet still-recalcitrant—problem: age dependence in organizational mortality processes. Thus we confront a situation in which several reasonably well developed theory fragments have withstood an attempt to formulate a coherent single theory expressed in first-order logic (Hannan 1998). We took as our challenge the task of showing that representing the arguments with an appropriate nonmonotonic logic would succeed where the classical tools had not.

We claim that our approach has passed this test. We came up with a formalization that incorporates several theory fragments that could not be reconciled in formalizations based upon first-order logic. Moreover, we arrived at a consistent picture that surprised us. We concentrated on getting the local structure of the process right by concentrating on the specific arguments that applied to given phases of an organizational life course, and we did not expect a strongly consistent global structure to emerge. When we shift from a ground-level to a bird's-eye view, we see that the mortality hazard is higher in each later phase than in each earlier phase, despite the fact that the hazard does not rise monotonically within the phases. This unintended result seems pleasing, because much well-designed empirical research has begun to find such a global pattern.

APPENDIX A: LOGICAL SYMBOLS

Classical (Truth-functional) Connectives

$\neg$	Negation: The sentence ϕ is false just in case $\neg\phi$ is true
$\wedge$	Conjunction: $\phi \wedge \psi$ is true just in case ϕ is true and ψ is true
$\cup$	Disjunction: $\phi \cup \psi$ is true just in case ϕ is true and/or ψ is true
$\exists$	Existential quantifier: $\exists x$ is read as "for some object x"
$\forall$	Universal quantifier: $\forall x$ is read as "for every object x"
$\rightarrow$	Material implication: $\phi \rightarrow \psi$ is true just in case $(\phi \wedge \neg\psi)$ is false

Nonmontonic Connectives

$\mathfrak{N}$	Nonmonotonic "normally" quantifier: $\mathfrak{N}x$ reads as "for an object x it is normally the case (in the absence of more specific information to the contrary)"
$\mathfrak{P}$	Nonmonotonic "presumably" quantifier: $\mathfrak{P}x$ reads as "at the current stage of the theory, it is presumably the case for all objects x"

Languages

$\mathcal{L}_F$	Language of first-order logic
$\mathcal{L}_W$	Language of working theories
$\mathcal{L}_T$	Language of theory testing

Stage of a theory

W	Set of (still) possible worlds
C	Semantic representation of the causal stories in a theory
$\langle \mathbf{W}, \mathbf{C} \rangle$	Stage of a theory, an ordered pair of sets

Specificity Relation

$\mathcal{I}(\phi)$	Intension of the open formula ϕ, which gives, for every possible world, the objects that satisfy ϕ
$\sqsubseteq_\mathbf{W}$	$\mathcal{I}(\phi) \sqsubseteq_\mathbf{W} \mathcal{I}(\psi)$ means that $\mathcal{I}(\phi)$ is a subset of $\mathcal{I}(\psi)$ in every still-possible world

APPENDIX B: FREEZING THE FIRST UNIFICATION

Premise $F_1.1^*$: Reliability/accountability grows with age after endowment.

$$\forall o, p, t_1, t_2 [\{(o \Subset p) \wedge (\xi \leq \alpha_{o,p}(t_1) < \alpha_{o,p}(t_2)) \wedge EE_{o,p}(\xi)\}$$

$$\longrightarrow \{\rho_{o,p}(t_1) < \rho_{o,p}(t_2)\}].$$

This premise differs from Premise $F_1.1$ in two respects. Its variables are bound by a universal quantifier ($\forall$) instead of the generic quantifier; and the applicability domain is restricted to age intervals starting after ξ. The latter restriction comes from restricting the domain to the portion of the age range in which the process is not overruled. The next two frozen premises differ from their corresponding causal stories only in that their variables are bound by a universal quantifier instead of the generic quantifier.

Premise $F_1.2^*$: Higher reliability/accountability lowers the hazard.

$$\forall o, p, t_1, t_2 [\{(o \Subset p) \wedge (\rho_{o,p}(t_1) < \rho_{o,p}(t_2))\} \longrightarrow \{\mu_{o,p}(t_1) > \mu_{o,p}(t_2)\}].$$

Premise $F_2.1^*$: Before exhaustion, initial endowments decline with age.

$$\forall o, p, t_1, t_2 [\{(o \Subset p) \wedge (\alpha_{o,p}(t_1) < \alpha_{o,p}(t_2) < \xi) \wedge EE_{o,p}(\xi)\}$$

$$\longrightarrow \{\epsilon_{o,p}(t_1) > \epsilon_{o,p}(t_2) > 0\}].$$

We retain two strict (first-order) rules:

Premise $F_2.2$: A larger endowment provides stronger immunity.

Premise $F_2.3$: A stronger immunity lowers the hazard.

This reformulation yields three restricted versions of the theorems derived with our nonmonotonic logic. Although they are restricted, these frozen theorems are universal, holding without exception.

Theorem 1: Mortality hazards increase with age during endowment.

$$\forall o, p, t_1, t_2 [\{(o \in p) \wedge (\alpha_{o,p}(t_1) < \alpha_{o,p}(t_2) < \xi) \wedge EE_{o,p}(\xi)\}$$
$$\longrightarrow \{\mu_{o,p}(t_1) < \mu_{o,p}(t_2)\}].$$

Theorem 2: Mortality hazards increase over intervals that span the end of endowment.

$$\forall o, p, t_1, t_2 [\{(o \in p) \wedge (\alpha_{o,p}(t_1) < \xi \leq \alpha_{o,p}(t_2)) \wedge EE_{o,p}(\xi)\}$$
$$\longrightarrow \{\mu_{o,p}(t_1) < \mu_{o,p}(t_2)\}].$$

Theorem 3. Mortality hazards decline with age after the end of endowment.

$$\forall o, p, t_1, t_2 [\{(o \in p) \wedge (\xi \leq \alpha_{o,p}(t_1) < \alpha_{o,p}(t_2)) \wedge EE_{o,p}(\xi)\}$$
$$\longrightarrow \{\mu_{o,p}(t_1) > \mu_{o,p}(t_2)\}].$$

REFERENCES

Barron, David N. 1992. "An Ecological Analysis of the Dynamics of Financial Institutions in New York State, 1914–1934." Ph.D. dissertation, Cornell University.

Barron, David N., Elizabeth West, and Michael T. Hannan. 1994. "A Time to Grow and a Time to Die: Growth and Mortality of Credit Unions in New York, 1914–1990." *American Journal of Sociology* 100:381–421.

Barwise, Jon, and John Etchemendy. 1992. *The Language of First-Order Logic*, 3d ed. CSLI Lecture Notes No. 34. Chicago: University of Chicago Press.

Brewka, G., J. Dix, and K. Konolige. 1997. *Nonmonotonic Reasoning: An Overview.* CSLI Lecture Notes No. 73. Chicago: University of Chicago Press.

Carlson, Gregory N. 1977. *Reference to Kinds in English*. Ph.D. dissertation, University of Massachusetts, Amherst.

———. 1995. "Truth-Conditions of Generic Sentences: Two Contrasting Views." Pp. 224–37 in *The Generic Book,* edited by G. N. Carlson and F. J. Pelletier. Chicago: University of Chicago Press.

Carroll, Glenn R., and Michael T. Hannan. 1989. "Density Delay in the Evolution of Organizational Populations: A Model and Five Empirical Tests." *Administrative Science Quarterly* 34:411–30.

———. 2000. *The Demography of Corporations and Industries.* Princeton, NJ: Princeton University Press.

Descartes, René. 1897–1913. *Oeuvres de Descartes*, edited by C. Adam and P. Tannery. Paris: J. Vrin.

Diesing, Molly. 1995. "Bare Plural Subjects and the Stage/Individual Contrast." Pp. 107–154 in *The Generic Book,* edited by G. N. Carlson and F. J. Pelletier. Chicago: University of Chicago Press.

Dowty, David R., Robert E. Wall, and Stanley Peters. 1980. *Introduction to Montague Semantics.* Dordrecht, Netherlands: Kluwer Academic.

Freeman, John, Glenn R. Carroll, and Michael T. Hannan. 1983. "The Liability of Newness: Age Dependence in Organizational Death Rates." *American Sociological Review* 48:692–710.

Gamut, L. T. F. 1991. *Logic, Language and Meaning.* Vol. 2, *Intensional Logic and Logical Grammar.* Chicago: University of Chicago Press. [Gamut is a collective pseudonym for J. F. A. K. van Benthem, J. A. G. Groenendijk, D. H. J. de Jongh, M. J. B. Stokhof, and H. J. Verkuyl.]

Hannan, Michael T. 1998. "Rethinking Age Dependence in Organizational Mortality: Logical Formalizations." *American Journal of Sociology* 104:85–123.

Hannan, Michael T., and John Freeman. 1977. "The Population Ecology of Organizations." *American Journal of Sociology* 82:929–64.

———. 1984. "Structural Inertia and Organizational Change." *American Sociological Review* 49:149–64.

Kratzer, Angelika. 1995. "Stage-Level and Individual-Level Predicates." Pp. 125–75 in *The Generic Book,* edited by G. N. Carlson and F. J. Pelletier. Chicago: University of Chicago Press.

Krifka, Manfred, Francois Jeffrey Pelletier, Gregory N. Carlson, Alice ter Meulen, Gennaro Chierchia, and Godehard Link. 1995. "Genericity: An Introduction." Pp. 1–124 in *The Generic Book,* edited by G. N. Carlson and F. J. Pelletier. Chicago: University of Chicago Press.

McCarty, J. 1980. "Circumscription—a Form of Nonmonotonic Reasoning." *Artificial Intelligence and Logic Programming* 13:27–39.

Makinson, D. 1994. "General Nonmonotonic Logic." Pp. 35–110 in *Handbook of Logic in Artificial Intelligence and Logic Programming: Nonmonotonic Reasoning and Uncertain Reasoning*, Vol. 3, edited by D. M. Gabbay, C. J. Hogg, and J. A. Robinson. Oxford: Oxford University Press.

Péli, Gábor, László Pólos, and Michael T. Hannan. 2000. "Back to Inertia: Theoretical Implications of Alternative Styles of Logical Formalization." *Sociological Theory* 18:193–213.

Pólos, László, and Michael T. Hannan. 2000. "Reasoning with Partial Knowledge." Research Paper No. 1638, Graduate School of Business, Stanford University.

———. 2001. "Nonmonotonicity in Theory Building." Pp. 405–38 in *Dynamics of Organizations: Computational Modeling and Organization Theories,* edited by A. Lomi and E. Larsen. Cambridge, MA: AAAI Press/MIT Press.

Pólos, László, Michael T. Hannan, and Glenn R. Carroll. Forthcoming. "Foundations of a Theory of Social Forms." *Industrial and Corporate Change.*

Pólos, László, Michael T. Hannan, and Jaap Kamps. 1999. "Aging by Default." Pp. 207–19 in *Proceedings of the Fourth Dutch–German Workshop on Nonmonotonic Reasoning Techniques and Their Applications,* edited by H. Rott, C. Albert, G. Brewka, and C. Wittveen. Amsterdam: ILLC Scientific Publications.

Schubert, Lenhardt, and Francis J. Pelletier. 1988. "An Outlook on Generic Sentenc-es." Pp. 357–372 in *Genericity in Natural Language: Proceedings of the 1988 Tübingen Conference,* edited by M. Krifka. Tübingen, Germany: Universität Tübingen.

Stinchcombe, Arthur L. 1965. "Social Structure and Organizations." Pp. 142–93 in *Handbook of Organizations,* edited by J. G. March. Chicago: Rand McNally.

Thomason, Richmond H. 1988. "Theories of Nonmonotonicity and Natural Language Generics." Pp. 395–406 in *Genericity in Natural Language: Proceedings of the 1988 Tübingen Conference,* edited by M. Krifka. Tübingen, Germany: Universität Tübingen.

van Benthem, Johan F. A. K. 1996. "Logic and Argumentation Theory." In *Logic and Argumentation,* edited by J. van Benthem, S. van Eemereren, R. Grootendorst, and F. Veltman. Amsterdam: Royal Dutch Academy of Sciences.

Veltman, Frank. 1996. "Defaults in Update Semantics." *Journal of Philosophical Logic* 25:221–61.

5

A LOGICAL TOOLKIT FOR THEORY (RE)CONSTRUCTION

Jeroen Bruggeman*
Ivar Vermeulen*

The social sciences have achieved highly sophisticated methods for data collection and analysis, leading to increased control and tractability of scientific results. Meanwhile, methods for systematizing these results, as well as new ideas and hypotheses, into sociological theories have seen little progress, leaving most sociological arguments ambiguous and difficult to handle, and impairing cumulative theory development. Sociological theory, containing many valuable ideas and insights, deserves better than this. As a way out of the doldrums, this paper presents a systematic approach to computer-supported logical formalization, that is widely applicable to sociological theory and other declarative discourse. By increasing rigor and precision of sociological arguments, they become better accessible to critical investigation, thereby raising scientific debate to a new level. The merits of this approach are

We are grateful to Jaap Kamps and Gábor Péli for their comments on an earlier version, and to an anonymous reviewer for comments on a later version. Basic ideas for the heuristics presented were developed by László Pólos, Gábor Péli, Breanndán Ó Nualláin, Michael Masuch, Jaap Kamps, and the authors of this paper, who all worked at CCSOM, now called the *Applied Logic Laboratory*, in Amsterdam. CCSOM was supported from 1990 until 1995 by the Netherlands Organizations for Scientific Research through a PIONIER project awarded to Michael Masuch (#PGS50-334). Bruggeman did part of this work at the Rijksuniversiteit Groningen and at the Universiteit Twente. He can be contacted at the Department of Sociology and Anthropology, Universiteit van Amsterdam, Oudezijds Achterburgwal 185, 1012 DK Amsterdam, Netherlands, bruggeman@pscw.uva.nl.

Ivar Vermeulen is at ALL, UvA, Nieuwe Achtergracht 166, 1018 VW Amsterdam, ivar@ccsom.uva.nl.

*University of Amsterdam

183

*demonstrated by applying it to an actual fragment from the socio-
logical literature.*

The very first lesson that we have a right to demand that logic
shall teach us is how to make our ideas clear; and a most important one it is, depreciated only by minds who stand in need of it.
To know what we think, to be masters of our own meaning, will
make a solid foundation for great and weighty thought. It is most
easily learned by those whose ideas are meagre and restricted; and
far happier they than such as wallow helplessly in a rich mud of
conceptions.   —*C. S. Peirce, How to Make Our Ideas Clear*

1. INTRODUCTION

Social scientists communicate most of their ideas and findings in natural
language. Compared to everyday conversation, though, scientific discourse is more regulated. In relating ideas to the pertaining literature, for
example, and in analyzing empirical data and displaying empirical results,
authors of scientific publications commit to certain rules and procedures.
As a consequence, their findings are laid open to scrutiny, criticism, and
falsification by peers who can check for themselves the claims published.
These self-imposed mechanisms of control and tractability distinguish scientific discourse from other kinds of discourse.

The main assignments for most social scientists are to hypothesize
about social phenomena and to test their hypotheses empirically. Although
in game theory and some other fields, hypotheses are inferred through
mathematical derivations, most theoretical reasoning in the social sciences takes place in natural language. The upside is that nearly all are able
to understand the arguments made, or at least believe they can. The down-
side, however, is that the flexibility of natural language comes at a cost: It
is notoriously ambiguous, both conceptually and logically. Moreover, natural language has no clear-cut benchmarks with respect to soundness and
consistency. Consequently, a theoretical argument in natural language can
easily be misinterpreted, and the logical validity of such an argument can
be hard to verify, thereby challenging and sometimes violating the rules
of the game. The amount of ambiguity present in social science theory
would certainly not be tolerated if it would concern collecting data or
analyzing empirical findings. Imagine a world void of methods and statistics, in which the researcher is left to analyze and evaluate empirical phenomena only with common sense. Nevertheless, we seem to accept such a
state of affairs for our treasured theories.

In a number of recent publications, an argument has been made to use formal logic in conjunction with sophisticated computer tools, to represent and (re)construct sociological theory (Péli et al. 1994; Hannan 1998; Kamps and Pólos 1999). On the one hand, formal logic shares with mathematics rigor and precision. Moreover, it has clear-cut benchmarks for soundness and consistency. On the other hand, formal logic shares with natural language, to a large extent, its sentential structure. The latter makes it possible for a formalized argument to stay relatively close to its natural language counterpart, whereas mathematics often seems to represent an argument in an unrecognizable manner.

The most important reason to use formal logic is that it makes it possible to reflect on scientific reasoning systematically and rigorously.[1] Logic forces the user to disambiguate the logical structure of an argument, and to lay bare each argumentative step, thereby revealing loopholes (i.e., implicit assumptions), invalid inferences, and inconsistencies. The fact that in logic one can actually *prove* claims, by following a small number of clear-cut rules of inference, is an advantage over informal theorizing that can hardly be overestimated.[2] On top of that, logic makes it possible to infer new and sometimes unforeseen conclusions from established empirical facts and generalizations. If conclusions based on true assumptions are proved, they do not need empirical support in their own right and can be transferred immediately to the set of statements we know to be true about the world.

Furthermore, logic forces us to think more rigorously about the concepts that occur in an argument. Many concepts have different and conflicting denotations within a field of science, or even within one theory. Also, relations between concepts may be implicitly assumed but must be specified explicitly in order for an argument to go through.

For reducing conceptual as well as logical ambiguity, choices must be made. At least as important as a formal representation of an argument is the explicated knowledge and motivation for the choices made along

---

[1] Some argue that because logical calculi are generally limited to two values, true and false, mathematical equations have fewer limitations than do logical calculi (Freese 1980, p. 199). In a two-valued logic, however, one can use any mathematical function and relation, and one can reason about any mathematical equation. Moreover, just like logical statements, mathematical statements are either true or false.

[2] Although finding a proof can be an art, checking a proof object (i.e., a fully written down proof) is simple, and can be fully automated. In first-order logic, which we use for our formalizations, both proof finding and proof checking can be automated, as well as model generating to check consistency.

the way. Once these choices are documented, reviewers and readers who do not agree with certain propositions can trace back exactly the point where they think something might have gone wrong. Both formalization and its documented choices increase control and tractability of scientific discourse—already achieved for empirical research—and may catalyze scientific debate.

Not every argument made in the social sciences asks for rigorous logical scrutiny. Some arguments are simple and straightforward, and their logical validity is easy to establish. However, as domains described become more complex, arguments may also become more complex and harder to handle. Readers may get the feeling that there is something flawed about an argument but not be able to put a finger exactly on the troubling spot. Other readers may discuss a well-known theory with colleagues, only to discover that they had a completely different understanding of it all along. In such cases, a natural tendency is to thoroughly reinvestigate those parts of a publication that can be feasibly investigated—for example, the statistical evidence claimed to support a theory, and to draw one's own conclusions from there.

Social science theory needs to be taken more seriously than that. It should be taken for what it is supposed to be: explanations of social phenomena, cast in logically valid arguments. Theory should be more than a context that helps to interpret correlations found in a data set. We should start judging social science theory by its own merits, and we need a way to judge it.

This paper attempts to provide such a way. It presents a five-step approach to computer supported logical formalization. Our approach takes a scientific text containing an argument as a point of departure (but social theorists may take their own ideas instead), and helps to produce a formal, sound, and consistent theory as a point of termination. The latter is not a termination point for theory development, though. To the contrary, a formal representation of a theory is a stepping stone for comparison, further development, and integration of theory. In this respect, the use of formal logic can contribute significantly to the accumulation and growth of knowledge in the social sciences.[3]

Our five-step approach is designed to target formalization systematically. Each subsequent step has the output of its preceding step as an input, and for each step, a number of heuristics (i.e., tricks of the trade) is

---

[3] The field should then, of course, not focus on problems that are mere artifacts of formalization (Hansson 2000), as happens, for instance, in some fields of economics.

presented in this paper, that help to gain insight in, and understanding of, a theory, its logic, and its concepts. The first three steps in our approach, constituting a so-called *rational reconstruction*, focus on reducing logical and conceptual ambiguity, by (1) marking sentences in the text that capture the core theory, (2) analyzing and sharpening key concepts and phrases, and (3) axiomatizing informally with the aid of a conceptual model. If the rational reconstruction is done well, a (4) formalization in logic, which in turn is (5) formally tested by computer, is relatively straightforward.[4]

To illustrate the merits of our approach, we use an example from an actual social science theory. This example has the degree of ambiguity that is typical for the social sciences, and that makes a rational reconstruction difficult. The example is chosen to highlight the rational reconstruction part, since worked out examples of formal representations of sociological theories are readily available in recent literature (Péli et al. 1994; Péli 1997; Bruggeman 1997; Kamps and Masuch 1997; Péli and Masuch 1997; Hannan 1998; Kamps and Pólos 1999; Carroll and Hannan 2000).

In sum, we present a systematic, and documenting, approach to computer supported logical formalization, involving heuristics on the one hand, and software—freely available on the Web—on the other. After further motivating and explicating our five-step approach in Sections 2 and 3, we apply it to a sociological example in Section 4. In Section 4, we also treat the application of specific software—i.e., a theorem prover and a model generator. The heuristics are dispersed over Sections 2, 3, and 4. The paper ends with a discussion and conclusions in Section 5.

Although this paper can be read by social scientists with no background in formal logic, those who themselves want to formalize should

---

[4]The heuristics we use are from or inspired by mathematics (Pólya 1945), logic (Tarski 1941; Frege 1961; Quine 1986; Hodges 1998; Andréka et al. 1998b), philosophy (Popper 1959; Quine 1961; Hempel 1966; Lakatos 1976), economics (Debreu 1959), game theory (Farquharson 1969), linguistics (Gamut 1991, Van Benthem 1994), computer science (Wos 1996), artificial intelligence (Kamps 1998; Kamps 1999a, Kamps 1999b), social science (Simon 1954; Coleman 1964; Blalock 1969), psychology (De Groot 1961), biology (Woodger 1937), and last but not least from the formalization projects at CCSOM (see acknowledgments at the beginning of this chapter). The sequence of our formalization steps is similar to approaches in computer science (Groenboom et al. 1996) and computer simulation in social science (Sastry 1997). Ideas to infer and prove theorems computationally date back centuries (Gardner 1983), although currently used theory (Beth 1962; Feigenbaum and Feldman 1963) and well-developed software are more recent (Wos et al. 1991). Ideas for formalization originate in logical positivism (Ayer 1959; Neurath 1970), and the term rational reconstruction (*rationale Nachkonstruktion*) as we use it is due to Carnap (1928).

acquire some knowledge of set theory (Halmos 1960; Enderton 1977) and logic (Enderton 1972; Barwise and Etchemendy 1999), as well as in-depth knowledge of the theory they want to formalize; they should then acquire as much experience as needed in formalization.

2. RATIONAL RECONSTRUCTION

In the social sciences, texts presenting theory have complex arguments stated in natural language, sometimes interspersed with graphics or mathematics. A frequently occurring problem is to find theory in these texts, and to distinguish theory from auxiliary parts, like examples, metaphors, analogies, summaries of the work of predecessors, empirical issues, motivations, and the like. Furthermore, texts are frequently ambiguous and their arguments may have loopholes. A rational reconstruction focuses on these problems.

2.1. *Step 1: Marking the Core Theory*

To extrapolate theory from a text, one has to know what to look for. As a benchmark, let us look at theories represented in logic. A formal theory is a set of sentences in a given formal language with an inference system; the set of sentences is "closed" under logical deduction and conclusions are validly inferred from premises according to the rules of inference.[5] This somewhat simple definition of theory, discarding intended domain, not to mention empirical and relevance criteria, has been advocated in social science by Homans (1967, 1980), among others, and suits our practical purpose fine. An important reason to choose formal logic and its definitions is that in natural language there are no precise benchmarks either for theory or for logical properties like soundness and consistency.

As a heuristic to find theory in a text under investigation, and following the definition of theory, we focus on the main claims or conclusions, and subsequently on their supportive arguments. These arguments branch "upward" until no further support for the conclusion, or for intermediate conclusions, can be found in the text. The limiting case

[5] For a formal definition, we refer to the technical literature (Hodges 1983; Van Dalen 1994; Van Benthem and Ter Meulen 1997). A more sophisticated view on theory, taking the dynamics of theory development into account, is in the writings of the structuralist approach (Balzer et al. 1987). See van Benthem (1982) for a broader perspective on formal theory.

is a statement without supportive argument—i.e., an argumentative "tree" consisting of only one node.

The claims and supportive arguments taken together may be considered a relevant set of sentences for a formalization attempt, and we see it as the *core theory*. The first step in our approach, then, is to mark the sentences belonging to this core theory (Fisher 1988). The remainder of the text is important too, because it indicates how the core theory should be interpreted.[6] A list of sentences quoted literally from the text is the output of step 1 of our approach. Along with this output, it is worthwhile to write down questions about the text on first or second reading, when looking at it with a fresh eye, and to see if later in the formalization process they can be answered. For theory builders, it is obvious which shortcuts they can make in step 1.

Posing questions to a core theory, or to a text at large, usually points out a great deal of ambiguity. Ambiguity leads to a combinatorial explosion of readings, as our example in Section 4 will show. This is fine for poetry but dangerous for scientific theories. "The implication is clear: those of us doing verbal theory in sociology need to get beyond ancestor worship and political posturing and begin the hard work of making our ideas clear enough to profit from formalization" (Kiser 1997, p. 154). We distinguish two kinds of ambiguity: conceptual, to be dealt with in step 2, and logical, to be addressed in step 3.

2.2. *Step 2: Analyzing key concepts*

To prevent a plethora of readings from a set of sentences, the key concepts and phrases should be disambiguated. Analyzing and sharpening key concepts in the core theory is the second step in our approach. For each concept (or phrase) the formalizer must find out what the objects are, what the concept refers to, what properties the objects have, and in what relations they stand. "Physical objects are postulated entities which round out and simplify our account of the flux of experience" (Quine 1961), which can also be said about sociological objects; they are not analyzed beyond the conceptualization in question. To paraphrase a well–known example: If we want to explain that Socrates is mortal, and we know that men are mortal, it helps to know the fact that Socrates is a member of the set of

---

[6]In some texts, one or a few instances (i.e., examples) of an intended theory are described in detail, but it is left to the reader to find the appropriate generalizations (Plato 1987). In some other texts, the intended theory is to be distilled from analogies or metaphors.

men. The facts that Socrates lived in Athens in the 5th century B.C. and that his wife had a quick temper can remain unexplored.

Elaborations of concepts can sometimes be found in the source text, and in other cases the reader is thrown back on other resources. Recourse may be taken to other writings of the same authors, to the authors in person, to standard textbooks, or to accepted wisdom in that particular branch of science. Furthermore, looking for relations between key concepts, which can be tacit in the source text, can yield important additional information to reconstruct an argument.

The output of step 2 is a "dictionary" of key concepts. Along with disambiguation, a dictionary should increase the parsimony of the theory by relating concepts to each other, if possible. The formalizer should try to define as many possible concepts in terms of as few as possible "primitive" (i.e, undefined) concepts. In order to decide whether or not a concept can be left undefined, the following can be applied as a rule of thumb: Within the set of undefined concepts, no concept should be a synonym, an element of, or a subset of another concept in the set.

A dictionary reduces conceptual ambiguity, but it does not illuminate the logical structure of the core theory. One wonders if conclusions are sufficiently supported, or if there are tacit background assumptions or flaws in the argument, and if there are redundant assumptions that may be deleted.

2.3. *Step 3: Informal axiomatization*

In the third step, the line of argumentation is analyzed. The goal is to represent the core theory as a set of relatively simple sentences, with a clear logical structure. To achieve soundness, the sentences in a core theory should match each other, by allowing synonymous concepts and phrases to match. Therefore frivolous requests for stylistic variation should be temporarily suspended, and the concepts as defined in the dictionary should be implemented all through the core theory. Then, complex sentences of the core theory are broken up into simpler ones.[7] If the sentences describe certain related events (or changes), as explanatory theories do, the logical structure of each individual sentence can be clarified by taking the events

---

[7] On the one hand, oversimplification should be avoided when discourse is disambiguated, but on the other hand "formal theories can support delicate structures that would be much more difficult to uphold and handle in the less unambiguous setting of an informal language" (Hansson 2000, p. 166).

(or changes) described in the sentence, and connecting them explicitly by the logical connectives ("... *and* ...", "... *or* ...", "*if* ... *then* ...", and "... *if and only if* ..."; furthermore, there is the logical negation, "it is *not* the case that ...").

When logically relating the events, usually logical ambiguity shows up, and sometimes a great deal of it.[8] Contrary to the problem of conceptual ambiguity, the problem of logical ambiguity has received little attention in the social sciences, whereas even in relatively simple sentences, common sense "logical" thinking may easily fall short (Young 1988). To appreciate the difficulties posed by logical ambiguity, one should realize that for n events described in a core theory, $2^{(2^n)}$ logical sentences can be formed—if the discursive theory does not impose restrictions (see Appendix A). So if a sentence describes three events, not clearly related by the author, the formalizer has to choose the representation that best covers the intended meaning of the original sentence out of $2^{(2^3)} = 256$ possible readings.

An important category of mistakes due to logical ambiguity is confusing a causal and a conditional (i.e., "if ... then ...") statement, or confusing the latter and "when ... then ..." statements. A logical consequent and a causal consequence are not necessarily related, and a logical implication does not necessarily describe a sequence of events.[9] Section 3 will present a more systematic treatment of logical ambiguity.

Once logical ambiguities have been resolved, or the number of alternatives reduced to a feasible number, then for each resulting sentence, its role in the argument is tagged. These roles can be a premise or a conclusion. A major conclusion is called a theorem, an intermediate conclusion a lemma. Premises can be assumption or definition. If a background assumption is added to fill a loophole in the argument, it is a premise too.

To keep track of the logical relations between the premises and conclusions, and to spot gaps in the argument where one expects relations, a diagram (or any other model; Spencer Brown, pp. 5–14) is a use-

---

[8] According to Popper (1959), weak (i.e., permissive) assumptions are to be preferred above stronger (i.e., more prohibiting) versions of the same assumptions, and strong theorems are to be preferred above weak ones, in order to increase the explanatory power of the theory. Following Popper's argument, those readings should be preferred that contribute to the explanatory power of the theory.

[9] "When ... then ..." can be regarded as a conditional statement restricted to a time point or interval. If for all time points t it holds that *if A at t, then B at t*, we can also say *when A then B*.

ful device. If loopholes in the argument show up in the diagram, the sources for filling them are the same as for the concepts in the previous step.

The modified core theory plus added background knowledge and missing assumptions forms the informal axiomatization, the output of step 3, which completes the rational reconstruction. This part is far more difficult than the formalization proper, and it requires the inventiveness and imagination of the formalizer to make appropriate and well-argued decisions in the reconstruction.

A rational reconstruction might appear to be firm ground to evaluate soundness and consistency, in particular with the aid of a conceptual model. Formalizations of several social science theories have pointed out, however, that informal scientific arguments may exhibit logical flaws and loopholes even after a rational reconstruction.

3. FORMALIZATION

To overcome the shortcomings of informal theory, the set of sentences that resulted from the rational reconstruction is represented in formal logic, and the formal representation is tested for logical properties.

3.1. *Step 4: Formalization Proper*

For formalization, it is best to use a logic as simple as possible. Standard logic—i.e., first-order logic (Hodges 1983)—turned out to be strong enough in all cases we are familiar with and is intuitively straightforward, and there exists useful and well tested software for it (see step 5). Although probably most scientific theories can be formalized in first-order logic (Quine 1990, p. 158), sometimes other logics can be more convenient—for instance, to express intentionality or belief revision (Gabbay and Guenthner 1989; Van Benthem and Ter Meulen 1997). If a more sophisticated logic is chosen, the advantages of intuitive tractability and computer support go by the board, while (tacit) ontological assumptions might slip in. Moreover, the purpose of logical formalization should be to increase comprehension, not to create complexity for its own sake. If standard logic does not seem to work, it is best to consult an expert logician first. We have seen several novices blaming standard logic for their own misunderstandings of it, and for their ill-performed rational reconstructions too. For examples of theories from various disciplines represented in first-order logic, see Kyburg (1968).

3.2. *Step 5: Formal Testing*

When all statements of the core theory are represented formally, attempts should be made to prove the theorem candidates. Proving by hand helps to achieve a higher level of understanding of the theory and its logical structure, and logical problems can be discovered and repaired—in a process that may be briefly put, "improving by proving" (Lakatos 1976, p. 37). But first the formal representation should be consistent. The reason for this order is that (in standard logic) from falsehood everything follows. An inconsistent theory is therefore automatically sound, but only those theorem candidates ought to be valid that follow from a consistent set of premises.

If a theory is inconsistent—i.e., if it says that both ϕ and not-ϕ are true—it cannot describe any possible state of affairs in the world, and cannot have a model (an instance of the theory) too (Chang and Keisler 1990).[10] This also means that an inconsistent theory can empirically be neither supported nor rejected, and empirical research is futile. Since the target theory should be consistent, one has to show that it has at least one model in which all sentences are true. As a matter of fact, to show that there is a model for the set of premises is sufficient, because then also the premises and the statements that logically follow from the premises have a model, due to the completeness of standard logic (Chang and Keisler 1990).

For first-order logic, a computer can evaluate soundness and consistency, and avoid human error. To produce a formal model of a theory, one can use an automated model generator, like MACE,[11] and let it run on the set of premises. MACE will try to construct a model for the set of premises by assigning objects to variables and functions, and by assigning truth values to relations. The user should let MACE look for simple models first—that is, models with as few as possible objects. If MACE fails, models with more objects should be sought after, which increases computational complexity considerably, though.

It is important to stress that logical formalization in most cases cannot demonstrate the inconsistency of a social science text, only that some readings of an ambiguous text are inconsistent. The appropriate action

---

[10] For simple examples of models of theories, see any introduction to logic.

[11] Both automated model generator MACE and automated theorem prover OTTER can be downloaded from http://www-unix.mcs.anl.gov/AR/otter/.

after a failed consistency–check is always to reconsider one's formalization, rather than rejecting the original theory. Formalizing, then, is not
establishing the ultimate reading but trying to establish a well-argued reading, thereby making choices explicit, facilitating empirical testing, and
raising the level of discussion (Suppes 1968).

One can test the derivability or soundness of theorems using an
automated theorem prover, like OTTER (Wos et al. 1991). The theorem
prover is given a set of (noncontradictory) premises, and the negation of
the theorem to be proved. If the theorem prover finds a contradiction, then
the negated theorem is false. (*Ergo*: The theorem is true.) Again, if this
test fails, the formalizers may have to backtrack to earlier steps, or may
have to repair their own mistakes.

A theorem prover does not only tell whether or not a theorem can
be proven, it actually gives a formal proof (although hard to read from the
output file). Using this information, the formalizer can see which theorems build upon which premises, which in turn elucidates the argumentative structure of the theory. Moreover, it may turn out that in the derivation
of the theorems, certain premises have remained unused. For parsimony,
they may be omitted from the formal representation.

Finally, a theorem prover can give valuable information regarding
consistency in cases where for reasons of computational complexity,
MACE is not able to produce a model. This can be done by attempting to
derive a nonsensical theorem, of which one is sure that it should not follow from the premises—for example, $\forall x \, Nonsense(x)$, which means, for
all x it holds that x is nonsense. If the proof attempt succeeds, the set of
premises in all likelihood is inconsistent.

3.3. *New Results*

If the theory is consistent and sound, then it makes sense to test it empirically. Although empirical testing is beyond the scope of this paper, it is
related to formalization in at least two ways. First, operationalization
should be facilitated by the conceptual clarity provided by step 2. Second,
the conceptual model, or another intermediate result in the formalization
process, may suggest new theorems. These new theorem candidates can
also be formalized and formally tested, and the current theory can be
extended if the new theorems are formally true. Moreover, these extensions of the theory are additional input for empirical research, or may
support formerly unexplained empirical findings.

When presenting formal results to an audience untrained in reading formulas, a summary in natural language is helpful, and an enigmatic style of presentations is always to be avoided (Hansson 2000). In our formalization papers, we also accompanied each formula with an English phrase that captures its essence.

4. THE FIVE-STEP APPROACH AT WORK

To illustrate our five-step approach, we use an example sentence. Any declarative sentence would do, but we draw from our experience in organizational ecology (Carroll and Hannan 2000).[12] In this particular theory, social organizations are seen as inert, which means that most of them cannot adapt readily and in a timely fashion to their environment (Hannan and Freeman 1984). Organizational ecology studies the dynamics of populations of organizations from a Darwinian selection perspective.

4.1. *Marking the Core Theory*

In resource partitioning theory, an important part of organizational ecology, we had seven sentences in the core theory, of which the first— quoted literally from the source text (Carroll and Hannan 1995, p. 216)— says the following:

> Early in these markets, when the arena is crowded, most
> firms vie for the largest possible resource base.

One may come up with several questions when reading the sentence: What is the state of affairs "early" in these markets? What is a "market" (a set of firms, a set of resources, or both, or perhaps something else)? What is an "arena" (perhaps a synonym of market)? What does "crowding" mean (perhaps strong competition)? Does crowding have an ordering relation (nominal, ordinal, interval, ratio)? How many is "most" with respect to the number of firms that do not "vie for the largest possible resource base"? What do the latter firms do? What makes a resource base the "largest pos-

---

[12] Although we use a sentence from organizational ecology as a working example, this paper is intended neither to criticize nor to contribute to this theory. A fully worked out formalization of this theory fragment can be found in Vermeulen and Bruggeman 2001.

sible" (limited competencies, the number or size of competing organizations, the limited amount of available resources, or all of these factors)?

Without a great deal of effort, to all of these questions we found
several plausible answers. These answers amounted to 48 conceptually
different readings of the phrase "most firms vie for the largest possible
resource base," which by no means exhaust all possible readings (see
Appendix A). A more economic way to deal with the core theory is to pin
down the meaning of key concepts and phrases first, rather than studying
all these different readings at length.

Although biologically trained formalizers might feel tempted to
apply differential equations to model population dynamics in general, and
resource partitioning theory in particular, we will not. Our aim is to stay
as close as possible to the source text, whereas introducing mathematical
models from another discipline also brings in background assumptions
that are possibly not supported by the authors of our source text. New
theory construction, inspired by but not based upon a source text, is a
different enterprise than pursued in this case study.

4.2. *Analyzing Key Concepts*

In sharpening the key concepts that occur in the example sentence, we use
additional information from the source text and related writings in organizational ecology. Each population is associated with a *resource base*, a
set of resources. Individual firms tap their resources from subsets of the
resource base. These subsets are called *niches*.[13] The extent to which the
niches of two firms overlap (i.e., between 0 to 100 percent of common
resources for which they compete) determines the strength of the *competition* between these firms. In Figure 1, two organizations, A and B, compete for resources in the same resource base.

A population of firms in the domain of resource partitioning theory
contains *generalist* and *specialist* firms. Organizations that appeal to a
wide range of resources are defined as generalist organizations. In the
example sentence, "most firms vie for the largest possible resource base."
From this we opt for the reading that "early in these markets" most organizations are generalist. As there is no information with regard to the
ratio of generalist and specialist organizations, we say only that at the

---

[13] For the example here, we do not need to digress into the distinction often
made between fundamental and realized niches.

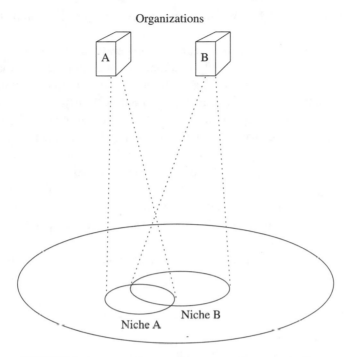

FIGURE 1. A resource base and two competing organizations.

"early" time, the population contains more generalist organizations than specialist organizations.

The source text does not provide definitions of the concepts of market, arena, and crowding. In a paper that has a coauthor in common with the source text, we found a mathematical definition for crowding of a set of resources by firms. In our example sentence, the arena is crowded, and we inferred that arena denotes a set of resources from which firms tap. In other words, arena and resource base are synonymous. To keep the example simple, we do not implement the mathematical definition here, but just say that "early in these markets" crowding has the value "high."

In the last phrase of our example sentence ("most firms vie for the largest possible resource base"), the concept of resource base is used as a synonym of organizational niche.

The text states that the theory of resource partitioning applies to certain kinds of markets, characterized by economies of scale and several other boundary conditions. The concept of market thus appears to denote those parts of the universe where the authors of resource partitioning theory intend it to apply.

The temporal reference "early" is generally a relative one. For a point in time to qualify as "early in a market," it should be later than the market's beginning, and early relative to other points in time for which we know the market to exist. So, in order to define "early," we could first define some fixed time point, and use it to define the relative time point "early." On the other hand, "early" is the earliest mentioned time in the source text, as it is the point at which the process of resource partitioning starts. Before this time nothing of relevance to the process of resource partitioning happens. Because our formalization effort aims at formalizing the theory of resource partitioning, rather than market dynamics in general, we choose the beginning to be fixed, not relative, and we call it t_0, the starting point.

With regard to the example sentence, our dictionary looks as follows:

Dictionary

- **early in these markets:** starting point (t_0)
- **arena:** resource base
- **crowded:** crowding is high
- **resource base:** (here) organizational niche
- **firm that vies for the largest possible resource base:** generalist
- **most firms vie for the largest possible resource base:** there are more generalists than specialists in the population

We now substitute the dictionary in the example sentence:

> At t_0, when crowding of the resource base is high, there are more generalists than specialists in the population.

4.3. Informal Axiomatization

In the third step, the structure of argument is investigated. The logical structure of the example sentence is by no means clear. Consider the following four plausible readings of the sentence out of a much larger number (see Appendix A):

1. **If** it is t_0 **and** crowding of the resource base is high, **then** there are more generalists than specialists in the population.
2. **If** it is t_0 **and** there are more generalists than specialists in the population, **then** crowding of the resource base is high.
3. **If** it is t_0, **then both** crowding of the resource base is high **and** there are more generalists than specialists in the population.
4. It is t_0 **if and only if** both crowding of the resource base is high **and** there are more generalists than specialists in the population.

In cases of logical ambiguity, the sentence in question, the other core sentences, or the remainder of the text may restrict the number of readings.

In addition to the source text, we may investigate the different readings systematically by using propositional logic. Although this logic is generally too simplistic to well represent scientific theories, it is precisely its simplicity that makes it a helpful tool in the rational reconstruction.

We first draw a table that lists all possible states of affairs that might occur with respect to the events (propositions) described in the example statement. Next, we apply Popper's view that a statement can only add information to a theory if it is falsifiable by some state(s) of affairs. If no state of affairs can falsify a statement, the statement is a tautology, and should be omitted from the theory.

Our example statement is falsified by states of affairs 2 to 4 (marked with an **F** in Table 1). On the basis of Table 1, there is a simple procedure

TABLE 1
Falsifying States of Affairs for the Example Sentence

	it is t_0	crowding [...] is high	[...] more gen's than spec's [...]	
1.	true	true	true	
2.	true	true	false	**F**
3.	true	false	true	**F**
4.	true	false	false	**F**
5.	false	true	true	
6.	false	true	false	
7.	false	false	true	
8.	false	false	false	

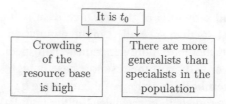

FIGURE 2. Conceptual model for the example sentence.

(Gamut 1991, p. 56) to arrive at a corresponding logical statement that is falsified in exactly these three cases. This statement corresponds to reading 4 above.

> If it is t_0 then both crowding of the resource base is high and there are more generalists than specialists in the population.

In parallel to the informal axiomatization, a diagram or conceptual model depicting implicative logical relations between events as described by the premises often proves to be useful. Theorems and lemmas can be informally checked by tracing the implicative arrows backward, from (desired) outcomes to their premises.

In a diagram (Figure 2) depicting the logical structure of our one-sentence theory, the events are boxed, while arrows connecting boxes indicate implicative relations. Note again that logical relations may not coincide with causal relations or sequences of events.[14] After analyzing the logic of the individual statements in the argument, one has to look at the logical relations between the statements, which goes beyond our one-sentence example.

4.4. *Formalization Proper*

The sentence that resulted from the rational reconstruction is now represented in first-order logic (see Appendix B). First-order logic has symbols for constants, functions, and relations that users may tailor to their needs.

---

[14] In this specific case, the informal definition of "when ... then ..." given in footnote 9 would actually allow us to use "when ... then..." instead of "if ... then ...," because the antecedent and the consequent are both at the same time.

In addition to these symbols, there are variables, two quantifiers, $\forall$ (for all) and $\exists$ (there exists), and five logical connectives, $\wedge$ (and), $\vee$ (or), $\rightarrow$ (if ... , then ...), $\leftrightarrow$ (if and only if), and $\neg$(not).

There are no general rules for representing informal sentences in formal logic. Only small fragments of natural language have been formalized (Van Benthem and Ter Meulen 1997). Furthermore, the representation of events described in a statement can range from one simple predicate to complicated subsentences. Only practice and trial and error can guide the formalizer's decisions. In our example sentence, the translation is rather straightforward.

We use a one-place relation constant SP to indicate the starting point, and a two-place relation constant RB to denote the resource base at a time. The two-place function symbol cr denotes the level of crowding of a resource base at a time. The relation symbol $High$ has one argument, and its meaning is obvious. Two one-place function symbols, n_g and n_s, denote the number of generalist firms and specialist firms in the population at a time, respectively. For the "larger than" relation, the binary relation symbol $>$ is used.

Assumption: *If it is t_0, then both crowding of the resource base is high and there are more generalists than specialists in the population.*

$$\forall t, r \quad [SP(t) \wedge RB(t, r)] \rightarrow [High(cr(r, t)) \wedge (n_g(t) > n_s(t))]$$

Read: For all t and r, it holds that if t is the starting point and r is the resource base at t, then the crowding of r at t is high and the number of generalists at t is higher than the number of specialists at t.

4.5. Formal Testing

Logical properties of the formal representation of the theory can now be tested. We show how consistency and soundness can be tested by computer.

4.5.1. Automated model generating

To check the consistency of the formal representation, we invoke MACE. For MACE input, which is the same as OTTER's, see Section 4.5.2. To see how MACE output should be read, consider Table 2, a possible interpretation of the $>$ relation in a model of cardinality 2 (*i.e.*, 2 elements).

TABLE 2
(False) Interpretation
of > by MACE

>	0	1
0	F	T
1	F	T

The model has two objects, named 0 and 1.[15] Table 2 states that $0 > 1$ and $1 > 1$ are true, and the other two combinations are false. Clearly, MACE does not know how to interpret the $>$ relation symbol. To solve this problem, three meaning postulates are added that accurately define the properties of $>$:

MP 1: $\forall xy \quad \neg(x > x)$

Read: For all x, it holds that it is not the case that $x > x$ (irreflexivity).

MP 2: $\forall xy \quad (x > y) \rightarrow \neg(y > x)$

Read: For all x and y, it holds that if $x > y$, then it is not the case that $y > x$ (asymmetry).

MP 3: $\forall xyz \quad [(x > y) \wedge (y > z)] \rightarrow (x > z)$

Read: For all x, y, and z, it holds that if $x > y$ and $y > z$, then $x > z$ (transitivity).

Once these meaning postulates are added, the first model that MACE comes up with is one shown in Table 3. Unfortunately, in this model there is no starting point or resource base, crowding is not high, and there are not more generalists than specialists at any time. In this situation, wherein the antecedent of the statement is false, the statement is vacuously true. A relevant, nontrivial model is wanted, not just any model. To this aim, we have to assume that there actually exists a starting point in the model as

---

[15]Note that in MACE, 0 and 1 are names for objects that might just as well have been called Abbott and Costello. In contrast to the *numbers* 0 and 1, the *names* 0 and 1 are not related by, for example, an ordering relation.

TABLE 3
Irrelevant Model of the Example Sentence by MACE

>	0	1		SP	0	1		RB	0	1		High	0	1		cr	0	1
0	F	F			F	F		0	F	F			F	F		0	0	0
1	T	F						1	F	F						1	0	0

ns	0	1		ng	0	1
	0	1			0	1

well as a resource base. We do this by adding the following background assumption to the theory:

$$\textbf{BA: } \exists tr \quad SP(t) \wedge RB(t,r)$$

Read: There exist a t and an r, such that t is the starting point of resource partitioning and r is the resource base at t.

With this formula added, one of the models MACE comes up with is one shown in Table 4. In this model, if t is assigned to object 0, then t is the starting point; r is the resource base at $t = 0$ if it is assigned to object 1. Furthermore, $cr(r,t)$ is 0, and 0 is *High*; $n_g(0)$ is 1, and $n_s(0)$ is 0, hence $n_g(0) > n_s(0)$.

Proving consistency for a single or few sentences, as we did in this example, is generally not hard. In this case, MACE provided 1536 models. If more sentences are added to the theory, the number of possible models with the same (low) cardinality usually decreases, and consistency may get harder to prove. If within a given cardinality no models are found, the formalizer switches to a higher cardinality and has MACE try to find models there.

TABLE 4
Relevant Model of the Example Sentence by MACE

>	0	1		SP	0	1		RB	0	1		High	0	1		cr	0	1
0	F	F			T	F		0	F	T			T	T		0	0	0
1	T	F						1	F	F						1	0	0

ng	0	1		ns	0	1
	1	0			0	0

It is possible that the tested theory, or a particular reading of it, is consistent but that the task of model generating is too complex for the computer. To stay on the safe side, one may then attempt to demonstrate inconsistency directly, which is a simple task for a computer if the theory at hand is inconsistent indeed. For this purpose, an automated theorem prover is well suited.

4.5.2. *Automated Theorem Proving*

Once one or more nontrivial models of a theory are found, the formalizer may call upon OTTER to check the theory's soundness. The theorem prover is given a consistent set of premises and the negation of a theorem candidate. If the theorem prover finds the negated theorem candidate to be inconsistent with the set of premises, the theorem is sound.

Although logic is the science of reasoning, in a one sentence example theory not much reasoning is going on.[16] To demonstrate how OTTER can be used, we give it our example statement, add the antecedent of this statement to the set of premises, and have OTTER derive the consequent. After going through this kindergarten example, readers may try for themselves to have OTTER derive more exciting theorems from a different set of premises.

In OTTER, the logical conjunction ($\land$) is represented by &, the implication ($\rightarrow$) by -> and the negation ($\neg$) by -. The quantifiers ($\forall$ and $\exists$) are represented by `all` and `exists`, respectively.

OTTER's input looks as follows:

```
% Meaning Postulate 1
all x (-(x > x)).
% Meaning Postulate 2
all x y ((x > y) -> -(y > x)).
% Meaning Postulate 3
all x y z ( ((x > y) & (y > z)) -> (x > z) ).


% Background Assumption
exists t r ( SP(t) & RB(t,r) ).
```

---

[16] Formal inferencing, in contrast to rational reconstruction, is already treated in the literature extensively. For sociological examples, see for instance (Péli et al. 1994; Péli 1997; Péli and Masuch 1997; Kamps Pólos 1999).

```
% Assumption
all t r ((SP(t) & RB(t,r)) -> (High(cr(r, t)) & (n_g(t) >
n_s(t))))).
```

```
% Negation of conclusion
- (exists t, r ( High(cr(r,t)) & (n_g(t) > n_s(t)) )).
```

The first three lines of the input are the meaning postulates that describe the properties of symbol $>$. The fourth line is the background assumption stating that there actually is a t which is the starting point and that at this starting point r is the resource base. The fifth line is the OTTER representation of the example statement, and the last line is the negation of the conclusion that crowding at t is high and there are more generalists than specialists.

OTTER establishes a proof in less than 0.01 seconds, and gives the following output:

```
-----> EMPTY CLAUSE at 0.00 sec ----> 12 [hyper,10,6,11]
$F.
```

```
Length of proof is 2. Level of proof is 1.
```

```
---------------- PROOF ----------------
```

```
4 [] -SP(x)| -RB(x,y)|High(cr(y,x)).
5 [] -SP(x)| -RB(x,y)|n_g(x) > n_s(x).
6 [] -High(cr(x,y))| -(n_g(y) > n_s(y)).
8 [] SP($c3).
9 [] RB($c3,$c2).
10 [hyper,9,5,8] n_g($c3) > n_s($c3).
11 [hyper,9,4,8] High(cr($c2,$c3)).
12 [hyper,10,6,11] $F.
```

```
------------ end of proof -------------
```

In steps 4 to 9 of the proof, OTTER rewrites the set of statements into the so-called "disjunctive normal form" (Fitting 1996). In the steps that follow, OTTER applies "hyper-resolution," a logical inference rule, to the rewritten statements until in step 12 the "empty clause" is derived. This means that an inconsistency is found, so the conclusion is sound.

When using an automated theorem prover, avoid unnecessarily complex formulas, as well as formulas that are not necessary in a particular proof. Try to restrict the ranges of quantifiers if possible. For example, if a property $G(x)$ is true only for organizations, $O(x)$, in the domain, then stating this fact formally, $\forall x (G(x) \rightarrow O(x))$, helps the theorem prover to shorten its proof trace. Following these guidelines can in some cases bring a proof that initially exceeds the memory capacity of the computer within a feasible range, or within the range of patience of the formalizer.

Notice again that neither an automated model generator nor a theorem prover has common sense knowledge. As we showed in the example, the human formalizer has to define the "larger than" symbol, among others.

5. DISCUSSION AND CONCLUSIONS

Systematic theory improvement, addressing logical and conceptual ambiguity and its underlying problems, had its adherents in the sixties (Hage 1965; Stinchcombe 1968; Blalock 1969). Since the seventies, though, such attempts have been largely abandoned, and many sociologists now look for sophistication in data collection and statistical modeling rather than theory building (Hage 1994). "Our graduate students spend years learning formal data analysis, but most do not even spend a day studying formal logic or mathematical theory"(Kiser 1997, p. 153).

From now on, it may make sense for graduates to spend some time studying logic (and mathematics, for that matter). With our formalization approach and a computer at hand, logical and conceptual problems can be more fruitfully addressed than in the past, hence made more clear and explicit, and consequently be solved in numerous occasions. A well-documented formalization enhances opportunities for critical investigation of scientific arguments, and may thereby catalyze cumulative theory development. As illustrated in our formalization experience, however, there are no simple tricks to translate a text presenting theory into a formal representation. Background knowledge of the theory and its intended domain—that may be tacit in the text—and careful conceptual as well as logical considerations are necessary first. Formal logic can subsequently add precision and rigor in the next step.

To achieve precision and rigor, mathematical modeling (Rapoport 1959; Coleman 1990) and computer simulation (Sastry 1997) are better known in the social sciences than logical formalization is, and they nicely complement the latter. They are well suited to build and analyze *models* (e.g., of social processes), in particular complex ones with many interacting variables (Axelrod 1997; Gilbert and Troitzsch 1999).[17] Formal logic, on the other hand, is better suited to analyze complex *theories*, as logic can be seen as critical reflection on reasoning, defining, and computing (Barendregt 1995). Moreover, logic does not require the imposition of strong assumptions about metrics (Péli 1997; Hannan 1997), and better fits qualitative reasoning.

To refute a theory, or at least one assumption in it, one model as counterexample—i.e. a model in which a conclusion is false and its assumptions believed to be true—is sufficient. One model is also sufficient to show the consistency of a theory. For consistency and refutation, an automated model generator is therefore equally useful as a computer simulation or a mathematical model (Kamps 1998; Kamps 1999a; Kamps 1999b). It goes without saying that along with analyzing existing theories, all three strands of formal techniques can help in the development of new theories.

In sum, our formalization approach consists of five steps, each with a specific input and output, and a documentation of choices made along the way. It is widely applicable to the social sciences and other declarative discourse. The first three steps taken together can be seen as a hermeneutic exercise, in which a better understanding of the discursive theory is obtained; in other words, this is a rational reconstruction, which in turn is the basis for the formalization proper. The formalization process then proceeds as high-tech hermeneutics wherein the formal representation of the theory is used to improve the comprehension of the theory and vice versa. In the last step, the formal representation is tested for logical properties like soundness and consistency, and possibly extended by new theorems, whereas redundant premises are deleted. New results can be obtained not

---

[17] Applied to texts presenting theory, mathematical modeling and computer simulation can show that in *some* models, both assumptions and conclusions are true (provided the text provides sensible theory). If the conclusions of a theory are inferred logically, then in *all* models where the assumptions are true, the conclusions must also be true (Kamps and Pólos 1999). Notice that both mathematics and declarative text can be represented in logic. Mathematics (other than logic) is precise but not very formal, because proofs are rarely formalized to a degree that a computer can check them.

only in the last step, because in each step, something about the theory can be learned.

APPENDIX A: EXAMPLE SENTENCE

The example sentence says that "Early in these markets, when the arena is crowded, most firms vie for the largest possible resource base." We present different readings of this sentence, and start with the phrase "... most firms vie for the largest possible resource base."

1. ... most organizations appeal to the largest resource base possible, given the competitive forces in the population.
2. ... most organizations realize the largest resource base possible, given the competitive forces in the population.
3. ... most organizations appeal to the largest resource base possible, given their core competencies.
4. ... most organizations realize the largest resource base possible, given their core competencies.
5. ... most organizations appeal to the largest resource base possible, given the size of their fundamental niche.
6. ... most organizations realize the largest resource base possible, given the size of their fundamental niche.
7. ... most organizations appeal to the largest resource base possible, given the size of the resource base.
8. ... most organizations realize the largest resource base possible, given the size of the resource base.
9. ... most organizations attempt to appeal to the largest resource base possible, given current competitive forces in the population.
10. ... most organizations attempt to realize the largest resource base possible, given current competitive forces in the population.
11. ... most organizations attempt to appeal to the largest resource base possible, given expected competitive forces in the population.
12. ... most organizations attempt to realize the largest resource base possible, given expected competitive forces in the population.
13. ... most organizations attempt to appeal to the largest resource base possible, given their current core competencies (strong inertia).
14. ... most organizations attempt to realize the largest resource base possible, given their current core competencies (strong inertia).

15.　... most organizations attempt to appeal to the largest resource base possible, given their expected core competencies (weak inertia).
16.　... most organizations attempt to realize the largest resource base possible, given their expected core competencies (weak inertia).
17.　... most organizations attempt to appeal to the largest resource base possible, given the current size of their fundamental niche.
18.　... most organizations attempt to realize the largest resource base possible, given the current size of their fundamental niche.
19.　... most organizations attempt to appeal to the largest resource base possible, given the expected size of their fundamental niche.
20.　... most organizations attempt to realize the largest resource base possible, given the expected size of their fundamental niche.
21.　... most organizations attempt to appeal to the largest resource base possible, given the current size of the resource base.
22.　... most organizations attempt to realize the largest resource base possible, given the current size of the resource base.
23.　... most organizations attempt to appeal to the largest resource base possible, given the expected size of the resource base.
24.　... most organizations attempt to realize the largest resource base possible, given the expected size of the resource base.

These 24 interpretations do not address the question whether the resource base (which here refers to the organizational niche) should be interpreted (1) in terms of niche width theory (Freeman and Hannan 1983) (i.e., the *diversity* of resources in the niche), or (2) as the number (or value, or volume) of resources. This ambiguity doubles the number of possible interpretations, generating a total of 48. At this point we stop, and we ignore conceptual ambiguities in the terms "early," "most," "markets" (referring to sets of organizations, sets of resources, or unions of both types of sets?), and "arena."

What needs to be addressed next is the logical ambiguity of the sentence. Does the crowding of the arena early in the market imply a certain behavior of most organizations, or does the behavior of most organizations early in the market imply that the arena is crowded? It may also be the case that the two events occur early in the market without an implicative relation, or that the occurrence of both events implies the starting point of resource partitioning. Without much effort we found 12 plausible logical readings of the sentence. We use square brackets to avoid ambiguity.

1. **If** it is early in these markets **and** the arena is crowded, **then** most organizations (...)
2. **If** it is early in these markets **and** most organizations (...), **then** the arena is crowded.
3. **If** the arena is crowded **and** most organizations (...), **then** it is early in these markets.
4. **If** it is early in these markets, **then** [the arena is crowded **if and only if** most organizations (...)].
5. **If** the arena is crowded, **then** [it is early in these markets **if and only if** most organizations (...)].
6. **If** most organizations (...), **then** [it is early in these markets **if and only if** crowding is high].
7. **If** it is early in these markets, **then** [the arena is crowded **and** most organizations (...)].
8. **If** the arena is crowded, **then** [it is early in these markets **and** most organizations (...)].
9. **If** there are more generalists than specialists, **then** [it is early in these markets **and** most organizations (...)].
10. It is early in these markets **if and only if** [the arena is crowded **and** most organizations (...)].
11. The arena is crowded **if and only if** [it is early in these markets **and** most organizations (...)].
12. Most organizations (...) **if and only if** [it is early in these markets **and** the arena is crowded].

It is important to note that the logical readings mentioned above differ not only *syntactically* (that is, according to the fact that different connectives are applied) but also *semantically* (that is, all 12 readings have a distinct logical meaning). The easiest way to see this is by subjecting the sentence to a propositional logical evaluation. First, we break up the sentence into subsentences. These subsentences ("it is early in these markets," "the arena is crowded," and "most organizations vie for the largest possible resource base") we consider to be propositions. These propositions are independent in the sense that we can imagine different domains in which they can be found either to hold or not to hold, in every possible combination. Altogether, eight different domains can be distinguished, ranging from a domain where all three propositions hold, to a domain where all three propositions do not hold. In general, for n propositions, 2^n

domains can be distinguished. To form a propositional sentence from propositions, we use logical connectives. The types of connectives we use, and the order in which we use them, determine by which domains the sentences formed are falsified. If two sentences are falsified by a different set of domains, they are semantically different. If they are falsified by the same set of domains, they are semantically equivalent. For our three propositions, we could distinguish eight domains. With eight domains, we can distinguish 256 sets of domains that may falsify a sentence, ranging from the empty set (no possible domain falsifies the sentence, *ergo*, the sentence is a tautology), to the full set (all possible domains falsify the sentence, *ergo*, the sentence is a contradiction). In general, with m domains, we can distinguish 2^m sets of domains that may falsify a sentence. So, with three propositions, we can form $2^{(2^3)} = 256$ semantically different sentences, each of them falsified by a different set of domains. For our example sentence, we found 12 of the 256 semantically different interpretations plausible.

Table 5 shows that indeed all presented readings have a distinct logical meaning, as they are falsified by different sets of domains. In our formalization, we chose the seventh reading. As the example sentence has—at least—48 different plausible conceptual readings and—again, at least—12 plausible logical ones, it turns out that this one sentence has $(48 \times 12 =)$ 576 different plausible readings all together. A theory consisting of, say, seven equally ambiguous sentences would have $576^7 = 21,035,720,123,168,587,776$ plausible readings.

TABLE 5

Falsifying States of Affairs for 12 Plausible Readings of the Example Sentence

It is early [...]	Arena is crowded	Most org's [...]	Falsifying domains for statements 1 to 12:											
			1	2	3	4	5	6	7	8	9	10	11	12
True	True	True												
True	True	False	F				F	F		F	F		F	F	F
True	False	True		F			F		F	F		F	F	F	
True	False	False							F		F			
False	True	True			F		F	F		F	F	F	F	F
False	True	False							F		F			
False	False	True								F		F		
False	False	False												

APPENDIX B: FIRST-ORDER LOGIC

Like other languages, the language of first-order logic has (1) a set of *symbols*, (2) a *syntax*, that allows the user to form valid expressions, and (3) *semantics*, that give the meaning of the expressions. Unlike natural languages, first-order logic has a formal notion of consequence. This notion is realized by (4) a *model*, that tells whether a statement is true or not, and (5) a *proof system*, that enables a (true) statement to be proved.

Symbols

In first-order logic, there are seven categories of symbols:

1. Constants   such as *c*
2. Relations   also called predicates, such as *R*
3. Functions   such as *f*
4. Variables   such as *x* and *y*
5. Logical operators   of which we distinguish two kinds:
    (i) *connectives*: negation ¬, conjunction ∧,
                       disjunction ∨,
                       implication →, and
                       equivalence ↔
    (ii) *quantifiers*: universal, ∀, and existential, ∃
6. Identity   ≈
7. Grouping symbols   parentheses, (), and [], and commas

Categories 1-3 constitute the *nonlogical* symbols, the other categories are the *logical* symbols, that are the same for each first-order language.

Syntax

The syntactic rules allow us to form valid expressions from the symbols. In first-order logic, there are two types of expressions, *terms* and *formulas*.

Definition 1: *Terms*

- *All variables and constants are terms.*
- *If f is a function symbol, and $t_1, \ldots, t_n$ are terms, then $f(t_1, \ldots, t_n)$ is a term.*

Terms can be compared to words; they are the building blocks of formulas. Only *well-formed* formulas can have a meaning.

Definition 2: *Well-formed formulas, or wffs*

- *If R is a relation symbol, and $t_1, \ldots, t_n$ are terms, then $R(t_1, \ldots, t_n)$ is a wff. This type of formula is known as an atomic formula. If R is a relation between two terms, we sometimes use the infix notation, $t_1 R t_2$, rather than the prefix notation, $R(t_1, t_2)$.*
- *If t_1 and t_2 are terms, then $(t_1 \approx t_2)$ is a wff.*
- *If $\phi_1, \ldots, \phi_n$ are wffs, and x is a variable, then $\neg\phi_1$, $(\phi_1 \wedge \ldots \wedge \phi_n)$, $(\phi_1 \vee \ldots \vee \phi_n)$, $(\phi_1 \rightarrow \phi_2)$, $(\phi_1 \leftrightarrow \phi_2)$, $\forall x \phi_1$, and $\exists x \phi_1$ are wffs.*

A *wwf* in which each variable is within the scope of a quantifier is called a *sentence*.

Semantics

In order to determine the meaning of a formula, we need to be able to interpret the logical as well as the nonlogical symbols. The logical symbols—variables, connectives, quantifiers, and the equality symbol—have a fixed meaning, which is informally given below. Let ϕ be a formula, then

$\neg\phi_1$	means	*not ϕ_1*
$(\phi_1 \wedge \ldots \wedge \phi_n)$	"	*ϕ_1 and ... and ϕ_n*
$(\phi_1 \vee \ldots \vee \phi_n)$	"	*ϕ_1 or ... or ϕ_n*
$(\phi_1 \rightarrow \phi_2)$	"	*if ϕ_1 then ϕ_2*
$(\phi_1 \leftrightarrow \phi_2)$	"	*ϕ_1 if and only if ϕ_2*
$(x \approx y)$	"	*x equals y*
$\forall x \phi_1$	"	*for all x, ϕ_1 holds*
$\exists x \phi_1$	"	*there exists an x, for which ϕ_1 holds*

Models

To interpret the meaning of the nonlogical symbols—constants, relations, and functions—we need a *model*. A model consists of a non-empty set of objects (a *universe*) and an interpretation function (an *assignment*), that maps the nonlogical symbols to elements of the universe. An example of a universe is a market, which can be regarded as a set of firms, consumers, and some auxiliary objects. Relations can be defined over the objects, such as competitive relations between firms pairwise, or a supplier/consumer relation. Possible functions are a firm's size, or a consumer's budget. The assignment's function is to map, for example, the symbol $s(c)$ to "the size of firm c."

A model determines the *truth value* of a sentence. Let $\mathcal{M}$ be a model and ϕ a sentence. Then $\mathcal{M} \vDash \phi$ means that ϕ is true in, or *satisfied by*, $\mathcal{M}$. Let Σ be a set of sentences. $\Sigma \vDash \phi$ denotes that every model that satisfies Σ, also satisfies ϕ. We say that ϕ is a *logical consequence* of Σ.

Proof Systems

$\Sigma \vdash \phi$ denotes that there exists a *proof* of ϕ from Σ. That means that $\phi \in \Sigma$, or ϕ is a tautology, or ϕ can be inferred from Σ by applying some *rules of inference*. A set of inference rules—a *proof system*—can be defined that is both *sound*, such that *if* $\Sigma \vdash \phi$ *then* $\Sigma \vDash \phi$, and *complete*, such that *if* $\Sigma \vDash \phi$ *then* $\Sigma \vdash \phi$.

Examples of proof systems that are both sound and complete include *natural deduction*, intended to emulate modes of reasoning that are natural to humans, and *resolution*, which is commonly applied by computational theorem provers like OTTER.

For readers who want to learn more about first-order logic, there are many excellent resources (at the introductory level, Barwise and Etchemendy 1999; for a linguistic approach, at the introductory level, Gamut 1991; for an overview, Hodges 1983; and at an advanced level Van Dalen 1994; for automated theorem proving, Fitting 1996).

REFERENCES

Andréka, H., J. X. Madarász, I. Németi, C. Sági, and I. Sam. 1998. "Analyzing the Logical Structure of Relativity Theory via Model Theoretic Logic." Mathematical Institute of the Hungarian Academy of Sciences. Unpublished manuscript.

Axelrod, R. 1997. *The Complexity of Cooperation*. Princeton, NJ: Princeton University Press.

Ayer, A. 1959. *Logical Positivism*. New York: Free Press.

Balzer, W., C. U. Moulines, and J. D. Sneed. 1987. *An Architectonic for Science*. Dordrecht, Netherlands: Reidel.

Barendregt, Henk. Informal Discussion. October 1995.

Barwise, J., and J. Etchemendy. 1999. *Language, Proof and Logic*. Stanford, CA: Center for the Study of Language and Information.

Beth, E. W. 1962. *Formal Methods*. Dordrecht, Netherlands: Reidel.

Blalock, H. M. 1969. *Theory Construction*. Englewood Cliffs, NJ: Prentice-Hall.

Bruggeman, J. 1997. "Niche Width Theory Reappraised." *Journal of Mathematical Sociology* 22:201–20.

Carnap, R. 1928. *Der Logische Aufbau der Welt*. Berlin, Germany: Weltkreis.

Carroll, G. R., and M. T. Hannan, eds. 1995. *Organizations in Industry*. Oxford, England: Oxford University Press.

———. 2000. *The Demography of Corporations and Industries*. Princeton, NJ: Princeton University Press.

Chang, C., and H. J. Keisler. 1990. *Model Theory*, 3d ed. Amsterdam, Netherlands: North-Holland.

Coleman, J. S. 1964. *An Introduction to Mathematical Sociology*. New York: Free Press.

———. 1990. *Foundations of Social Theory*. Cambridge, MA: Harvard University Press.

De Groot, A. D. 1961. *Methodologie: Grondslagen van onderzoek en denken in de gedragswetenschappen*. The Hague, Netherlands: Mouton.

Debreu, G. 1959. *Theory of Value*. New Haven, CT: Yale University Press.

Enderton, H. B. 1972. *A Mathematical Introduction to Logic*. New York: Academic Press.

———. 1977. *Elements of Set Theory*. New York: Academic Press.

Farquharson, R. 1969. *Theory of Voting*. Oxford, England: Blackwell.

Feigenbaum, F. A., and J. Feldman, eds. 1963. *Computers and Thought*. New York: McGraw-Hill.

Fisher, A. 1988. *The Logic of Real Arguments*. Cambridge, England: Cambridge University Press.

Fitting, M. 1996. *First-Order Logic and Automated Theorem Proving*, 2d ed. New York: Springer.

Freeman, J., and M. T. Hannan. 1983. "Niche Width and the Dynamics of Organizational Populations." *American Journal of Sociology* 88:1116–45.

Freese, L. 1980. "Formal Theorizing." *Annual Review of Sociology* 6:187–212.

Frege, C. 1961. *Funktion, Begriff, Bedeutung*. Göttingen, Germany: Vandenhoeck.

Gabbay, D., and F. Guenthner, eds. 1983–1989. *Handbook of Philosophical Logic*. Dordrecht, Netherlands: Reidel.

Gamut, L. 1991. *Logic, Language, and Meaning*. Chicago, IL: University of Chicago Press.

Gardner, M. 1983. *Logic Machines and Diagrams*. Brighton, England: Harvester Press.

Gilbert, N., and K. C. Troitzsch. 1999. *Simulation for the Social Scientist*. Buckingham, England: Open University Press.

Groenboom, R., E. Saaman, E. Rotterdam, and C. R. de Lavalette. 1996. "Formalizing Anaesthesia: A Case Study in Formal Specification." Pp. 120–39 in M. Gaudel and J. Woodcock, eds., *Industrial Benefit and Advances in Formal Methods*, No. 1051 in Lecture Notes in Computer Science. New York: Springer.

Hage, J. 1965. "An Axiomatic Theory of Organizations." *Administrative Science Quarterly* 10(3): 289–320.

———, ed. 1994. *Formal Theory in Sociology*. Albany: State University of New York Press.

Halmos, P. R. 1960. *Naive Set Theory*. New York. Springer.

Hannan, M. T. 1997. "On Logical Formalization of Theories from Organizational Ecology." Pp. 145–49 in *Sociological Methodology 1997*, edited by A. E. Raftery. Cambridge, MA: Blackwell Publishers.

———. 1998. "Rethinking Age Dependence in Organizational Mortality: Logical Formalizations." *American Journal of Sociology* 104:126–64.

Hannan, M. T., and J. Freeman. 1984. "Structural Inertia and Organizational Change." *American Sociological Review* 49:149–64.

Hansson, S. O. 2000. "Formalization in Philosophy." *The Bulletin of Symbolic Logic* 6:162–75.

Hempel, C. C. 1966. *Philosophy of Natural Science*. Englewood Cliffs, NJ: Prentice-Hall.

Hodges, W. 1983. "Elementary Predicate Logic." Pp. 1–31 in *Handbook of Philosophical Logic*, vol. 1, edited by D. Gabbay and F. Guenthner. Dordrecht, Netherlands: Reidel.

———. 1998. "An Editor Recalls Some Hopeless Papers." *Bulletin of Symbolic Logic* 4:1–16.

Homans, C. C. 1967. *The Nature of Social Science*. New York: Harcourt, Brace and World.

———. 1980. "Discovery and the Discovered in Social Theory." Pp. 17–22 in *Sociological Theory and Research*, edited by H. Blalock. New York: Free Press.

Kamps, J. 1998. "Formal Theory Building Using Automated Reasoning Tools." Pp. 478–87 in *Principles of Knowledge Representation and Reasoning: Proceedings of the Sixth International Conference (KR '98)*, edited by A. C. Cohn, L. K. Schubert, and S. C. Shapiro. San Francisco, CA: Morgan Kaufmann.

———. 1999a. "On Criteria for Formal Theory Building: Applying Logic and Automated Reasoning Tools to the Social Sciences." Pp. 285–90 in *Proceedings of the Sixteenth National Conference on Artificial Intelligence (AAAI-99)*, edited by J. Hendler and D. Subramanian. Menlo Park, CA: AAAI Press/MIT Press.

Kamps, J. 1999b. "On the Process of Axiomatizing Scientific Theories: Using Justification Criteria in the Context of Discovery." Pp. 49–58 in *Proceedings of the AISB'99 Symposium on Scientific Creativity*, Society for the Study of Artificial Intelligence and Simulation of Behaviour.

Kamps, J., and M. Masuch. 1997. "Partial Deductive Closure: Logical Simulation and Management Science." *Management Science* 48(9):1229–45.

Kamps, J., and L. Pólos. 1999. "Reducing Uncertainty: A Formal Theory of Organizations in Action." *American Journal of Sociology* 104:1776–812.

Kiser, E. 1997. "Comment: Evaluating Qualitative Methodologies." Pp. 151–58 in *Sociological Methodology 1997*, edited by A. E. Raftery. Cambridge, MA: Blackwell Publishers.

Kyburg, Jr., H. E. 1968. *Philosophy of Science: A Formal Approach*. New York: Macmillan.

Lakatos, I. 1976. *Proofs and Refutations*. Cambridge, England: Cambridge University Press.

Neurath, O. 1970. "Foundations of the Social Sciences." Pp. 1–51 in *Foundations of the Unity of Science*, edited by O. Neurath, R. Carnap, and C. Morris, Vol. 2. Chicago, IL: University of Chicago Press.

Peirce, C. S. 1931. *Collected Papers*. Cambridge, MA: Harvard University Press.

Péli, C. 1997. "The Niche Hiker's Guide to Population Ecology: A Logical Reconstruction of Organizational Ecology's Niche Theory." Pp. 1–46 in *Sociological
Methodology 1997*, edited by A. E. Raftery. Cambridge, MA: Blackwell Publishers.

Péli, C., J. Bruggeman, M. Masuch, and B. Ó. Nualláin. 1994. "A Logical Approach to
Formalizing Organizational Ecology." *American Sociological Review* 59:571–93.

Péli, C., and M. Masuch. 1997. "The Logic of Propagation Strategies: Axiomatizing a
Fragment of Organizational Ecology in First-Order Logic." *Organization Science*
8:310–31.

Pólya, C. 1945. *How to Solve It*. Princeton, NJ: Princeton University Press.

Popper, K. 1959. *The Logic of Scientific Discovery*. London, England: Hutchinson.

Quine, W. V. O. 1961. *From a Logical Point of View*. New York: Harper and Row.

———. 1986. *Philosophy of Logic*, 2d ed. Cambridge, MA: Harvard University Press.

———. 1990. *Quiddities*. Harmondsworth, England: Penguin.

Rapoport, A. 1959. "Uses and Limitations of Mathematical Models in Social Sciences." In *Symposium on Sociological Theory*, edited by L. Gross. Evanston, IL:
Row Peterson.

Sastry, M. A. 1997. "Problems and Paradoxes in a Model of Punctuated Organizational Change." *Administrative Science Quarterly* 42:237–75.

Simon, H. A. 1954. "Some Strategic Considerations in the Construction of Social Science Models." Pp. 388–415 in *Mathematical Thinking in the Social Sciences*, edited
by P. F. Lazarsfeld. Glencoe, IL: Free Press.

Spencer Brown, C. 1957. *Probability and Scientific Inference*. London, England:
Longman.

Stinchcombe, Arthur, L. 1968. *Constructing Social Theories*. New York: Harcourt.

Suppes, P. 1968. "The Desirability of Formalization in Science." *Journal of Philosophy* 65:651–64.

Tarski, A. 1941. *Introduction to Logic*. New York: Oxford University Press.

Van Benthem, J. 1982. "The Logical Study of Science." *Synthese* 51:431–72.

———. 1994. "Logic and Argumentation." Presented at the Third Conference of the
International Society for the Study of Argumentation, Amsterdam, Netherlands.

Van Benthem, J., and A. Ter Meulen, eds. 1997. *Handbook of Logic and Language*.
Amsterdam, Netherlands: North-Holland.

Van Dalen, D. 1994. *Logic and Structure*, 3d ed. Berlin, Germany: Springer-Verlag.

Vermeulen, I., and J. Bruggeman. 2001. "The Logic of Organizational Markets: Thinking Through Resource Partitioning Theory." *Computational and Mathematical
Organization Theory* 7:87–111.

Woodger, J. 1937. *The Axiomatic Method in Biology*. Cambridge, England: Cambridge University Press.

Wos, L. 1996. *The Automation of Reasoning*. San Diego, CA: Academic Press.

Wos, L., R. Overbeek, E. Lusk, and J. Boyle. 1991. *Automated Reasoning*, 2d ed. New
York: McGraw-Hill.

Young, R. 1988. "Is Population Ecology a Useful Paradigm for the Study of Organizations?" *American Journal of Sociology* 94:1–24.

6

REGRESSION MODELS WITH PARAMETRICALLY WEIGHTED EXPLANATORY VARIABLES

Kazuo Yamaguchi*

This paper describes linear regression models with parametrically weighted explanatory variables and related logistic regression models that estimate parameters characterizing (1) the effects of weighted variables on the dependent variable and (2) weights for the components of weighted variables. The models also characterize parsimoniously the interaction effects between weighted variables and covariates on the dependent variable by the use of various constraints on parameters. In particular, the models are concerned with testing the significance of variation with covariates in the weights of weighted variables separately from the significance of variation with those covariates in the effects of weighted variables.

The usefulness of these models in sociological research is demonstrated by an illustrative analysis of the class identifications of married working women using education, occupational prestige, and income as three variables weighted between own and spousal attributes, and using year, age, race, part-time–full-time distinction, and employment status as covariates.

This research is partly supported by the National Science Foundation research grant SBR-9904948 and by the Alfred P. Sloan Center of Family, Work, and Children at the University of Chicago. I wish to thank anonymous referees of *Sociological Methodology* for their comments on an earlier draft. Address correspondence to Kazuo Yamaguchi, University of Chicago/NORC, 1155 East 60th Street, Chicago, IL 60637. Email: kyamagu@midway.uchicago.edu.

*University of Chicago

219

1. INTRODUCTION

This paper describes regression models with parametrically weighted explanatory variables and the usage of such models in sociology. These models employ a set (or sets) of variables that are optimally weighted to explain the dependent variable. A parametrically weighted variable implies a linear combination $\Sigma_i w_i x_i$ of a set of variables $\{x_i\}$ with weight parameters $\{w_i\}$ along with a constraint on the parameters. Examples of such constraints include the sum of 1 for a set of weights or a variance of 1 for the weighted variable when all $x_i s$ are standardized. While regression models that employ such weighted explanatory variables are relatively simple in structure, they appear in different forms for different methodological purposes in different substantive applications. An example is the method used for calculating the *sheaf coefficient*, introduced by Heise (1972), to express the effects of a set of variables by a single quantity. The method reflects an optimal weighting of a set of variables to explain the dependent variable. Heise introduced the sheaf coefficient for its use in path analysis especially for a set of dummy variables for a categorical variable such as ethnicity, but the method can be used more generally to obtain a standardized regression coefficient for the combined effect of any set of explanatory variables.

Another important example in the use of parametrically weighted explanatory variables is a group of models, called *diagonal mobility models* or *diagonal reference models*, introduced by Sobel (1981, 1985) to assess the effects of social mobility, or the effects of inconsistency between husbands' and wives' statuses, on dependent variables, such as fertility (Sobel 1985; Sorenson 1989) and voting behavior (Weakliem 1992; De Graaf and Nieuwbeerta 1995). Diagonal reference models use states for individuals who did not experience mobility or those of couples between whom statuses are consistent as reference states for comparison. Generally, the models, which are described formally later, are very useful for situations where we have a pair of key categorical variables with one-to-one correspondences in categories, and the main substantive focus of the situation is to assess the effects of disagreement in the states of these two variables, such as the effects of social mobility and the effects of status inconsistency between husbands and wives, on dependent variables.

Other regression models with parametrically weighted explanatory variables are useful for different reasons and varying situations. Analyzing the class identification of married working women is a situation representative of the use of the models introduced in this paper. For this analysis, researchers have examined three alternative hypotheses and assessed their relative explanatory power (e.g., Goldthorpe 1983; Beeghley and Cochran 1988; Davis and Robinson 1988; Erikson and Goldthorpe 1992). One hypothesis, the *independence hypothesis*, posits that the class identifications of married working women depend on their own individual class attributes, typically represented by education, occupational prestige, and income, and do not depend on their husbands' class attributes. An alternative hypothesis, the *status-borrowing hypothesis*, posits that the class identifications of married working women depend on their husbands' class attributes, and do not depend on their own class attributes. The third hypothesis, the *status-sharing hypothesis*, posits that the class identifications of married working women depend on both their own and their spouses' class attributes, typically represented by the arithmetic means of the couples' education, occupational prestige, and income.

Suppose that we consider a model in which *weighted* averages of married women's and their husbands' class attributes affect married women's class identifications, such that $wx_1 + (1 - w)x_2$ affects y, where x_1 and x_2 are married women's and their husbands' class attributes respectively and w and $1 - w$ are their weights. The three hypotheses stated above all correspond to special cases of this model with varying weights; the independence hypothesis is represented by a model that gives 1.0 weight to own attributes (i.e., $w = 1$, and thereby 0.0 weight to spousal attributes), the status-borrowing hypothesis is represented by a model that gives 0.0 weight to own attributes (i.e., $w = 0$, and thereby 1.0 weight to spousal attributes), and the status-sharing hypothesis is represented by a model that gives 0.5 weights to both own and spousal attributes (i.e., $w = 1 - w = 0.5$). It follows that these three models can be generalized by a single model that specifies the relative weight w of own attribute to be an unknown parameter rather than a fixed constant. We can employ such a generalized model to estimate weights that predicts the dependent variable best, and then identify their confidence intervals in order to assess which hypothesis agrees with the data.

The weights that best predict the dependent variable usually vary with each class attribute—that is, weights between own and spousal attributes differ among education, occupational prestige, and income. The weights may also vary more generally with each individual. In other words, different hypotheses (independence, status borrowing, or status sharing) may hold, depending not only on whether it is about education, occupational prestige, or income but also on the individual. Such population heterogeneity in the weights may show systematic variation with observable individual and family characteristics such as age, race, employment status, and whether the wife's income is greater than the husband's income. Therefore, weights between own and spousal class attributes should depend on covariates. The dependence of weights on a covariate represents a particular hypothesis on class identification about the interaction effects between a pair of class-attribute variables and the covariate. The hypothesis is that for a pair of class-attribute variables, such as own income and spousal income, it holds that the two interaction effects—one between own income and the covariate and the other between spousal income and the covariate—sum to zero so that the covariate affects only the relative sizes of the own-income effect and spousal-income effect, while it keeps the sum of these two effects the same. Generally, covariate effects on weights thus represent tests on hypotheses about the set of interaction effects under a *zero-sum constraint*. I will describe this more formally later. Such a test is substantively meaningful because, for example, we may hypothesize that while the importance of income in determining class identification did not change over time, married working women place more weight on their own income than on their husbands' income in more recent years.

We can also test a hypothesis, with a set of *equality constraints* on parameters, that such weight changes with a covariate are uniform across class attributes, in order to test whether a group of women is generally more "independent" than others. For a group of relatively independent women, the weights of their own class attributes compared with their husbands' would be uniformly greater than other women for all three class attributes.

The use of weighted variables also permits another substantively meaningful test. It is a test on the interaction effects of a weighted variable (or a set of weighted variables) with covariates without changes in weights. For example, we may hypothesize that the importance of income in determining class identification has increased in more recent years without changes in the relative sizes of the own-income effect and the spousal-income effect. This represents a test on the set of interaction effects of a covariate with a pair of class-attribute variables under an *equi-proportionality constraint* such that while the two income effects increase over time, the rate of increase is the same between the own-income effect and the spousal-income effect. I will also describe this more formally later.

Furthermore, if we standardize class attributes so that their scales are comparable, we can also test, with a set of *equality constraints* on parameters, a hypothesis that the interaction effects between the set of weighted variables and a covariate are uniform across class attributes such that the effects of objective class attributes on subjective class identification are uniformly greater for a certain group of people than for others.

Although I described weighted variables using the case of weighting own and spousal attributes, models with parametrically weighted variables can also be applied by using weighted variables that have more than two components. For example, we may employ own composite status and spousal composite status as variables defined as weighted averages of the corresponding education, occupational prestige, and income, all standardized for scale comparability. We can then test whether the weights of education, occupational prestige, and income vary with covariates. For example, we may hypothesize that education, in comparison to two other class attributes, is more important as a determinant of class identification for younger people than for older people. We can also test whether this hypothesis holds uniformly for both own composite status and spousal composite status.

The purpose of using weighted variables here is thus (1) to estimate weights and their standard errors to test whether they significantly differ from particular values such as 0, 0.5, or 1, (2) to test whether the weights systematically vary with covariates to reveal characteristics of population heterogeneity in the *relative* importance of mutually related variables, and (3) to test whether the effects of weighted variables systematically vary with covariates to reveal characteristics of population heterogeneity in the *combined* effects of the mutually related variables.

We can also employ categorical weighted variables for the purpose of analysis described above. For example, we can characterize education and occupation by using a set of categories instead of using the number of years of education and occupational prestige scores. While a model that employs a weighted categorical variable was introduced by Sobel (1982, 1985), this model was developed for a different purpose, and the incorporation of Sobel's method of using diagonal reference groups into models for the purpose described above leaves some methodological issues to be solved. I discuss such issues later when Sobel's model is formally described.

For the purpose of analyzing (1), (2), and (3) stated above, however, a straightforward extension is possible regarding the use of weighted variables for pairs or groups of categorical variables that have the same set of categories. The extension replaces, for example, a pair of own and spousal class-attribute variables that have a common interval scale, as in the number of years of education or occupational prestige scores, by a pair of categorical variables by imposing, among categories, *a latent unidimensional order that is common between own and spousal variables*. The commonality of a latent scale can be imposed by assuming *equiproportionality* between the effects of two categorical variables, one for own class attribute and the other for spousal class attribute. We can also test the interaction effects of a categorical weighted variable and other covariates, as in the case of the usage of weighted variables with interval scales.

The models with parametrically weighted variables have a form of bilinear regression for the effects of weighted explanatory variables. Log-bilinear models are well known as extensions of log-linear models (Goodman 1979 1986; Clogg 1982a,b; Clogg and Shihadeh 1994; Xie 1991; Yamaguchi 1990). Regression expressions for such log-bilinear models have also been introduced (Anderson 1984; Diprete 1990). Similar log-bilinear models have been described to characterize interaction effects in hazard rate models as well (Xie 1994). What these models have in common is that a bilinear form is introduced to characterize association, either between two categorical variables or between a categorical variable and a set of interval-scale variables, and thus to provide a more parsimonious expression than either the full category-by-category or the full category-by-variable interactions.

The models introduced in this paper are also concerned with providing a parsimonious characterization of interaction effects between pairs or groups of mutually related variables and other variables by the use of equiproportionality constraints, zero-sum constraints, and equality constraints. The attainment of parsimony is one of two major aims. The other aim is to estimate the parameters, expressed in a specific bilinear form, in order to assess the significance of relative weights among mutually related variables, and to assess the variability in relative weights with covariates separately from the variability in the combined effect of these mutually related variables.

This paper describes the use of parametrically weighted explanatory variables for linear regression models and for logistic regression models—though the idea can easily be extended to generalized linear models (McCullagh and Nelder 1989) with various link functions.

2. MODELS

2.1. *Basic Models*: *Models with Weighted Interval-Scale Covariates*

I first describe the case where weighted variables have interval scales. In the next section, I extend it to include categorical weighted variables. Let y_i be the dependent variable for respondent i, and $\mathbf{x}_{ij} = (x_{ij1}, \ldots, x_{ijK})$, $j = 1, \ldots, J$, be the covariate vector of respondent i for the jth "to-be-weighted" covariate of y_i. Each covariate vector has a set of K components to be weighted, which correspond to the components either of the pair ($K = 2$) or of the group ($K > 2$). For example, if we use three weighted covariates—namely, education, occupational prestige, and income, weighted for own attributes and spousal attributes—then the number of covariates, J, is 3, and the number of components for each covariate, K, is 2. Alternatively, if we use two weighted covariates—namely, own composite status and spousal composite status, each of which is a weighted average of the corresponding education, occupational prestige, and income (each attribute standardized for comparability across variables with different measurement units)—then the number of covariates, J, is 2, and the number of components for each covariate, K, is 3.

Let $\mathbf{w}_j = (w_{j1}, \ldots, w_{jK})$ be the corresponding weights for $\mathbf{x}_{ij}$, where we assume for the baseline model of equation (1) below that $\Sigma_k w_{jk} = 1$ holds for each j. We denote by u_{ij} the jth nonweighted covariate of y_i. When the model does not include the interaction effects of weighted variables and other covariates of y, the equation for a dependent variable y_i which has an interval scale, is expressed as

$$y_i = \beta_0 + \Sigma_j \beta_j (\Sigma_k w_{jk} x_{ijk}) + \Sigma_m \alpha_m u_{im} + \epsilon_i, \tag{1}$$

where β_j is the effect of the jth *weighted covariate*, which is $\Sigma_k w_{jk} x_{ijk}$, and α_m is the effect of the mth nonweighted covariate u_{im}. We assume here that each ϵ_i is a normally-distributed random error that is independently and identically distributed with variance σ^2.[1]

Equation (1) is a simple bilinear reparameterization of the linear regression equation because for a linear regression equation $y_i = \beta_0 + \Sigma_j \Sigma_k \beta_{jk} x_{ijk} + \Sigma_m \alpha_m u_{im} + \epsilon_i$ applied to the same data set, we obtain identities (a) $\beta_j = \Sigma_k \beta_{jk}$ and (b) $w_{jk} = \beta_{jk}/\Sigma_k \beta_{jk}$ between the regression coefficients β_{jk} of this linear regression and β_j and w_{jk} in equation (1) with weighted variables. Hence, the effect of the jth weighted variable β_j is the *sum* of the K effects of the components of this weighted variable, and weight w_{jk} is the *ratio* of the effect of the kth component variable to the sum of the K effects.

Consider now that there exist some interaction effects of variable z_n with the components $\mathbf{x}_j \equiv (x_{j1}, \ldots, x_{jK})$ of the jth weighted variable. Then such interaction effects can be expressed as (1) the dependence of the effect β_j of the jth weighted variable on z_n, or (2) the dependence of the weight $\mathbf{w}_j = (w_{j1}, \ldots, w_{jK})$ of the jth weighted variable on z_n, or (3) both (1) and (2). A model that hypothesizes one of these effects, but not both effects, has either a *zero-sum constraint* (the case in which the effect of z_n on β_j is absent) or an *equiproportionality constraint* (the case in which the effect of z_n on $\mathbf{w}_j$ is absent) among parameters that characterize the interaction effects of $\mathbf{x}_j$ and z_n. Let us express this more formally.

Suppose we denote by β_{jk} the effect of x_{jk} and by β_{jkn} the effect of $x_{jk} z_n$ in the standard linear-regression expression. Then, a model with the hypothesis that the effect of z_n on β_j is absent has a zero-sum constraint because the hypothesis is equivalent with the condition that the K elements of β_{jkn} for given j sum to zero. A model hypothesizing that the effect of z_n on $\mathbf{w}_j$ is absent has an equiproportionality constraint because the hypothesis is equivalent with the condition that the set of β_{jkn}/β_{jk} for $k = 1, \ldots, K$, does not depend on k unless $\beta_{jkn} = \beta_{jk} = 0$.

Furthermore, we can also hypothesize and test whether the effects of z_n on the sum ($\beta_j = \Sigma_k \beta_{jk}$, where β_{jk} is the regression coefficient for x_{jk} in the standard regression expression) or the ratio ($w_{jk} = \beta_{ik}/\Sigma_k \beta_{jk}$) are uniform across J weighted variables—although the uniform effect on the sum is meaningful only if $\mathbf{x}_j$, $j = 1, \ldots, J$, are all standardized for scale

[1] Although the present paper does not test such an extended model, it is easy as in the standard linear regression model to extend the model described here to a new model that assumes a generalized log-gamma distribution for the error term. The extended model provides a one-parameter extension for the normally distributed error term and allows positive or negative skewness of the error distribution.

comparability. The uniform effect on the ratio is meaningful regardless of this standardization.

Formally, in the expression for a model with parametrically weighted variables, we can hypothesize

$$\beta_j = \lambda_{0j} + \Sigma_n \lambda_{jn} z_n \tag{2}$$

$$w_{jk} = \gamma_{0jk} + \Sigma_n \gamma_{jkn} z_n \quad k = 1, \ldots, K, \tag{3}$$

where in equation (3), $\Sigma_k \gamma_{0jk} = 1$ and $\Sigma_k \gamma_{jkn} = 0$ are both assumed in order to make weights w_{jk} sum to 1 across K groups. When the effects of z_n on w_{jk} are uniform, $\gamma_{jkn} = \gamma_{kn}$ holds in equation (3). Similarly, when the effects of z_n on β_j are uniform, then $\lambda_{jn} = \lambda_n$ holds in equation (2).

While we test whether each covariate z_n affects the kth weight of all covariates $\mathbf{x}_j, j = 1, \ldots, J$, uniformly—i.e., whether $\gamma_{jkn} = \gamma_{kn}$ holds in equation (3), we assume for the intercept weights, γ_{0kj}, that they depend on covariate $\mathbf{x}_j$, such that the "baseline" weights between own and spousal attributes in determining class identification differ among education, occupational prestige, and income. Only the effects of covariates $\mathbf{z}$ on weights are tested for possible simplification to γ_{kn}. Similarly, λ_{0j} are assumed to differ among education, occupational prestige, and income in equation (2) and only the effects of covariates $\mathbf{z}$ on β_j are tested for possible simplification to λ_n.

For models that extend the model of equation (1), the *sum-and-ratio expression* characterized by the pair of equations (2) and (3) is not the only expression possible for the interaction effects of weighted variables and $\mathbf{z}$. The other expression is the *unconstrained-weight expression*. The unconstrained-weight expression does not assume the dependence of β_j on covariates, as in equation (2), but instead removes constraint $\Sigma_k \gamma_{jkn} = 0$ from equation (3) since condition $\Sigma_k \gamma_{jkn} \neq 0$ can reflect change in magnitude of the interaction effect of z_n with the jth weighted variable on y. More specifically, using the unconstrained-weight expression, we can test whether a particular effect γ_{jkn} of covariate z_n on weight w_{jk} may differ from zero while all other γ_{jmn}, $m \neq k$, are set at zero. This is very similar to testing the significance of a particular variable-by-variable interaction effect—namely, the effect of $x_{jk} z_n$. However, with the unconstrained-weight expression, γ_{jkn} tests the significance of the change in the relative proportion—i.e., tests the interaction effect as a proportional increase ($\gamma_{jkn} > 0$) or a proportional decrease ($\gamma_{jkn} < 0$) of the sum effect β_j, rather than as an additive change as in the case of testing the significance of

$x_{ijk} z_{in}$ in the OLS regression. This is because when, for a given $\mathbf{x}_j$ and z_n, $\lambda_{jn} = 0$ and $\gamma_{jkn} \neq 0$ only for a particular k, the interaction effect of x_{jk} and z_n is $\lambda_{j0} \gamma_{jkn} [= \beta_j \gamma_{jkn}]$. In terms of significance, however, the alternative expressions normally yield the same results. Thus the unconstrained-weight expression permits a juxtaposition of the tests on sum and ratio and the tests on individual variable-by-variable interaction to attain a model with the most efficient characterization for the interaction effects.

With the use of multiple nonzero γ_{jkn}, which are not constrained to sum to 0 across K groups for the jth weighted variable and covariate z_n, an increase in the effect of the jth weighted variable with z_n can be characterized by $\Sigma_k \gamma_{jkn} > 0$, and a decrease in the effect of the jth weighted variable with z_n can be characterized by $\Sigma_k \gamma_{jkn} < 0$. We can also hypothesize and test whether the effects of covariates on unconstrained weights are uniform across weighted variables—i.e., whether $\gamma_{jkn} = \gamma_{kn}$ holds. Note that "the constraint" here refers to the zero-sum constraint for the set of γ_{jkn}, and that in the unconstrained-weight expression, we often set other γ_{jmn}, m $\neq$ k, at zero while the effect of a particular weight, γ_{jkn}, is tested for significance.

There are two situations where the unconstrained-weight expression is more effective than the sum-and-ratio expression. One is the case involving the usage of a categorical weighted variable, which is described in the next section. The other is a situation where a covariate z_n interacts only with a particular component of a weighted variable. For example, the recency of years may increase the effect of own income but not the effect of spousal income on class identification. While the sum and the ratio of the effects of own income and spousal income are both affected by this interaction effect, the interaction effect is more efficiently characterized by an increase in the weight for own income without changes in the weight for spousal income in the unconstrained-weight expression. This is because in the unconstrained-weight expression, the interaction effect is characterized by a change in one parameter in this situation, rather than changes in two parameters (one effect on the sum and the other effect on the ratio) which occur in the sum-and-ratio expression. It is possible that while the single effect is significant in the former expression, the two effects both become nonsignificant in the latter expression due to redundancy.

We can obtain *standardized* regression coefficients for weighted covariates, which allow a descriptive comparison among the effects of weighted covariates, such as among education, occupational prestige, and income, each weighted between husband and wife. We can thus see which variables are the more important determinants of y when covariates in each group are optimally weighted to maximize the explanatory power of the model. This standardized regression coefficient is the sheaf coefficient for the set of components of the weighted variable.

When we have a dichotomous dependent variable y_i instead of a continuous dependent variable, we can simply replace the linear link function with the logit function such that for $P_i \equiv \text{Prob}(y_i = 1 | \mathbf{x}, \mathbf{u})$

$$\text{logit}(P_i) = \beta_0 + \Sigma_j \beta_j \Sigma_k w_{jk} x_{ijk} + \Sigma_m \alpha_m u_{im}, \qquad (4)$$

while applying either the sum-and-ratio expression or the unconstrained-weight expression for the interaction effects of weighted variables and other covariates $\mathbf{z}$, as in the case of the dependent variable with an interval scale.

2.2. Models with Categorical Weighted Covariates

We can use categorical weighted variables. I illustrate their use below by models having a single categorical weighted variable—though models can also employ two or more categorical weighted variables.

Suppose we use a pair of categorical education variables for the wife x_{11} and the husband x_{12} (where $K = 2$) instead of a pair of the number of years of education, in order to reflect a nonlinear effect of education on class identification. We assume a common unidimensional latent scale for these educational variables. For simplicity, I assume that other weighted covariates $\mathbf{x}_j, j = 2, \ldots, J$, have an interval scale. Then the equation, without having an interaction effect of the categorical weighted variable with other covariates $\mathbf{z}$ of y, is given as

$$y_i = \beta_0 + \sum_{m=1}^{M-1} \beta_{1m} [w_1 D_{iml} + (1 - w_1) D_{im2}]$$

$$+ \sum_{j=2}^{J} \beta_j [w_j x_{ij1} + (1 - w_j) x_{ij2}] + \Sigma_m \alpha_m u_{im} + \epsilon_i. \qquad (5)$$

In this equation, D_{iml} and D_{im2}, for $m = 1, \ldots, M - 1$, are respectively the set of dummy variables to distinguish M categories of variables x_{11} and x_{12}—i.e., own education and spousal education, β_{1m}, for $m = 1, \ldots,$ $M - 1$, is the set of common effects of education, and w_1 is the relative weight of own education effect. Note that in contrast to the use of

$2(M-1)$ regression coefficients for the two sets of dummy variables for x_{11} and x_{12}, the model of equation (5) imposes equiproportionality between the effects of x_{11} and those of x_{12}, yielding the use of M parameters (one for w and $M-1$ for β_{1m}). The equiproportionality implies that the two sets of educational effects, one for own education and the other for spousal education, have the same relative distance among categories.

Suppose now that a covariate z_n has an interaction effect with education on y. As described before, the interaction effect can involve both (a) variation with z_n in the effect of weighted education on y and (b) variation with z_n in the relative weight between own education and spousal education. In addition, there is a third possibility in the use of categorical weighted education; (c) variation with z_n in relative distances among educational levels in their effects on y.

Suppose that we first consider the sum-and-ratio expression in which the set of beta coefficients, β_{1m}, $m = 1, \ldots, M-1$, and weight w_1 for the education variable vary linearly with z_n such that

$$\beta_{1m} = \lambda_{01m} + \Sigma_n \lambda_{1mn} z_n \tag{6}$$

$$w_1 = \gamma_{01} + \Sigma_n \gamma_{1n} z_n, \tag{7}$$

where $1 - w_1 = 1 - \gamma_{01} - \Sigma_n \gamma_{1n} z_n$ hold for the weights summing to 1 across the effects of own and spousal education.

In equation (6), the set of λ_{1mn} makes relative distances among the effects of different education levels (element [c] stated above) as well as the effect of the weighted educational variable (element [a] stated above) vary with z_n—while γ_{1n} in equation (7) makes the relative weight between own and spousal education vary with z_n (element [b] stated above).

However, with the pair of equations (6) and (7), we cannot test whether the effect of weighted education varies with z_n, without changing relative distances among educational levels (or by retaining the same non-linear latent scale of education independent of z_n). Such a test will require β_{1m}, $m = 1, \ldots, M$, to change equiproportionally with z_n. Then, it is necessary to characterize the effect of z_n on the set of β_{1m} as the multiplier to the baseline value of β_{1m}, $\beta_{1m,0}$, such that $\beta_{1m} = \beta_{1m,0}(1 + \Sigma_n \lambda_{1mn} z_n)$. This expression makes the model partially trilinear because of the involvement of the product of three parameters, $\beta_{1m,0} \lambda_{1mn} w_1$, as the coefficient for $D_{1m} z_n$ (and $\beta_{1m,0} \lambda_{1mn}(1 - w_1)$ as the coefficient for $D_{2m} z_n$). However, this trilinear form is more parsimoniously expressed in a bilinear form, and parameters are more stably estimable, if $\beta_{1m,0} w_1$ and $\beta_{1m,0}(1 -$

w_1) are replaced by two parameters w_{11} and w_{12} without loss of generality. In other words, by using the unconstrained-weight expression, we can test proportional variations with z in the effects of a categorical weighted variable on y. By such a characterization, interaction effects of categorical weighted education and z retain the same latent scale of education, regardless of z. Generally, we can employ the sum-and-ratio expression as well as the unconstrained-weight expression for interaction effects involving the categorical weighted variable and choose one that attains a better fit, or a more parsimonious fit, with the data.

2.3. *Notes on Related Models and Methods*

1. Sheaf coefficient, latent variable, and assumed "direction of causality"

Although the models introduced above distinguish the sum and ratios for the effects of a set of variables, the standardized regression coefficient for the sum is a sheaf coefficient whose concept was introduced by Heise (1972). Heise's method as well as the models described in this paper are concerned with a useful bilinear parametric expression for regression equation, based on the optimal linear combination for a set of explanatory variables under a constraint on parameters that linearly combine the variables.

Heise described an important difference between his idea of sheaf coefficient and the idea behind the use of multiple indicators for a latent variable (or latent variables) in confirmatory factor analysis, such as those currently employed in Jöreskog's LISREL program (Jöreskog and Sörbom 1984) and Bentler's EQS program (Bentler 1995). According to Heise's expression, the sheaf coefficient is concerned with "a determinant *of* the construct," regarding the relationship between a latent construct and its indicators, while in the confirmatory factor analysis, indicators are "determined *by* the construct," thereby assuming the opposite causal direction between the latent construct and its indicators. Technically, this also leads to the fact that in the use of the sheaf coefficient, no constraints are imposed on the relationship among indicator variables of the latent construct, because the indicator variables are assumed to be exogenous variables, but no error term is allowed for the latent construct in order for the model's parameters to be identifiable (Heise 1972). In contrast, in confirmatory factor analysis, the latent variable is subject to random errors, but it is assumed that the indicator variables satisfy some conditional independence controlling for latent variables in order for the model's parameters to be identifiable.

As in the sheaf coefficient, models with parametrically weighted variables assume that the latent construct—i.e., a weighted variable—is determined by its component variables rather than being a common determinant of its component variables. Models introduced in this paper assume, as in the sheaf coefficient, that the weighted variables are not subject to random errors. An extension for a model with random error terms for weighted variables is possible, however, under either the zero-sum constraints on β parameters or equiproportionality constraints on weight parameters. This is because the degrees of freedom generated by such constraints may yield information for the estimation of parameters of the error distribution. Such an extension is not described in this paper, however.

Unlike the sheaf coefficient, whose only concern is to measure the combined effect of a set of indicator variables, the models introduced in this paper are concerned with both the sum (which measures the combined effect) and the ratios which measure the relative importance among the effects of a set of indicator variables, and the parsimonious modeling of variation with covariates in the sum and the ratios. In addition, for categorical variables, while the sheaf coefficient is concerned with producing a single measure for the effects of a set of dummy variables, the regression model with parametrically weighted categorical variables is concerned with estimating relative weights among the combined effects of categorical variables having an identical set of categories, by imposing equiproportionality constraints on the component effects of the multiple sets of dummy variables.

Despite apparent dissimilarity between the factor-analytic approach and the approach taken in this paper, there is one commonality between the two. The use of a latent variable instead of its indicators, say x_1 and x_2, in the regression may eliminate the misleading lack of significance in their unique effects, say b_1 and b_2. In the case of models introduced in this paper, high near multicollinearity of b_1 and b_2, indicated by a high correlation of the two, yields a much smaller standard error for the sum effect $b_1 + b_2$, compared with their components b_1 or b_2, and, therefore, the use of combined effect rather than the unique effects is more effective in detecting significance. The use of the effect of latent variable in confirmatory factor analysis also possesses similar effectiveness.

2.   Notes on Sobel's model for a categorical weighted variable

Sobel's "baseline" diagonal reference model in assessing mobility effects assumes that the expected outcome y for people who experience mobility from origin i to destination j is a parametrically weighted average of the mean of y among people who stay in state i and the mean of y among people who stay in state j, with a weight parameter indicating the relative influence of the origin state compared with the destination state. This baseline model represents a hypothesis of no mobility effect because the expected outcome for people who experience mobility becomes the weighted average of the expected outcomes for two referent groups of people who do not experience mobility. Mobility effects, whose effects need to be parameterized in some way, can then be reflected by a systematic deviation in y as a function of mobility patterns from such a weighted average. Sobel also introduced an extended model (1985) where the origin effects and the destination effects of nonmobile referent groups on y depend on covariates so that mobility effects can be assessed by controlling for population heterogeneity.

It is possible to incorporate the idea behind Sobel's diagonal reference model into the present purpose of using a set of weighted variables and testing alternative forms of interaction effects between weighted and nonweighted variables. However, this becomes technically much more complicated than the method described in the previous section and leaves several methodological issues to be solved. I describe these issues by taking an example of education as a categorical weighted variable. The idea behind Sobel's diagonal reference model is that in the baseline model given below, we let the outcome for every subject with level m for own education and level n for spousal education characterized by the weighted average of the mean outcomes of the two referent groups of people; one group with level m for both own and spousal education and the other group with level n for both own and spousal education. Suppose that we assume no other weighted variables and no interaction effect between education and other covariates. Then Sobel's model can be specified by using his extended model (Sobel, 1985) with covariates as follows.

Let $E(y_m|\mathbf{u})$, where $\mathbf{u}$ is the set of nonweighted covariates of y, be the predicted mean of y for each education level m obtained from a linear equation of the mean as a function of $\mathbf{u}$ *among people for whom the level of education is the same between the subject and her spouse* such that

$$E(y_m|\mathbf{u}) = a_m + \mathbf{b}'_m \mathbf{u}. \tag{8}$$

Then the baseline model for subject i whose level of education is m and whose spousal education is n is given as

$$y_{i,mn} = w_1 E(y_m|\mathbf{u}) + (1 - w_1)E(y_n|\mathbf{u}) + \epsilon_i$$

$$= w_1(a_m + \mathbf{b}'_m \mathbf{u}) + (1 - w_1)(a_n + \mathbf{b}'_n \mathbf{u}) + \epsilon_i. \qquad (9)$$

Note that this baseline model assumes no effect of differences between own and spousal educational levels on y. The parameters w_1 for equation (9) and parameters a_m and $\mathbf{b}_m$ for equation (8) are estimable by the method described by Sobel (1985). We can also introduce into equation (9) parameters to reflect the effects of educational status inconsistency between the subject and her spouse. However, our primary interest in the present application is not to apply a model of equation (9) and its extension for status-inconsistency effects, but to apply a model that includes interaction effects of education with other covariates $\mathbf{z}$. This extension, however, leaves some methodological issues to be solved.[2] In addition, the Sobel model cannot easily be extended to include more than one categorical weighted variable.[3] Hence, if our primary interest is to use several weighted variables in a model and to express the interaction effects between weighted and nonweighted variables parsimoniously, the use of the Sobel model needs further methodological developments.

[2] As I described before, the interaction effects of categorical education and $\mathbf{z}$ involve the dependence of the sum and the ratio of the two component education effects on $\mathbf{z}$ and the dependence of relative distances among the effects of different educational levels on $\mathbf{z}$. As an extension for equation (9), we may employ a model where the relative weight of own education w_1 depends on $\mathbf{z}$—though this makes parameter estimation more complicated. However, the variation in the effect of weighted education with $\mathbf{z}$ is not parametrically estimable—at least not as an extension for equations (8) and (9). This is because the dependence of coefficients $\mathbf{b}_m$ on the level of education m in equation (8) implies that interaction effects of education and $\mathbf{u}$ are assumed among the reference group of people for whom $m = n$ holds. Hence if $\mathbf{z}$ is included in $\mathbf{u}$ and if we assume that the same interaction effects apply to the nonreferent group (i.e., people for whom $m \neq n$ holds) as well, the dependence of weighted education effect on $\mathbf{z}$ is already nonparametrically controlled. The same applies to variability with covariates $\mathbf{z}$ in relative distances among the effects of different educational levels. Hence, in the Sobel model we cannot parametrically test some aspects of interaction effects of the weighted variable and $\mathbf{z}$.

[3] The Sobel model cannot easily be extended to include more than one categorical weighted variable. Note that by making $\mathbf{b}_m$ independent of educational level m, while keeping intercept a_m to be level-specific in equation (8), the Sobel model permits a control for the effects of $\mathbf{u}$ on y without involving the interaction effects of the weighted variable and $\mathbf{u}$ in equation (9). Therefore, in principle, we may include other weighted variables simply as a part of control variables $\mathbf{u}$. However, if we wish to use two categorical weighted variables each with Sobel's diagonal reference expression, such an analysis will require a model that simultaneously estimates two kinds of "mobility effects" or "status inconsistency effects." Such a model has not been developed, however. In the meantime, we can thus assess the effects of just one categorical weighted variable in a model.

3. METHOD OF PARAMETER ESTIMATION

I employed maximum-likelihood estimation with the alternate Newton-Raphson algorithm. We can effectively employ the alternation between (1) the estimation of covariate effects on the dependent variable, including the effects of weighted variables, and (2) the estimation of covariate effects on weights, with simultaneous estimation of all parameters at the end of iterations in order to estimate the variance-covariance matrix of parameter estimates. The parameter estimates are largely insensitive to initial values because the likelihood function is well shaped. A FORTRAN program to estimate parameters, WGTREG.FOR, used in the analysis below, has been made available from Statlib. See the appendix to this chapter for more details about parameter estimation and program WGTREG.FOR.

4. DATA AND VARIABLES

The sample is selected from the respondents of the General Social Survey (GSS) for 17 different years during the period of 21 years from 1978 to 1998. The years 1981, 1992, 1995, and 1997 were excluded because some key variables were not collected during those periods. The sample was restricted to women aged 20–65, married, employed at the time of survey, with employed spouses, and with two earners in their families. The sample was restricted to these respondents because the GSS collected data on respondents' individual income and family income, but not on spousal income. For two-earner families where both husband and wife are employed, we could estimate spousal income as family income minus the respondent's individual income, and we employed such estimates for spousal income. We also excluded respondents with missing data for the dependent variable (subjective class identification) and key covariates (own and spousal education, occupational prestige, and employment status, respondent's income, and family income). The sample thus retained is made up of 2,631 women.

The dependent variable is class identification, having four ordered categories (upper, middle, working, and lower class), as an interval scale variable. The weighted variables are education, occupational prestige, and income weighted between own and spousal statuses. Education is based either on the number of years of education or consists of five categories (0–11 years, 12 years, 13–15 years, 16 years, 17–20 years) depending on the model. Occupational prestige is divided by 100 and income is adjusted for yearly change in the average Consumer Price Index to reflect changes in the purchasing value of a dollar due to inflation and is divided by 10,000 after the adjustment.

As nonweighted covariates, I employ (1) year (year minus 1978), (2) age (age minus 20), (3) race (1: blacks; 0: nonblacks), (4) part-time job (versus full-time job), and (5) self-employed (versus employee). These covariates are included as predictors of the dependent variable and are examined for possible interactions with weighted variables.

In Yamaguchi and Wang (2001), a companion paper on class identification, I present comprehensive substantive analyses based on the GSS data including the analyses of both married men and women with more covariates. The analyses also include models with a dichotomous dependent variable with a logit link function, and models where the weighted variables are own composite status and spousal composite status weighted among education, occupational prestige, and income. In contrast, the analyses below are illustrative, and are concerned with demonstrating the usefulness of the models introduced in this paper.

5. APPLICATION: AN ANALYSIS OF CLASS IDENTIFICATION AMONG MARRIED WORKING WOMEN

Table 1 presents results from three models (1, 2, and 3). Models 1 and 2 do not include any interaction effect between weighted and nonweighted covariates, and they differ only in the interval versus categorical treatment for the weighted education variable. These two models include only the main effects of three weighted and five nonweighted covariates. Model 3, which retains the categorical expression for education, is the best-fitting model among those that hypothesize interaction effects between three weighted variables and five covariates—except that I retained one nonsignificant coefficient because of its substantive relevance to a key hypothesis.

The following describes the procedural method for identifying model 3 to be the best model among those models that hypothesize the interaction effects between three weighted variables and five covariates. For each of the five covariates (year, age, race, part-time, and self-employment), I first tested four alternative forms of interactions—(1) "sum and ratio," (2) "sum only," (3) "ratio only," and (4) no interaction—where "sum and ratio," for example, implies that the covariate affects both β_j and w_j. I then tested two other forms—(5) unconstrained weight

TABLE 1
Results from Models Using Three Status Variables as Weighted Variables

	Model 1		Model 2		Model 3
	b	β	b	β	b
I. Weighted predictors					
(1A) Education (years)	0.057	0.230	—		—
	(7.75)				
(1B) Education (versus 12)	—		—	0.595	—
0–11 years	—		−0.004		−0.070
			(0.87)		(1.60)
13–15 years	—		0.137		0.155
			(4.13)		(4.59)
16 years	—		0.340		0.365
			(8.50)		(8.99)
17 years or more	—		0.408		0.426
			(9.04)		(9.36)
(2) Income	0.371	0.283	0.369	0.282	0.238
	(13.84)		(13.81)		(4.85)
(3) Prestige	0.401	0.081	0.370	0.074	0.381
	(3.44)		(1.86)		(3.33)
II. Interaction effects of weighted predictors and nonweighted predictors					
(1) Income × year	—		—		0.009
					(2.73)
(2) Income × self-employed	—		—		0.158
					(2.58)
III. Nonweighted predictors					
(1) Year	−0.004		−0.003		−0.012
	(2.48)		(2.27)		(3.56)
(2) Age	0.002		0.002		0.002
	(2.83)		(2.43)		(2.40)
(3) Black	−0.167		−0.161		0.035
	(5.10)		(4.91)		(0.53)
(4) Part-time	0.034		0.030		0.016
	(1.45)		(1.30)		(0.67)
(5) Self-employed	0.056		0.053		−0.067
	(1.85)		(1.74)		(0.96)
(6) Constant	1.102		1.854		1.961

continued

TABLE 1
continued

	Model 1		Model 2		Model 3	
	b	β	b	β	b	
IV. Weights on:	own status		own status		own status	spousal status
(1) Intercept Education	0.575		0.572		0.528	[0.472]
	(7.75)		(8.19)		(8.03)	
Income	0.533		0.528		0.462	[0.538]
	(17.72)		(17.37)		(7.69)	
Prestige	0.352		0.345		0.362	[0.638]
	(2.06)		(1.86)		(2.05)	
(2) Year: Income	—		—		0.000	[0.000]
					(0.00)	
(3) Black: Education	—		—		—	−0.821
						(3.93)
Income	—		—		—	−0.400
						(2.85)
(4) Self-employed:	—		—		0.151	[−0.151]
All three statuses					(2.94)	
V. Log sigma squared	−1.411		−1.418		−1.437	
VI. Log-likelihood	−1876.22		−1866.61		−1842.31	

Note: b: unstandardized coefficients; β: standardized coefficient.
Numbers in parentheses are asymptotic z statistics.
Numbers in brackets are those obtained due to constraints that intercept weights sum to 1 and the effect of the particular covariate on weights sum to zero.

for own status, and (6) unconstrained weight for spousal status—when form 1 is found to be the best in the first step. Since forms 2 through 6 are nested within form 1, we can identify the best-fitting form by the likelihood ratio test for each of the 15 combinations of five covariates and three weighted variables. The test results may depend on whether other interaction effects are included in the model, however. Hence, I first identified the best form for each 15 cases by assuming no other interaction effects, and then confirmed afterward that the same pattern is still the best when all other significant interaction effects found in the first step are included in the model. In the present application, no change was necessary in the second step, thereby uniquely identifying the tentative best-fitting model.

However, we are also interested in identifying the model that hypothesizes uniform effects across three weighted variables if such a model provides more parsimony. Owing to an elimination of redundancy in parameterization, it is quite possible that the set of nonsignificant effects in the same direction may gain significance with the estimation of such uniform effects. Therefore, we need to test uniform effects before individually nonsignificant effects are eliminated from the model. In order to do this, I first examined for each covariate the results from the model that uses the full sum and ratio expression for the three weighted variables—i.e., the model that employs six parameters to characterize the interaction effects of a covariate with the three weighted variables. When the model with these full sets of λ_{jn} and γ_{jkn} parameters suggested a possibility of a uniform effect because of similar amounts in the estimates of λ_{jn} or γ_{jkn} across all three cases, I tested models that combine such uniform effects with characteristics found in the tentatively best-fitting model identified above. This procedure ultimately required only one change. The tentatively best-fitting model used three parameters to characterize the interaction effects of self-employment with the three weighted variables: (1) the effect of (income) $\times$ (self-employment) on the sum, (2) the effect of (income) $\times$ (self-employment) on the ratio, and (3) the effect of (education) $\times$ (self-employment) on the ratio. However, the use of two parameters—namely, (1) the effect of (income) $\times$ (self-employment) on the sum and (2) the uniform effect of (education, prestige, income) $\times$ (self-employment) on the ratio—was found to be more parsimonious. It was concluded that the model thus identified is the best-fitting model. Model 3 of Table 1 adds one nonsignificant parameter—namely, the effect of (income) $\times$ (year) on the ratio, to the best-fitting model because the nonsignificance of this interaction effect is theoretically relevant.

First I focus on the results of models 1 and 2 regarding the effects of the three weighted variables. The results show that education, occupational prestige, and income all affect class identification significantly. The relative importance among these three class attributes (indicated by their *standardized* coefficients) varies according to whether we measure education by the number of years of education or by a set of categories. Occupational prestige is consistently the least important predictor. Model 1, which uses the number of years of education, shows much less explanatory power for education than model 2 and thereby makes education the second most important predictor next to income. However, model 2, which treats education categorically, shows that education is the most important predictor of subjective class. Model 2 also shows that there is no significant difference in class identification between those with 12 years of education and those with less than 12 years of education, but that with each additional level of education above 12 years, there is a significant increase in the level of subjective class, with the widest gap between those who have bachelor's degrees and those without.

For each class attribute, models 1 and 2 show similar results regarding the average weight of own status compared with husband's status. However, there is one important qualitative difference between the two results. Note that since we assume no interaction effects between weighted and nonweighted covariates, these weights reflect the average tendency. For both education and income, the status-sharing hypothesis holds because the weights for own attribute are not significantly different from 0.5— they differ significantly from 0 and 1. For occupational prestige, the weight for own status is greater than 0 at the 5 percent level of significance in the results of model 1, but it is not significantly greater than 0 in the results of model 2. Generally, model 1, which uses the number of years of education, tends to overestimate the effect of occupational prestige. This is because the model attributes to the effect of occupational prestige a part of the nonlinear effect of education not captured by the number of years of education. The results of model 2 indicate that after the elimination of such an overestimation of the effect of occupational prestige, the prestige of own occupation becomes nonsignificant. Model 2 thus indicates that the status-borrowing hypothesis cannot be rejected for occupational prestige. In any case, married working women derive their subjective classes from their husband's occupation rather than from their own occupation— although they derive their subjective classes nearly equally from their own and their husbands' statuses regarding education and income.

Nonweighted predictors show, consistently in both the results of models 1 and 2, that controlling for other variables, (1) women identify themselves with lower classes in more recent years, (2) older women identify themselves with higher classes as they age, (3) African-American women identify themselves with lower classes than women of other races, and (4) class identification is affected neither by having a part-time work rather than a full-time work nor by being self-employed rather than an employee.

Model 3 shows that three covariates—namely, year, race, and self-employment—have unique patterns of interaction effects with weighted variables. The interaction effect of weighted income and year indicates that income has a greater effect on married women's class identification in more recent years. Note that the effect of the year on the weight between own and spousal income is nonsignificant and virtually nonexistent. (The log-likelihood has the same value as in Table 1 without this parameter estimate.) This is the only interaction effect that involves the year variable. Hence, there is no significant tendency that married working women's class identification has come to depend more on their own class attributes rather than on their spousal attributes in more recent years. However, this result is restricted to married working women, and since the rate of women's labor force participation has increased over time, a trend toward increased "independence" may hold if we include all married women.

The interaction effects involving race are best indicated by the unconstrained-weight expression because race interacts only with the effects of spousal class attributes. Compared with other women, African-American women have much reduced weights for their husbands' education and income in identifying their class subjectively—while weights for their own class attributes remain the same as other women. These weight reductions are to such an extent that neither spousal education nor spousal income affects their class identifications. Hence, unlike women of other races, the "independence hypothesis" holds for African-American women. One thing is noteworthy here. This "independence" is attained without increasing the importance of their own class attributes in deriving their subjective class. Regarding the effects of their own class attributes on class identification, African-American women are not different from other women. Accordingly, the subjective class of African-American women depends less on objective class attributes than women of other races.

The interaction effects involving employment status are the most complicated. The most parsimonious expression is characterized by two coefficients presented in Table 1. First, self-employed women have a significantly greater relative weight for own class attributes than spousal class attributes in deriving their subjective class. This is a *uniform* effect that applies equally to education, occupational prestige, and income. Second, there is a positive interaction effect between weighted income and self-employment such that the effect of income on class identification is greater for self-employed women than for women who are employees. These two results come from the following characteristics of the interaction effects between self-employment and class attributes. As for income, the effect of own income is greater for self-employed women than for other women, while the effect of spousal income does not differ significantly, thereby leading to an increase in both the sum of own income effect and spousal income effect and the ratio of own income effect for self-employed women. Regarding the other two class attributes—i.e., education and occupational prestige—the relative weights of their own attributes compared with spousal attributes tend to increase without changes in the sum of the effects of own and spousal attributes. These results also show that like African-American women, self-employed women are more independent than other women in deriving their subjective class. But unlike African-American women for whom the objective basis of their subjective class is weaker than women of other races, self-employed women's subjective class depends more strongly on their objective class situations than women who are employees because of the increased income effect.

6. CONCLUSION

While regression models with parametrically weighted variables are simple in structure, they can provide meaningful and parsimonious characterizations of the interaction effects between pairs/groups of mutually related variables and other covariates on dependent variables. The models are bilinear reparameterizations of linear regression models (or logistic regression models for dichotomous dependent variables) with various constraints on parameters for the interaction effects, and the parameters can be stably estimated by the maximum-likelihood estimation. The usefulness of these models were demonstrated by the illustrative analysis of class identification, which differentiated patterns of the interaction effects of year, race, and self-employment with weighted education, occupational prestige, and income.

The models described here will be useful for many studies beyond the current application. One such area of research includes various studies of individual and family outcomes with couples' data. For example, one may analyze marital satisfaction as a function of subjects' and their spouses' education, income, and employment status, or analyze the division of household labor between subjects and their spouses among dual-worker families as a function of subjects' and spouse's education, occupation, income, and gender-role attitudes. As in the application presented in this paper, interesting substantive questions are those concerning the relative weights between the husband's and wives' attributes and variation of those weights with covariates. The models introduced here will also be useful to researchers who plan to use a group of variables (such as depression, drug use and health, employment status) measured at two points in time in predicting outcomes (such as marital dissolution). One can assess the relative importance of the effect of a more recent state (time 2) compared to a past state (time 1) for each variable when both affect the outcome, and how the relative importance of a more recent state varies with covariates such as race/ethnicity and education in predicting the outcome. The two time points need not be two fixed time points; one may employ own education and parents' education as a group of variables in predicting own status attainment, or employ first-job status and current-job status as a pair of variables in predicting current income, health, etc. If the pair or the group of variables is categorical—such as a pair of sets of occupational categories or a pair of sets of educational levels—the method described in this paper will be especially useful if a researcher wishes to impose a common nonlinear latent scale for the variables in the group in predicting the outcome.

APPENDIX: METHODS OF PARAMETER ESTIMATION AND PROGRAM WGTREG.FOR

Although this paper employed the maximum-likelihood estimation using the Newton-Raphson algorithm, the estimates for parameters other than $\log(\sigma)$ are identical to the least-square estimates because of the standard assumption of normality, linearity, and homoscedasticity for the error term. Since the equation is bilinear rather than linear as a function of parameters, the least-square method should employ the alternating least-square estimation, which alternates iteratively the estimation of the set of lambda parameters (parameters for the effects of weighted variables and their dependence on covariates) and that of the set of gamma parameters (parameters for weights and their dependence on covariates), with the set of parameters for the effects of nonweighted variables included in both steps. The maximum-likelihood estimation also employs the same alternating procedure but differs from the least square estimates in that it simultaneously estimates the logarithm of the variance of the error term.

Although the alternating least-square estimation is very easy to program, each model to be tested may employ a distinct set of constraints on the parameters, such as zero-sum constraints, equiproportionality constraints, and equality constraints, while the set of explanatory variables included in the model is the same. This implies that design matrices that require only slight modifications from each other need to be specified individually. In order to eliminate such redundancy, I have written a FORTRAN program for which various alternative forms of constraints can be specified by simply assigning a number for each covariate. This FORTRAN program, WGTREG.FOR, is available free of charge from Statlib by sending the E-mail message "send WGTREG.FOR from general" to statlib@stat.emu.edu. The program is written in FORTRAN77 and requires FORTRAN compiling and linkage software for FORTRAN 77 or 90 to make it executable. The program manual is attached as comments in the beginning of the program. For those without a FORTRAN compiler, a copy of the executable program of WGTREG.FOR and its WORD program manual are also available from the author on request.

REFERENCES

Anderson, J. A. 1984. "Regression and Ordered Categorical Variables." *Journal of Royal Statistical Society*, Ser. B4, 6:1–30.

Beeghley, Leonard, and John Cochran. 1988. "Class Identification and Gender-Role Norms among Employed Married Women." *Journal of Marriage and the Family* 50:719–29.

Bentler, Peter M. 1995. *EQS Program Manual*. Multivariate Software, Inc.

Clogg, Clifford C. 1982a. "Some Models for the Analysis of Association in Multiway Contingency Tables Having Ordered Categories." *Journal of the American Statistical Association* 77:803–15.

———. 1982b. "Using Association Models in Sociological Research: Some Examples." *American Journal of Sociology* 88:113–34.

Clogg, Clifford C., and Edward S. Shihadeh. 1994. *Statistical Models for Ordinal Variables*. Newbury Park, CA: Sage.

Davis, Nancy J., and Robert V. Robinson. 1988. "Class Identification of Men and Women in the 1970s and 1980s." *American Sociological Review* 53:103–12.

De Graaf, Nan Dirk, and Paul NieuwBeerta. 1995. "Class Mobility and Political Party Preference: Individual and Contextual Effects." *American Journal of Sociology* 100:997–1027.

DiPrete, Thomas A. 1990. "Adding Covariates to Loglinear Models for the Study of Social Mobility." *American Sociological Review* 55:440–64.

Erikson, Robert, and John H. Goldthorpe. 1992. "Individual or Family? Results from Two Approaches to Class Assignment." *Acta Sociologia* 35:95–105.

Goodman, Leo A. 1979. "Simple Models for the Analysis of Association Having Ordered Categories." *Journal of the American Statistical Association* 74:537–52.

———. 1986. "Some Useful Extension of Usual Correspondence Analysis Approach and Usual Log-linear Models Approach in the Analysis of Contingency Tables." *International Statistical Review* 54:243–70.

Goldthorpe, John H. 1983. "Women and Class Analysis: In Defence of Conventional View." *Sociology* 17:465–88.

Heise, David R. 1972. "Employing Nominal Variables, Induced Variables, and Block Variables in Path Analysis." *Sociological Methodology* 1:147–173.

Jackman, Mary R., and Robert W. Jackman. 1983. *Class Awareness in the United States.* Berkeley: University of California Press.

Jöreskog, Karl G., and Dag Sörbom. 1984. *LISREL VI: Analysis of Linear Structural Relationships by Maximum Likelihood, Instrumental Variables, and Least Square Methods.* Scientific Software: Mooresville, IN.

McCullagh, Peter, and John A. Nelder. 1989. *Generalized Linear Models,* 2d ed. London: Chapman-Hill.

Simpson, Ida Harper, David Stark, and Robert A. Jackson. 1988. "Class Identification Processes of Married, Working Men and Women." *American Sociological Review* 53:284–302.

Sobel, Michael. 1981. "Diagonal Mobility Models: A Substantively Motivated Class of Designs for the Analysis of Mobility Effects." *American Sociological Review* 46:893–906.

———. 1985. "Social Mobility and Fertility Revisited: Some New Models for the Analysis of the Mobility Effects Hypothesis." *American Sociological Review* 50:699–712.

Sorenson, Ann Marie. 1989. "Husbands' and Wives' Characteristics and Fertility Decisions: A Diagonal Mobility Model." *Demography* 26:125–135.

Weakliem, David. 1992. "Does Social Mobility Affect Political Behavior?" *European Sociological Review* 8:153–165.

Xie, Yu. 1991. "The Log-Multiplicative Layer-Effect Model for Comparing Mobility Tables." *American Sociological Review* 57:380–95.

———. 1994. "Logmultiplicative Models for Discrete-Time, Discrete-Covariate Event-History Data." *Sociological Methodology* 24:301–41.

Yamaguchi, Kazuo. 1990. "Some Models for the Analysis of Asymmetric Association in Contingency Tables Having Ordered Categories." Pp. 181–211 in *Sociological Methodology 1990,* edited by Clifford C. Clogg. Cambridge, MA: Blackwell Publishing.

Zipp, John F., and Eric Plutzer. 1996. "Wives and Husbands: Social Class, Gender and Class Identification in the United States." *Sociology* 30:235–52.

FIXED-EFFECTS NEGATIVE BINOMIAL REGRESSION MODELS

Paul D. Allison*
Richard P. Waterman*

This paper demonstrates that the conditional negative binomial model for panel data, proposed by Hausman, Hall, and Griliches (1984), is not a true fixed-effects method. This method—which has been implemented in both Stata and LIMDEP—does not in fact control for all stable covariates. Three alternative methods are explored. A negative multinomial model yields the same estimator as the conditional Poisson estimator and hence does not provide any additional leverage for dealing with over-dispersion. On the other hand, a simulation study yields good results from applying an unconditional negative binomial regression estimator with dummy variables to represent the fixed effects. There is no evidence for any incidental parameters bias in the coefficients, and downward bias in the standard error estimates can be easily and effectively corrected using the deviance statistic. Finally, an approximate conditional method is found to perform at about the same level as the unconditional estimator.

1. INTRODUCTION

A major attraction of panel data is the ability to control for all stable covariates, without actually including them in a regression equation. In general, this is accomplished by using only within-individual variation to estimate the parameters and then averaging the estimates over individuals. Regression models for accomplishing this are often called fixed-effects models.

*University of Pennsylvania.

Fixed-effects models have been developed for a variety of different data types and models, including linear models for quantitative data (Mundlak 1978), logistic regression models for categorical data (Chamberlain 1980), Cox regression models for event history data (Yamaguchi 1986; Allison 1996), and Poisson regression models for count data (Palmgren 1981).

Here we consider some alternative fixed-effects models for count data. First, we show that the fixed-effects negative binomial model proposed by Hausman, Hall, and Griliches (1984) (hereafter HHG) is not a true fixed-effects method. Next we consider a negative multinomial model, which leads back to the estimator for the fixed-effects Poisson model. We then use simulated data to compare an unconditional negative binomial estimator with the fixed-effects Poisson estimator. The negative binomial estimator does not appear to suffer from any "incidental parameters" bias, and is generally superior to the Poisson estimator. Finally, we investigate an approximate conditional likelihood method for the negative binomial model. Its performance on the simulated data is roughly comparable to that of the unconditional negative binomial estimator.

2. THE FIXED-EFFECTS POISSON MODEL

The fixed-effects Poisson regression model for panel data has been described in detail by Cameron and Trivedi (1998). The dependent variable y_{it} varies over individuals ($i = 1, \ldots, n$) and over time ($t = 1, \ldots, T_i$). It is assumed to have a Poisson distribution with parameter μ_{it}, which in turn depends on a vector of exogenous variables $\mathbf{x}_{it}$ according to the loglinear function

$$\ln \mu_{it} = \delta_i + \beta \mathbf{x}_{it}, \tag{1}$$

where δ_i is the "fixed effect."

One way to estimate this model is to do conventional Poisson regression by maximum likelihood, including dummy variables for all individuals (less one) to directly estimate the fixed effects. An alternative method is conditional maximum likelihood, conditioning on the count total $\sum_t y_{it}$ for each individual. For the Poisson model, this yields a conditional likelihood that is proportional to

$$\prod_i \prod_t \left(\frac{\exp(\beta \mathbf{x}_{it})}{\sum_s \exp(\beta \mathbf{x}_{is})} \right)^{y_{it}}, \tag{2}$$

which is equivalent to the likelihood function for a multinomial logit model for grouped data. Note that conditioning has eliminated the δ_i parameters from the likelihood function.

For logistic regression models, it is well known that estimation of fixed-effects models by the inclusion of dummy variables yields inconsistent estimates of β (Hsiao 1986) due to the "incidental parameters" problem (Kalbfleisch and Sprott 1970), while conditional estimation does not suffer from this problem. For Poisson regression, on the other hand, these two estimation methods—unconditional maximization of the likelihood and conditional likelihood—always yield identical estimates for β and the associated covariance matrix (Cameron and Trivedi 1998). Hence, the choice of method should be dictated by computational convenience.

The fixed-effects Poisson regression model allows for unrestricted heterogeneity across individuals but, for a given individual, there is still the restriction that the mean of each count must equal its variance:

$$E(y_{it}) = \text{var}(y_{it}) = \mu_{it}. \tag{3}$$

In many data sets, however, there may be additional heterogeneity not accounted for by the model.

As an example, let's consider the patent data analyzed by HHG and reanalyzed by Cameron and Trivedi (1998). The data consist of 346 firms with yearly data on number of patents from 1975 to 1979. Thus, y_{it} is the number of patents for firm i in year t. This variable ranged from 0 to 515 with a mean of 35 and a standard deviation of 71. A little over half of the firm years had patent counts of five or less. The regressor variables include the logarithm of research and development expenditures in the current year and in each of the previous five years. All the fitted models also include four dummy variables corresponding to years 1976 to 1979.

To analyze the data, we created a separate observation for each firm year, for a total of 1730 working observations. We then estimated a fixed-effects Poisson regression model by conventional Poisson regression software,[1] with 345 dummy variables to estimate the fixed effects. Results for the research and development variables are shown in the first two columns of Table 1. These numbers differ somewhat from those in Cameron and Trivedi (1998), but they are identical to the corrected results reported in their website (http://www.econ.ucdavis.edu/faculty/cameron/).

---

[1]We used the GENMOD procedure in SAS.

TABLE 1
Conditional Regression Models for Number of Patents

	Conditional Poisson		Conditional Negative Binomial			
	Coefficient	Standard Error	Coefficient	Standard Error	Coefficient	Standard Error
LogRD-0	.322	.046	.363	.085	.272	.071
LogRD-1	−.087	.049	.156	.099	−.098	.077
LogRD-2	.079	.045	.174	.090	.032	.071
LogRD-3	.001	.041	.015	.083	−.020	.066
LogRD-4	−.005	.038	.029	.076	.016	.063
LogRD-5	.003	.032	.136	.062	−.010	.053
Log SIZE					.207	.078
SCIENCE					.018	.198
Intercept					1.660	.343

A potential problem with these results is that there is still some evidence of overdispersion in the data. The ratio of the deviance to the degrees of freedom is 2.04 (deviance = 2807 with 1374 d.f.) and the ratio of the Pearson goodness-of-fit chi-square to the degrees of freedom is 1.97 (chi-square = 2709 with 1374 d.f.). For a good-fitting model, these measures should be close to 1. Substantial departures from this ratio may indicate a problem with the model specification, and also suggest that the estimated standard errors may be downwardly biased.

3. THE HHG NEGATIVE BINOMIAL MODEL

HHG deal with the problem of overdispersion by assuming that y_{it} has a negative binomial distribution, which can be regarded as a generalization of the Poisson distribution with an additional parameter allowing the variance to exceed the mean. There are several different ways to parameterize the negative binomial distribution, and the choice can be consequential for regression models. In the HHG model, the negative binomial mass function can be written as

$$f(y_{it}|\lambda_{it},\theta_i) = \frac{\Gamma(\lambda_{it}+y_{it})}{\Gamma(\lambda_{it})\Gamma(y_{it}+1)}\left(\frac{\theta_i}{1+\theta_i}\right)^{y_{it}}\left(\frac{1}{1+\theta_i}\right)^{\lambda_{it}} \qquad (4)$$

where Γ is the gamma function. The parameter θ_i is assumed to be constant over time for each individual while λ_{it} depends on covariates by the function

$$\ln \lambda_{it} = \beta \mathbf{x}_{it}. \tag{5}$$

The decision to decompose λ_{it} as a function of the covariates is somewhat surprising, since λ is usually regarded as an overdispersion parameter. That's because (4) becomes the Poisson mass function as $\lambda \to \infty$.

The mean and variance of y_{it} are given by

$$E(y_{it}) = \theta_i \lambda_{it}$$

$$\text{var}(y_{it}) = (1 + \theta_i)\theta_i \lambda_{it}. \tag{6}$$

Under this model, the ratio of the variance to the mean is $1 + \theta_i$, which can vary across individuals but, as already noted, is constant over time.

HHG further assume that for a given individual i, the y_{it} are independent over time. These assumptions imply that $\sum_t y_{it}$ also has a negative binomial distribution with parameters θ_i and $\sum_t \lambda_{it}$. Conditioning on these total counts, the likelihood function for a single individual is given by

$$\frac{\Gamma\left(\sum_t y_{it} + 1\right)\Gamma\left(\sum_t \lambda_{it}\right)}{\Gamma\left(\sum_t y_{it} + \sum_t \lambda_{it}\right)} \prod_t \frac{\Gamma(\lambda_{it} + y_{it})}{\Gamma(\lambda_{it})\Gamma(y_{it} + 1)}, \tag{7}$$

thereby eliminating the θ_i parameters. The likelihood for the entire sample is obtained by multiplying together all the individual terms like (7). This likelihood may be maximized with respect to the β parameters using conventional numerical methods. In fact, the method has been implemented in at least two commercial statistical packages, Stata (www.stata.com) and LIMDEP (www.limdep.com).

In the middle two columns of Table 1, we report results of applying this method to the patent data,[2] using the same covariates as Cameron and Trivedi (1998). The numbers reported here are the same as the corrected numbers given in their website. Note that the coefficients are

---

[2] To estimate the model, we used the NLMIXED procedure in SAS. This required the specification of the log-likelihood for a single individual.

similar in magnitude to those for the conditional Poisson method, but the estimated standard errors are appreciably larger because the model allows for overdispersion.

Unfortunately, this negative binomial model and its conditional likelihood does not really fit the bill as a fixed-effects method. The basic problem is that the θ_i parameters that are conditioned out of the likelihood function do not correspond to different intercepts in the log-linear decomposition of λ_{it}. HHG's rationale is that if we write $\theta_i = \exp(\delta_i)$, equations (5) and (6) imply that

$$E(y_{it}) = \exp(\delta_i + \beta x_{it})$$

$$\mathrm{var}(y_{it}) = (1 + e^{\delta_i})E(y_{it}).$$

Therefore, it appears that this model does allow for an arbitrary intercept δ_i for each individual. The problem with this approach is that the δ_i's play a different role than x_{it}. Specifically, changes in x_{it} affect the mean directly, and affect the variance only indirectly through the mean. But changes in δ_i affect the variance both indirectly, through the mean, and directly. If we regard δ_i as representing the effects of omitted explanatory variables, then there is no compelling reason why these variables should have a different kind of effect from that of x_{it}.

To put it another way, suppose we begin with equations (6) and specify

$$\lambda_{it} = \exp(\delta_i + \beta \mathbf{x}_{it} + \gamma z_i),$$

where δ_i is an individual-specific intercept and z_i is a vector of time-invariant covariates. Then conditioning on the total count for each individual does *not* eliminate δ_i or γz_i from the likelihood function.

Symptomatic of this problem is that using HHG's conditional likelihood in (7), one can estimate regression models with both an intercept and time-invariant covariates, something that is usually not possible with conditional fixed-effects models. The last two columns of Table 1 show results for estimating the conditional negative binomial model with an intercept and two time-invariant covariates.[3] Both the intercept and one of the two covariates are statistically significant at beyond the .01 level.

---

[3] SIZE is the firm book value in 1972. SCIENCE is an indicator variable equal to 1 if the firm is in the science sector.

4. A NEGATIVE MULTINOMIAL MODEL

We now consider an alternative parameterization of the negative binomial model that is a more natural generalization of the Poisson model. The mass function for a single y_{it} is given by

$$f(y_{it}|\mu_{it},\lambda_i) = \frac{\Gamma(\lambda_i + y_{it})}{\Gamma(\lambda_i)\Gamma(y_{it} + 1)} \left(\frac{\mu_{it}}{\mu_{it} + \lambda_i} \right)^{y_{it}} \left(\frac{\lambda_i}{\mu_{it} + \lambda_i} \right)^{\lambda_i}, \qquad (8)$$

with mean and variance functions

$$E(y_{it}) = \mu_{it}$$

$$\text{var}(y_{it}) = \mu_{it}(1 + \mu_{it}/\lambda_i). \qquad (9)$$

Note that the mean is allowed to vary with time, but the overdispersion parameter λ_i is assumed to be constant for each individual. To model dependence on covariates, we let

$$\ln \mu_{it} = \delta_i + \beta \mathbf{x}_{it}. \qquad (10)$$

Cameron and Trivedi (1998) refer to this as an NB2 model, to distinguish it from the previous NB1 model.

If we assume (along with HHG) that the event counts are independent across time for each individual, then this model is not tractable for deriving a conditional likelihood. That's because $\sum_t y_{it}$ does not itself have a negative binomial distribution, so it's awkward to condition on it. More technically, under this specification, there is no complete sufficient statistic for the δ_i's that is a function of the data alone.

As an alternative approach, let's assume that the y_{it} have a negative multinomial distribution, a well-known multivariate generalization of the negative binomial distribution (Johnson and Kotz 1969). For a single individual, the joint mass function is given by

$$f(y_{i1},\ldots,y_{iT}|\lambda_i,\mu_{i1},\ldots,\mu_{iT}) = \frac{\Gamma\left(\lambda_i + \sum_t y_{it}\right)}{\Gamma(\lambda_i)y_{i1}!\ldots y_{iT}!} \left(\frac{\lambda_i}{\lambda_i + \sum_t \mu_{it}} \right)^{\lambda_i}$$

$$\times \prod_t \left(\frac{\mu_{it}}{\lambda_i + \sum_t \mu_{it}} \right)^{y_{it}} \qquad (11)$$

with μ_{it} specified as in (10).[4] This multivariate distribution has the property that the marginal distribution of each y_{it} is negative binomial as defined in (8). Furthermore, the sum $\sum_t y_{it}$ has a negative binomial distribution with parameters $\sum_t \mu_{it}$ and λ_i. Unlike the HHG model, this one does *not* assume that event counts in different time intervals are independent for a given individual. In fact, the correlation (Johnson and Kotz 1969) between y_{it} and $y_{is}(s \neq t)$ is

$$\rho(y_{it}, y_{is}) = \sqrt{\left(\frac{\mu_{it}}{\mu_{it} + \lambda_i}\right)\left(\frac{\mu_{is}}{\mu_{is} + \lambda_i}\right)} \qquad (12)$$

To derive a fixed effects estimator for β, we can condition the joint mass function on the total $\sum_t y_{it}$, which yields

$$f\left(y_{i1}, \ldots, y_{iT} \middle| \sum_t y_{it}\right) = \frac{y_{i1}! \ldots y_{iT}!}{\Gamma\left(1 + \sum_t y_{it}\right)} \prod_t \left(\frac{\mu_{it}}{\sum_t \mu_{it}}\right)^{y_{it}}$$

$$\propto \prod_t \left(\frac{\exp(\beta \mathbf{x}_{it})}{\sum_s \exp(\beta \mathbf{x}_{is})}\right)^{y_{it}} \qquad (13)$$

Thus, conditioning gives us a distribution that doesn't depend on the parameter λ_i but is proportional to the conditional likelihood for the Poisson model in equation (2). In other words, the fixed-effects negative multinomial model leads to the same conditional estimator of β as the fixed-effects Poisson model.[5]

So it seems that the negative multinomial approach doesn't accomplish anything with respect to overdispersion. To understand this, recall that the negative binomial distribution can be generated by compounding a Poisson random variable with a gamma random variable. The negative multinomial can be generated by compounding a set of independent Poisson random variables with a single gamma random variable. Thus, the overdispersion in the negative multinomial can be thought of as arising from a single random variable that is common to all the event counts

----

[4]This distribution is the same as the one described by Cameron and Trivedi (1998, p. 288) as a Poisson random-effects model with gamma distributed random effects.
   [5]See Guo (1996) for an application of the negative multinomial model in a random-effects setting.

for a given individual (which is why the correlation in [12] is not zero). Conditioning on the total count for each individual removes all the unobserved heterogeneity, both that arising from the δ_i fixed-effects and the unobserved heterogeneity that is intrinsic to the negative multinomial distribution.

5. CONVENTIONAL APPROACHES TO OVERDISPERSION

We have seen that the HHG method does not condition out the fixed effects, while the negative multinomial method conditions out too much to be useful. What's left? A relatively simple approach is to estimate the β coefficients under the fixed-effects Poisson model but to adjust the standard errors upward for overdispersion. A commonly used adjustment is to multiply the standard errors by the square root of the ratio of the goodness-of-fit chi-square to the degrees of freedom. (Either Pearson's chi-square or the deviance could be used.) The first two columns of Table 2 show the Poisson coefficients and adjusted standard errors for the patent data. The coefficients are the same as those in Table 1. The standard errors were obtained by multiplying the standard errors in Table 1 by 1.404, the square root of Pearson's chi-square divided by the degrees of freedom.

An alternative approach is to estimate an unconditional negative binomial model. That is, to specify a conventional NB2 regression model, with dummy variables to estimate the fixed effects. Results of doing

TABLE 2
Regression Models with Overdispersion Corrections

	Fixed-Effects Poisson		Unconditional Negative Binomial	
	Coefficient	Adjusted Standard Error	Coefficient	Standard Error
LogRD-0	.322	.064	.356	.093
LogRD-1	−.087	.068	.021	.102
LogRD-2	.079	.063	.007	.096
LogRD-3	.001	.058	.008	.089
LogRD-4	−.005	.053	.117	.081
LogRD-5	.003	.045	.011	.067

that for the patent data are shown in the last two columns of Table 2.[6] The coefficients are similar to those obtained with a Poisson specification, but the negative binomial standard errors are notably larger than the Poisson standard errors, even though the latter are already adjusted for overdispersion.

There are two potential problems with the unconditional negative binomial method. First, since there is a potential incidental parameters problem, it is questionable whether the coefficient estimates are consistent. As yet, there is no proof of this one way or the other. Second, in the case of large sample sizes, it may be computationally impractical to estimate coefficients for large numbers of dummy variables. Greene (2001) has shown that the computational problem can be readily overcome for this and many other nonlinear fixed-effects models, although conventional software would have to be modified to implement his methods.

To investigate the performance of the unconditional negative binomial estimator and the fixed-effects Poisson estimator, we generated simulated data under the following model. For 100 individuals ($i = 1, \ldots, 100$) and two time periods ($t = 1, 2$), let y_{it} have a negative binomial distribution with conditional mean μ_{it} and overdispersion parameter λ (constant over individuals and time). Assume that y_{i1} and y_{i2} are independent, conditional on μ_{it}. Restricting the panel to only two time periods produces conditions most likely to yield evidence of bias due to the incidental parameters problem. Using samples of only 100 cases facilitates the use of conventional software to estimate the unconditional models (by including 99 dummies).

The conditional mean is specified as

$$\mu_{it} = \eta \exp(\beta x_{it} + \gamma z_i),$$

where x_{it} and z_i have standard normal distributions with correlation ρ. The variable z_i will be treated as unobserved. It can be interpreted as representing all the stable, unobserved characteristics of individual i that have some effect on y_{it}. Conditional on z_i, the observed variables x_{i1} and x_{i2} are uncorrelated. Unconditionally, their correlation is ρ^2.

As a baseline model, we set $\beta = 1$, $\gamma = 1$, $\lambda = 1$, and $\rho = 0$. For these parameter values, we generated data for 500 samples, each of size 100. (With two observations per case, the working sample size was 200.) For each sample, we estimated β using a conventional negative binomial

---

[6] Estimates were obtained with SAS PROC GENMOD.

regression program with x as the predictor, along with 99 dummy variables to capture the fixed effects. We then estimated β via a fixed-effects Poisson regression model, with an overdispersion correction for the standard errors. (Standard errors were multiplied by the square root of the ratio of the Pearson chi-square goodness-of-fit statistic to its degrees of freedom.)

This process was replicated over a range of plausible values for each parameter, with other parameters held at their baseline values. For each set of parameter values, Table 3 gives the mean of the coefficient estimates, standard error (standard deviation across the repeated samples), root mean squared error, and proportion of times that the nominal 95 percent confidence intervals contained the true value. For ease of comparison, the baseline model is replicated within each subpanel of Table 3. These baseline

TABLE 3
Simulation Results for Negative Binomial and Poisson Models

Model	Negative Binomial					Poisson			
	β	SE	RMSE	95% CI Coverage	Non-Conv.	β	SE	RMSE	95% CI Coverage
$\lambda = .2$	.978	.326	.327	.854	0	1.045	.458	.460	.724
$\lambda = .5$	.966	.191	.194	.854	3	1.011	.278	.278	.746
$\lambda = 1$ (base)	.982	.145	.146	.826	156	1.018	.202	.203	.778
$\lambda = 10$	.995	.063	.063	.902	500	1.005	.078	.078	.866
$\lambda = 50$	.996	.052	.052	.952	500	1.002	.053	.053	.928
$\gamma = 0$	.966	.124	.129	.846	327	1.003	.144	.144	.900
$\gamma = .5$	.966	.139	.143	.819	281	1.005	.169	.169	.850
$\gamma = 1$ (base)	.974	.138	.140	.838	140	1.016	.202	.203	.782
$\gamma = 1.5$	.967	.142	.146	.860	53	.999	.281	.281	.640
$\beta = 0$	.008	.116	.116	.872	1	.006	.163	.163	.730
$\beta = .5$	.474	.124	.126	.850	25	.490	.164	.164	.794
$\beta = 1$ (base)	.978	.131	.132	.866	144	1.014	.194	.194	.800
$\beta = 1.5$	1.454	.151	.158	.806	261	1.513	.279	.279	.726
$\eta = 1$	.978	.167	.168	.836	452	1.025	.221	.222	.860
$\eta = 2$	.974	.137	.139	.870	353	1.008	.189	.189	.836
$\eta = 4$ (base)	.968	.139	.142	.844	152	1.009	.211	.211	.758
$\eta = 6$	.972	.125	.128	.850	60	1.004	.202	.202	.752
$\eta = 8$	.977	.131	.133	.840	19	1.006	.209	.209	.760
$\rho = 0$ (base)	.959	.140	.146	.822	139	.989	.197	.197	.780
$\rho = .50$	.972	.160	.162	.846	38	1.011	.311	.311	.646
$\rho = .75$	.978	.204	.205	.872	6	1.016	.451	.451	.588

Note: SE is the standard error, RMSE is the root mean squared error, and CI is the confidence interval.

estimates were made from new random draws in each subpanel, which should provide some feel for the sampling variability of these estimates.

One potential problem that occurred with the negative binomial estimator was that, for many of the samples, the estimate for the overdispersion parameter λ did not converge. The number of nonconvergent samples is shown in Table 3. For the baseline model, this happened in about 20 percent of the samples. For other models, the percentage of convergent samples ranged from zero for true $\lambda = 50$ to 100 for true $\lambda = .2$. Nonconvergence for λ did not seem to affect the estimates for β, however. For all models with appreciable numbers of nonconvergent samples, we compared the means and standard errors of β for the convergent and nonconvergent samples. In no case was there a statistically significant difference, so the results in Table 3 are based on all samples combined.

The general conclusions to be drawn from Table 3 are these:

- There is little evidence for incidental parameters bias. Both the negative binomial and Poisson estimates appear to be approximately unbiased under all conditions, although the negative binomial estimates are always a bit too low.
- Root mean squared errors are appreciably lower for the negative binomial estimator, except when $\lambda = 50$ when the negative binomial distribution is very close to a Poisson distribution.
- Both estimators have confidence intervals that are too small, yielding coverage rates that are often considerably lower than the nominal 95 percent level. The Poisson estimator is much worse in this regard, especially for some of the more extreme parameter values. Although not obvious from the table, these reduced coverage rates stem from standard error estimates that are generally too small.

Now for the details. Variation in λ is crucial for comparing the negative binomial with the Poisson because it controls the degree of overdispersion. More specifically, as $\lambda \to \infty$, the negative binomial converges to the Poisson. Interestingly, both estimators do better in both RMSE and CI coverage when λ is large rather than small, although the degradation in performance with decreasing λ is more rapid for the Poisson estimator.

The parameter γ controls the variance of the stable, unobserved heterogeneity. The performance of the negative binomial estimator is hardly affected at all by changes in γ. But for the Poisson, increases in γ produce both substantial increases in RMSE and major decreases in CI coverage. Variations in the true value of β also show little impact on the performance of the negative binomial estimator. For the Poisson estimator, the CI coverage remains fairly stable with variations in β, but there is some evidence for an increase in the RMSE as β gets larger.

The parameter η is a scale factor that affects both the mean and variance of the counts. For these models, $\eta = 1$ produces a mean of about 3.8 while $\eta = 8$ yields a mean of 23. This is potentially important because when the mean is small, large proportions of the sample will have a count of 0 and it becomes increasingly difficult to discriminate between a Poisson distribution and a negative binomial distribution. In Table 3, we see that for $\eta = 1$, the Poisson estimator actually does a little better than the negative binomial estimator in CI coverage, although its RMSE is still about 30 percent larger. As η gets larger, the coverage rate for the Poisson estimator deteriorates, while remaining stable for the negative binomial estimator.

Finally, we examine the impact of ρ, the correlation between the observed variable x and the source of unobserved heterogeneity. When $\rho = 0$, as with all the models examined thus far, we satisfy the assumptions of a random effects model and could, presumably, do better using a random-effects negative binomial or Poisson estimator. When $\rho \neq 0$, random-effects estimators are likely to be biased, while fixed-effects estimators should remove that bias. Table 3 shows that both the negative binomial and Poisson estimators do a good job of avoiding bias in the estimate of β. However, with increasing ρ, the performance of the negative binomial estimator remains stable, while the Poisson estimator deteriorates substantially in both RMSE and CI coverage.

In sum, the message of Table 3 is that, under the specified model, the unconditional fixed-effects negative binomial estimator is virtually always a better choice than the fixed-effects Poisson estimator. But it is still troubling that the negative binomial estimator is accompanied by underestimates of the standard errors, leading to insufficient coverage of confidence intervals. It is natural to ask whether there is some way to adjust the standard errors upward. Table 4 shows the consequences of multiplying the standard errors by the square root of the ratio of the deviance to its degrees of freedom,[7] where the deviance is defined as

$$D = \sum_i \sum_t \{y_{it} \log(y_{it}/\mu_{it}) - (y_{it} + \lambda)\log[(y_{it} + \lambda)/(\mu_{it} + \lambda)]\}. \quad (14)$$

[7] With SAS PROC GENMOD, this correction can be implemented with the DSCALE option on the MODEL statement.

TABLE 4
Confidence Interval Coverage for Negative Binomial Model with Deviance
Overdispersion Correction.

Model	95% CI Coverage	Model	95% CI Coverage
$\lambda = .2$	.982	$\beta = 0$	.960
$\lambda = .5$	.972	$\beta = .5$	.972
$\lambda = 1$ (baseline)	.956	$\beta = 1$ (baseline)	.948
$\lambda = 10$	.956	$\beta = 1.5$	.940
$\lambda = 50$	.956	$\eta = 1$	.954
$\gamma = 0$	.966	$\eta = 2$	.964
$\gamma = .5$	.956	$\eta = 4$ (baseline)	.956
$\gamma = 1$ (baseline)	.960	$\eta = 6$	.968
$\gamma = 1.5$	.952	$\eta = 8$	.952
		$\rho = 0$ (baseline)	.962
		$\rho = .50$	.964
		$\rho = .75$	.950

With this correction, confidence intervals have close to their nominal coverage for all parameter values considered in the simulation. Somewhat surprisingly, standard error correction using the Pearson chi-square goodness-of-fit statistic did not produce any noticeable improvement over the conventional model-based standard error estimates (results not shown). Also, use of the deviance-based correction did not improve the confidence interval coverage for the Poisson estimator.

6. AN APPROXIMATE CONDITIONAL ESTIMATOR

Previously we remarked that conditional inference is not feasible for the NB2 model (with event counts independent over time for each individual) because there is no complete, sufficient statistic for the incidental parameters that is a function of the data alone. However, Waterman and Lindsay (1996a), following the work of Small and McLeish (1989), have introduced an approximate method that mimics the beneficial properties of conditional inference, even in situations where a straightforward conditioning approach fails. This methodology is termed the projected score method.

In conventional maximum likelihood estimation, the log-likelihood is differentiated to produce the score function. This function is then set equal to zero, and the solutions to this equation are the MLE's. The projected score method brings the score function itself to the center of attention, and engineers a version of the score function that has properties equivalent to the conditional score function if it existed; the desirable property is that among all estimating functions that are insensitive to the incidental parameters, it provides the maximal information.

Here are some details of the method. Let β be a vector of parameters of interest and let δ be a vector of nuisance (incidental) parameters. Let $U_0(\beta, \delta)$ be the conventional score function—that is, the first derivative of the log-likelihood function with respect to β. Let $U_\infty(\beta, \delta)$ denote the optimal estimating function, which is defined as follows. We restrict attention to all square, integrable functions $g(\beta, \delta)$ that satisfy the strong unbiasedness condition,

$$E\{g(\beta_0, \delta_0)\} = 0,$$

for all true values of δ, and for any values of β_0 and δ_0. This condition implies that the estimating function is insensitive to the values of the nuisance parameters, which is what we desire in a conditional method. Among functions that satisfy this condition, the optimal estimating equation is the one whose solution has lowest asymptotic variance. This function exists whenever certain regularity conditions are satisfied (Waterman and Lindsay 1996a). When a complete sufficient statistic exists, this optimal estimating function is identical to the score function for the conditional likelihood.

It can be shown (Waterman and Lindsay 1996a) that the optimal estimating function U_∞ can be expressed as an infinite series. Consider a single individual i with nuisance parameters δ_i. Define $V_\alpha = f^{(\alpha)}/f$ where f is the density function and $f^{(\alpha)}$ is the αth derivative of f with respect to δ_i. Then, we have for individual i

$$U_\infty(\beta, \delta) = U_0(\beta, \delta) - \sum_{\alpha=1}^{\infty} \rho_\alpha V_\alpha,$$

where the ρ_a are coefficients that depend on the parameters but not the data.

We approximate U by the first r terms of this series:

$$U_r(\beta, \delta) = U_0(\beta, \delta) - \sum_{\alpha=1}^{r} \rho_\alpha V_\alpha$$

Clearly one could construct an entire sequence of approximations to the optimal estimating function, but the hope is that the first approximation, denoted as the U_2 estimating function, is close enough for practical purposes. Waterman and Lindsay (1996b) show a number of examples for which this is the case. The way in which these approximate score functions are engineered to be close to the optimal one is identical to the way a least squares line is engineered to be close to the data. That is, a regression approach is used to obtain estimated values of ρ_a, but here the objects of interest are functions rather than data points. This is achieved by taking a set of derivatives of the score functions and their cross products and then finding expectations, so that the mathematical operations are differentiation and expectation. The effort in accomplishing this is minimized by using symbolic software, such as Mathematica or Maple, which can derive the functions with relatively modest input from the analyst. Once the projected score function has been obtained, the ML solutions can be obtained using standard software packages.

Using the U_2 approximation, we applied the projected score method to the NB2 model, which was the basis for the simulation study of the previous section. (Mathematica and R programs for accomplishing this are available from the authors.) Simulation results are displayed in Table 5.

Comparing the projected score estimates in Table 5 with the unconditional estimates in Tables 3 and 4, we find noticeably less bias in the projected score estimates for every condition. On the other hand, the standard errors for the projected score estimates are somewhat larger than those for the unconditional estimates in every case but one. Combining these results into the root mean squared errors, we find that the unconditional method does better in 13 out of the 21 conditions. With respect to confidence interval coverage, the projected score method is always appreciably better than the unconditional method using the uncorrected standard errors (Table 3). But when the unconditional estimates are corrected by the deviance (Table 4), the resulting confidence interval coverage is always closer to the nominal level than the coverage of the projected score method.

In sum, it does not appear that the projected score method based on the U_2 approximation offers any substantial advantage over the unconditional method with corrected standard errors, at least with respect to estimating β, the regression coefficients. However, the projected score method was much better at estimating λ, the overdispersion parameter. The number of convergence failures was far lower using the projected score method. Furthermore, if we restrict our attention to samples in which the estimate

TABLE 5
Simulation Results for Projected Score Method

Model	β	SE	RMSE	Projected Score Negative Binomial 95% CI Coverage	Non-Convg.
$\lambda = .2$	.994	.336	.336	.929	22
$\lambda = .5$	.993	.211	.211	.916	7
$\lambda = 1$ (baseline)	.988	.139	.139	.934	1
$\lambda = 10$	1.002	.069	.069	.919	7
$\lambda = 50$	1.001	.053	.053	.933	65
$\gamma = 0$	.995	.136	.136	.932	0
$\gamma = .5$	.997	.141	.141	.924	0
$\gamma = 1$ (baseline)	.996	.140	.140	.944	0
$\gamma = 1.5$	1.003	.143	.143	.927	4
$\beta = 0$	.005	.125	.125	.940	0
$\beta = .5$	.504	.133	.133	.936	1
$\beta = 1$ (baseline)	1.004	.140	.140	.936	0
$\beta = 1.5$	1.493	.155	.155	.934	2
$\eta = 1$	1.004	.178	.178	.930	0
$\eta = 2$	1.008	.164	.164	.932	1
$\eta = 4$ (baseline)	.989	.141	.142	.920	0
$\eta = 6$	1.000	.136	.136	.914	1
$\eta = 8$	1.002	.132	.132	.934	0
$\rho = 0$ (baseline)	.993	.140	.140	.924	0
$\rho = .50$	.996	.141	.141	.920	0
$\rho = .75$	1.007	.136	.136	.948	0

of λ converged, the unconditional estimates of λ had substantially greater upward bias than the projected score estimates (not shown in the tables). In principle, the projected score method could be improved by using more terms in the approximation.

7. CONCLUSION

The negative binomial model of Hausman, Hall, and Griliches (1984) and its associated conditional likelihood estimator does not accomplish what is usually desired in a fixed-effects method, the control of all stable covariates. That is because the model is based on a regression decomposition of the *overdispersion* parameter rather than the usual regression decomposition of the mean. Symptomatic of the problem is that programs that implement the conditional estimator have no difficulty estimating an intercept or coefficients for time-invariant covariates.

A good alternative is to do conventional negative binomial regression with direct estimation of the fixed effects rather than conditioning them out of the likelihood. Greene (2001) has demonstrated the computational feasibility of this approach, even with large sample sizes. Simulation results strongly suggest that this estimation method does not suffer from incidental parameters bias, and has much better sampling properties than the fixed-effects Poisson estimator. Bias in standard error estimates can be virtually eliminated by using a correction factor based on the deviance.

The approximate conditional score method is another attractive alternative. The approximation used here showed slightly less bias in the coefficient estimates but slightly more sampling variability than the unconditional estimator. This performance could be improved still further by using a higher-order approximation. Furthermore, estimation of the overdispersion parameter was much better with the approximate conditional method than with the unconditional method.

REFERENCES

Allison, Paul D. 1996. "Fixed Effects Partial Likelihood for Repeated Events." *Sociological Methods and Research* 25:207–22.

Cameron, A. Colin, and Pravin K. Trivedi. 1998. *Regression Analysis of Count Data.* Cambridge, England: Cambridge University Press.

Chamberlain, Gary A. 1980. "Analysis of Covariance with Qualitative Data." *Review of Economic Studies* 47:225–38.

Guo, Guang. 1996. "Negative Multinomial Regression Models for Clustered Event Counts." Pp. 113–32 in *Sociological Methodology 1996*, edited by Adrian E. Raftery. Washington, DC: American Sociological Association.

Greene, William. 2001. "Estimating Econometric Models with Fixed Effects." Unpublished manuscript, available at http://www.stern.nyu.edu/~wgreene.

Hausman, Jerry, Bronwyn H. Hall, and Zvi Griliches. 1984. "Econometric Models for Count Data with an Application to the Patents–R&D Relationship." *Econometrica* 52:909–38.

Hsiao, C. 1986. *Analysis of Panel Data.* Cambridge, England: Cambridge University Press.

Johnson, Norman L., and Samuel Kotz. 1969. *Discrete Distributions.* New York: Wiley.

Kalbfleisch, John D., and David A. Sprott. 1970. "Applications of Likelihood Methods to Models Involving Large Numbers of Parameters" (with discussion). *Journal of the Royal Statistical Society*, Ser. B, 32:175–208.

Mundlak, Y. 1978. "On the Pooling of Time Series and Cross Section Data." *Econometrica* 46:69–85.

Palmgren, Juni. 1981. "The Fisher Information Matrix for Log-Linear Models Arguing Conditionally in the Observed Explanatory Variables." *Biometrika* 68:563–66.

Small, C. G., and D. L. McLeish. 1989. "Projection as a Method for Increasing Sensitivity and Eliminating Nuisance Parameters." *Biometrika* 76:693–703.

Waterman, Richard P., and Bruce G. Lindsay. 1996a. "Projected Score Methods for Approximating Conditional Scores." *Biometrika* 83:1–13.

———. 1996b. "A Simple and Accurate Method for Approximate Conditional Inference Applied to Exponential Family Models." *Journal of the Royal Statistical Society*, Ser. B, 58:177–88.

Yamaguchi, Kazuo. 1986. "Alternative Approaches to Unobserved Heterogeneity in the Analysis of Repeated Events." Pp. 213–49 in *Sociological Methodology 1986*, edited by Nancy Brandon Tuma. Washington, DC: American Sociological Association.

$$\mathfrak{X} \, 8 \, \mathfrak{X}$$

COMPARING NETWORKS ACROSS SPACE AND TIME, SIZE AND SPECIES

Katherine Faust*
John Skvoretz†

We describe and illustrate methodology for comparing networks from diverse settings. Our empirical base consists of 42 networks from four kinds of species (humans, nonhuman primates, nonprimate mammals, and birds) and covering distinct types of relations such as influence, grooming, and agonistic encounters. The general problem is to determine whether networks are similarly structured despite their surface differences. The methodology we propose is generally applicable to the characterization and comparison of network-level social structures across multiple settings, such as different organizations, communities, or social groups, and to the examination of sources of variability in network structure. We first fit a p* model (Wasserman and Pattison 1996) to each network to obtain estimates for effects of six structural properties on the probability of the graph. We then calculate predicted tie probabilities for each network, using both its own parameter estimates and the estimates from every other network in the collection. Comparison is based on the similarity between sets of predicted tie probabilities. We then use correspondence analysis to represent the similarities among all 42 networks and interpret the resulting configuration using information about the species and relations involved. Results

*University of California, Irvine
†University of South Carolina
We acknowledge the helpful comments of the editor and anonymous reviewers. For their encouragement and suggestions on the research, we thank H. Russell Bernard, Linton Freeman, and A. Kimball Romney. We thank Tracy Burkett and Douglas Nigh for making their data available to us.

show that similarities among the networks are due more to the kind
of relation than to the kind of animal.

1. INTRODUCTION

Much of social network analysis examines a single network at a time.
Commonly the analyses comprise case studies of network properties or
processes within a single community. For example, dominance relations
among chimpanzees are described and the structure of the network analyzed. Or the liking and disliking relations among novices in a monastery
are described and the patterning in these networks related to observations
about group structure and dynamics. The problem of comparing networks
arises more rarely, and when it does the usual context is that of comparing
two relations mapped on the same population during the same time period.
For example, possible associations between friendship and advice seeking among corporate managers may be studied by comparing the two
relations.

In this paper we expand the scope of comparison by describing a
general way in which two, three, . . . , many networks can be compared
at the same time even though they differ widely in size, type of relation, species of the units, and time and space of the observations. The
general question concerns determining whether the networks are similarly structured despite their surface differences. The method we propose and illustrate allows us not only to compare two networks at a
time but to look at the overall patterning of similarities among a large
collection of networks from diverse settings. Our empirical base consists of 42 different networks from four kinds of species (humans, nonhuman primates, nonprimate mammals, and birds), varying in size from
7 to 103 units, and covering distinct types of relations such as influence, grooming, and agonistic encounters. Although we illustrate the
methodology on a collection of relatively exotic networks, it can be easily applied to a wide range of more familiar substantive situations, such
as comparing advice networks among managers in different firms, friendships among schoolchildren in different classrooms, referrals between
service agencies in various communities, and so on.

Six of these networks are diagrammed in Figure 1. The diversity in
our collection is apparent from the figures. All are directed graphs. In
some, the original data refer to counts. We dichotomize these data, regarding any nonzero count as indicating the presence of a tie. Network 1(a)
derives from the observation of agonistic encounters between red deer: A

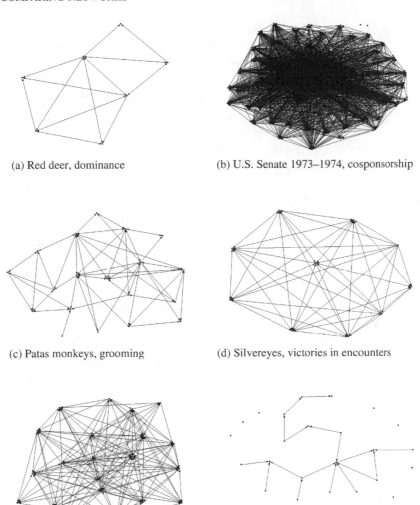

(a) Red deer, dominance   (b) U.S. Senate 1973–1974, cosponsorship

(c) Patas monkeys, grooming   (d) Silvereyes, victories in encounters

(e) Krackhardt's managers, advice   (f) Cows, social licking

FIGURE 1. Graphs of six networks.

tie exists from animal i to animal j if the first defeated the second in an encounter (Appleby 1983). Network 1(b) diagrams the cosponsorship ties among U.S. senators in the Ninety-third Congress (1973–1974): A tie exists from senator i to senator j if the first cosponsored at least one bill introduced by the second (Burkett 1997). Network 1(c) graphs grooming relations among patas monkeys: The presence of a tie from monkey i to monkey j indicates that the first groomed the second at least once (Kaplan and Zucker 1980). Network 1(d) depicts victories in encounters among birds called silvereyes: The presence of a tie from i to j indicates that silvereye i was victorious in at least one encounter with j (Kikkawa 1980). Network 1(e) graphs the advice relations among a group of high-tech managers: There is a tie from manager i to manager j if i reports going to j for advice (Krackhardt 1987). Finally, network 1(f) diagrams social licking among cows: There is a tie from cow i to cow j if the first licks the second (Reinhardt and Reinhardt 1981).

Our problem of the comparison of networks can now be posed rather dramatically: Is the network of cosponsorship among senators structurally more similar to the network of social licking among cows, the network of grooming among monkeys, or the network of advice among managers? Or, are the networks of victory in encounters among silvereyes and of dominance among red deer similarly structured? Such questions are substantively interesting and theoretically provocative, but they cannot be addressed systematically without general methods for the comparison of networks. Such methods would enable us to answer certain questions: What structural features are similar or different among networks of different kinds of organisms or different kinds of relations? Which kinds of networks tend to be similarly structured and which tend to be different? The present work contributes to research on these deeper issues.

In the next section we review the relatively sparse literature on the comparison of networks. We then outline the formal background for our approach. We use the p^* modeling framework to build and estimate models for the probability of a graph as a function of its structural properties. The estimates from these models, in turn, form the basis from which the similarity or dissimilarity of pairs of networks is calculated. Correspondence analysis provides a way of representing the similarities among all networks under consideration. We then interpret the resulting configuration using information about the networks and their structural properties. We apply this strategy to 42 networks and discuss the results.

2. COMPARING NETWORKS

The vast majority of social network studies are case studies of individual communities. Nevertheless, comparison of networks can, and does, proceed along several lines. The most straightforward case is the comparison of two networks over the same set of actors. For instance, two different relations could be measured on the same set of actors or the same relation could be measured on one set of actors at two time points. Methodology for comparison of two relations measured on the same set of actors dates to the early years of social network analysis (Katz and Powell 1953) and has been elaborated by Hubert and colleagues in a matrix permutation context (Hubert and Baker 1978; Baker and Hubert 1981). Moreover, statistical models for multiple relations are well developed (Wasserman 1987; Pattison and Wasserman 1999). There are also models for longitudinal networks, where the same relation is measured on the same set of actors at two (or more) points in time (Wasserman and Iacobucci 1988; Snijders 1996; Snijders and VanDuijn 1997).

Another type of comparison, replication, arises when the same relation is measured on two (or more) different sets of actors. Researchers are usually concerned with whether the networks exhibit similar structural properties or relationships or whether nonnetwork properties of the groups are associated with network-level properties. Examples include both classics, such as Laumann and Pappi's study of elite networks in the communities of Altneustadt and Towertown (Laumann and Pappi 1976) and Hallinan's (1974) studies of sentiment structures in school groups, and more recent studies such as Shrader, Lincoln, and Hoffman's (1989) study of networks in 36 agencies, Johnson and Boster's study of winter-over research teams at the South Pole (Johnson, Boster, and Palinkas n.d.), the National Longitudinal Study of Adolescent Health replication of friendship networks across schools (Bearman, Jones, and Udry 1997), and Rindfuss and Entwisle's studies of networks of kinship and social and economic relations in 51 villages in Nang Rong District, Thailand (Rindfuss et al. 2000). Until recently, methodology for the comparison of replicated networks was primarily descriptive. For example, Breiger and Pattison's comparison of elite structures in two communities used joint homomorphic reduction of the semigroup algebras in the two communities (Breiger and Pattison 1978). Recently, however, Anderson et al. (1999) and Martin (1999) describe statistical approaches that evaluate whether a common set of parameter estimates provides adequate fit to two or more networks.

A fourth type of comparison arises when data on roughly similar relations are available from different settings with different sets of actors. Unlike the situation just described, which is "pure" replication, relations in this case are only roughly comparable. The classic series of studies by Davis (1979) and by Holland and Leinhardt (1978) using the sociometric data bank of several hundred sociomatrices is a case in point. The studies asked whether sociometric data from diverse sources tended to exhibit greater than chance tendencies for transitivity, balance, or clustering. They calculated standard transitivity statistics on each network and then examined the distribution of the scores. Another example is studies of informant accuracy in different settings (for example, Bernard and Killworth 1977; Bernard, Killworth, and Sailer 1980), where observational data were collected in different ways depending on the setting (e.g., monitoring radio transmissions among ham radio operators, or observing interactions in the office or fraternity). Similarly, Freeman (1992) compiled examples of observations of interactions among people in seven different communities to explore the question of which of two alternative grouping models was more consistent with the observed interactions. In these examples of comparison, interest centers on whether hypothesized structural patterns or relationships are found across a range of roughly similar settings.

Common to the examples cited is the fact that the comparisons involve communities of identical actor types, usually humans. Only rarely have comparisons been made between networks of different kinds of organisms—for example, different animal species (Sade and Dow 1994). A notable exception is Maryanski's (1987) comparison of weak and strong ties in gorilla and chimpanzee social networks.

A more abstract and methodologically more challenging type of comparison arises when networks not only have different actor sets but also vary greatly in size, have substantively different relations, and include actors that are different kinds of organisms. The methods we propose address this problem. Our overarching question is whether pairs or sets of networks are similarly structured despite being based on substantively different relations measured on quite different kinds of organisms. An important contrast between our approach and previous methods for network comparison is that it measures directly the similarity between pairs of networks rather than simply determining whether (or to what degree) each exhibits specific structural tendencies. That is, our method provides an index, akin to a correlation coefficient, that quantifies the degree of similarity between two networks. An additional contrast with previous methods derives from the number of networks our method compares simultaneously. In the most straightforward case of comparison—two networks over the same set of actors—several measures of association can be calculated and evaluated—for example, using matrix permutation tests (Hubert and Baker 1978; Baker and Hubert 1981) or estimating multiplexity parameters in statistical models for multiple relations (Wasserman 1987; Pattison and Wasserman 1999). Extending comparisons to more than two networks requires calculating similarities between all pairs of networks and analyzing these simultaneously. In the method we propose, the idea is to represent the similarities among all networks in the set being compared via scaling or clustering techniques to depict graphically the similarity space of networks.

In overview, our approach consists of four steps: (1) We characterize each network in terms of a set of structural properties using a statistical model for the probability of the graph; (2) we measure the similarity between networks based on parameter estimates for the structural properties in the models as they predict network tie probabilities; (3) we represent the similarities among the networks using a spatial model; and (4) we interpret the resulting spatial configuration using information about the networks. Each of these steps involves decisions about possible alternative approaches, which we discuss as they arise in our description below and consider in detail in the discussion.

3. FORMAL BACKGROUND

Our aim is to assess whether two, three, . . ., many networks are similarly structured despite their surface differences. We argue that two networks are similarly structured to the extent that they exhibit the same structural tendencies, to the same degree. Obviously there are numerous structural tendencies that could be used to characterize networks, and selection centers on which properties are argued to be theoretically important for characterizing the networks at hand. Some widely used properties provide the basis for our comparison: mutuality, transitivity, cyclical triples, and star configurations (in-stars, out-stars, and mixed stars), as illustrated below. To be precise, we focus on predicting the probability of a network from a profile of structural properties of the network. Two networks are similarly structured to the extent that the probabilities of both networks depend on the same set of structural properties, used as predictor variables in the models, and on each property to the same degree.

We draw upon recent developments in the statistical modeling of networks—in particular, the development of models known as p^* models (Anderson et al. 1999; Crouch et al. 1998; Pattison and Wasserman 1999; Wasserman and Pattison 1996; Robins, Pattison, and Wasserman 1999). Statistical models for networks were long based on the assumption of dyadic independence. Dyadic independence means that the presence or absence of a tie in the ij dyad is independent of the presence or absence of a tie in any other dyad. It is widely recognized that this assumption clearly oversimplifies matters. As one example of the inappropriateness of the dyadic independence assumption, triadic effects such as the presence of an ij tie being significantly more likely if there are several others k who have ties to i and to j abound in real social networks. Modeling these effects is beyond the capability of statistical models that assume dyadic independence. The new statistical approaches, the p* family of models, explicitly model nonindependence among dyads by including parameters for structural features that capture hypothesized dependencies among ties.

In the p* framework, the probability of a digraph G is expressed as a log-linear function of a vector of parameters $\boldsymbol{\theta}$, an associated vector of digraph statistics $x(G)$, and a normalizing constant $Z(\boldsymbol{\theta})$:

$$P(G) = \frac{\exp(\boldsymbol{\theta}'x(G))}{Z(\boldsymbol{\theta})}. \tag{1}$$

The normalizing constant ensures that the probabilities sum to unity over all digraphs. The $\boldsymbol{\theta}$ parameters express how various "explanatory" properties of the digraph affect the probability of its occurrence. Different models use different profiles of digraph properties. Our models use a profile of six structural properties: mutuality, out 2-stars, in 2-stars, mixed 2-stars, transitive triples, and cyclical triples, as diagrammed in Figure 2.

Taken together, these effects constitute a Markov graph model (Frank and Strauss 1986) in which the probability of the ij tie depends only on other ties in which i and j might be involved but not on ties that involve neither i nor j. This model includes substantively interesting dyadic and triadic effects and provides a base to which higher order network properties (such as subgrouping or graph connectivity) might later be added. These effects are assumed to be homogeneous. The homogeneity assumption means that a particular structural property has the same effect regardless of the specific individual nodes involved. Obviously when comparing networks of different individuals the homogeneity assumption is desirable. Under the assumption of homogeneity, then, our model stipulates that the probability of a graph is a log-linear function of the number of mutual dyads, the number of out 2-stars, the number of in 2-stars, etc. If the resulting parameter estimate for a specific property is large and positive, then graphs with that property have large probabilities. For example, if the mutuality property has a positive coefficient, then a graph with many mutual dyads has a higher probability than a graph with few mutual dyads. Or, if the cyclical triple property has a negative coefficient, then a graph with many cyclical triples has a lower probability than a graph with few cyclical triples. Thus, the resulting parameter estimates associated with

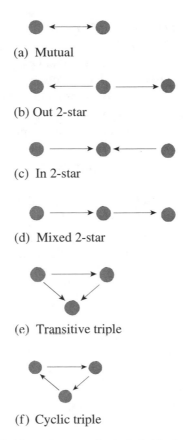

(a) Mutual

(b) Out 2-star

(c) In 2-star

(d) Mixed 2-star

(e) Transitive triple

(f) Cyclic triple

FIGURE 2. Network properties included in the p* models.

the structural properties capture the importance of their respective properties for characterizing the network under study.

Conceptually, the models are easy to understand. The real difficulty comes in trying to estimate the effect coefficients. Consider the estimation problem. Suppose we assigned a set of values to the effect coefficients. Then for each digraph realization over the set of all digraphs for a particular node set of size g, we could calculate the numerator of equation (1). Summing the numerator over all realizations yields the normalizing constant in the denominator of equation (1). The probability of a particular digraph realization is then given by the ratio of its numerator to the normalizing constant. One particular realization is the observed digraph. The estimation problem can be thought of as finding an assignment of values to effect coefficients that maximizes the probability of the observed digraph. Conceptually, of course, these are the maximum-likelihood estimates of the effect parameters. One could imagine estimation by a numerical search procedure through an orthogonal space of parameter values. But the number of combinations to be searched and the number of digraph realizations to be calculated on each pass are so huge for even relatively small networks that such a procedure is simply not practicable. Clearly, direct analysis via the solution of simultaneous differential equations for values that maximize equation (1) is equally out of the question.

The literature proposes a way of out of this impasse. The estimation approach, suggested by Strauss and Ikeda (1990) and elaborated by Wasserman and Pattison (1996), uses equation (1) to express the probability of tie, conditional on the rest of the digraph:

$$P(x_{ij} = 1 | G^{-ij}) = \frac{P(G^+)}{P(G^+) + P(G^-)}, \tag{2}$$

where G^{-ij} is the digraph including all adjacencies except the i,j^{th} one. The digraph G^+ is defined by the adjacency matrix plus $x_{ij} = 1$ while G^- is defined as the adjacency matrix plus $x_{ij} = 0$. This equation expresses the probability that $x_{ij} = 1$ conditional on the rest of the graph. Note that equation (2) does not depend on the normalizing constant because upon rewriting we get

$$P(x_{ij} = 1 | G^{-ij}) = \frac{\exp(\theta' x(G^+))}{\exp(\theta' x(G^+)) + \exp(\theta' x(G^-))}. \tag{3}$$

The conditional odds of the presence of a tie from i to j versus its absence is expressed by

$$\frac{P(x_{ij} = 1 | G^{-ij})}{P(x_{ij} = 0 | G^{-ij})} = \frac{\exp(\theta' x(G^+))}{\exp(\theta' x(G^-))}. \tag{4}$$

From equation (4), we derive the log of the odds or *logit* model:

$$logit\ P(x_{ij} = 1 | G^{-ij}) = \theta' [x(G^+) - x(G^-)]. \tag{5}$$

The quantity in brackets on the right side is a vector of differences in the profile of structural properties (which are assumed in equation (1) to affect the probability of the digraph) when x_{ij} changes from 1 to 0. Finally, we can derive an equation for the probability that $x_{ij} = 1$, conditional on the rest of the digraph, from equation (5):

$$P(x_{ij} = 1 | G^{-ij}) = \frac{\exp(\theta'(x(G^+) - x(G^-)))}{1 + \exp(\theta'(x(G^+) - x(G^-)))}. \tag{6}$$

The estimation method proposed by Strauss and Ikeda (1990) forms a pseudolikelihood function for the graph in terms of the conditional probabilities for x_{ij} as follows:

$$PL(\theta) = \prod_{ij} P(x_{ij} = 1 | G^{-ij})^{x_{ij}} P(x_{ij} = 0 | G^{-ij})^{1-x_{ij}} \tag{7}$$

Strauss and Ikeda prove that equation 7 can be maximized using maximum-likelihood estimation of the logistic regression, equation (5), assuming the x_{ij}'s are independent observations. Thus the p* family of models can be estimated, albeit approximately, using logistic regression routines in standard statistical packages. However, since the logits are not independent, the model is not a true logistic regression model and statistics from the estimation must be used with caution. Because goodness-of-fit statistics are pseudolikelihood ratio statistics, it is questionable whether the usual chi-square distributions apply, and standard errors have only "nominal" significance (see Crouch and Wasserman 1998). These reservations have little or no importance in our use of the p* framework. We are not concerned with exactly how good a fit a particular model has to a particular network. Nor are we concerned with identifying just those coefficients that are statistically "significant." Instead we use estimates from the model in conjunction with the calculated changes in graph statistics to calculate an estimated probability for each ij tie in the network.

For each of our data sets, we estimate a p* model that expresses the probability of a tie being present (conditional on the rest of the graph) as a function of the six structural properties diagrammed in Figure 2. Fitting the p* model results in estimates of θ's for the effects of each of the graph properties hypothesized to affect the likelihood of a tie. These estimates express the importance of the properties for the probability of the graph, but they can also be used (via equation (6)) to calculate the probabilities of the individual ties in the network. We use all parameter estimates to calculate predicted probabilities regardless of their level of statistical significance.

With these considerations in hand, we may return to the question of whether two networks are similarly structured. Consider two networks,

A and B, in which the θ's from the p* model (equation (6)) are similar in direction and magnitude. We would argue that these two networks are similarly structured in that the same structural tendencies are important, and important to the same degree, in predicting tie probabilities in both networks. In such a case we should be able to predict the tie probabilities in one network not only from its own parameter estimates but also from the parameter estimates of its "twin." On the other hand, this would not be the case if the p* models for two networks resulted in quite different estimates of the θ's.

An important general principle for comparison is that the magnitudes of the effects should be independent of scale differences in the explanatory variables in the models. The networks we compare vary widely in size and density, leading to distributional differences in the explanatory variables—the change statistics $x(G^+) - x(G^-)$. Thus, for comparison, the effects should be expressed as standardized logistic regression coefficients. Two networks are similarly structured if network structural properties have the same impact, net of distributional differences in the explanatory variables; that is, if the impact is the same in standardized terms.

Comparison can now proceed at different levels. First, we could directly compare the standardized parameter estimates from models for different networks. Alternatively, we could use sets of parameter estimates to get predicted tie probabilities for the networks and then compare these predicted probabilities. We use the second mode of comparison for three reasons: (1) We are interested in the collection of structural effects that characterize the network rather than individual parameter comparisons; (2) we are fundamentally interested in the structure of the network as manifested in the tie probabilities predicted by the network structural effects; and (3) resemblance between networks based on predictions from the parameter estimates may be asymmetric; parameter estimates from network A may predict ties in network B better than parameter estimates from B predict ties in A.

The task of comparing networks proceeds by using the standardized parameter estimates for one data set to predict tie probabilities for every other data set in the collection, in a pair-wise fashion. Predictions are made using equation (6) but entering the standardized parameter estimates from one network and the standardized change statistics $(x(G^+) - x(G^-))$ from the network that is being predicted. We do this for each pair of networks. The result is a set of predicted tie probabilities for each network, one based on its own p* parameter estimates and the rest based on the estimates from the other networks. The next step assesses the relative similarity between one set of parameter estimates and another set of estimates via their predicted tie probabilities. We now turn to a description of this step in the comparison process.

4. DATA AND METHODOLOGY OF COMPARISON

Table 1 lists the 42 data sets we use to illustrate our methodology of comparison. The networks range in size from 7 red deer stags to 104 U.S. senators. The ties composing the networks also vary from grooming relations and advice seeking to victories in agonistic encounters. Each of the networks that we compare is represented by a 0,1 adjacency matrix (created by dichotomizing all nonzero entries equal 1 if the original relation was valued). More details about each of the data sets can be found in the Appendix.

The strategy of comparison consists of four steps: (1) for each data set, we estimate a p^* model that expresses the conditional probability of a tie as a function of six structural factors: mutuality, out 2-stars, in 2-stars, mixed 2-stars, transitive triples, and cyclical triples (since we use standardized estimates there is no intercept); (2) we use these standardized parameter estimates and the standardized change scores in these structural factors to calculate the predicted probability of a tie in each i,j pair in each data set using as coefficients the parameter estimates from its own model and from each of the remaining 41 models. Thus for each data set, we have 42 sets of predicted probabilities, one from each set of parameter estimates including the set of estimates from the focal data set itself. The third step calculates a (dis)similarity score between the predicted probabilities from the estimates on the focal data set and each of the other 41 sets of predicted probabilities. The fourth and final step uses correspondence analysis to represent the proximities among all of the networks, using as input the 42 by 42 matrix of (dis)similarity scores. To illustrate the methodology, we can follow through the steps for the six networks diagrammed in Figure 1.

For these six networks, the results of the p^* model estimation are displayed in Table 2. The estimates vary considerably and many of the coefficients are not statistically significant at the $p < .05$ level. However, all estimates are retained in the prediction equation regardless of their nominal statistical significance. In one case, "cows, licking," the full model cannot be estimated due to multicolinearity among the predictor variables. In that case and three others like it, we use the model that is estima-

TABLE 1
List of Networks

Label	Network	Relation	mut	trans	cycle	ostar	istar	mstar	N
								p* parameter profile	
1. s93	U.S. Senate, 1973–74	Influence/cosponsorship		+	−	+	+		103
2. s94	U.S. Senate, 1975–76	Influence/cosponsorship		+		+	+	−	101
3. s95	U.S. Senate, 1977–78	Influence/cosponsorship	+	+		+		−	104
4. s96	U.S. Senate, 1979–80	Influence/cosponsorship	+	+		+		−	101
5. s97	U.S. Senate, 1981–82	Influence/cosponsorship	+	+		+		−	101
6. s98	U.S. Senate, 1983–84	Influence/cosponsorship	+	+		−	−	−	101
7. s99	U.S. Senate, 1985–86	Influence/cosponsorship	+	+		−	−		102
8. s100	U.S. Senate, 1987–88	Influence/cosponsorship	+	+		−	−	−	101
9. s101	U.S. Senate, 1989–90	Influence/cosponsorship	+	+		−	−	−	102
10. krack	Krackhardt's managers	Advice	+			+	+		21
11. sampin	Sampson's Monastery	Influence, positive	+	+			+		18
12. sampnin	Sampson's Monastery	Influence, negative	+	−		−		−	18
13. sampnpr	Sampson's Monastery	Blame	+	−	+	+	+		18
14. samppr	Sampson's Monastery	Praise	+	+		−			18
15. ua02	Athanassiou & Nigh TMT 2	Advice				+			12
16. ue02	Athanassiou & Nigh TMT 2	Worked together	+		+	+			12
17. ua06	Athanassiou & Nigh TMT 6	Advice				+		+	11
18. ue06	Athanassiou & Nigh TMT 6	Worked together			−				11
19. chimp1	Chimpanzees	Pant grunt calls	−		+			−	9
20. chimp2	Chimpanzees	Agonistic					−	−	9
21. chimp3	Chimpanzees	Grooming	+						9
22. macaca	*Macaca mulatta*	Grooming	+	+				−	16

23. macaqa	*Macaca sylvanus*	*i* carries baby away from *j*	+		+				8
24. macaqb	*Macaca sylvanus*	*i* leaves baby w/*j*	–			–			8
25. macaqc	*Macaca sylvanus*	*i* w/baby approaches *j*	–		+				8
26. macaqd	*Macaca sylvanus*	*j* w/baby approached by *i*	–	+	+	–	–		8
27. macaqu	*Macaca artaides*	Aggression	–						14
28. patasf	Patas monkeys, female	Fight	–						18
29. patasg	Patas monkeys	Groom	+		+	+			19
30. vervet1a	Vervet monkeys, juveniles	Aggressive/submissive							14
31. vervet1m	Vervet monkeys, juveniles	Aggressive/submissive		–	+	+			14
32. vervet2a	Vervet monkeys, juveniles	Aggressive/submissive	–						11
33. vervet2m	Vervet monkeys, juveniles	Aggressive/submissive						–	11
34. cowg	Cows, *bos indicus*	Grazing preference	+				+		29
35. cowl	Cows, *bos indicus*	Licking	+	+			+		29
36. hyenaf	Hyaena, female, *crocuta crocuta*	Dominance	–		+				25
37. hyenam	Hyaena, male, *crocuta crocuta*	Dominance	–	+	+				13
38. ponies	Highland ponies	Threat	–						17
39. reddeer	Red deer stags, *cervus elaphus L.*	Dominance	+						7
40. silver	Silvereyes, *zosterops lateralis*	Victory in encounter							10
41. sparrow	Harris' sparrows	Dominance	–	+					26
42. tits	Willow tits	Dominance							8

281

TABLE 2
p* Parameter Estimates for Six Networks

	Red Deer	Senate 93rd	Patas	Silvereyes	Managers	Cows, Lick
Intercept	4.291	−5.773*	−2.308*	3.801	−3.676*	−4.179*
Mutual	6.520*	−0.074	1.813*	1.057	1.714*	2.032*
O-Star	−0.795	0.061*	0.152*	−0.347	0.260*	0.115
I-Star	−8.482	0.066*	−0.045	−0.741	0.249*	0.488*
M-Star	2.689	0.002	−0.131	−0.443	−.152*	−0.458
Trans	2.085	0.007*	0.092	0.450	0.039	1.402*
Cycle	−5.973	−0.017*	0.647*	0.180	0.102	...

*Significant at p < .05

ble and contains the greatest number of original structural factors. The omitted one(s) are set equal to zero. Inspection of the parameter estimates reveals several similarities and differences. For instance, mutuality has a positive effect in all six networks but "Senate 93rd". Transitivity has a positive effect in all six networks—that is, completing a triple transitively tends to be an important property in all of them, although the size of the effect varies considerably from one network to another.

Table 3 presents six sets of predicted tie probabilities for a portion of the red deer network, one made by its own parameters and the others by the estimates from the other five networks. In general, if another network has a structure similar to the "red deer" network, then its model should provide predicted probabilities that are close to the probabilities predicted from the "red deer" model itself. That is, we would expect the average difference between predictions to be small.

To calculate the dissimilarity between the predicted probabilities, we use the Euclidean distance function:

$$d(t, y) = \sqrt{\frac{\sum_{i,j} (p_t(i,j) - p_y(i,j))^2}{g_t(g_t - 1)}}, \tag{8}$$

where $p_t(i,j)$ is the standardized tie probability for pair (i,j) predicted from the target network t's model, $p_y(i,j)$ is the standardized tie probability for pair (i,j) predicted from network y's model, and g_t is the number of nodes in network t. Results for our six illustrative networks are given

TABLE 3
Predicted Tie Probabilities for Red Deer Dominance

				Model Providing Predictions			
i	j	Obs x_{ij}	Red Deer	Senate 93rd	Patas	Silvereyes	Managers	Cows, Lick
1	2	1	0.99097	0.60750	0.80128	0.78903	0.75413	0.50732
1	3	1	0.96682	0.60753	0.69805	0.66990	0.82355	0.59876
1	4	1	0.99978	0.32027	0.66999	0.66996	0.60650	0.40379
1	5	1	0.99535	0.61614	0.74646	0.74403	0.76769	0.53816
1	6	1	0.98674	0.32624	0.38869	0.38818	0.37927	0.3266
1	7	1	0.87031	0.63108	0.40235	0.41386	0.58531	0.48569
2	1	1	0.99264	0.80810	0.70941	0.74697	0.78741	0.63561
2	3	1	0.37954	0.52914	0.56319	0.63587	0.53177	0.47484
2	4	1	0.99802	0.24093	0.66128	0.68044	0.57629	0.42665
2	5	1	0.99847	0.54663	0.65779	0.72511	0.70561	0.56147
2	6	0	0.59946	0.62525	0.43461	0.47461	0.66197	0.54392
2	7	1	0.69987	0.54721	0.40736	0.51333	0.56865	0.53659
3	1	1	0.60305	0.55773	0.56403	0.44505	0.45961	0.47982
3	2	0	0.69020	0.65131	0.65062	0.64060	0.66261	0.59907
3	4	0	0.39391	0.35465	0.44473	0.47845	0.24874	0.35147
3	5	1	0.89568	0.27196	0.64230	0.70525	0.44261	0.48479
3	6	0	0.35590	0.36566	0.32775	0.41485	0.34780	0.46709
3	7	0	0.13754	0.68110	0.35404	0.52912	0.56595	0.65571
	...	...	...	...	...	...	...	...

in Table 4. We find, for instance, that the model that best predicts the "red deer" target (other than the "red deer" model itself) is the model for encounters between silvereyes. The model of social licking among cows best predicts, as a target, cosponsorship among U.S. senators in the Ninety-

TABLE 4
Distances Between Networks

Target Network	Model Providing Predictions					
	Red Deer	Senate 93rd	Patas	Silvereyes	Managers	Cows, Lick
Red Deer	0	0.07082	0.05098	0.04568	0.05477	0.06412
Senate 93rd	0.00505	0	0.00232	0.00229	0.00117	0.00128
Patas	0.01969	0.01186	0	0.00714	0.00680	0.00706
Silvereyes	0.03438	0.02214	0.00724	0	0.01861	0.01610
Managers	0.02386	0.00580	0.00997	0.00977	0	0.00616
Cows, Lick	0.01678	0.00565	0.00427	0.00662	0.00533	0

Third Congress. However, that network of cosponsorship ties is best predicted by the model for advice seeking between managers, among the five alternatives. Note that the matrix of distances is not symmetric. In fact, there is no reason to expect symmetry—the (i, j) cell expresses the distance between the predicted probabilities of target network i's ties from network j's model, while the (j, i) cell expresses the distance between the predicted probabilities of target network j's ties from network i's model. The final step takes the full matrix version of Table 4 (transformed to similarities) and scales it using correspondence analysis. These results are reported and interpreted in the next section.

5. REPRESENTING SIMILARITIES AMONG NETWORKS: CORRESPONDENCE ANALYSIS

We use correspondence analysis to represent the similarities among the networks. Correspondence analysis (Greenacre 1984; Weller & Romney, 1990) is a data analytic technique for studying two-way arrays such as contingency tables or similarity matrices. It is one of several closely related scaling approaches, also including dual scaling (Nishisato 1994), homogeneity analysis (Gifi, 1990), and optimal scaling. It aims to represent proximity data in a low-dimensional space using scores for categories of the variables. These scores then serve as coordinates in graphical displays in which points represent the categories of the variables and the distance between points represents the similarity between their respective entities. We use as input the matrix of distances between networks, appropriately transformed into similarities by subtracting each value from a large positive number. As Carroll, Kumbasar, and Romney (1997) show, this is equivalent to multidimensional scaling of the original distances. The advantage of correspondence analysis is that it can be used to analyze nonsymmetric matrices, such as the distances between the target networks and the networks providing the model predictions. In our application, two networks will be close in space if the predictions provided by their models are similar, in the sense that they similarly predict other networks in the collection.

Correspondence analysis is accomplished through a singular value decomposition of an appropriately scaled matrix. Entries in the input matrix are divided by the square root of the product of the row and column marginal totals, prior to singular value decomposition. Let $\mathbf{F}$ be a rectangular matrix of positive entries. $\mathbf{R}$ and $\mathbf{C}$ are diagonal matrices with entries equal to the row and column totals of $\mathbf{F}$, respectively. Correspondence analysis consists of a singular value decomposition of the matrix $\mathbf{R}^{1/2}\mathbf{FC}^{1/2}$

$$\mathbf{R}^{1/2}\mathbf{FC}^{1/2} = \mathbf{UDV}, \qquad (9)$$

where $\mathbf{D}$ is a diagonal matrix of singular values, and $\mathbf{U}$ and $\mathbf{V}$ are row and column vectors, respectively. For visual displays, $\mathbf{U}$ and $\mathbf{V}$ are rescaled. We use principal coordinates, where, on each dimension, the weighted mean is equal to 0 and the weighted variance is equal to the singular value squared. In the following graphs we present the column scores from correspondence analysis of the matrix of similarities among the networks. Column scores show similarities among networks in terms of the predictions they make for other networks. Row scores would show similarities among the targets being predicted. We should note that for our analyses using the row scores leads to essentially the same results and conclusions as those presented here.

To interpret the correspondence analysis configuration, we employ information about the networks and about the species and relations that are involved. There are four kinds of species: human, nonhuman primate, mammal, and bird. Relations are first categorized by how they were collected: observation or report by respondent. Obviously this is confounded with the type of animal since only humans provided reports of their ties to others. We then categorize the relation as either positive or negative. Grooming, advice seeking, cosponsorship, and working together are considered positive, whereas dominance, agonistic encounters, and blaming are negative. This leads to four types: observed positive, observed negative, reported positive, or reported negative.[1] We also use information about the structural tendencies exhibited by each network, including the extent and direction of each of the structural properties included in the p^* models, based on the nominal significance of the coefficients (θ's) from the p^* model: positive, none, or negative. We use a cutoff value of a .05 significance level only as a heuristic to determine whether the tendency is positive or negative.

---

[1] We also tried a four-category coding for the kind of relation: groom, agonistic, influence, and other. The conclusions from that analysis are similar to the ones reported here for the four group categorization.

6. RESULTS OF THE CORRESPONDENCE ANALYSIS

Let us turn now to the full set of 42 networks. Figure 3 presents the first
two dimensions of column scores from the correspondence analysis. The
first three dimensions of the correspondence analysis accounted for 24.7,
12.9, and 11.1 percent of the variance, respectively. The column scores
plotted in Figure 3 pertain to the model providing the predictions. Networks that are in close proximity in this figure are similar in the extent to
which their p^* parameter estimates predict other networks in the set. Looking at Figure 3, we see in the center toward the top a grouping of networks
including cosponsorship in all of the U.S. senates except the Ninety-third
and Ninety-fourth (labeled s95 through s101), dominance among willow
tits (tits), advice among Krackhardt's high-tech managers (krack), and
dominance among male hyenas (hyenam). On the far right of the figure,
we see aggressive/submissive relations among juvenile vervet monkeys
(vervet1a and vervet2a, vervet2m), dominance among sparrows (spar-

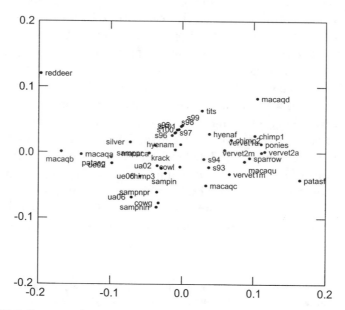

FIGURE 3. Correspondence analysis of similarities between networks from p^* model
parameters, column scores.

row), threats among highland ponies (ponies), pant-grunt calls between chimpanzees (chimp1), and patas monkeys fighting (patasf).

In Figure 3 networks that are close to one another tend to exhibit similar structural properties. How can we interpret the overall spatial patterning in this figure? First, we use information about the structural features of the networks themselves, as seen in the directions and magnitudes of their p* parameter estimates. For each network, we code it as positive, negative, or none on each of the structural features based on the direction and nominal significance of the estimated coefficient for that property, as described above. Table 1 reports these codings for each network as the p* parameter profile. For example, we can see that the Ninety-third Senate has positive tendencies for transitive triples, out-stars, and in-stars and a negative tendency for cyclic triples. We then draw confidence ellipses around the networks with each property on the correspondence analysis configuration.[2] The results for mutuality, transitivity, and cycles are presented in Figures 4 through 6.

We examine the extent to which networks with specific structural tendencies occupy distinct regions of the correspondence space using an analysis of variance with the dimension scores as the dependent variables and the three category classifications of structural tendencies as factors, using the procedure described in Kumbasar, Romney, and Batchelder (1994) and Romney, Batchelder, and Brazill (1995). An analysis of variance comparing column dimension scores along the first three dimensions between three categories of structural properties gives the proportion reduction in error (PRE) in dimension scores due to the categorical grouping variables, as measured by the correlation ratio squared, η^2. Table 5 presents these statistics for the first three dimensions of the correspondence analysis. From these results it is clear that the first dimension distinguishes networks in which mutuality is an important property from those in which it is not, or in which there is a tendency away from mutuality ($\eta^2 = 0.43$). Transitivity is an important contrast along the second dimension ($\eta^2 = 0.27$).

We use the same procedure to study whether similarities among networks are patterned by animal type (human, nonhuman primate, nonprimate mammal, or bird) or by relation type (observed positive, observed negative, reported positive, reported negative). The confidence ellipses

---

[2] The confidence ellipse is centered on the means of the dimension 1 and dimension 2 coordinates. Its orientation is determined by the covariance of the two variables. We present 68.27 percent confidence ellipses.

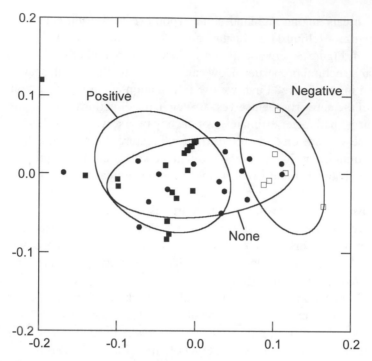

FIGURE 4. Confidence ellipses for mutuality overlaid on correspondence analysis of similarities between networks from p* model parameters.

for animal type and for relation type, overlaid on the correspondence analysis configurations, are in Figures 7 and 8. Results in Table 5 show that the kind of animal is not an important distinction along any of the first three dimensions of the correspondence analysis. Whether the relation is observed or reported is important along both of the first two dimensions ($\eta^2 = 0.10$ and $\eta^2 = 0.20$), and whether the relation is positive or negative is an important distinction along the first and third dimensions ($\eta^2 = 0.12$ and $\eta^2 = 0.13$). Relation type, coded into four categories, is an important aspect of the second dimension ($\eta^2 = 0.26$). Overall the type of relation appears to be more important than the type of animal in distinguishing among the networks.

Further investigation of the associations between the relation type and properties of the networks reveals some interesting relationships for our sample of networks. Observed positive relations (for example, grooming between nonhuman primates and cosponsorship between senators) tend

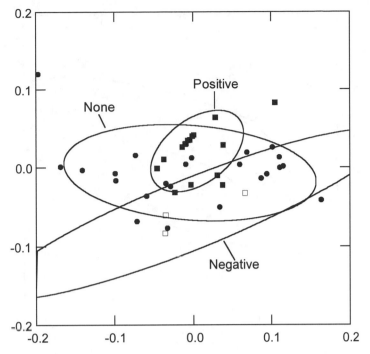

FIGURE 5. Confidence ellipses for transitivity overlaid on correspondence analysis of similarities between networks from p* model parameters.

to be mutual, as do reported negative relations (blame and negative influence). In general, transitivity is characteristic of observed positive relations, and a tendency away from transitivity is characteristic of reported negative relations. Whether these associations hold in larger samples of networks is a topic for future research.

7. DISCUSSION

We have described a methodology for comparing networks from diverse settings including vastly different species and relational contents. This methodology allows one to assess not only what structural features are important in a given network but also how similar various networks are in terms of these properties. Important features of our approach are the calculation of an index of (dis)similarity between each pair of networks, and

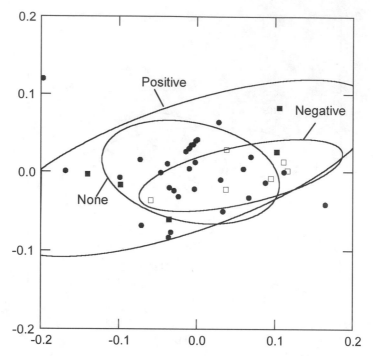

FIGURE 6. Confidence ellipses for cyclic triples overlaid on correspondence analysis of similarities between networks from p* model parameters.

then the representation of these similarities among the diverse networks using correspondence analysis. Information about characteristics of the networks, including the kinds of actors and types of relations, is then used to interpret this spatial configuration.

In our results it appears that the kind of relation involved rather than the species underlies similarities among the networks. It is the nature of relation that determines the structural features of its network. For example, agonistic relations, whether between red deer or highland ponies, are similarly structured. This leads to the speculation that distinctions among species in network structures are due to differences in the distributions of relations in which they typically engage. This also naturally suggests that greater efforts should be devoted to measuring the typical range of relations for a species. For example, it would be useful to have observational data on different kinds of human interactions (though interviewing chimpanzees about who they go to for advice is probably out of the question).

TABLE 5

Proportion Reduction in Error Measures (η^2) for Correspondence Analysis Dimensions by Network Structural Properties, Type of Animal, and Type of Relation

Dimension	Mutual[a]	Transitive Triples[a]	Cyclic Triples[a]	Type of Animal[b]	Observed or Reported Relation	Positive or Negative Relation	Type of Relation[c]
1	0.43**	0.00	0.09	0.09	0.10*	0.12*	0.19
2	0.01	0.27**	0.00	0.05	0.20**	0.00	0.26*
3	0.03	0.10	0.13	0.16	0.02	0.13*	0.14

*p < .05
**p < .01
[a]Mutual, transitive, and cycle coded: positive, none, negative.
[b]Human, nonhuman primate, non-primate mammal, bird.
[c]Observed positive, observed negative, reported positive, reported negative.

291

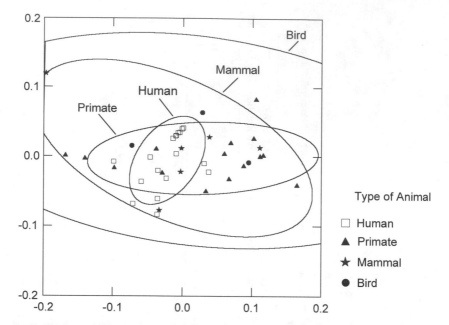

FIGURE 7. Confidence ellipses for type of animal overlaid on correspondence analysis of similarities between networks from p* model parameters.

Our methodology of comparison consists of four steps: (1) characterizing the structural properties of each network using a statistical model, (2) comparing pairs of networks based on parameter estimates for the effects of these structural properties, (3) representing spatially the similarities among the networks, and (4) interpreting the resulting configuration using information about the networks. At each juncture there are alternative approaches that might be used. Thus it is important to consider the principles on which we base our choices and the robustness of our results in light of decisions about particular alternatives.

First, we use the p* family of statistical models to estimate the effects of network structural properties on the probability of the graph. In the present analysis, the model includes six relatively local properties (mutuality, out 2-stars, in 2-stars, mixed stars, transitive triples, and cyclic triples). This collection of effects constitutes a Markov graph model but can easily be expanded to include other structural properties. Building models with lower-order effects before adding more complex higher-order effects is standard practice in statistical modeling, and one that we

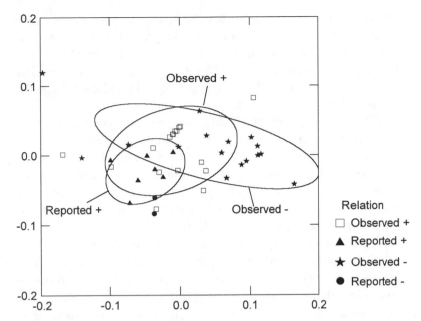

FIGURE 8. Confidence ellipses for type of relation overlaid on correspondence analysis of similarities between networks from p* model parameters.

follow here. In addition, there are alternatives to the p^* modeling framework that also could be used to estimate effects of network structural properties—for example, Friedkin's local density model (Friedkin 1998) could be used to estimate tie probabilities.

The second step is to compare networks based on the structural parameters in the models. We base our choice here on the principle that networks of different sizes and of different densities can have similar structures. We view size and density as differences of scale rather than as differences of theoretical significance. This leads us to use standardized regression coefficients and standardized explanatory variables for predicting tie probabilities. Comparison is then based on predicted tie probabilities, using a network's own parameter estimates and the parameter estimates from other networks. Resemblance between networks is measured using Euclidean distance. Other measures of similarity (such as a correlation coefficient) would also be possible. We have explored other modes of comparison, using predicted probabilities from unstandardized regression coefficients, and using predicted logits rather than predicted probabilities. In all cases the results and substantive conclusions are substantially similar to those we present here. We have only preliminarily explored another alternative—namely, direct comparison of the parameter estimates themselves. Our preliminary investigation on the current data indicates this comparison would yield the same substantive conclusions.

The third step in our methodology represents spatially the (dis)similarities among the collection of networks. Since the matrix of (dis)similarities is not symmetric we use correspondence analysis rather than other scaling options that require symmetric input data. Finally, we interpret the resulting configuration of similarities among networks by systematically examining which features of the networks are related to the spatial configuration from the correspondence analysis.

This research may be extended in several directions. First, the method can easily be used to compare multiple networks in a wide variety of situations. For example, one could compare friendship networks in multiple schools, communications relations in multiple organizations, or interorganizational transactions in multiple communities. Thus our method can be used to address fundamental questions about variability or similarity in network structure and organization. Importantly, however, our methodology is not restricted to comparing networks where the same relation has been measured in all settings. Second, in future research it will be important to explore two extensions to the models for tie probabilities or strengths. The first extension would handle valued relations. In this paper, we have, perhaps somewhat arbitrarily, dichotomized all relations. The second extension would include additional structural features in the p^* models used to characterize the networks. We have used a limited set of relatively local properties in our models. Certainly graph-level properties, such as network centralization, the diameter of the graph, or the average path length between points could also be included. Theoretically, the addition of these long-range effects may prove quite interesting if it turns out that they have different impacts in the networks of humans as opposed to the networks of other animals.

APPENDIX: LIST OF DATA SOURCES

This appendix lists the 42 networks, describes the relations, gives a reference for the source of the data, and reports the label used in Table 1 and

Figure 2. Where data are published, the table number and page of the source are given. Numbers correspond to numbers listed in Table 1.

- 1–9. *U.S. Senate.* Cosponsorship in nine senates. Records whether senator *i* cosponsored at least one bill introduced by senator *j* during that session of the Senate. Data provided by Burkett (1997). Labels: s93, s94, s95, s96, s97, s98, s99, s100, s101.
- 10. *Krackhardt's high-tech managers.* Each manager was asked who they went to for help or advice at work; Krackhardt (1987). Data available in Wasserman and Faust (1994) and in UCINET (Borgatti, Everett, and Freeman 1999). Label: krack.
- 11–14. *Sampson's monastery.* Four relations reported between monks in the monastery: positive influence (Table D15, p. 471), negative influence (Table D15, p. 471), blame (Table D16, p. 472), and praise (Table D16, p. 472); data from Sampson (1968). Data are also available in UCINET (Borgatti, Everett, and Freeman 1999). Labels: sampin, sampnin, sampnpr, samppr.
- 15–18. *Athanassiou and Nigh's top management teams (TMT).* There are two teams (02 and 05) and two relations: from whom each manager sought advice and how extensively they had worked together; Athanassiou and Nigh (1999). Data provided by the second author. Labels: ua02, ua05 (advice), ue02, ue05 (work with).
- 19–21. *Chimpanzees.* Three relations: pant-grunt calls (Table 9.3, p. 119), initiation of dyadic agonistic confrontations (Table 9.4, p. 119), and initiation of grooming (Table 9.14a, p. 126); data from Nishida and Hosaka (1996). Labels: chimp1, chimp2, and chimp3.
- 22. *Macaca Mulatta.* One relation: grooming (Table 1, p. 274); data are from Sade (1989). Label: macaca.
- 23–26. *Macaques, macaca sylvanus.* Four relations: male carried baby away from another (Table 7a, p. 71), label macaqa; male left another with a baby (Table 7b, p. 71), label macaqb; male carrying a baby approached another male (Table 5a, p. 69), label macaqc; male approached another male who was with a baby (Table 5b, p. 69), label macaqd; data from Deag (1980).
- 27. *Stumptail Macaques (Macaca artaides).* The relation is aggression (Table 2, p. 247); data are from Dow and de Waal (1989). Label: macaqu.
- 28–29. *Patas monkeys.* Two relations: fighting (Table III, p. 202) and grooming (Table V, p. 205); data from Kaplan and Zucker (1980). Labels: pataf and patag.

- 30–33. *Vervet monkeys* (*Cercopithecus aethiops sabaeus*), juveniles from two troops (1 and 2) and two conditions (mother present and mother absent): dyadic aggressive/submissive interactions, both mothers present (Table I, p. 775), labels: vervet1m and vervet2m; dyadic aggressive/submissive interactions, both mothers absent (Table II, p. 776), labels: vervet1a and vervet2a; data from Horrocks and Hunte (1983).
- 34–35. *Cows, bos indicus.* Two relations: social licking (Figure 7, p. 130) and social grazing (Figure 4, p. 126); data from Reinhardt and Reinhardt (1981). Labels: cowl, cowg.
- 36–37. *Hyaena, crocuta crocuta.* Dominance, among females and among males. Dominance among adult females (Table I, p. 1513) and dominance among males (Table V, p. 1519); data from Frank (1986). Labels: hyenaf, hyenam.
- 38. *Highland ponies.* The relation is threats (Table 2, p. 3); data from Roberts and Browning (1998), originally in Clutton-Brock, Greenwood, and Powell (1976). Label: ponies.
- 39. *Red deer stags, Cervus elaphus L.* Winner and loser in encounters (Figure 1(a), p. 601); data from Appleby (1983) and also in Freeman, Freeman, and Romney (1992) and Roberts (1994). Label: reddeer.
- 40. *Silvereyes, zosterops lateralis.* One relation, victories in encounters (Table 1, p. 94); data from Kikkawa (1980). Label: silver.
- 41. *Sparrows, zonotrichia querula.* One relation: dominance, both attacks and avoidances (Figure 2, p. 19); data from Watt (1986). Label: sparrow.
- 42. *Willow tits, parus montanus.* One relation: dominance (Table 1, p. 1492); data from Tufto, Solberg, and Ringgsby (1998). Data originally from Lahti, Koivula, and Orell (1994). Label: tits.

REFERENCES

Appleby, Michael. 1983. "The Probability of Linearity in Hierarchies." *Animal Behaviour* 31:600–608.

Anderson, Carolyn, J., Stanley Wasserman, and Bradley Crouch. 1999. "A p* Primer: Logit Models for Social Networks." *Social Networks* 21:37–66.

Athanassiou, Nicholas, and Douglas Nigh. 1999. "The Impact of U.S. Company Internationalization on Top Management Team Advice Networks: A Tacit Knowledge Perspective." *Strategic Management Journal* 20:83–92.

Baker, Frank, and Lawrence Hubert. 1981. "The Analysis of Social Interaction Data." *Sociological Methods and Research* 9:339–61.

Bearman, P. S., J. Jones, and J. R. Udry. 1997. "National Longitudinal Study of Adolescent Health: Research Design." Carolina Population Center. Unpublished manuscript.

Bernard, H. Russell, and Peter D. Killworth. 1977. "Informant Accuracy in Social Network Data II." *Human Communications Research* 4:3–18.

Bernard, H. Russell, Peter D. Killworth, and Lee D. Sailer. 1980. "Informant Accuracy in Social Network Data IV: A Comparison of Clique-Level Structure in Behavioral and Cognitive Network Data." *Social Networks* 2:191–218.

Borgatti, Stephen, Martin Everett, and Linton Freeman. 1999. UCINET 5.0 for Windows. Analytic Technologies.

Breiger, R. L., and P. Pattison. 1978. "The Joint Role Structure of Two Communities' Elites." *Sociological Methods and Research* 7:213–26.

Burkett, Tracy. 1997. "Cosponsorship in the United States Senate: A Network Analysis of Senate Communication and Leadership, 1973–1990." Ph.D. dissertation. University of South Carolina.

Carroll, J. Douglas, Ece Kumbasar, and A. Kimball Romney. 1997. "An Equivalence Relation Between Correspondence Analysis and Classical Multidimensional Scaling for the Recovery of Euclidean Distances." *British Journal of Mathematical and Statistical Psychology* 50:81–92.

Clutton-Brock, T. H., P. J. Greenwood, and R. P. Powell. 1976. "Ranks and Relationships in Highland Ponies and Highland Cows." *Z. Tierpsychol* 41:202–16.

Crouch, Bradley, and Stanley Wasserman. 1998. "A Practical Guide to Fitting p* Social Network Models." *Connections* 21:87–101.

Davis, James A. 1979. "The Davis/Holland/Leinhardt Studies: An Overview." Pages 51–62 in *Perspectives on Social Network Research*, edited by Paul W. Holland and Samuel Leinhardt. New York: Academic Press.

Deag, John M. 1980. "Interactions Between Males and Unweaned Barbary Macaques: Testing the Agonistic Buffering Hypothesis." *Behaviour* 75:54–81.

Dow, Malcolm M., and Frans B. M. de Waal. 1989. "Assignment Methods for the Analysis of Network Subgroup Interactions." *Social Networks* 11:237–55.

Frank, Ove, and David Strauss. 1986. "Markov Graphs." *Journal of the American Statistical Association* 81:832–42.

Frank, Laurence G. 1986. "Social Organization of the Spotted Hyaena Crocuta Crocuta. II: Dominance and Reproduction." *Animal Behaviour* 34:1510–27.

Freeman, Linton. 1992. "The Sociological Concept of 'Group': An Empirical Test of Two Models." *American Journal of Sociology* 98:152–66.

Freeman, Linton C., Sue C. Freeman, and A. Kimball Romney. 1992. "The Implications of Social Structure for Dominance Hierarchies in Red Deer." *Animal Behaviour* 44:239–45.

Friedkin, Noah. 1998. *A Structural Theory of Social Influence*. Cambridge, UK: Cambridge University Press.

Gifi, Albert. 1990. *Nonlinear Multivariate Analysis*. New York: Wiley.

Greenacre, Michael. 1984. *Theory and Applications of Correspondence Analysis*. New York: Academic Press.

Hallinan, Maureen T. 1974. "A Structural Model of Sentiment Relations." *American Journal of Sociology* 80:364–78.

Holland, Paul W., and Samuel Leinhardt. 1978. "An Omnibus Test for Social Structure Using Triads." *Sociological Methods and Research* 7:227–56.

Horrocks, Julia, and Wayne Hunte. 1983. "Maternal Rank and Offspring Rank in Vervet

Monkeys: An Appraisal of the Mechanisms of Rank Acquisition." *Animal Behaviour* 31:772–82.

Hubert, Lawrence, and Frank Baker. 1978. "Evaluating the Conformity of Sociometric Measurements." *Psychometrika* 43:31–41.

Johnson, Jeffrey C., James S. Boster, and Lawrence Palinkas. n.d. "The Evolution of Networks in Extreme and Isolated Environments." Unpublished manuscript.

Kaplan, J. R., and E. Zucker. 1980. "Social Organization in a Group of Free-ranging Patas Monkeys." *Folia Primatologica* 34:196–213.

Katz, Leo, and James H. Powell. 1953. "A Proposed Index of the Conformity of One Sociometric Measurement to Another." *Psychometrika* 18:249–56.

Kikkawa, Jiro. 1980. "Weight Change in Relation to Social Hierarchy in Captive Flocks of Silvereyes, *Zosterops Lateralis*." *Behaviour* 74:92–100.

Krackhardt, David. 1987. "Cognitive Social Structures." *Social Networks* 9:104–34.

Kumbasar, Ece, A. Kimball Romney, and William H. Batchelder. 1994. "Systematic Biases in Social Perception." *American Journal of Sociology* 100:477–505.

Lahti, K., K. Koivula, and M. Orell. 1994. "Is the Social Hierarchy Always Linear in Tits." *Journal of Avian Biology* 25:347–48.

Laumann, E. O., and F. Pappi. 1976. *Networks of Collective Action: A Perspective on Community Influence Systems*. New York: Academic Press.

Martin, John. 1999. "A General Permutation-Based QAP Analysis Approach for Dyadic Data from Multiple Groups." *Connections* 22:50–60.

Maryanski, A. P. 1987. "African Ape Social Structure: Is There Strength in Weak Ties?" *Social Networks* 9:191–215.

Nishida, Toshisada, and Kasuhiko Hosaka. 1996. "Coalition Strategies Among Male Chimpanzees of the Mahale Mountains, Tanzania." Pp. 114–134 in *Great Ape Societies*, edited by William C. McGrew, Linda F. Marchant, and Toshisada Nishida. New York: Cambridge University Press.

Nishisato, Shizuhiko. 1994. *Elements of Dual Scaling: An Introduction to Practical Data Analysis*. Hillsdale, NJ: Lawrence Erlbaum.

Pattison, Philippa, and Stanley Wasserman. 1999. "Logit Models and Logistic Regressions for Social Networks: II. Multivariate Relations." *British Journal of Mathematical and Statistical Psychology* 52:169–93.

Reinhardt, Viktor, and Annie Reinhardt. 1981. "Cohesive Relationships in a Cattle Herd (Bos Indicus)." *Behaviour* 76:121–51.

Rindfuss, Ronald R., Aree Jampaklay, Barbara Entwisle, Yothin Sawangdee, Katherine Faust, and Pramote Prasartkul. 2000. "The Collection and Analysis of Social Network Data in Nang Rong, Thailand." Presented at the IUSSP Conference on Partnership Networks, February, Chiang Mai, Thailand.

Roberts, John M., Jr. 1994. "Fit of Some Models to Red Deer Dominance Data." *Journal of Quantitative Anthropology* 4:249–58.

Roberts, John M., Jr., and Bridget A. Browning. 1998. "Proximity and Threats in Highland Ponies." *Social Networks* 20:227–38.

Robins, Garry, Philippa Pattison, and Stanley Wasserman. 1999. "Logit Models and Logistic Regressions for Social Networks. III. Valued Relations." *Psychometrika* 64:371–94.

Romney, A. Kimball, William H. Batchelder, and Timothy Brazill. 1995. "Scaling

Semantic Domains." Pp. 267–94 in *Geometric Representations of Perceptual Phenomena: Papers in Honor of Tarow Indow's 70th Birthday*, edited by Duncan Luce et al. Hillsdale, NJ: Lawrence Erlbaum.

Sade, Donald Stone. 1989. "Sociometrics of *Macaca Mulatta* III: N-path Centrality in Grooming Networks." *Social Networks* 11:273–92.

Sade, Donald Stone, and Malcolm Dow. 1994. "Primate Social Networks." Pp. 152–66 in *Advances in Social Network Analysis*, edited by Stanley Wasserman and Joseph Galaskiewicz. Thousand Oaks: Sage.

Sampson, S. 1968. "A Novitiate in a Period of Change: An Experimental and Case Study of Social Relationships." Ph.D. dissertation. Cornell University.

Shrader, Charles B., James R. Lincoln, and Alan N. Hoffman. 1989. "The Network Structures of Organizations: Effects of Task Contingencies and Distributional Form." *Human Relations* 42:43–66.

Snijders, T. A. B. 1996. "Stochastic Actor-Oriented Dynamic Network Analysis." *Journal of Mathematical Sociology* 21:149–72.

Snijders, T. A. B., and M. A. J. Van Duijn. 1997. "Simulation for Statistical Inference in Dynamic Network Models." Pp. 493–512 in *Simulating Social Phenomena*, edited by R. Conte, R. Hegselmann, and P. Terna. Berlin: Springer.

Strauss, David, and Michael Ikeda. 1990. "Pseudolikelihood Estimation for Social Networks." *Journal of the American Statistical Association* 85:204–12.

Tufto, Jarle, Erling Johan Solberg, and Thor-Harald Ringgsby. 1998. "Statistical Models of Transitive and Intransitive Dominance Structures." *Animal Behaviour* 55:1489–98.

Wasserman, Stanley. 1987. "Conformity of Two Sociometric Relations." *Psychometrika* 52:3–18.

Wasserman, Stanley, and Katherine Faust. 1994. *Social Network Analysis: Methods and Applications*. Cambridge, England: Cambridge University Press.

Wasserman, Stanley, and Dawn Iacobucci. 1988. "Sequential Social Network Data." *Psychometrika* 53:261–82.

Wasserman, Stanley, and Philippa Pattison. 1996. "Logit Models and Logistic Regressions for Social Networks: I. An Introduction to Markov Graphs and p*." *Psychometrika* 61:401–25.

Watt, Doris, J. 1986. "Relationship of Plumage Variability, Size, and Sex to Social Dominance." *Animal Behaviour* 34:16–27.

Weller, Susan C., and A. Kimball Romney. 1990. *Metric Scaling: Correspondence Analysis*. Newbury Park, CA: Sage.

9

NEIGHBORHOOD-BASED MODELS FOR SOCIAL NETWORKS

Philippa Pattison*
Garry Robins*

We argue that social networks can be modeled as the outcome of processes that occur in overlapping local regions of the network, termed local social neighborhoods. Each neighborhood is conceived as a possible site of interaction and corresponds to a subset of possible network ties. In this paper, we discuss hypotheses about the form of these neighborhoods, and we present two new and theoretically plausible ways in which neighborhood-based models for networks can be constructed. In the first, we introduce the notion of a setting structure, a directly hypothesized (or observed) set of exogenous constraints on possible neighborhood forms. In the second, we propose higher-order neighborhoods that are generated, in part, by the outcome of interactive network processes themselves. Applications of both approaches to model construction are presented, and the developments are considered within a general conceptual framework of locale for social networks. We show how assumptions about neighborhoods can be cast within a hierarchy of increasingly complex models; these models represent a progressively greater capacity for network processes to "reach" across a network through long cycles or semipaths. We argue that this class of models holds new promise for the development of empirically plausible models for networks and network-based processes.

We are grateful to the Australian Research Council for support of the work presented here; and to Peter Bearman, Ronald Breiger, Noah Friedkin, David Gibson, Mark Handcock, Laura Koehly, Miller McPherson, Ann Mische, Martina Morris, Tom Snijders, Ross Stolzenberg, Harrison White, and several anonymous reviewers for valuable comments on the work.
*University of Melbourne

301

1. INTRODUCTION

The importance of network structure for a wide variety of social processes has been convincingly demonstrated in many different domains,
including interpersonal influence (Friedkin 1998), the spread of disease
(Klovdahl 1985; Kretzschmar and Morris 1996), and information diffusion (Valente 1995). Yet the success of attempts to build adequate models
for network-dependent processes is critically dependent on our understanding of the *structure* of social networks and particularly on our capacity to
construct adequate models for network structure. Frank and Strauss (1986)
took a significant step in addressing the problem of model construction
when they introduced the class of Markov random graphs. Within this
class of models, it is possible to relinquish the statistically convenient but
empirically implausible assumption of the independence of network ties
in different dyads (that is, of ties linking nonidentical *pairs* of people).
Relaxation of the dyad-independence assumption has led to the construction of new and demonstrably more successful classes of random graph
models for networks (Pattison and Wasserman 1999; Skvoretz and Faust
1999; Robins, Pattison, and Wasserman 1999; Wasserman and Pattison
1996). In this paper, we propose a more general theoretical framework for
building models of network structure, and we show how the approach
leads to a hierarchy of models within which hypotheses about the nature
of network structure can be explored.

Like many who have previously attempted to understand network
structure, we begin with the premise that network structures are, at least
in part, generated "locally." We see the major challenge facing model-
builders as that of understanding the precise form and extent of appropriate local dependencies. Our approach leads to a generalization of a number
of well-known classes of statistical models for network structures and is,
at the same time, sympathetic to some important theoretical claims about
the localized nature of important network processes (e.g., Abbott 1997;
Granovetter 1973; Johnsen 1986).

Before articulating some more general ways in which the term
"local" might be understood, we note that a number of significant contributions to the social networks literature have demonstrated how certain
systematicities in local *triadic* social network structures can give rise to
particular global network properties. Prominent examples include balance theory and its generalizations (e.g., Cartwright and Harary 1956;
Davis 1967), Granovetter's (1973, 1982) strength-of-weak-ties argument

and Johnsen's (1986) analysis of microstructures underlying the formation of friendship networks. In each of these examples, systematic features of local network structure that are specifiable at the level of small network substructures—triples of individuals and the ties that connect them—are seen to have potentially profound implications for aspects of global network structure. Below, we argue that such claims can be represented using models in which network ties are modeled as random variables that are subject to various kinds of regular, "locally specified" constraints.

The insistence on a stochastic formulation as well as a local one may seem surprising, but work by Watts on the Small World Phenomenon (Watts and Strogatz 1998; Watts 1999a, b) has demonstrated how the introduction of even a small proportion of random network ties to a "regular" network structure can have a dramatic effect on the connectivity properties of a network. In addition, considerations of scale encourage a stochastic approach. As White (1992) has argued, "no larger ordering which is deterministic either in cultural assertion or social arrangement could sustain and reproduce itself across so many and such large network populations as in the current world. Some sort of stochastic environment must be assumed and requires modeling" (pp. 164–65).

1.1. *Beyond Triads*

Despite the well-established claims for the importance of regularities in triadic network configurations, few approaches to network modeling have considered *extra-triadic* features as the basis for building models for global structures. Rather, higher-order local configurations—for instance, those involving four or more actors—are assumed to arise as the concatenation of lower-order dyadic and triadic configurations. It is not clear, however, that this assumption can always be justified, either theoretically or empirically. For instance, theoretical arguments about generalized exchange (e.g., Bearman 1997) suggest the importance of cycles involving more than three actors. In addition, we may not be able to explain the presence of long paths in a network as accidental conjunctions of shorter paths involving no more than three actors. For example, people may use their friends to get in touch with other individuals with certain qualities. If those qualities are individual attributes, then this process can be represented as a path involving three people. But if the quality is a network-related property—for instance, being "well-connected" or being connected in a particular way—then more than three actors are implicated, even though the process is local. Indeed, such a network process may itself create new boundaries for "locality" as it unfolds.

So, in order to explore the importance of longer cycles and paths in networks, we need to construct models that incorporate local structures involving more than three actors. And as longer cycles and paths may be crucial to certain global properties of the network (e.g., connectivity), it is apparent that we need theoretical conceptualizations and empirical methods that expand the possibility of what counts as local. We argue below that what is "local" in a network needs to be conceptualized carefully, and may even need to incorporate features that are exogenous to a network. To the extent that this claim is justified for certain types of networks, it has implications not only for the models that we might need to construct but also for the type of observations that we might usefully make in network studies.

In what follows, then, we consider hybrid definitions of "locality" that comprise triadic or other types of dependencies constrained by exogenous features. We also introduce methods to model notions of "locality" that emerge from the network processes themselves, thereby allowing us to investigate claims about longer cycles and paths. We base these innovations on a theoretical consideration of what we term *social locales* and *social neighborhoods*.

1.2. *Social Locales and Neighborhoods*

Our local approach to model-building recognizes the socially situated nature of social action, the fact that social action takes place within *social locales* (e.g., Abbott 1997; Feld 1981; White 1992). But what do we mean by the term "social locale"? Is a locale defined by geographical location, a set of network ties, or some aspect of community or culture? Like White (1992), we argue that all of these are likely to be implicated in the notion of locale. We do not attempt a precise definition here, but we propose that locale be regarded as a complex relational entity that links the geographical, social, cultural, and psychological aspects of the context for social action.[1] The importance of social locale in developing models for network structure is that the (often unobserved) characteristic of context

---

[1]Feld (1981) introduced a related notion of *focus*, "a social, psychological, legal, or physical entity around which joint activities are organized" (p.1016), and he argued that foci underpin aspects of patterning in social networks.

implicit in the notion of locale is the generator of contingencies among possible network ties.

Consider, for example, the so-called forbidden triad in Granovetter's (1973) theory. The triad comprises a triple of individuals in which two pairs of individuals are each linked by a strong tie, and the remaining pair by neither a strong nor weak tie. Granovetter's proposition that such triads are scarce can be seen as a claim that an individual with strong ties to two others is unlikely to be able to maintain these dyadic relations as components of separate locales. Rather, a locale encompassing all three individuals is likely to emerge (through, for example, representations in discursive forms, or common physical settings) and the locale is likely to have implications for the potential ties that it contains. The original dyadic locales may persist, but they are likely to be augmented by higher-order triadic locales. More generally, we see locales as overlapping and as operating at different "scales," from possibly more intimate dyadic contexts to broader and progressively more public and communal social settings.

We argue that previous approaches to the development of network models have made implicit assumptions about the nature of locale. At the simplest level, locales have been regarded as entities that correspond to single possible network ties, instantiating a class of (Bernoulli) models in which each tie is assumed to be negotiated independently of each other tie (Frank 1981). The general implausibility of the claim that the tie from one individual to another is negotiated independently of the tie from the second to the first led to the somewhat more general notion of locale as *dyad*. In this formulation, a locale corresponds to a pair of individuals and the possible interdependent ties between them, but network processes occurring within separate dyadic locales are assumed to be independent of one another. This assumption underpins the so-called p_1, or dyad-independent, class of models (Holland and Leinhardt 1981; Wasserman 1987; Wasserman and Galaskiewicz 1984). The notion that locales are restricted to dyads has also been criticized and Frank and Strauss made a significant generalization with the introduction of Markov random graphs. They proposed that a pair of possible network ties that share *one or more* actors belong to a common locale, and so introduced a model for network structure in which locales are potentially overlapping. The overlapping nature of locales means that the outcome of processes in one locale may have some impact on processes within another locale, thus lending a self-organizing quality to the resulting characterization of network structure.

The characterization just presented is based on two implicit assumptions. First, it is assumed that network ties are subject to both local and random processes. Second, it is assumed that systematicities in the arrangement of network ties emerge from regular, interactive processes occurring within social locales. Each locale is associated with a subset of possible network ties that we term the *local social neighborhood* of the locale. The neighborhood of the locale comprises its potential interpersonal relational components, with the geographical, psychological, and sociocultural aspects stripped away. The significance of this construct for building network models is that network data are often observed in isolation from these other contextual aspects, and the neighborhood may be the only aspect of a locale that is available for modeling. We note that this sense of social neighborhood is distinct from existing network concepts such as cliques or blocks. Cliques and blocks are defined in terms of observed ties in a network, whereas a social neighborhood specifies interdependencies among *possible* ties—that is, among relational variables, irrespective of their observed values.

In building models for networks, a major step is to specify the form of local social neighborhoods—that is, the form of the regions within which contingent social processes are assumed to occur. The approach we describe below begins to construct a general framework within which hypotheses about neighborhood form can be developed and empirically examined. The foundation of the framework is the p^* class of models (Frank and Strauss 1986; Pattison and Wasserman 1999; Robins, Pattison, and Wasserman 1999; Wasserman and Pattison 1996). The models are derived by assuming that possible ties that do not share a common locale are conditionally independent. The Hammersley-Clifford theorem (Besag 1974) is then used to derive a general implied parametric form (see Frank and Strauss 1986; Pattison and Wasserman 1999; Wasserman and Pattison 1996). The theorem establishes that nonzero parameters of a probability model for the network correspond to subsets of possible network ties that are assumed to be mutually conditionally dependent. By construction, each of these subsets corresponds to a collection of mutually contingent possible ties and corresponds to a local social neighborhood. In other words, the notion of social neighborhood is intrinsic to the p^* class of models.

The purpose of this paper is threefold. The first (Section 2) is to review some possible hypotheses about the form of local neighborhoods, including the Markovian assumption introduced by Frank and Strauss (1986). We argue that, while the theoretical rationale for this assumption is often strong, there are also reasons to consider both more restricted and more general assumptions about neighborhood form, and we note that certain of these lead to technical problems for the p^* class of models.

Our second aim is therefore to propose two possible approaches to constructing plausible and more general classes of neighborhood assumptions, based on a more general notion of locale. In one approach (Section 3), we introduce the notion of *exogenous settings* that impose boundaries on possible neighborhoods. These exogenous setting structures can be used in a variety of ways to represent external constraints on possible network processes—for example, to limit the assumed size of neighborhoods or to represent spatiotemporal or external, organizational constraints. In the other approach (Section 4), we allow that neighborhoods can be created in part by the network processes themselves, and so can be seen both as a product of the interactive processes underlying the generation of network ties, and as the potential sites within which future processes are located. These developments depend on the introduction of the notion of partial conditional dependencies among network ties and we present a corresponding generalization of the Hammersley-Clifford theorem for the associated dependence structures. Our third aim is to present several applications of these approaches, and thereby demonstrate their potential value in the development of social network models (Section 5). We conclude with a brief discussion in Section 6 of parallel work that allows other forms of flexibility in neighborhood dependence structures, and with some speculations about future steps that might guide social network modeling.

2. THE p^* CLASS OF MODELS AND LOCAL NEIGHBORHOOD HYPOTHESES

A social network can be regarded as a designated set of nodes and their pairwise interconnections. In many applications, the nodes correspond to individuals and interconnections correspond to interpersonal ties (e.g., person i regularly communicates with person j), but, in general, a network may represent any collection of connections among a specifiable set of social units.

Let $N = \{1, 2, \ldots, n\}$ be a set of network nodes and let the two-way $n \times n$ (binary) array $\mathbf{x}$ denote an observed network on N: that is, $x_{ij} = 1$ if there is an observed tie from node i to node j, and $x_{ij} = 0$ otherwise. (See Appendix A for a full list of symbols.) Also let $\mathbf{X}$ denote a *random* graph or network on N, with each *possible tie* (i, j) regarded as a random variable X_{ij}. The possible tie (i, j) may be regarded as *directed* (and distinct from X_{ji}) or it may be *nondirected* (and identical to X_{ji}). We refer mainly to nondirected graphs in the discussion below.

As foreshadowed above, a potential problem with constructing models for $\Pr(\mathbf{X} = \mathbf{x})$ is that an assumption of independent variables is unlikely to be tenable; rather, ties are likely to be interdependent by virtue of shared locales. As a result, a modeling approach needs to give explicit recognition to possible interdependencies. Frank and Strauss (1986) recognized that some fundamental theorems for interdependent observations developed in spatial statistics could be applied to arbitrary dependence structures, including structures specifying assumed dependencies among network ties. Application of these results yields a general expression for $\Pr(\mathbf{X} = \mathbf{x})$ from a specification of which pairs of possible ties are conditionally independent, given the values of all other ties (Frank and Strauss 1986).

More specifically, potential dependencies among possible network ties may be represented by a *dependence graph* $\mathbf{D}$. The node set M of the dependence graph indexes the set of possible ties,[2] and the edge set $E = \{((i,j),(k,l))\colon X_{ij}$ and X_{kl} are conditionally dependent, given that $X_{mh} = x_{mh}$ for $(m,h) \in M\backslash\{(i,j),(k,l)\}\}$ specifies which pairs of possible ties are assumed to be conditionally dependent.[3] In the terms we have introduced above, possible ties are assumed to be conditionally dependent if they occupy a common locale, or neighborhood. Invoking the Hammersley-Clifford theorem (Besag 1974) yields an expression for $\Pr(\mathbf{X} = \mathbf{x})$ in terms of parameters and substructures corresponding to cliques of $\mathbf{D}$; that is

$$\Pr(X = x) = p^*(x) = (1/c)\exp\{\Sigma_{A \subseteq M}\lambda_A z_A(x)\},$$

where

a.   the summation is over all subsets A of M;
b. $z_A(x) = \Pi_{(i,j)\in A}x_{ij}$ is the *network statistic* corresponding to subset A of M;

---

[2] Often, $M = \{(i,j)\colon i,j \in N, i < j\}$ in the nondirected case, but, more generally, we allow that any subset of (i,j) combinations can define the set of possible ties.

[3] X_{ij} and X_{kl} are *conditionally independent*, given $X_{mh} = x_{mh}$ for $(m,h) \in M\backslash\{(i,j),(k,l)\}$ if

$$\Pr(X_{ij} = x_{ij}, X_{kl} = x_{kl} | X_{mh} = x_{mh} \text{ for } (m,h) \in M\backslash\{(i,j),(k,l)\})$$

$$= \Pr(X_{ij} = x_{ij} | X_{mh} = x_{mh} \text{ for } (m,h) \in M\backslash\{(i,j),(k,l)\})$$

$$\times \Pr(X_{kl} = x_{kl} | X_{mh} = x_{mh} \text{ for } (m,h) \in M\backslash\{(i,j),(k,l)\});$$

otherwise they are *conditionally dependent*.

c. $c = \Sigma_{\mathbf{X}} \exp\{\Sigma_A \lambda_A z_A(\mathbf{x})\}$ is a normalizing quantity; and

d. the parameter $\lambda_A = 0$ for all $\mathbf{x}$ unless A is a clique of $\mathbf{D}$ (where a *clique* of $\mathbf{D}$ is a nonempty subset A of M such that A comprises a single possible tie, or $(((i,j),(k,l)) \in E$ for all $(i,j), (k,l) \in A)$.

(See Frank and Strauss [1986] and Wasserman and Pattison [1996] for a detailed discussion of the models for nondirected and directed graphs, respectively.) This formulation can be generalized to both polytomous network data, where the entries in $\mathbf{X}$ can take a range of values signifying different strengths of tie (Robins et al. 1999), and to multivariate network data, where a number of edges of different types may be observed between pairs of nodes (Pattison and Wasserman 1999).

Since it is assumed that possible ties are conditionally dependent only if they occupy a common social neighborhood, the subsets A for which the parameter λ_A is nonzero are all subsets of a local social neighborhood. (These subsets are themselves social neighborhoods.) It is in this sense that the form of social neighborhoods determines the form of the network model. The statistic $z_A(\mathbf{x})$ is a binary-valued measure corresponding to A that is computed from $\mathbf{x}$. It takes the value 1 if all of the possible ties in the subset A are present in $\mathbf{x}$, and 0 otherwise. The subset A corresponds to a subgraph configuration in $\mathbf{x}$—namely, the subgraph obtained when all possible ties in A are present in $\mathbf{x}$. Thus, if the parameter λ_A is large and positive, the probability of observing the network $\mathbf{x}$ is enhanced if the configuration corresponding to A is present in $\mathbf{x}$ (net of other effects). More intuitively, if all ties in A are present— and so $z_A(\mathbf{x}) = 1$—then the model reflects—through the parameter λ_A—the effect of the network configuration on the probability of the network. Since the subsets of A are also neighborhoods, the model can represent the effects of higher-order, over and above lower-order, configurations. In principle, therefore, the model allows us to determine the extent to which lower-order building blocks contribute to the existence of higher-order configurations.

2.1. *Markovian Neighborhoods*

A critical step in model construction is the specification of the form of local social neighborhoods, but what form should they take? Frank and Strauss (1986) introduced what we term here *Markovian neighborhoods*. A pair of possible ties X_{ij} and X_{kl} belong to a common neighborhood (and so are conditionally dependent) whenever they have a node in common—

i.e., whenever $\{i,j\} \cap \{k,l\} \neq \varnothing$. This Markovian dependence structure specifies the independence, *conditional on the state of all other variables in the network*,[4] of any two variables X_{ij} and X_{kl} that correspond to possible ties with no node in common.

The assumption of Markovian neighborhoods reflects a natural intuition about processes that generate social relationships: Social ties are not independent of each other, but their dependence is expressed through any persons directly involved in the ties in question. The assumption is also a natural graph-theoretical generalization of the dyad-independence assumption, since it asserts that dependencies arise not just in potential tie cycles of length two (that is, in dyadic structures), but also in any potential semi-path of length two.[5]

For nondirected graphs, the configurations corresponding to Markovian neighborhoods take one of a relatively small number of forms: edges; triads; and starlike structures (see Figure 1). If a homogeneity assumption is also made (that parameters corresponding to isomorphic neighborhoods are equal),[6] then the probability model for X has a single parameter corresponding to each of the distinct configurations in Figure 1. Each configuration corresponds to an isomorphism class $[A]$ of neighborhoods A, and the statistic $z_{[A]}(x)$ corresponding to class $[A]$ is then a count of the number of observed configurations of that form. The

---

[4]In contrast to dyad-independent models, the conditionality is necessary, for if X_{ij} is not independent of X_{jk}, and in turn X_{jk} is not independent of X_{kl}, then X_{ij} cannot be said to be independent of X_{kl}, even if $\{i,j\} \cap \{k,l\} = \varnothing$. Conditional dependence here is, in fact, equivalent to the claim that X_{ij} and X_{kl} are independent, given the states of variables $X_{ik}, X_{ki}, X_{jk}, X_{kj}, X_{il}, X_{li}, X_{jl}$ and X_{lj}—that is, the variables in the intersection of the maximal neighborhoods of the possible ties (i,j) and (k,l). More generally, once the state of variables in the neighborhood of (i,j) is known, then the state of other variables provides no information about X_{ij}. In fact, it is possible to construct some artificial examples where conditionality on all other variables and conditionality based on variables corresponding to the intersection of neighborhoods are not equivalent. These examples typically arise because of a logical relation among the variables, which will not be the case in the types of networks that we consider. See Lauritzen (1996) for further discussion.

[5]A *semipath of length k* in a directed graph is a set $\{(i_1,i_2),(i_2,i_3),\ldots,(i_k,i_{k+1})\}$ of node pairs such that either (i_h,i_{h+1}) or (i_{h+1},i_h) is an edge in the graph, for each $h = 1,2,\ldots,k$. A *cycle* of length k is a set $\{(i_1,i_2),(i_2,i_3),\ldots,(i_k,i_1)\}$ of edges linking k distinct nodes $i_1, i_2,\ldots,i_k$.

[6]In general, two configurations A and A' are *isomorphic* if there is a 1-1 mapping φ on N such that $(i,j) \in A$ if and only if $(\varphi(i),\varphi(j)) \in A'$. If we assume that $\lambda_A = \lambda_{A'}$ whenever A and A' are isomorphic, the model then takes the form $\Pr(X = x) = (1/c)\exp\{\Sigma_{[A]} \lambda_{[A]} n_{[A]}(x)\}$, where $[A]$ is the class of cliques in $\mathbf{D}$ isomorphic to A, and $n_{[A]}(x) = \Sigma_{A \in [A]} z_A(x)$ is the corresponding *sufficient statistic*.

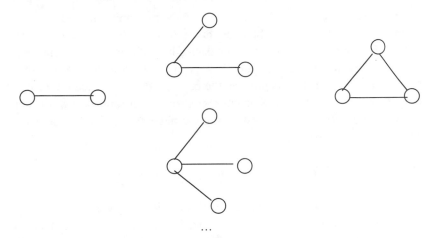

FIGURE 1. Configurations with three or fewer edges corresponding to Markovian neighborhoods for a graph.

model for the global network structure X expresses the probability of a network in terms of propensities for these triadic and starlike configurations to occur.

Model parameters are often currently estimated using a maximum pseudo-likelihood procedure (Strauss and Ikeda 1990), but other Markov chain Monte Carlo estimation approaches are also under investigation (e.g., Corander, Dahmström, and Dahmström 1998; Crouch and Wasserman 1998; Snijders in press). Computational details of the maximum pseudo-likelihood approach for Markovian and other models considered here are presented in Appendix B.[7]

Compared to models with only edge and dyadic neighborhoods, empirical support for models with Markovian neighborhoods has been strong in a number of applications involving a broad range of network types (e.g., Lazega and Pattison 1999; Pattison and Wasserman 1999; Robins 1998; Robins et al. 1999; Wasserman and Pattison 1996). This support is not surprising in light of strong theoretical claims about triadic depen-

---

[7] The development of feasible methods for maximum-likelihood estimation is an area of active research (for example, Corander et al. 1998; Crouch and Wasserman 1998; Snijders 2001). Preliminary results suggest that it is useful to pursue the development of more plausible models for networks in parallel with this work, since the performance of estimators is critically dependent on model properties.

dencies such as those reviewed earlier; indeed, empirical findings have already mirrored aspects of balance theory (e.g., Pattison and Wasserman 1999), Granovetter's strength-of-weak-ties hypothesis (e.g., Robins et al. 1999), and local clustering effects (Lazega and Pattison 1999). Yet whether Markovian neighborhoods provide the most precise specification of local neighborhoods for network structures is uncertain, and below we consider the theoretical task of evaluating the necessity and sufficiency of a Markovian formulation.

2.2. Beyond Markovian Neighborhoods

It is easy to conceive of hypothetical situations in which the generic Markovian neighborhoods that we have just described are at once too broadly and too narrowly specified. On the one hand, it is possible that the ties X_{ij} and X_{kl} arise within a common social locale even though i, j, k, and l are all distinct (for instance, they may all meet regularly in a group setting, or be connected by common interests), and they may, accordingly, be conditionally dependent. On the other hand, X_{ij} and X_{ik} may never occupy the same settings: Even though individual i is common to the two possible ties, the possible tie (i, j) may occupy a distinct set of social locales to those containing the possible tie (i, k), and, as a result, it is plausible that the two possible ties are in fact conditionally independent of one another. Indeed, in large networks individuals may not be aware of all of the possible ties of those to whom they are themselves tied, nor even of all other nodes in the network; in addition, contextual factors may be such that certain potential Markov dependencies are never realized. In other words, these hypothetical examples raise the possibility that the generic Markovian neighborhoods introduced above do not map directly onto an as-yet-unspecified structure of social locales that underpin conditional dependencies among variables.

We consider below two possible ways of constructing more general, and arguably more plausible, specifications of neighborhood form. In the first, a setting structure is directly hypothesized (or even observed) and considered as a set of exogenous constraints on the model. These assumed exogenous constraints take the form of substantive limitations on possible tie interactions and are used to hypothesize directly that certain model parameters are zero. In the second, neighborhoods are proposed to be generated in part by the unfolding interactive processes themselves. In this second case, the neighborhood structure for the model of a system of tie variables depends on the *realization* of the model; that is, whether two possible ties are conditionally dependent may depend on whether a particular subset of possible ties is actually observed to be present.

Before describing these two approaches to modifying a generic Markovian neighborhood specification, we note that a simple generic extension of the Markovian assumption is problematic for the p^* class of models. In particular, if we allow that X_{ij} and X_{lm} are conditionally dependent for all $((i,j),(l,m)) \in E$, then the dependence graph $\mathbf{D}$ is complete. In this case, every subset of nodes in M corresponds to a neighborhood, and even with a general homogeneity assumption, the resulting p^* model cannot be estimated. Of course, in order to render the model estimable, one can choose to set particular parameters to zero, and the first approach that we describe below provides a way of proposing a principled set of choices. Our second approach introduces a modified form of conditional dependence assumptions and so arguably retains a more explicit link between conditional dependence assumptions and model form. In the applications presented in Section 5, both approaches are used.

3. SETTING STRUCTURES

The first approach is to hypothesize a setting structure directly. That is, we assume that possible ties are conditionally dependent only when they share a potential "site of social action" (White 1995a) or *social setting* (also, Feld 1981). Each setting is assumed to correspond to some subset of possible network ties.[8] The notion of setting is intended, for the moment, to be a very general and skeletal one. It may correspond to some spatio-temporal context, such as a group of people gathered together at the same time and place, or it may refer to a collection of possible ties that are connected in some more abstract sociocultural space (for instance, pairs of persons linked by their political commitments). Settings may even reflect some external "design" constraints, such as organizational structure, task

[8] In fact, although we do not pursue the possibility here, it is likely that these subsets of possible ties are associated with sociocultural locales that include jointly produced interpretive frames through which actions of the participants can be understood. White (1995a,b) coined the term *network-domain* to refer to this intercoordination of sets of (possible) network ties and cultural domains. He proposed that these network domains as well as *switchings* between them are the primitive entities through which the regularities and discontinuities in sociocultural processes might come to be understood.

requirements in organizational settings, or hardware capabilities in communication networks. We have deliberately chosen an abstract formalization of the concept of setting, given the current limited state of theoretical and empirical articulation (but see Mische and Pattison 2000). And, for the moment, we simply propose that settings impose limits on local neighborhoods. Like neighborhoods, they may in general overlap, and possible ties may occupy many neighborhoods within many settings simultaneously. But mutual conditional dependencies among a set of ties (that is, neighborhoods) are assumed to be restricted so that they occur only within common settings. That is, two possible ties are assumed to be conditionally independent if they do not occupy a common setting, and they may or may not be conditionally independent if they do. Thus a setting is a weaker notion than a neighborhood, since the membership of two possible ties in a common setting is only a necessary but not sufficient condition for conditional dependence.

Formally, we define a *setting* $s \subseteq M$ as a subset of possible ties on a set N of nodes and a *setting structure* S simply as a collection of settings on N. We assume that if s is a setting in S, then so is any subset of s. Thus we can think that a setting structure is a *closed hypergraph*[9] on the set M that indexes all possible ties on the node set N.

Suppose that $\mathbf{X}$ is a random network with generic dependence structure $\mathbf{D}$ whose edge set is E (for example, $\mathbf{D}$ may assume Markovian neighborhoods). Also, let H denote the set of all cliques of $\mathbf{D}$; H is also a closed hypergraph on E (Robins 1998). Then a random graph model *confined* by the setting structure S has *the setting-restricted* clique set $H_S = H \cap S$; H_S is also a closed hypergraph on E.[10] Thus, in the restricted dependence structure, a collection of possible ties is mutually conditionally dependent only if it lies in some common setting. A setting structure hypothesis thus provides one approach to setting parameters in a model to zero: By restricting the clique set of the dependence graph to H_S, we impose the assumption $\lambda_A = 0$ for any $A \notin H_S$.

For a given dependence structure, setting structure hypotheses and homogeneity assumptions are usually both invoked. These two sets of

---

[9] A *hypergraph* H consists of a set V of elements and a collection E of subsets of V, termed edges. It is assumed that each element of V belongs to at least one edge, and that no edge is empty (e.g., Berge 1989). The hypergraph is *closed* if every subset of an edge in E is also an edge.

[10] The closure of H and H_S ensures that the corresponding probability models are hierarchical.

assumptions are not completely independent, however, as a setting structure hypothesis may set the parameters corresponding to some members of an isomorphism class $[A]$ to zero, but not others. We assume below that setting structure hypotheses have primacy—that is, that the homogeneity assumption applies to all cliques $A \in H_S$.

Several different forms for possible setting structures can be distinguished. If S comprises a single setting corresponding to the set M of all possible ties, then it is termed *universal*. In this case, the setting-restricted clique set H_S is simply the clique set H associated with the generic dependence structure $\mathbf{D}$.

Setting structures may also be defined for disjoint groups. Suppose that $N = \cup_g N_g$ is a disjoint union of the node set N, and let S_g be the universal setting structure defined on N_g. Then $S = \{S_g\}$ defines a disjoint subgroup structure and the model for $\Pr(X = x)$ can be decomposed into the form $\Pi_g \Pr(X_g = x_g)$, where X_g denotes the random network on the node set N_g, and x_g is its corresponding realization.[11] Such a form was described by Anderson, Wasserman, and Crouch (1999). Note that homogeneity of parameters corresponding to isomorphic neighborhoods may be assumed either within groups, or both within and between groups. Indeed, comparisons between models making these different homogeneity assumptions may yield useful insights into the heterogeneity of parameters across groups, as Anderson et al. (1999) demonstrated.

More generally, it may be appropriate to regard settings as group-like in structure but potentially overlapping (e.g., Freeman and White 1993; Mische 1998). In particular, if we conceptualize a setting in terms of the potential links among a subset N_s of individuals who are, say, co-present in a particular location, co-members of a particular group, or who share certain aspirations, then settings take the form $s_s = \{(i,j) : i, j \in N_s$ and $i \neq j\}$ and a potentially *overlapping subgroup setting structure* results.

Versions of overlapping subgroup setting structures can be used to explore the interaction between neighborhoods specified in network terms (as in the Markovian case) and neighborhoods defined in terms of regions in physical or social space. For example, as White (1992) has argued, physical space is likely to be important to the notion of locale, and it is impor-

---

[11] In this case it is also possible to think of the restriction arising at the level of the dependence graph, not just at the level of its cliques. That is, if we define a *setting-restricted dependence graph* $\mathbf{D}_S$ *with edge set* $E \cap \{\cup_g (M_g \times M_g)\}$, where M_g is the set of possible ties on N_g, then the clique set of $\mathbf{D}_S$ is simply H_S. The restriction acts to ensure that only pairs of possible ties from the same group give rise to an edge in $\mathbf{D}_S$.

tant to develop an understanding of the relationship between physical space and local neighborhoods. If we assume that individuals have some spatial distribution, we can use spatially defined setting structures of different forms and extents to explore the properties of the very different neighborhood structures that network- and spatially restricted neighborhoods imply.

An overlapping subgroup structure also arises if we assume that settings are restricted to a maximum of k individuals, so that each setting comprises ties among a subgroup of individuals of size no greater than k. Such setting structures are implicit when we restrict neighborhoods according to the number of nodes that they involve. For instance, with a generic Markov assumption, and $k \geq 3$, such a setting structure leads to a model in which star configurations involving more than k nodes have zero parameters, a model that has proved useful in many empirical applications for $k = 3$ (see also Robins 1998).

To illustrate how overlapping subgroup setting structures may be invoked, we use organizationally defined overlapping subgroups to set certain model parameters to zero in one of the applications presented in Section 5. As indicated above, the parameters are set to zero prior to the imposition of a homogeneity constraint on isomorphic within-setting forms.

More generally, a setting structure comprises a collection of subsets of possible ties, subject to the requirement that each subset of a setting is also a setting. For example, a general setting structure form that has proved technically useful, especially in multivariate applications, is one in which the number of ties in a setting is restricted to some maximum (e.g., see Lazega and Pattison 1999).

4. PARTIAL CONDITIONAL DEPENDENCE ASSUMPTIONS

It was observed above that the general assumption that X_{ij} and X_{kl} are conditionally dependent for distinct i, j, k, l leads to a complete dependence graph and associated problems. In fact, though, such a general assumption is likely to be unreasonable in any but the smallest face-to-face group contexts. Rather, if there is a conditional dependence between X_{ij} and X_{kl} for distinct i, j, k, l, it is likely to result from the fact that these possible ties occupy a common setting. In the section above, we introduced hypothesized setting structures as a means of using information about settings to restrict generic dependence assumptions. In this section, we consider the possibility that the interactive processes giving rise to network ties are themselves a source of social settings, so that new settings are created as network ties are generated: For instance, the possible ties X_{ij} and X_{kl} might become conditionally dependent if there is an observed tie between j and k or between l and i.

In other words, we might assume that longer-range dependencies (that is, those involving X_{ij} and X_{kl} for distinct i, j, k, l) are restricted by such conditions as

$$((i,j),(k,l)) \in E \text{ for distinct } i, j, k, l \text{ only if } x_{ik} = 1 \text{ or } x_{il} = 1$$

$$\text{or } x_{jk} = 1 \text{ or } x_{jl} = 1.$$

We noted above that the Markov assumption introduces conditional dependencies among possible ties forming semipaths of length two, and that this can be seen as a natural graph-theoretical extension of the assumption of dependence among possible ties forming cycles of length two.[12] The condition just posited extends the assumption of conditional dependence among possible ties forming a path of length 3 (and the middle tie must be present for the assumed conditional dependence among the first and last possible ties in the path).[13]

The condition introduces the notion of *partial conditional independence* with respect to some subset of ties: X_{ij} and X_{kl} are conditionally independent for certain observed values of other variables (e.g., if $x_{ik} = 0$ and $x_{il} = 0$ and $x_{jk} = 0$ and $x_{jl} = 0$) but conditionally dependent for certain other observed value combinations (e.g., if $x_{ik} = 1$ or $x_{il} = 1$ or $x_{jk} = 1$ or $x_{jl} = 1$).

To capture the idea in general, we define a *partial dependence structure* $\mathbf{D}_B$ *for a subset* $B \subset M$ of possible ties. The node set of $\mathbf{D}_B$ is the set $M \backslash B$ of possible ties that are in M but are not in B and the edge set of $\mathbf{D}_B$ is given by $\{((i,j),(k,l)): X_{ij} \text{ and } X_{kl} \text{ are conditionally dependent, given that } X_{mh} = x_{mh} \text{ for } (m,h) \in M \backslash B \text{ and } X_{mh} = 0 \text{ for } (m,h) \in B\}$. In other words, two possible ties are linked by an edge in $\mathbf{D}_B$ if they are assumed to be conditionally dependent even when all of the possible ties in the set

---

[12] In fact, an intermediate model between the dyad-independent model and the Markov model is the *(2)-path* model described by Pattison and Wasserman (1999), in which X_{ij} and X_{kl} are conditionally dependent whenever $j = k$—that is, when X_{ij} and X_{kl} form a possible 2-path.

[13] It is interesting to note that the construction we propose here is similar to that suggested by Baddeley and Möller (1989), who were concerned to formulate spatial interaction models for randomly positioned objects in a way that would satisfy certain geometrical or topological conditions but also retain good probabilistic and statistical properties.

B have observed values of 0. More importantly, two ties are *not* linked by an edge in $\mathbf{D_B}$ if they are assumed to be conditionally independent when all of the possible ties in the set B have observed values of 0. Note that if $((i,j),(k,l)) \in \mathbf{D_B}$ then $((i,j),(k,l)) \in \mathbf{D}$; thus, $\mathbf{D_B}$ is a subgraph of $\mathbf{D}$ for all $B \subset M$. It is possible though that $((i,j),(k,l))$ may be an edge in $\mathbf{D}$ but not in $\mathbf{D_B}$, for some B, signifying that X_{ij} and X_{kl} are conditionally independent when $x_{mh} = 0$ for all $(m,h) \in \mathrm{B}$. We refer to two conditionally dependent possible ties as *partially conditionally independent* with respect to a set of possible ties B (a set that includes neither tie) if the pair of ties represents an edge in $\mathbf{D}$ but not in $\mathbf{D_B}$.[14] We show in Appendix C the following:

Proposition:

If $A \subseteq M \backslash B$ and A is not a clique in $\mathbf{D_B}$ for some subset B of M, then $\lambda_A = 0$ in $\Pr(X = x)$.

In other words, if there exists *any* subset B of possible ties for which $A \cap B = \varnothing$ and the set A of possible ties is not a clique in $\mathbf{D_B}$, then the parameter λ_A corresponding to A must be zero. The following is therefore established:

Corollary:

The parameter λ_A is non-zero in the model $p^*(x)$ if and only if A is a clique in $\mathbf{D}$ and in all $\mathbf{D_B}$ for which $A \cap B = \varnothing$.

For example, suppose, as suggested above, that in addition to the assumption that X_{ij} and X_{kl} are conditionally dependent if $(i,j) \cap (k,l) \neq \varnothing$, we assume that X_{ij} and X_{kl} are conditionally dependent for distinct i, j, k, and l if $x_{ik} = 1$ or if $x_{il} = 1$ or if $x_{jk} = 1$ or if $x_{jl} = 1$ but are conditionally independent otherwise. Then $((i,j),(k,l))$ is an edge in $\mathbf{D}$ but $((i,j),(k,l))$ is not an edge in $\mathbf{D_B}$, for $B = \{(i,k),(i,l),(j,k),(j,l)\}$. Thus, for $A =$

[14] Partial conditional independence is a generalization of the more familiar notion of conditional independence. Conditional independence is the expression of the statistical independence of two variables given the state of a third variable (Dawid, 1979, 1980). In the case of partial conditional independence, we assert that two variables are statistically independent if and only if a third variable is in a *particular* state.

$\{(i,j),(k,l)\}$, $\lambda_A = 0$ even though for $A = \{(i,j),(j,k),(k,l)\}$, λ_A may be nonzero. It follows from this conditional dependence structure that non-Markovian parameters correspond to certain connected configurations comprising 4 or more nodes that satisfy the condition that every pair of edges lies on a path of length 3. We refer to this model as the *3-path* random graph model. For nondirected graphs, there are nonzero model parameters corresponding to configurations in which every pair of edges lie on a path of length 3; configurations on 4 nodes satisfying the condition are shown in Figure 2. Note that these configurations contain longer paths and cycles than the Markov configurations of Figure 1.

A positive model parameter corresponding to one of these higher-order configurations would reflect a tendency for networks to be more probable if they possess many such higher-order configurations. For example, a model with a positive parameter for a 3-path (the first configuration in Figure 2) would indicate that, given a particular tendency toward edges and 2-paths, networks with many 3-paths are more likely. In example 2 below, we also suggest how models with positive parameters for 4-cycles (the third configuration in Figure 2) might be interpreted.

For directed graphs, both *3-semipath* and *3-path* random directed graph model can be formulated, with two possible ties conditionally dependent if they lie on a 3-semipath, or 3-path, respectively. In the applications presented below, we use the 3-path model for nondirected graphs; for directed graphs, though, it is an empirical question as to which might provide the most useful model in a given modeling context.

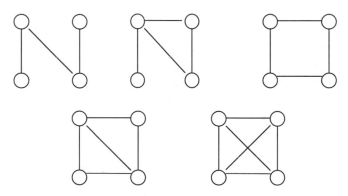

FIGURE 2. Non-Markovian configurations corresponding to nonzero parameters in a 3-path random graph model.

   The steps just described allow us to embed models with Markovian neighborhoods in classes of models with more complex dependence structures. This embedding has two important theoretical consequences. First, it permits a more detailed assessment of the class of Markovian models. Only by comparing Markovian models with models that make plausible but more complex neighborhood assumptions can we explore the sufficiency of the Markovian neighborhood assumption. Second, it permits us to examine some more complex dependencies that are suggested by several theoretical claims, including arguments for the presence of *generalized exchange* and hence for *cyclic* patterns of network ties (e.g., Bearman 1997); arguments about the nature of strategic activity in networks, including brokering and mediating behaviors (e.g., Mische 1998; Mische and Robins 2000); and arguments for indirect social influence (e.g., Robins, Pattison, and Elliott 2001).

   In theoretical terms, it is worth emphasizing that extra-Markovian dependence assumptions allow us to explore the possibility of "action at a distance," whereby individual ties may be shaped by events or opinions that are not contiguous to the individuals concerned. For instance, *generalized exchange* (Bearman 1997; Breiger and Ennis 1997; Yamagishi and Cook 1993) requires extra-Markovian neighborhood assumptions. Although exchange *within* dyads is often governed by a norm of reciprocity, *generalized exchange* is governed by reciprocity with a difference: Those who receive also give but they give to someone else. The result is a system of cycles where "values have to flow through all parties in a cycle before a giver can become a taker, that is, receive a gift in return" (Bearman 1997, p.1389). A Markov assumption is adequate to model cycles of order three (e.g., see Pattison and Wasserman 1999) but Bearman's analysis revealed cycles of order 8 in a generalized system of marital exchange within aboriginal kinship systems. To investigate the relevance of cyclic structures within a network, we need to assume that a possible tie is conditionally dependent on other possible ties with which it might form cycle-constituting paths. Thus partial conditional dependence assumptions such as those described above are required. An example of this approach for cycles of order 4 is presented in the applications below.

   A final observation on partial conditional dependence structures is that the associated models may not be hierarchical. We observed earlier that the cliques of a dependence graph define a closed hypergraph, since, for a dependence structure, every subset of a clique is necessarily also a clique. Similarly, setting-confined clique sets are also closed hypergraphs by virtue of the construction of setting structures. In the case of models associated with partial conditional dependence structures, however, it is possible for a model to have a nonzero parameter corresponding to λ_A, even though $\lambda_{A'}$ is fixed to be zero for some $A' \subset A$. In this case, the collection of cliques with nonzero parameters defines a hypergraph that is not closed. The interpretation of the parameter λ_A is made relative to constituent substructures A' for those A' that correspond to connected configurations and that are included in the model (rather than for all such A'). This point is illustrated in the interpretation of models for the last two applications below.

5. APPLICATIONS

We present two applications that draw on the approaches to neighborhood formulation that we have described.

5.1. *Friendship-Setting Structures from Organizational Constraints*

In the first example, we use a familiar network data set to illustrate the application of an overlapping subgroup setting structure. The data come from Roethlisberger and Dickson's (1939) classic study, *Management and the Worker*, and we use some of the information about work arrangements supplied by the authors and discussed by Homans (1951) to model the network of friendships in the Bank Wiring Room.

As both Roethlisberger and Dickson and Homans report, the 14 workers in the Bank Wiring Room occupied particular locations in the room and their work arrangements dictated certain functional interdependencies. Here we use the two types of organizational constraints illustrated in Homans (1951, fig. 1, p. 56) to generate setting structure hypotheses. The first is the arrangement of workers into soldering units. Each unit comprised four workers, with three engaged in wiring and one in soldering. The units were (W1, W2, W3, S1), (W4, W5, W6, S2), and (W7, W8, W9, S3). A slightly different structure was associated with work inspections, with inspection units comprising (W1, W2, W3, S1, W4, W5, W6, I1) and (W5, W6, S2, W7, W8, W9, S3, I2).

Here we assume that the setting structure for the Bank Wiring Room comprises the collection of these subgroups as well as all pairs of workers in the room. The rationale for this hypothesis is twofold. First, friendship ties are possible among all members of the room, hence we include all possible ties in the setting structure. Second, more complex dependencies involving two or more possible friendship ties are most likely to have their source in the likely more intensive work-related interactions among members of a work unit; accordingly, we include functional work units in the setting structure. Of course, there may be social settings outside of work that contribute to possible tie dependencies and that are not captured by this setting structure; such dependencies are not modeled by this hypothesized structure and are likely to be associated with lack of fit.

In Table 1, we report the fit of 5 models to the Friendship network in the Bank Wiring Room (the data are presented in Homans, 1951, p. 69, fig. 6). The first is the homogeneous Bernoulli model and it is presented for comparative purposes. (The model assumes a generic dependence structure in which all possible friendship ties are independent, so that the cliques in H correspond to edge configurations and each has the same parameter.) For each of the fitted models, Table 1 shows two heuristic indices of model fit: -2 times the log of the maximized pseudolikelihood function (-2LPL: see Appendix B); and the mean absolute residual (MAR) for each possible tie).[15] We rely on heuristic measures of fit since the distribution of -2LPL is not known (as for other applications of maximum pseudolikelihood estimation; see Besag 1977; Strauss and Ikeda 1990). The pseudolikelihood parameter estimates are also shown in Table 1; computational details are given in Appendix B. The second and third rows of the table show two Markov models for a universal setting structure; the fourth and fifth rows show the same models confined by the setting structure described above. (Note that additional restrictions are imposed in both cases, since only a subset of possible Markov configurations are used.)

It is evident from the table that the inclusion of a 2-star parameter improves model fit in the presence of the restricted setting structure hypothesis, but that the improvement is only marginal if the setting structure is assumed to be universal. Comparison of parameter estimates shows that the edge parameter is estimated to be substantially more negative and the star parameter substantially more positive for the restricted setting structure case. In the restricted set of neighborhoods associated with the set-

---

[15] The mean absolute residual is computed as the average value of $|x_{ij} - z_{ij}|$, where z_{ij} is the estimated value of $Pr(X_{ij} = 1 | X_{mh} = x_{mh}$ for $(m,h) \in M\backslash\{(i,j)\})$, computed from the conditional logit form of the p^* model, namely, logit $Pr(X_{ij} = 1 | X_{mh} = x_{mh}$ for $(m,h) \in M\backslash\{(i,j)\} = \Sigma_B \lambda_B \Pi_{Xkl \in B \backslash \{Xij\}} x_{kl})$, where B is the set of substructures including the possible tie X_{ij}.

TABLE 1
Fit of Models to Friendship Ties in the Bank Wiring Room

Model	Number of Parameters	−2LPL	MAR	Edge	Parameter Estimates	
					2-star	triangle
Universal Setting Structure						
Bernoulli	1	74.6	0.245	−1.79 (.30)	—	—
2-parameter Markov	2	71.1	0.238	−3.00 (.79)	.318 (.177)	—
3-parameter Markov	3	38.4	0.112	−2.66 (.93)	−.294 (.278)	3.19 (.805)
Organizational setting structure						
2-parameter Markov	2	52.1	0.176	−4.57 (1.1)	1.09 (.320)	
3-parameter Markov	3	35.3	0.103	−3.40 (.81)	.023 (.416)	3.02 (1.04)

323

ting structure hypothesis, therefore, there appears to be a tendency for friendship ties to be connected through particular individuals, and for isolated friendship ties to be rare.

For models possessing both 2-stars and triangles, there is less difference in the fit of the models with universal and restricted setting structures, and also a less clear difference in parameter estimates. The largest difference is in the 2-star parameter, which is close to zero when neighborhoods are setting-restricted and small and negative without the setting restriction. It is interesting that the effects of the setting-restriction are so substantially moderated once the triangle parameter is introduced. It is possible that, in this case, the triangle parameter largely has its effect within settings, so that the setting structure hypothesis and the triangle (clustering) effect are somewhat redundant. In other words, tendencies toward clustering in the Bank Wiring Room may arise principally from the organizational division of labor. This simple example suggests that formal organizational structure may play an important role in the evolution of informal networks, with balance and clustering effects to some degree constrained by formal boundaries.

5.2. *Work Organization in a New England Law Firm*

The second application is to data from a study conducted by Emmanuel Lazega in a U.S. law firm (see Lazega 1993; Lazega and van Duijn 1997; Lazega and Pattison 1999). All 71 lawyers in the firm were interviewed and provided information about a number of network ties among firm members. One of the questions sought information about work ties in the firm.[16] Here we consider the matrix of reciprocated work ties, in which $x_{ij} = 1$ if both i and j claim to work with each other, and $x_{ij} = 0$, otherwise. Since the ties are nondirected, Markovian neighborhoods correspond to edges, k-stars (for $2 \leq k \leq 70$), and triangles; see again Figure 1.

The purpose of our analyses is to examine the structure of these reciprocated Work ties, and to ask (1) whether they possess any regular, discernible form of local structuring, and (2) whether Markovian neigh-

---

[16] The question was as follows: "Here is the list of all the members of your Firm: Think back over the past year and check the names of the lawyers with whom you have worked. By 'worked with' I mean that you have spent time together on at least one case, that they have read or used your work product, or that you have read or used their work product; this includes professional work done within the firm like Bar Association work, administration, etc."

TABLE 2
Fit of Models to Reciprocated Work Ties in the Law Firm

Model	Number of Parameters	−2LPL	MAR
1. Bernoulli model	1	2119.0	0.258
2. Level 3 Markov model	4	1760.8	0.213
3. Level 4 3-semipath model	7	1579.2	0.191
4. Reduced 3-semipath model	6	1598.9	0.193

Source: From Lazega (1993).

borhoods are sufficient to describe any such local regularities. From a substantive point of view, any regularities in the social organization of Work ties are of considerable interest. On the one hand, Work ties are not centrally organized in a professional group such as a law firm and are clearly somewhat contingent on lawyers' availability and expertise. On the other hand, the firm and its members are critically dependent on a timely flow of work for their financial well-being. Thus the question of how work relationships come to be forged is a critical one, and regularities in the organization of work ties may suggest the emergence of social forms that serve to ameliorate this problem.

In the first two rows of Table 2 we report the fit of homogeneous Bernoulli and Markov models. In fitting the homogeneous Markov model, we assume that parameters corresponding to higher-order stars (i.e., $k > 3$) are zero, and so we invoke the assumption that settings comprise no more than four lawyers.[17] As comparison of the heuristic indices of fit indicates, the Markov model provides a substantial improvement over the Bernoulli model, and the estimated values of its parameters suggest that reciprocated Work ties exhibit quite substantial local clustering (parameter estimates appear in the top panel of Table 3). It is worth noting also that both star parameters have estimated values close to zero, indicating that there is no particular tendency for or against the generation of ties in ways that create 2-stars or 3-stars. The lack of a tendency for or against 2- or 3-stars suggests that there is no particular tendency for or against work partners with high degree. In this work network, in other words, there is

---

[17] See Robins et al. (1999) for a discussion of the role of higher-order stars in Markov models.

TABLE 3
Parameter Estimates for Markov and Reduced 3-Path Models
for Reciprocated Work Ties

Model	Configuration	PLE	Approximate Standard Error
Level 3 Markov			
	Edge	−2.785	.369
	2-star	−0.019	.030
	3-star	0.002	.002
	3-cycle	0.482	.035
Reduced 3-path Model			
	Edge	−3.669	.474
	2-star	0.307	.053
	3-star	−0.001	.002
	3-cycle	0.173	.047
	3-path	−0.019	.002
	4-cycle	0.086	.009

little evidence for high levels of centralization. Further, the low values of the star parameters suggest that the local clustering tendency is not accompanied by a tendency against unclosed 2-paths, leading to an overall structure with the character of a triangular tessellation.

In the third row of Table 2, we present the fit of the model in which we assume that the variables X_{ij} and X_{kl} are conditionally dependent if either (1) $\{i,j\} \cap \{k,l\} \neq \varnothing$ (as in the Markovian case) or (2) $\{i,j\} \cap \{k,l\} = \varnothing$ and x_{ik} or x_{il} or x_{jk} or x_{jl} is equal to 1; otherwise we assume that X_{ij} and X_{kl} are conditionally independent. The resulting partial dependence assumptions lead to neighborhoods that correspond to edges, stars, triads, and higher-order structures such as those shown in Figure 2. If we impose a setting structure of level 4, then the parameters of the model correspond to configurations with no more than four edges. Several of the parameters corresponding to these configurations are close to zero; their elimination leads to the model shown in the fourth row of Table 2; parameter estimates are given in Table 3. As the heuristic fit indices suggest, this model is an improvement over the Markov model, and the parameter corresponding to a 4-cycle of reciprocated Work ties is positive, suggesting that the probability of a Work network is enhanced by the presence of both 3-cycles and 4-cycles. Consistent with the interpretation made by

Lazega and Pattison (1999) in their analysis of directed Work ties, it appears that these results provide some evidence for the presence of a form of generalized exchange in the arrangement of Work ties. The cyclic structures do not encompass the entire group, as in the case of the Groote Eylandters analyzed by Bearman (1997); rather the 3-cycle and 4-cycle structures occur locally, and they may overlap with one another. It is also worth noting that the three-path parameter is negative. This implies that long unclosed paths are relatively rare, and that those 3-paths that are found are more likely to arise in local cyclic structures of length 4. It should be noted that the evidence is weak: In order to make a stronger claim, it would be useful to compare the model in the third and fourth rows of the table with one assessing the role of more densely connected subsets of four nodes, as well as with one possessing longer cycles. Nevertheless, the ability of this model to represent effects involving longer cycles provides a new empirical method for investigating generalized exchange.

6. PROSPECTS

In this paper, we have argued that social networks may be modeled as the outcome of processes that occur in overlapping local regions of the network, termed local social neighborhoods. Each neighborhood is conceived as a possible site of interaction and corresponds to a subset of possible ties. We have also argued that while there is growing evidence for the value of Markovian neighborhoods for network models, there are reasons to doubt the universal applicability of the Markovian neighborhood assumption. Accordingly, we presented two theoretically plausible ways in which Markovian and other neighborhood assumptions can be modified. The first is to introduce the notion of a setting structure—a directly hypothesized (or observed) set of exogenous constraints on possible neighborhood forms. The second is to propose higher-order neighborhoods that are generated in part by the outcome of interactive network processes themselves.

The two constructions that we introduced were deliberately presented at a very general level, since we believe we are not yet in a position to make strong claims about higher-order forms that are likely to be useful in a wide range of network modeling settings. Nonetheless, even though the applications of these constructions that were presented were illustrative only, they do point to the potential theoretical value of more carefully crafted hypotheses about network neighborhoods. In this final section, we briefly review the applications that we have presented and then suggest some potentially important additional applications. We also sketch some next steps in the exploration of neighborhood forms.

6.1. *Non-Markovian Neighborhoods*

The applications provide some initial evidence for the empirical value of models with non-Markovian neighborhoods. Higher-order structures in the organization of work in the law firm are both theoretically meaningful and lead to a substantially enhanced capacity to account for network data. In relation to substantive setting structure hypotheses, we have only explored one limited application to the small network of friendship ties in the Bank Wiring Room: Clearly, more extensive investigations, particularly in large networks where setting effects are likely to be more pronounced, are required. Nonetheless, the interesting pattern of results obtained from the Bank Wiring Room application suggests a possible interaction between setting structures and neighborhood forms. It may be the case that setting structure hypotheses will prove most useful where neighborhood assumptions are minimal and where networks are large. It may also be the case that the major impact of setting structure hypotheses of the type investigated for the Bank Wiring Room is for lower-order neighborhood forms, such as stars. Higher-order forms (such as triangles) are most likely to occur within settings anyway, and so to be somewhat redundant with them, whereas lower-order forms may be implicated in structures that bridge settings.

Within a general conceptual framework of the social locales underpinning social networks, we have presented various dependence assumptions as a hierarchy of increasingly complex dependence structures. The development of partial conditional dependence structures allows the fitting of models based on local configurations with increasing capacity to "reach" across the network through large cycles or long semipaths. In a graph theoretic sense, we can represent dependencies among possible ties within a hierarchy of structures with increasingly longer "reach." The hierarchy of models is presented in Table 4.

6.2. *Further Applications*

Many additional applications of the constructions that we have introduced have been suggested. For example, Mische and Robins (2000) use

TABLE 4
Some Classes of Dependence Assumptions Ties Are Conditionally Dependent
Within:

1-paths	Bernoulli models
2-cycles	Dyad-independent models
2-paths	2-path models
2-semipaths	Markov models
3-paths	3-path models
3-semipaths	3-semipath models
...	
Settings	Setting-restricted versions of the above models

partial conditional independence assumptions in modeling tripartite networks linking youth leaders, social and political organizations, and political events during the 1992 Brazilian impeachment movement. The resulting higher-order neighborhoods allow them to examine hypotheses about the roles of youth acting as mediators, brokers, or coordinators between organizations.

   In addition, these constructions are especially useful in a number of models that distinguish classes of variables and permit certain directed dependencies between variables in different classes. For example, Robins, Pattison, and Elliott (2001) constructed social influence models that examine contingencies between attributes of nodes and social organization. In these models, network ties and individual attributes form two distinct variable classes, and dependencies are assumed to be directed from the tie variables to the attribute variables. Mutual within-class dependencies are also assumed. These developments are noteworthy for two reasons. First, the neighborhoods associated with such models comprise variables that refer to potentially interdependent phenomena of different types; in principle, for instance, they might refer to such entities as possible ties, actor attributes, group memberships, and discursive forms. As a result, these models lead to a generalization of the notion of neighborhood from a collection of possible ties to more complex and, arguably more realistic, sociocultural forms—social locales, in the sense used earlier (Mische & Pattison 2000). A second important feature of these models is that they can instantiate the assumption of influence-at-a-distance (e.g., that the attributes of individuals i and/or j can influence the attribute of a third individual k). Such models require a partial conditional independence assumption. For example, it may be hypothesized that such effects are likely only when certain subsets of the network ties among i, j, and k are present. Similar approaches can be applied to social selection models, where the attributes of individuals are assumed to shape the formation of network ties (Robins, Elliott, and Pattison 2001).

Likewise, if the two classes comprise tie variables corresponding to two distinct measurement points, then a possible tie from i to j at time 2 might be assumed to be conditionally dependent on a possible tie from k to i at time 1 only if the tie from k to i is observed to be present at time 2 (i.e, only if it persists in time). Robins and Pattison (2001) refer to this as the *constant tie* assumption, and argue that it is plausible for some network ties.

6.3. *Challenges*

Many challenges remain. In statistical terms, the p^* class of models presents some important problems in a number of areas, including the estimation of parameters and their standard errors. Despite the promising steps that have been taken to obtain maximum likelihood parameter estimates for models in the p^* class, much work is required to further develop these techniques if they are to be applicable to models of the level of complexity that social theory is likely to demand. In addition, it would be useful to understand the dynamics of processes that have the models that we have constructed as their equilibrium distributions. The Metropolis-Hastings algorithm provides one clue, as it defines a "birth-and-death" process that necessarily converges to the model used to define it; Snijders's (2001) model for network evolution provides another.

On the substantive side, the constructions that we have introduced suggest both empirical and theoretical tasks. We need a better understanding of the role of various neighborhood forms and setting structure hypotheses that are useful in different empirical contexts. An especially interesting version of this challenge is to develop an understanding of the interdependence of physical space and network forms, as indicated earlier. The more complex model forms generated by these new constructions also invite richer and more specific theoretical articulation. The work by Mische and Robins (2000) provides one compelling illustration of how this might be done, but the development of a fuller understanding of the interdependencies among social actors in dynamic, network-based settings (Abbott 1997; Emirbayer 1997; Emirbayer and Goodwin 1994) poses an even greater challenge.

APPENDIX A: LIST OF SYMBOLS

$N = \{1, 2, \ldots, n\}$	Set of network nodes
x_{ij}	Observed tie between nodes i and j ($x_{ij} = 1$ if present; $x_{ij} = 0$ otherwise)
$\mathbf{x} = [x_{ij}]$	$n \times n$ (binary) array $\mathbf{x}$ denoting an *observed* network on N
X_{ij}	Random variable for the *possible tie* (i, j) between nodes i and j
$\mathbf{X} = [X_{ij}]$	$n \times n$ (binary) array $\mathbf{X}$ denoting a *random* graph or network on N
$\Pr(\mathbf{X} = \mathbf{x})$	Probability that the random network $\mathbf{X}$ is equal to $\mathbf{x}$
$\mathbf{D}$	Dependence graph $\mathbf{D}$
M	Node set of $\mathbf{D}$ (the set of all possible ties)
E	Edge set of $\mathbf{D}$ (pairs of possible ties assumed conditionally dependent)
A	Subset of possible ties in M
λ_A	Model parameter corresponding to the subset A of possible ties
$z_A(x) = \Pi_{(i,j) \in A} x_{ij}$	*Network statistic* corresponding to subset A of M
$c = \Sigma_{\mathbf{X}} \exp\{\Sigma_A \lambda_A z_A\}$	Normalizing quantity
$[A]$	Isomorphism class for a set A of possible ties
$z_{[A]}(x)$	Count of number of configurations in x corresponding to class $[A]$
$s \subseteq M$	Setting (subset of possible ties)
S	Setting structure (a collection of settings)
H	Set of all cliques of $\mathbf{D}$
$H_S = H \cap S$	Clique-set of $\mathbf{D}$ restricted by the setting structure S
$\mathbf{D}_B$	Partial dependence structure

APPENDIX B: PSEUDO-LIKELIHOOD ESTIMATION OF MODEL PARAMETERS

Given an observed network and a proposed p^* model, it is naturally of interest to estimate the model parameters from the observed network. In view of the difficulty of maximum-likelihood estimation of parameters (but see Corander, Dahmström, and Dahmström 1998; Crouch and Wasserman 1998; Snijders 2001; and also Ripley 1988), Strauss and Ikeda (1990) suggested an alternative *pseudo-likelihood* means of estimation. Following Besag (1977) and Strauss and Ikeda (1990), we define a *pseudo-likelihood function*:

$$PL(\boldsymbol{\lambda}) = \Pi_{i \neq j} \Pr(X_{ij} = 1 | X_{ij}^c)^{xij} \Pr(X_{ij} = 0 | X_{ij}^c)^{(1 - xij)},$$

where $\boldsymbol{\lambda} = [\lambda_A]$ is a vector of parameters and $X_{ij}^c = \{X_{kl}: k, l \in N, k \neq l,$ $(k, l) \neq (i, j)\}$. The *maximum pseudo-likelihood estimator (MPLE)* is defined as the value of $\boldsymbol{\lambda}$ that maximizes $PL(\boldsymbol{\lambda})$. Strauss and Ikeda (1990) established that MPLEs for $\boldsymbol{\lambda}$ are equivalent to MLEs for $\boldsymbol{\lambda}$ assuming independent observations x_{ij} in the following (conditional) logit model (Strauss and Ikeda 1990). Let $\boldsymbol{x}_{ij}^+$ denote the realization $\boldsymbol{x}$ with x_{ij} set to 1 and let $\boldsymbol{x}_{ij}^-$ denote the realization $\boldsymbol{x}$ with x_{ij} set to 0; recall also that $z_A(\boldsymbol{x})$ is the value of the statistic for the network $\boldsymbol{x}$ corresponding to the clique A of the dependence graph. Then

$$\text{logit } \Pr(X_{ij} = 1|X_{ij}^c) = \log[\Pr(X_{ij} = 1|X_{ij}^c)/\Pr(X_{ij} = 0|X_{ij}^c)]$$

$$= \Sigma_{A \subseteq M} \lambda_A[z_A(\boldsymbol{x}_{ij}^+) - z_A(\boldsymbol{x}_{ij}^-)]$$

$$= \Sigma_{A \subseteq M} \lambda_A(d_A)_{ij}$$

where $(d_A)_{ij} = [z_A(\boldsymbol{x}_{ij}^+) - z_A(\boldsymbol{x}_{ij}^-)]$ is the *change* in the value of the statistic $z_A(\boldsymbol{x})$ when x_{ij} changes from 1 to 0. Thus MPLEs can be obtained from standard logistic regression programs (with the observed x_{ij}s as the response variable, and the $(d)_{ij}$s as explanatory variables).

Let $\boldsymbol{d}_A = [(d_A)_{ij}]$ be the *change statistic matrix* corresponding to the clique A of $\mathbf{D}$. The matrix of change statistics needs to be computed for each clique A of $\mathbf{D}$. In Table A1, we give matrix expressions for $\boldsymbol{d}_A$ in the case of homogeneous Markov models for nondirected networks. The second and third panels of Table A1 provide expressions for the change statistic matrices used for the setting-restricted and non-Markovian models described in Section 5.

We note that in order to obtain MPLEs for model parameters, it is sufficient to fit a logistic regression model in which x_{ij} serves as the observation on a response variable, and $(d_A)_{ij}$ constitute explanatory variables. (The cases for the analysis are indexed by M.) The coefficient for $(d_A)_{ij}$ is the PLE for λ_A. Note that the number of explanatory variables is equal to the number of classes $[A]$ of cliques whose parameters are to be estimated.

APPENDIX C: PROOF OF PROPOSITION

Following Besag (1974), we define $Q(\boldsymbol{x}) = \ln\{\Pr(X = \boldsymbol{x})/\Pr(X = \mathbf{0})\}$, where $\mathbf{0}$ is the null graph; we also define $\boldsymbol{x}_{ij}^-$ according to $(x_{ij}^-)_{kl} = (x_{ij})_{kl}$ if $(k, l) \neq (i, j)$ and $(x_{ij}^-)_{ij} = 0$, that is, $\boldsymbol{x}_{ij}^-$ is the same as $\boldsymbol{x}$ but its (i, j) entry is set to 0. Likewise, $\boldsymbol{x}_{ij}^c$ is defined according to $(x_{ij}^c)_{kl} = (x_{ij})_{kl}$ if

TABLE A1

Computation of Change Statistics

Configuration Corresponding to A	Form of A	d_A
Homogeneous Markov Model for a Nondirected Graph		
Edge	$\{(i,j)\}$	$\boldsymbol{u}$
2-star	$\{(i,j),(i,k)\}$	$\boldsymbol{ux} + \boldsymbol{xu}$
3-star	$\{(i,j),(i,k),(i,l)\}$	$\boldsymbol{ux} * (\boldsymbol{ux}-1)/2 + \boldsymbol{xu} * (\boldsymbol{xu}-1)/2$
...		
Triangle	$\{(i,j),(i,k),(j,k)\}$	$\boldsymbol{xx}$
Additional Parameters in Example 1 (Overlapping Subgroup Setting Structure for a Nondirected Graph)		
2-star	$\{(i,j),(j,k)\}$	$\{\Sigma_{1\leq k\leq K}(-1)^{k-1}\Sigma_{Q:|Q|=k}[N_Q(\boldsymbol{x} * N_Q) + (\boldsymbol{x} * N_Q)N_Q]\}_{ij}$
3-cycle	$\{(i,j),(j,k),(k,i)\}$	$\{\Sigma_{1\leq k\leq K}(-1)^{k-1}\Sigma_{Q:|Q|=k}[(\boldsymbol{x} * N_Q)(\boldsymbol{x} * N_Q)]\}_{ij}$
Additional Parameters for Examples 2 and 3 (3-paths and 4-cycles in a nondirected Graph)		
3-path	$\{(i,j),(j,k),(k,l)\}$	$(\boldsymbol{uxx})_{ij} - (\boldsymbol{xx})_{jj} - \boldsymbol{x}_{ij}(\boldsymbol{ux})_{ii} + \boldsymbol{x}_{ij}$
		$+ (\boldsymbol{xux})_{jj} - \boldsymbol{x}_{ij}(\boldsymbol{ux})_{jj} - \boldsymbol{x}_{ij}(\boldsymbol{xu})_{ii} + \boldsymbol{x}_{ij}$
		$+ (\boldsymbol{xxu})_{ij} - \boldsymbol{x}_{ij}(\boldsymbol{xu})_{jj} - (\boldsymbol{xx})_{ii} + \boldsymbol{x}_{ij}$
4-cycle	$\{(i,j),(j,k),(k,l),(l,i)\}$	$(\boldsymbol{xxx})_{ij} - \boldsymbol{x}_{ij}(\boldsymbol{xx})_{jj} - \boldsymbol{x}_{ij}(\boldsymbol{xx})_{ii} + \boldsymbol{x}_{ij}$

Where:

1. $u_{ij} = 1$ if X_{ij} is a possible tie, and $u_{ij} = 0$, otherwise;

2. for matrices $\boldsymbol{a}$ and $\boldsymbol{b}$ and constant k:

$$(\boldsymbol{a} * \boldsymbol{b}) = [a_{ij}b_{ij}] \text{ (element-wise multiplication)}$$

$$\boldsymbol{a} + k = [a_{ij} + k];$$

3. Markov configurations are shown in Figure 1;

4. For example 1, there are K maximal subgroups, indexed by the set $P = \{1,2,\ldots,K\}$;

5. $(n_q)_{ij} = 1$ if X_{ij} is a possible tie in the qth maximal subgroup and $(n_q)_{ij} = 0$, otherwise;

6. $(N_Q)_{ij} = 1$ if $(n_q)_{ij} = 1$ for all $q \in Q \subseteq P$; and

333

$(k, l) \neq (i, j)$ and $(x_{ij}^c)_{ij}$ is regarded as missing; thus, x_{ij}^c is the same as x but its (i, j) entry is excluded.

Then

$$Q(x) - Q(x_{ij}^-) = \ln\left[\Pr(X = x)/\Pr(X = x_{ij}^-)\right]$$

$$= \ln[\Pr(X_{ij} = x_{ij}|X_{ij}^c = x_{ij}^c)/\Pr(X_{ij} = 0|X_{ij}^c = x_{ij}^c)]$$

It follows from the Hammersley-Clifford theorem that

$$Q(x) - Q(x_{ij}^-) = x_{ij}\left\{\Sigma_{A \subseteq M\setminus\{(i,j)\}} \lambda_{A \cup \{(i,j)\}} \Pi_{(k,l) \in A} x_{kl}\right\}$$

where $\lambda_{A \cup \{(i,j)\}} = 0$ unless $A \cup \{(i,j)\}$ is a clique of **D**.

Now suppose that C is not a clique of $\mathbf{D_B}$; that is, suppose without loss of generality that $((i,j),(k,l))$ is not an edge in $\mathbf{D_B}$ for some (k,l) with (i,j), $(k,l) \in C \subseteq M\setminus B$. Consider the function $Q(x) - Q(x_{ij}^-)$ for the case where $X_{mh} = 0$ for all $(m, h) \in B$. Since X_{ij} is conditionally independent of X_{kl} in this case, $Q(x) - Q(x_{ij}^-)$ must be independent of X_{kl} for all x_{ij}^c having $x_{mh} = 0$ for all $(m, h) \in B$. It therefore follows that $\lambda_{\{(i,j),(k,l)\}} = 0$ (by choosing $X_{mh} = 0$ for all $(m, h) \neq (i, j)$ or (k, l)).

Likewise, if (i, j), (k, l), $(p, q) \in C \subseteq M\setminus B$, we can choose $X_{mh} = 0$ for all $(m, h) \neq (i, j)$ or (k, l) or (p, q), from which it follows that

$$Q(x) - Q(x_{ij}^-) = \lambda_{\{(i,j),(k,l),(p,q)\}} x_{ij} x_{kl} x_{pq} = 0, \text{ and so } \lambda_{\{(i,j),(k,l),(p,q)\}} = 0.$$

A similar argument holds for all other subsets of C including (i, j) and (k, l), and so the result holds.

REFERENCES

Abbott, A. 1997. "Of Time and Space: The Contemporary Relevance of the Chicago School." *Social Forces* 75:1149–82.

Anderson, C., S. Wasserman, and B. Crouch. 1999. "A p^* Primer: Logit Models for Social Networks." *Social Networks* 21:37–66.

Baddeley, A., and J. Möller. 1989. "Nearest-Neighbor Markov Point Processes and Random Sets." *International Statistical Review* 57:89–121.

Bearman, P. 1997. "Generalized exchange." *American Journal of Sociology* 102: 1383–415.

Berge, C. 1989. *Hypergraphs: Combinatorics of Finite Sets*. Amsterdam, Netherlands: Elsevier Science Publishers.

Besag, J. E. 1974. "Spatial Interaction and the Statistical Analysis of Lattice Systems" (with discussion). *Journal of the Royal Statistical Society*, Series B, 36:96–127.

―――. 1977. "Efficiency of Pseudo-Likelihood Estimation for Simple Gaussian Random Fields." *Biometrika* 64:616–18.

Breiger, R., and J. Ennis. 1997. "Generalized Exchange in Social Networks: Statistics and Structure." *L'Annee Sociologique* 47:73–88.

Cartwright, D., and F. Harary. 1956. "Structural Balance: A Generalization of Heider's Theory." *Psychological Review* 63:277–92.

Corander, J., K. Dahmström, and P. Dahmström. 1998. "Maximum Likelihood Estimation for Markov Graphs." Unpublished technical report, Department of Statistics, Stockholm University.

Crouch, B., and S. Wasserman. 1998. "Fitting p^*: Monte Carlo Maximum Likelihood Estimation." Presented at the International Conference on Social Networks, May 28–31, Sitges, Spain.

Davis, J. A. 1967. "Clustering and Structural Balance in Graphs." *Human Relations* 20:181–87.

Dawid, A. P. 1979. "Conditional Independence in Statistical Theory" (with discussion). *Journal of the Royal Statistical Society*, Series B, 41:1–31.

―――. 1980. "Conditional Independence for Statistical Operations." *Annals of Statistics* 8:598–617.

Emirbayer, M. 1997. "Manifesto for a Relational Sociology." *American Journal of Sociology* 103:281–317.

Emirbayer, M., and J. Goodwin. 1994. "Network Analysis, Culture, and the Problem of Agency." *American Journal of Sociology* 99:1411–54.

Feld, S. 1981. "The Focused Organization of Social Ties." *American Journal of Sociology* 86:1015–35.

Frank, O. 1981. "A Survey of Statistical Methods for Graph Analysis." Pp. 110–55 in *Sociological Methodology 1981*, edited by S. Leinhardt. San Francisco: Jossey-Bass.

Frank, O., and D. Strauss. 1986. "Markov Graphs." *Journal of the American Statistical Association* 81:832–42.

Freeman, L., and D. R. White. 1993. "Using Galois Lattices to Represent Network Data." Pp. 127–46 in *Sociological Methodology 1993*, edited by Peter V. Marsden. Cambridge, MA: Blackwell Publishers.

Friedkin, N. 1998. *A Structural Theory of Social Influence*. New York: Cambridge University Press.

Granovetter, M. 1973. "The Strength of Weak Ties." *American Journal of Sociology* 78:1360–80.

―――. 1982. "The Strength of Weak Ties: A Network Theory Revisited." Pp. 105–30 in *Social Structure and Network Analysis*, edited by P. V. Marsden & N. Lin. Beverly Hills, CA: Sage.

Holland, P. W., and S. Leinhardt. 1981. "An Exponential Family of Probability Distributions for Directed Graphs." *Journal of the American Statistical Association* 76:33–50.

Homans, G. 1951. *The Human Group*. London: Routledge and Kegan Paul.

Johnsen, E. C. 1986. "Structure and Process: Agreement Models for Friendship Formation." *Social Networks* 8:257–306.

Klovdahl, A. 1985. "Social Networks and the Spread of Infectious Diseases: The AIDS Example." *Social Science and Medicine* 21:1203–16.

Kretzschmar, M., and M. Morris. 1996. "Measures of Concurrency in Networks and the Spread of Infectious Disease." *Mathematical Biosciences* 133:165–95.

Lauritzen, S. 1996. *Graphical Models.* Oxford, England: Oxford University Press.

Lazega, E. 1993. "Bureaucratie et collégialité dans les firmes américaines d'avocats d'affaires." *Droit et Société* 23/24:15–40

Lazega, E., and M. Van Duijn. 1997. "Position in Formal Structure, Personal Characteristics and Choices of Advisors in a Law Firm: A Logistic Regression Model for Dyadic Network Data." *Social Networks* 19:375–97.

Lazega, E., and P. Pattison. 1999. "Multiplexity, Generalized Exchange, and Cooperation in Organizations." *Social Networks* 21:67–90.

Mische, A. 1998. "Projecting Democracy: Contexts and Dynamics of Youth Activism in the Brazilian Impeachment Movement." Ph.D. dissertation, New School for Social Research.

Mische, A., and P. Pattison. 2000. "Composing a Civic Arena: Publics, Projects, and Social Settings." *Poetics* 27:163–94.

Mische, A., and G. L. Robins. 2000. "Global Structures, Local Processes: Tripartite Random Graph Models for Mediating Dynamics in Political Mobilization." Presented at the 2000 International Social Networks Conference, Vancouver, April 13–16.

Pattison, P. E., and S. Wasserman. 1999. "Logit Models and Logistic Regressions for Social Networks, II. Multivariate Relations." *British Journal of Mathematical and Statistical Psychology* 52:169–94.

Ripley, B. D. 1988. *Statistical Inference for Spatial Processes.* Cambridge, England: Cambridge University Press.

Robins, G. L. 1998. "Personal Attributes in Interpersonal Contexts: Statistical Models for Individual Characteristics and Social Relationships." Ph.D. dissertation, Department of Psychology, University of Melbourne.

Robins, G., P. Elliott, and P. Pattison. 2001. "Network Models for Social Selection Processes." *Social Networks* 23:1–30.

Robins, G., and P. Pattison. 2001. "Random Graph Models for Temporal Processes in Social Networks." *Journal of Mathematical Sociology* 25:5–41.

Robins, G., P. Pattison, and P. Elliott. 2001. "Network Models for Social Influence Processes." *Psychometrika* 66:161–90.

Robins, G., P. Pattison, and S. Wasserman. 1999. "Logit Models and Logistic Regressions for Social Networks, III. Valued Relations." *Psychometrika* 64:371–94.

Roethlisberger, F. J., and W. J. Dickson. 1939. *Management and the Worker.* Cambridge, MA: Harvard University Press.

Snijders, T. A. B. Forthcoming. "Markov Chain Monte Carlo Estimation of Exponential Random Graph Models." *Journal of Social Structure.*

———. Forthcoming. "The Statistical Evaluation of Social Network Dynamics. *Sociological Methodology 2001*, edited by Mark P. Becker and Michael E. Sobel. Cambridge, MA: Blackwell Publishers.

Skvoretz, J., and K. Faust. 1999. "Logit Models for Affiliation Networks." Pp. 253–80, in *Sociological Methodology 1999*, edited by Mark P. Becker and Michael E. Sobel. Cambridge, MA: Blackwell Publishers.

Strauss, D., and M. Ikeda. 1990. "Pseudolikelihood Estimation for Social Networks. *Journal of the American Statistical Association* 85:204–12.

Valente, T. 1995. *Network Models of the Diffusion of Innovations*. Creskill, NJ: Hampton Press.

Wasserman, S. 1987. "Conformity of Two Sociometric Relations." *Psychometrika* 52:3–18.

Wasserman, S., and J. Galaskiewicz. 1984. "Some Generalizations of p_1: External Constraints, Interactions, and Non-Binary Relations." *Social Networks* 6:177–92.

Wasserman, S., and P. E. Pattison. 1996. "Logit Models and Logistic Regressions for Social Networks, I. An Introduction to Markov Random Graphs and p^*." *Psychometrika* 60:401–25.

———. Forthcoming. *Multivariate Random Graph Distributions*. Springer Lecture Note Series in Statistics.

Watts, D. 1999a. "Networks, Dynamics, and the Small-World Phenomenon." *American Journal of Sociology* 105:493–527.

———. 1999b. *Small Worlds: The Dynamics of Networks Between Order and Randomness*. Princeton, NJ: Princeton University Press.

Watts, D., and S. Strogatz. 1998. "Collective Dynamics of 'Small-world' Networks." *Nature* 393:440–42.

White, H. C. 1992. *Identity and Control*. Princeton, NJ: Princeton University Press.

———. 1995a. "Where Do Languages Come From?" Center for the Social Sciences, Columbia University, Pre-print series.

———. 1995b. "Network Switchings and Bayesian Forks: Reconstructing the Social and Behavioral Sciences." *Social Research* 62:1035–63.

Yamagishi, T., and K. Cook. 1993. "Generalized Exchange and Social Dilemmas." *Social Psychological Quarterly* 56:235–48.

NAME INDEX

SUBJECT INDEX